D0025605

OPPORTUNITIES IN
Chemistry

Committee to Survey Opportunities in the
Chemical Sciences

Board on Chemical Sciences and Technology

Commission on Physical Sciences,
Mathematics, and Resources

National Research Council

NATIONAL ACADEMY PRESS
Washington, D.C.   1985

NATIONAL ACADEMY PRESS   2101 Constitution Avenue, N.W.   Washington, D.C. 20418

NOTICE: The project that is the subject of this report was approved by the Governing Board of the National Research Council, whose members are drawn from the councils of the National Academy of Sciences, the National Academy of Engineering, and the Institute of Medicine. The members of the committee responsible for the report were chosen for their special competences and with regard for appropriate balance.

This report has been reviewed by a group other than the authors according to procedures approved by a Report Review Committee consisting of members of the National Academy of Sciences, the National Academy of Engineering, and the Institute of Medicine.

The National Research Council was established by the National Academy of Sciences in 1916 to associate the broad community of science and technology with the Academy's purposes of furthering knowledge and of advising the federal government. The Council operates in accordance with general policies determined by the Academy under the authority of its congressional charter of 1863, which establishes the Academy as a private, nonprofit, self-governing membership corporation. The Council has become the principal operating agency of both the National Academy of Sciences and the National Academy of Engineering in the conduct of their services to the government, the public, and the scientific and engineering communities. It is administered jointly by both Academies and the Institute of Medicine. The National Academy of Engineering and the Institute of Medicine were established in 1964 and 1970, respectively, under the charter of the National Academy of Sciences.

Support for this project was provided by the American Chemical Society, the U.S. Air Force Office of Scientific Research under Grant No. AFOSR-83-0323, the Council for Chemical Research, Inc., the Camille and Henry Dreyfus Foundation, Inc., the U.S. Department of Energy under Grant No. DE-FG02-81ER10984, the National Institutes of Health under Grant No. CHE-8301035, the National Bureau of Standards under Contract No. NB835BCA2075, and the National Science Foundation under Grant No. CHE-8301035. Support was also provided by the following industrial companies: Aluminum Company of America, AT&T Bell Laboratories, Calgon Corporation, Celanese Research Company, Dow Chemical Company, Eastman Kodak Company, E.I. du Pont de Nemours and Company, Inc., Exxon Corporation, General Electric Company, GTE Laboratories, Inc., Johnson and Johnson Company, Mobay Chemical Company, Mobil Research and Development Corporation, Monsanto Company, Pfizer, Inc., Phillips Petroleum Company, PPG Industries, Inc., Proctor and Gamble Company, Shell Development Company, Standard Oil Company (Ohio), Stauffer Chemical Company, TRW, Inc., and U.S. Steel Corporation.

Library of Congress Catalog Card Number 85-62586

International Standard Book Number 0-309-03594-5, soft cover
International Standard Book Number 0-309-03633-X, hard cover

Printed in the United States of America

First Printing, October 1985
Second Printing, February 1986

Committee to Survey Opportunities in the Chemical Sciences

GEORGE C. PIMENTEL *(Chairman)*, University of California, Berkeley
ALLEN J. BARD, The University of Texas at Austin
FRED BASOLO, Northwestern University
JOHN H. BIRELY, Los Alamos National Laboratory
JOHN I. BRAUMAN, Stanford University
HARRY G. DRICKAMER, University of Illinois, Urbana
HANS-G. ELIAS, Dow Chemical Co.
MOSTAFA A. EL-SAYED, University of California, Los Angeles
DAVID A. EVANS, Harvard University
JOSEF FRIED, University of Chicago
GERHART FRIEDLANDER, Brookhaven National Laboratory
HARRY B. GRAY, California Institute of Technology
VLADIMIR HAENSEL, University of Massachusetts, Amherst
RALPH F. HIRSCHMANN, Merck Sharp & Dohme Research Laboratories
ISABELLA L. KARLE, U.S. Naval Research Laboratory
WILLIAM A. LESTER, JR., University of California, Berkeley
RUDOLPH A. MARCUS, California Institute of Technology
FRED W. McLAFFERTY, Cornell University
KOJI NAKANISHI, Columbia University
ALAN SCHRIESHEIM, Argonne National Laboratory
HOWARD E. SIMMONS, JR., E.I. du Pont de Nemours and Company, Inc.
WILLIAM P. SLICHTER, AT&T Bell Laboratories
GABOR A. SOMORJAI, University of California, Berkeley
EARL R. STADTMAN, National Institutes of Health
CHRISTOPHER T. WALSH, Massachusetts Institute of Technology
GEORGE M. WHITESIDES, Harvard University

WILLIAM SPINDEL, *Staff Director*, Board on Chemical Sciences and Technology (BCST)
ROBERT M. SIMON, *Staff Officer*, BCST
PEGGY J. POSEY, *Staff Officer*, BCST
ROBERT C. ROONEY, *Editor*, Commission on Physical Sciences, Mathematics, and Resources
MARTIN A. PAUL, *Technical Consultant*, BCST
MARY E. BUNDY, *Administrative Associate to Dr. Pimentel*
JEAN E. YATES, *Financial Coordinator*, BCST
RENEE R. HARRIS, *Senior Secretary*, BCST

Board on Chemical Sciences and Technology

ALLEN J. BARD *(Co-Chairman)*, The University of Texas at Austin
LEO J. THOMAS, JR. *(Co-Chairman)*, Eastman Kodak Company
FRED BASOLO, Northwestern University
STEPHEN J. BENKOVIC, Pennsylvania State University
JOHN H. BIRELY, Los Alamos National Laboratory
KENNETH B. BISCHOFF, University of Delaware
JOHN I. BRAUMAN, Stanford University
EUGENE H. CORDES, Merck Sharp and Dohme Research Laboratories
WILLIAM A. GODDARD III, California Institute of Technology
LOWELL P. HAGER, University of Illinois, Urbana
ARTHUR E. HUMPHREY, Lehigh University
DAVID W. McCALL, AT&T Bell Laboratories
FRED W. McLAFFERTY, Cornell University
LEO A. PAQUETTE, Ohio State University
GEORGE W. PARSHALL, E.I. du Pont de Nemours and Company, Inc.
GEORGE C. PIMENTEL, University of California, Berkeley
DAVID P. SHEETZ, Dow Chemical Co.
THRESSA C. STADTMAN, National Institutes of Health
MONTE C. THRODAHL, St. Louis, Mo.
NICHOLAS J. TURRO, Columbia University
GEORGE M. WHITESIDES, Harvard University

Commission on Physical Sciences, Mathematics, and Resources

HERBERT FRIEDMAN *(Chairman)*, National Research Council
CLARENCE R. ALLEN, California Institute of Technology
THOMAS D. BARROW, Standard Oil Company, Ohio (retired)
ELKAN R. BLOUT, Harvard Medical School
BERNARD F. BURKE, Massachusetts Institute of Technology
GEORGE F. CARRIER, Harvard University
CHARLES L. DRAKE, Dartmouth College
MILDRED S. DRESSELHAUS, Massachusetts Institute of Technology
JOSEPH L. FISHER, Office of the Governor, Commonwealth of Virginia
JAMES C. FLETCHER, University of Pittsburgh
WILLIAM A. FOWLER, California Institute of Technology
GERHART FRIEDLANDER, Brookhaven National Laboratory
EDWARD D. GOLDBERG, Scripps Institution of Oceanography
MARY L. GOOD, Signal Research Center, Inc.
J. ROSS MacDONALD, University of North Carolina
THOMAS MALONE, Saint Joseph College
CHARLES J. MANKIN, Oklahoma Geological Survey
PERRY L. McCARTY, Stanford University
WILLIAM D. PHILLIPS, Mallinckrodt, Inc.
ROBERT E. SIEVERS, University of Colorado
JOHN D. SPENGLER, Harvard School of Public Health
GEORGE WETHERILL, Carnegie Institution of Washington

RAPHAEL G. KASPER, *Executive Director*
LAWRENCE E. McCRAY, *Associate Executive Director*

iv

Preface

In 1965, the National Research Council published *Chemistry: Opportunities and Needs*. This report, under the leadership of Frank Westheimer, surveyed the state of the discipline at that time. In the 20 years since then, chemistry has undergone a virtual revolution—in its techniques, instrumentation, and capabilities. New frontiers lie before us.

These new vistas made evident the need for a new survey of chemical science and its intellectual and economic impact. That need, recognized by the Chemistry Section of the National Academy of Sciences, led in 1982 to meetings of a planning committee formed by the Board on Chemical Sciences and Technology of the National Research Council. The planning committee unanimously recommended that a new survey of chemistry be undertaken, and the Board approved. This report is the result.

A committee of 26 members broadly representative of the academic, industrial, and governmental research sectors, the geographic areas, and the major subdisciplines of chemistry was appointed to guide the study and to frame its conclusions and recommendations. Put briefly, the committee's charge was to describe:

- the contemporary research frontiers of chemistry;
- the opportunities for the chemical sciences to address society's needs; and
- the resources needed to explore these frontiers to advance human knowledge and to exploit chemistry's opportunities to enhance the well-being of humankind.

To achieve these goals, the committee organized itself into five task forces, which, in turn, called upon more than 350 chemical researchers to suggest topics, prepare commissioned papers on cutting-edge research, and provide critiques of the manuscript as it developed. An interim report was prepared in the fall of 1983 under the auspices of the Academies' Committee on Science, Engineering, and Public Policy, titled *Report of the Research Briefing Panel on Selected Opportunities in Chemistry*. The briefing report was based upon research directions of particular promise that became apparent early in this study. Its recommendations and priorities are entirely consonant with the more complete analysis presented here.

Of course, a single report can hardly cover every aspect of a set of disciplines as broad, vigorous, and dynamic as the chemical sciences. For example, chemical engineering is not explicitly discussed in detail; a complementary examination of the research frontiers in that field is clearly called for and is now under way. Nevertheless, I believe that this report does indeed capture the essence of the chemical sciences today. Its content represents an enthusiastic consensus of a broad spectrum from that community. The National Research Council, the scientific community, and I, myself, are all deeply indebted to the members of the committee, the many colleagues who assisted the task forces, and the able and conscientious reviewers whose suggestions and advice determined the substance of the report. I am also grateful to my staff at Berkeley and to the staff of the NRC's Board on Chemical Sciences and Technology who, under the leadership of William Spindel, provided throughout the term of the project the day-to-day support so essential to its successful completion.

The primary audience for this report is made up of those responsible for guiding science policy in the Congress and the Administration. We believe that the report will be useful to other audiences, too: the leaders of the chemical industry, the chemical research community, and also those inquisitive about science, about its relation to their own lives, and about the current directions of that most central of sciences, chemistry.

GEORGE C. PIMENTEL
Chairman, Committee to Survey
Opportunities in the Chemical Sciences

Contents

WORLD'S LARGEST INDEX

(so says the *Guinness Book of World Records*)

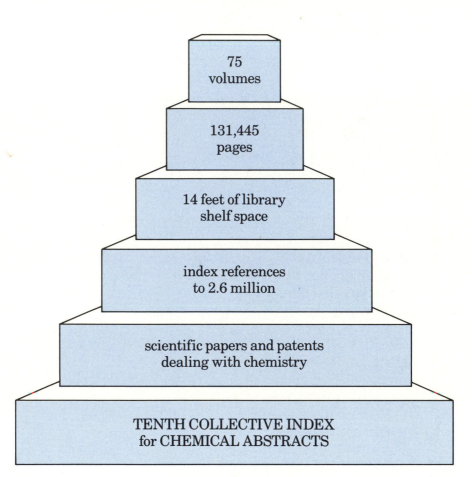

75
volumes

131,445
pages

14 feet of library
shelf space

index references
to 2.6 million

scientific papers and patents
dealing with chemistry

TENTH COLLECTIVE INDEX
for CHEMICAL ABSTRACTS

1977-1981

The sheer volume of this amazing collective index attests to
the worldwide activity and importance of chemistry today.

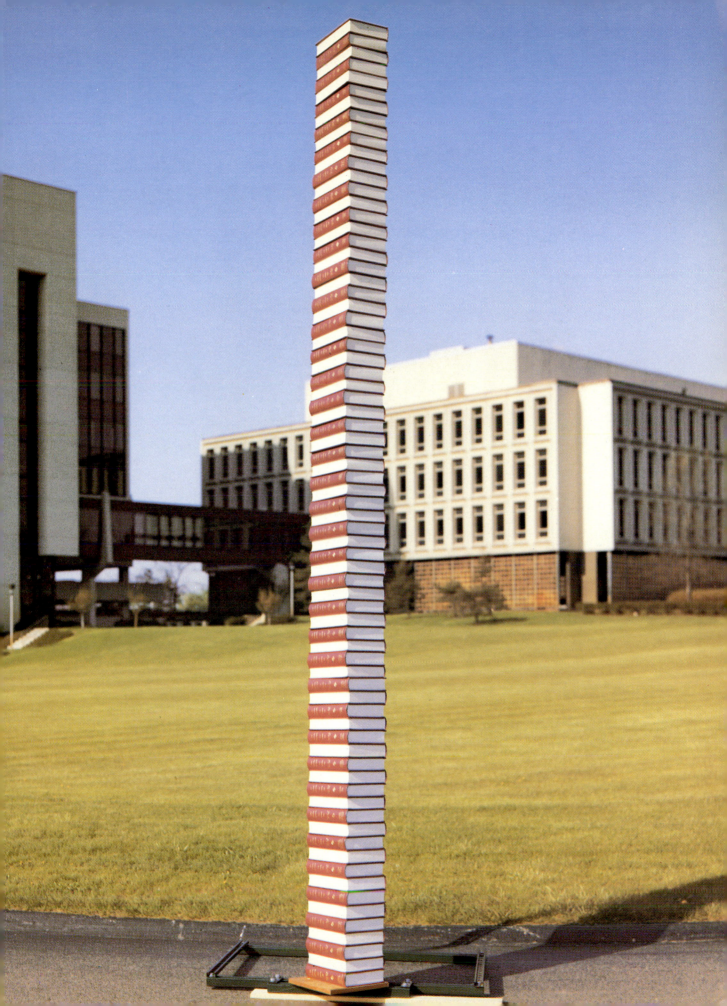

OPPORTUNITIES IN
Chemistry

CHAPTER I

Introduction

Two decades have passed since the publication of NRC Report 1292, *Chemistry: Opportunity and Needs*, edited by Frank H. Westheimer. The frontiers that it envisaged in 1965 have indeed fulfilled their promise, and almost all of the report's optimistic expectations have been realized. In fact, the advances have been so rapid and so penetrating that the structure of chemistry and its interactions with contiguous disciplines have qualitatively changed. Physics has provided a panoply of powerful diagnostic tools that extend the experimental horizons of chemistry. Chemical theory has advanced to full partnership in the discipline, substantially aided by the revolutionary advances made by computer scientists. Molecular biology has made remarkable progress in its elucidation of life processes and has placed before chemistry challenging problems that require explication at the molecular level. Hence it is timely for a new assessment of the status of chemistry, the opportunities that can be seen ahead, and the resources needed to pursue them. This report presents that assessment.

Chemistry is a central science that provides fundamental understanding needed to deal with many of society's needs. It is a critical component in man's attempt to feed the world population, to tap new sources of energy, to clothe and house humankind, to provide renewable substitutes for dwindling or scarce materials, to improve health and conquer disease, to strengthen our national security, and to monitor and protect our environment. Basic research in chemistry will help future generations to cope with their evolving needs and unanticipated problems.

Because of this responsiveness to human needs, chemistry has become a crucial element in the nation's economic well-being. The U.S. Chemicals and Allied Products industry employs more than a million people, makes annual manufacturing shipments totalling about $175 billion, and, currently, displays a $12 billion positive international balance of trade, second highest of all commodity groups. Our competitiveness in a range of international markets depends upon maintaining our present position of leadership in the chemical sciences. There is no area of basic science that offers a more secure investment in the nation's future.

Finally, our culture embraces the premise that learning about ourselves and our environment is an ample basis for encouraging scientific inquiry. Chemistry contributes substantially to this cultural enrichment. For example, nothing preoccupies humans more than questions about the nature of life and how to preserve it. Because all life processes are manifestations of chemical changes, understanding chemical reactivity is a requisite foundation for our ultimate understanding of life. Thus, chemistry, along with biology, contributes to human knowledge in areas of universal philosophical significance.

Fortunately, we find ourselves in a time of special opportunity for advances on all these fronts. The opportunity derives from our developing ability to probe and understand the elemental steps of chemical change and, at the same time, to deal with extreme molecular complexity. Progress is epitomized by the striking fact that the number of new compounds continues to increase at a rate that is faster than exponential. Powerful instrumental techniques furnish a crucial dimension. They account for the recent acceleration of progress that now promises especially high return from the investment of additional resources in the field of chemistry.

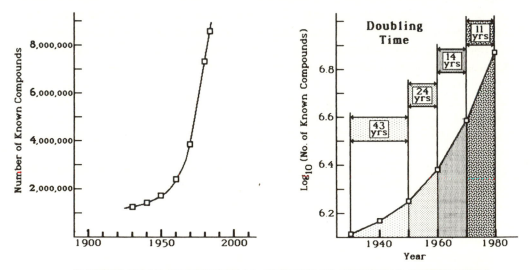

FASTER THAN EXPONENTIAL GROWTH IN CHEMICAL KNOWLEDGE

It will be helpful to describe here the organization of this report. Following this introductory chapter, an Executive Summary of the report makes up Chapter II. Each of the three Chapters III, IV, and V begins with three sections, A, B, and C, that focus on chemistry's responses to society's needs. Several of these sections are introduced, in turn, by a one-page vignette that presents in nontechnical language a case history illustrating chemistry's usefulness. The section then describes recent important accomplishments and identifies potentialities for the future. The potentialities stem from intellectual opportunities and opening research frontiers that are described in a Section D, where the vocabulary must sometimes be pitched at a more technical level than that used elsewhere in the report. Most of the frontiers depend upon sophisticated and expensive instrumentation that is described in a Section E, which highlights trends in instrument capabilities that account for chemistry's accelerating progress. The trends are usually accompanied by escalation in cost caused by the increasing complexity and capability of the equipment; this escalation is quantitatively evaluated. Chapter VI addresses issues of manpower and education and concerns itself primarily with factors that determine the effectiveness of doctoral education. Then, Chapter VII assesses the resources needed if the United States is to maintain a position of international leadership in chemistry. The assessment finds current funding levels inadequate to secure the substantial societal benefits to be derived from such leadership.

The current federal investment in chemical research is still historically rooted in a funding pattern appropriate to a test-tube and Bunsen burner era, an era long since eclipsed. The sophistication of a modern chemistry laboratory requires a much more vigorous and sustained financial commitment of both capital and supporting services. The cost is miniscule when weighed against the potential returns. We must encourage a scientific field brimming with opportunities for discovery that will advance human knowledge and strengthen the underpinnings of a critical industry, and we must attract a substantial share of our brightest young scientists to this rewarding task. This report presents a program that can accomplish these goals.

CHAPTER II

Executive Summary

SOCIETAL BENEFITS FROM CHEMISTRY

Chemistry provides fundamental understandings needed to deal with many societal needs, including many that determine our quality of life and our economic strength.

New Processes

The U.S. chemical industry has a current $12 billion positive balance of trade. Continued competitiveness depends upon constant improvement of existing processes and introduction of new ones. Advances in chemical catalysis and synthesis will be key to maintaining our current position of world leadership. (See Section III-A.)

More Energy

Ninety-two percent of our present energy consumption is based upon chemical technologies; this will remain true well into the 21st century. However, new chemistry-based energy sources will have to be tapped. They will include low-grade fuels for which better control of chemical reactivity is needed so that we can protect the environment while providing energy at reasonable cost. (See Section III-B.)

New Materials

The next two decades will bring many changes in the materials we use, including the materials in which we are clothed, housed, and transported. Chemistry will play an increasingly vital role in this interdisciplinary field because advances will depend upon ability to tailor new substances, including polymers, to replace and outperform traditional or scarce materials. (See Section III-C.)

6

More Food

To increase world food supply, we need improvements in the production and preservation of food, soil conservation, and the use of photosynthesis. In collaboration with contiguous disciplines, chemistry plays a central role as we seek to clarify in detail the chemistry of biological life cycles. Once clarified they can be nurtured and controlled, while undesired side effects are avoided through chemical identification and synthesis of hormones, growth regulators, pheromones, self-defense structures, and nutrients. (See Section IV-A.)

Better Health

All life processes—birth, growth, reproduction, aging, mutation, death—are manifestations of chemical change. Chemistry is now poised to clarify such complex biological processes at the molecular level. Hence it is making important contributions to physiology and medicine through rational drug design and, then, through synthesis of new compounds that promote health and alleviate specific ailments such as atherosclerosis, hypertension, Parkinson's disease, cancer, and disorders of the central nervous and immune systems. (See Section IV-B.)

Biotechnologies

Remarkable progress made in recent years by molecular biologists and biochemists in genetic engineering has been built upon basic chemical principles that determine the chemical structures and functional relationships between molecules and supermolecules (proteins, DNA) within biological systems. Full realization of the potentialities of the projected new biotechnologies will increasingly depend upon molecular-level understandings. Chemists will be active collaborators in the progress toward this goal. (See Section IV-C.)

Better Environment

A major contemporary concern is protecting the environment in the face of increasing world population, urbanization, and rising standards of living. Effective strategies for safeguarding our surroundings require that we know what's there, where it came from, and what we can do about it. Chemistry lies at the heart of the answers to each of these questions: it can provide analytical techniques that give early warning of emerging problems, recognition of their origins, and access to alternative products and processes to ameliorate undesired impacts. (See Section V-A.)

Continued Economic Competitiveness

The value of U.S. chemical sales is near $175 billion, and we have a positive balance of trade. Preservation of our quality of life depends significantly upon maintaining this position of leadership. Our future competitiveness will be dependent upon staying in the vanguard as the frontiers of chemistry change and upon supplying to industry a stream of talented young scientists who have been working at these frontiers and using state-of-the-art instrumentation. (See Section V-B.)

Increased National Security

Key factors underlying national security are a healthy populace and a dynamic, productive economy. In both spheres, chemistry plays an essential role. In addition, the nation must be able to deter armed conflict. Again, chemistry is a vital contributor; it enters all areas of defense from propulsion, weapons materials, and classical munitions to the most advanced strategic concepts. (See Section V-C.)

INTELLECTUAL FRONTIERS IN CHEMISTRY

Fortunately, this is a time of intellectual ferment in chemistry deriving from our increasing ability to probe and understand the elemental steps of chemical change and, at the same time, to deal with molecular complexity. Powerful instrumental techniques are a crucial dimension. We can anticipate exciting discoveries on a number of frontiers of chemistry.

Chemical Kinetics

Over the next three decades, we will see advances in our understanding of chemical kinetics that will match those connected with molecular structures over the last three decades. Lasers by themselves have spectacularly expanded experimental horizons for chemists. They can now probe chemical reactions on a time scale that is short compared to the lifetime of any transient substances that can be said to possess a molecular identity. Elementary reactions can be dissected, first, through detailed control of energy content of reactants and, then, through discrimination of energy distribution and recoil geometry among the products. Pathways for energy movement between and within molecules can now be experimentally tracked and theoretically resolved. These new avenues of study will clarify the factors that govern temporal aspects of chemical change. (See Section III-D.)

Chemical Theory

Chemistry is on the verge of a renaissance because of emerging ability to fold experiment and theory together to design chemical structures with properties of choice. With today's computers, accurate calculations can clarify transient situations not readily accessible to experimental measurements, such as intermediate steps in combustion processes. In some cases benefitting from the power of computers, theoretical understandings are developing across chemistry, including dynamics of reactive collisions, electron transfer reactions in solution, and statistical mechanical descriptions of the liquid state. (See Section III-D.)

Catalysis

Developing insights fueled by an array of powerful instrumentation are now moving catalysis from an art to a science. It is now possible to "see" molecules as they react on catalytic surfaces. Metal-organic compounds with purposeful steric specificity and reactivity can be prepared. Organic molecules with predetermined surface conformations that simulate enzymatic architectures can be synthesized. Coherence is appearing that encompasses surface, solution, electrochemical, photochemical, and enzymatic catalysis. Fundamental advances in these various facets of catalysis are forthcoming that will have great economic and technological impact. (See Sections III-A, III-B, V-D.)

Materials

Modern experimental techniques and chemical principles now permit systematic chemical strategies for discovery and design of novel materials. Hence, chemists are increasingly joining and expanding the specialist communities concerned with glasses, ceramics, polymers, alloys, and refractory materials. Coming years will see entirely new structural materials, liquids with orientational regularity, self-organizing solids, organic and ionic conductors, acentric and refractory materials. Chemists will have a central position on the most dramatic frontier of materials science, the design of molecular-scale memory and electrical circuit devices. (See Sections III-C, V-B, V-D.)

Synthesis

Modern instrumental techniques greatly facilitate discovery and testing of new reaction pathways and synthetic strategies. Our accelerating progress, which extends from invention of new families of inorganic compounds to the synthesis of ever-more complex organic structures, is erasing the border between inorganic and organic chemistry. Reactivity control in metal-organic molecules can now be achieved through insightful choice of molecular appendages; new soluble catalysts will result. Molecules with metal atom clusters at their cores can be synthesized to link the chemistry of bulk metals to that of simple metal-organic compounds. This linkage relates the action of dissolved and surface catalysts. Organic molecules of biological complexity can be structurally identified and precisely replicated; this opens the way to tailored biological function. (See Sections III-D, IV-A, IV-B, IV-D.)

Life Processes

The recent striking advances in biology have exposed problems of revolutionary significance that require analysis in terms of molecular interactions. With its ability to deal with molecular complexity, chemistry can play its role in investigating and clarifying the molecular origins of biological processes.

Working hypotheses for biological functions can be tested through deliberate synthesis of tailored molecules: natural product analogs, chemotherapeutic agents, proteins deliberately altered to provide new functions, genetic inserts. This will move us closer to real understanding of the basic workings of life processes in response to the strongest of human preoccupations, the nature and preservation of life. (See Sections IV-B, IV-C, IV-D, V-B.)

Analytical Methods

Conceptual advances in detection, characterization, and quantification of chemical species are benefitting chemistry and contiguous sciences on many fronts. Incorporation of computers is a key factor. Analytical separations based on a variety of chromatographic techniques are essential elements of the rapid progress in identification and synthesis of natural products. Novel ionization methods extend mass spectrometry to biologic macromolecules and other nonvolatile solids. Surface analysis and electroanalytical methods are helping to clarify important aspects of catalysis. Remote spectroscopic and a variety of laser techniques are furnishing timely contributions to environmental monitoring and protection. (See Sections V-A, V-D.)

PRIORITY AREAS IN CHEMISTRY (See Ch. VII.)

The strength of American science has been built by allowing creative, working scientists to decide independently where the best prospects lie for acquiring significant new knowledge. Many of the most far-reaching developments, both in concept and application, have come from unexpected directions. Thus, to list priority areas carries the risk of closing off or quenching some adventurous new directions with potential yet to be recognized.

Even so, it makes sense to concentrate some resources in specially promising areas. This can be done if we regard our research support as an investment portfolio designed to achieve maximum gain. A significant part of this investment should be directed toward consensually recognized priority areas but with a flexibility that encourages evolution in these areas as new frontiers emerge. A second substantial element in this portfolio should be support of creative scientists who propose to explore new directions and new ideas. Finally, a third element must be provision of the instrumentation and the infrastructure needed to assure the cost effectiveness of the entire portfolio.

Where this balance will fall for each of the funding sources will vary. Industrial research will weight heavily the currently recognized priority frontiers. At the other extreme, NSF must encourage the new avenues from which tomorrow's priority lists will be drawn. The other mission agencies should structure their portfolios between those extremes. With such a balanced portfolio in mind, the following priority areas are identified with the intent to achieve the greatest intellectual and societal returns.

Recommendation 1

Priority should be given to the following research frontiers:

  A. **Understanding Chemical Reactivity**
  B. **Chemical Catalysis**
  C. **Chemistry of Life Processes**
  D. **Chemistry Around Us**
  E. **Chemical Behavior Under Extreme Conditions**

Recommendation 1 should be implemented through initiatives sponsored by the relevant mission agencies, scaled by each agency in its own appropriate balance with its support of creative scientists expected to explore new directions and new ideas.

Initiative A.   Understanding Chemical Reactivity

We propose an initiative to apply the full power of modern instrumental techniques and chemical theory to the clarification of factors that control the rates of reaction and to the development of new synthetic pathways for chemical change.

Principal objectives are to sustain international leadership for the United States at the major fundamental frontier of chemistry—control of the rates of chemical reactions—and to provide the basis for U.S. competitive advantage in development of new processes, new substances, and new materials.

Initiative B.   Chemical Catalysis

We propose an initiative to apply the techniques of chemistry to obtain a molecular-level and coherent understanding of catalysis that encompasses heterogeneous, homogeneous, photo-, electro-, and artificial enzyme catalysis.

A principal objective here will be to provide the fundamental knowledge and creative manpower required for the United States to maintain competitive advantage in and to develop new catalysis-aided technologies.

Initiative C.   Chemistry of Life Processes

We propose an initiative to develop and apply the techniques of chemistry to the solution of molecular-level problems in life processes and to develop young research scientists broadly competent in both chemistry and the biological sciences.

A principal objective of this initiative will be to accelerate the conversion of qualitative biological information into techniques and substances useful in biotechnologies, in human and animal medicine, and in agriculture.

Initiative D.   Chemistry Around Us

We propose an initiative devoted to understanding the chemical make-up of our environment and the complex chemical processes that couple the atmosphere, oceans, earth, and biosphere, with special reference to man's conscious and inadvertent disturbance of this global reactor. Analytical chemistry and reaction dynamics define the core of this initiative.

Principal objectives of this initiative are to provide the basic chemical understandings needed to protect our environment and to extend detection of potentially hazardous substances well below toxicity bounds so that potential problems can be anticipated and ameliorated long before hazard levels are reached.

Initiative E. *Chemical Behavior Under Extreme Conditions*

We propose an initiative to explore chemical reactions under conditions far removed from normal ambient conditions. Chemical behaviors under extreme pressures, extreme temperatures, in gaseous "plasmas," and at temperatures near absolute zero provide critical tests of our basic understandings of chemical reactions and new routes toward discovery of new materials and new devices.

Principal objectives are to broaden our understanding of chemical change and to lead to new materials that will have application under extreme conditions of pressure, temperature, and exposure to specially challenging environments (e.g., fusion reactors, reentry vehicle heat shields, superconducting magnets).

EXPLOITING THE OPPORTUNITIES IN CHEMISTRY

The extent to which our nation will be able to benefit directly from these promising frontiers in chemistry is, in part, a matter of resources. This report shows that existing patterns of funding are anachronistic and inadequate. Average grant sizes are too small; for example, the average NSF grant will barely support the research activities of two or three students, while an active research group might range in size from six to sixteen (see Table VII-8 and the discussion preceding it). Furthermore, the grants do not provide support for the infrastructure needed to sustain the sophisticated scientific activities of today's chemistry (electronic, computer, and laboratory technicians, machinists and glass blowers, supplies). The inadequacy of support for "mid-cost" instrumentation (less than $1 million), both for shared use among several research groups and for specialized and dedicated use, requires painful trade-offs that tend to restrict capacity to fund new, young investigators entering chemistry. (See Figure, p. 302.) The instrumentation crisis is exacerbated because university chemistry departments are struggling to provide the operating and maintenance infrastructure needed to use this state-of-the-art equipment with maximum cost effectiveness. (See Tables VII-4 and VII-6.)

The listing of opportunities and potential rewards to society that will flow from them is impressive. That we cannot afford to lose these rewards is underscored by the economic importance of chemistry. Business and industry employ more doctoral chemists than the sum of those employed in the biological sciences, mathematics, physics, and astronomy combined (see Appendix Table A-4). Yet we find that the average federal investment in the crucial human resource in chemistry is only one fifth as much per Ph.D. as in other comparably important disciplines (see Table VII-1). Without a more determined U.S. commitment to the chemical sciences, there is substantial likelihood that our leadership position will be preempted abroad.

Chemistry in Industry

The Chemistry and Allied Products industry invests heavily in its own in-house research. This report should be of value to the industry as it decides upon the amount and focus of its own research investment. In addition, U.S. industry has an interest in the health and direction of university-based fundamental research. Industrial progress and competitiveness also depend upon access to a reservoir of fundamental knowledge constantly replenished by university-based research and upon a stream of talented young scientists familiar with the latest chemical frontiers and instrumental techniques. Hence, industry furnishes direct support to university research. Though modest in total (about $10 million each to chemistry and chemical engineering in 1983), it is extremely important because it facilitates movement of new discoveries into new applications and influences university research agendas.

Recommendation 2

New mechanisms and new incentives should be sought for strengthening links between industrial and academic research.

Recommendation 3

Industry should increase its support for university fundamental research in the chemical sciences. Tax incentives to encourage such gains should be explored.

The Federal Role in Fundamental Research

Industry can engage in only a modest amount of the most fundamental and adventurous research because the time horizon for application is remote. Yet, this "high-risk" research offers the most far reaching benefits to society and the intellectual basis for technological competitiveness. It is an appropriate place for public investment.

This report displays an array of opening research frontiers rich in potential for societal benefit. In this setting, an examination of funding patterns in a variety of disciplines that depend upon sophisticated instrumentation reveals that the federal investment in chemistry is not adequate and will not bring to society the full benefits to be realized.

Recommendation 4

The federal investment in chemistry should be raised to be commensurate with the practical importance of chemistry, both economic and societal, and with the outstanding intellectual opportunities it now offers.

Chemistry and the NSF Mission

Chemistry supported by the NSF is judged on its potential for adding to our understanding of nature. Since the most far-reaching technological changes tend to stem from unpredictable discoveries, the fundamental research supported by NSF is critical to this country's long-range technological future. The increasing dependence of our economy upon the health of our chemical industry coupled with the exciting intellectual opportunities in chemistry justify a considerably larger NSF support in all three of its crucial dimensions: shared instrumentation, dedicated instrumentation, and grant size. Such support is needed to assure a U.S. position of international leadership in the exploitation of the rich opportunities before us.

Recommendation 5

(a) NSF should begin a 3-year initiative to increase its support for chemistry by 25 percent per year for FY 1987, FY 1988, and FY 1989.

(b) The added increments should be directed toward increasing grant size, ensuring encouragement of young investigators, enhancing the shared instrumentation program, and increasing the amount directed toward dedicated instrumentation.

(c) NSF should build into its shared instrumentation program a federal capital investment averaging at 80 percent of instrument cost together with maintenance and operating costs for a 5-year period after purchase.

Chemistry and the Department of Energy Mission

For at least the next quarter century, 90 percent of our still growing energy use must come from chemical energy sources. At the same time, the quality and character of feedstocks will be changing in ways that challenge existing technologies and that make it harder to resolve society's concerns about environmental pollution. To meet these challenges, the Department of Energy currently invests in its Chemical Sciences Program only 5 percent and in its Biological Energy Research Program less than 1 percent of the total resources it directs toward 11 of its largest fundamental research programs. To assure our future access to abundant and clean sources of energy over the next three decades, DOE must make a much larger commitment to the chemical sciences. This commitment must engage more fully both the DOE National Laboratories and the larger chemistry community.

Recommendation 6

(a) **The DOE should establish a major initiative in those areas of chemistry relevant to the energy technologies of the future.**

(b) **In an appropriate number of our National Laboratories, the defined mission should be reshaped to include a major focus on one or more of the chemistry areas crucial to energy technologies.**

(c) **University research programs in energy-relevant areas of chemistry should be raised to be commensurate with those in the National Laboratories.**

(d) **Incremental growth in these programs by a factor of about 2.5 will be needed to exploit the opportunities before them. For cost effectiveness, this growth should be uniformly spread over the next 5 years. A $22 million incremental growth in the FY 1986 DOE chemistry budget would support an appropriate beginning.**

Chemistry and the NIH Mission

Progress in both medicine and chemistry now makes it possible to interpret complex biological events at the molecular level. Because of the ubiquitous role of chemistry in human health, NIH provides substantial support to chemists engaged in research at the broad interface of physiology/medicine/chemistry. Chemistry research relevant to the NIH mission concentrates largely in the Institute for General Medical Sciences. Characteristically, the grants are modest in size, and the award success rates have fluctuated widely over the last decade.

Recommendation 7

(a) **A fraction of any additional NIH funds in support of chemistry should be used to increase average grant size, including grants for young investigators and particularly for cross-disciplinary collaborative programs that link expertise in chemistry with that in other health-science disciplines.**

(b) **NIH should vigorously continue its attempts to stabilize its extramural grant program.**

(c) **NIH should maintain its extramural shared instrumentation program at a level approximately equal to that of NSF. The initial federal capital investment should include at least 80 percent of instrument cost, and maintenance and operating costs should be provided for 5 years after purchase.**

Chemistry and the Department of Defense Mission

Chemistry plays a critical part in our national security. It not only strengthens our ability to deter and prevent armed conflict, it also contributes strongly to the health of the economy and to the maintenance of the technical manpower pool needed to develop and deploy our increasingly sophisticated defense technologies. In the longer view, our future national security, our international economic posture, and our technical manpower supply dictate DOD attention to fundamental chemical research, including that conducted at universities. Yet DOD support of fundamental research has grown very little over the last 5 years; its investment in university research does not fulfull DOD's desire to maintain our manpower pool while providing indirect influence on university research agendas toward promising chemistry areas key to our defense posture.

Recommendation 8

(a) **The percentage of the DOD R&D budget directed to basic (6.1) research should be increased to restore the 1965 value of 5 percent.**

(b) **DOD support for university research in the chemical sciences should be raised to about 25 percent of the total federal support for basic research through real growth at 10 percent per year.**

(c) **Parallel growth should be provided to DOD in-house research programs of the 6.1 category in chemistry.**

(d) **Growth should concentrate attention on the special opportunities now offered through chemistry in the following broad research areas:**

—Strategic and critical materials
—Fuels, propellants, and explosives
—Atmospheric phenomena
—Chemical and biological defense
—Nuclear power and nuclear weapons effects

(e) **Interaction between DOD laboratories and universities should be encouraged and increased.**

(f) **DOD should continue its instrumentation program but with the addition of support for maintenance and operation.**

(g) **DOD should explore mechanisms to support new construction and renovation of university research facilities in particularly critical areas of chemistry.**

Chemistry and the Department of Agriculture Mission

The USDA devotes only a small portion of its R&D budget to chemistry research relevant to agriculture and animal health. But human needs are great, so we can ill afford to miss the relevant opportunities offered by chemistry.

Recommendation 9

The Department of Agriculture should initiate a substantial competitive grants program in chemistry with the aim of increasing extramural support of fundamental research in chemistry relevant to agriculture and animal health to an approximate par with the Department's intramural program.

Chemistry and the National Aeronautics and Space Administration Mission

The several initiatives proposed in this report present opportunities for improvement of the safety, range, and effectiveness of future space operations. Furthermore, NASA has unique capabilities for monitoring and mission-related concern about the changing chemical compositions of the troposphere and the stratosphere.

Recommendation 10

(a) The National Aeronautics and Space Administration should maintain a substantial commitment to the understanding of atmospheric chemistry.

(b) Increased attention should be directed toward special opportunities relevant to operations in space:

—high energy propellants;
—chemical behavior under extreme conditions;
—reaction kinetics and photochemistry under collision-free conditions.
—chemical aspects of life-sustenance in a closed system
—analytical methods for compositional monitoring in both the troposhere and the stratosphere

(c) NASA should more actively encourage academic chemists to address problems relevant to the NASA mission through competitive grants for fundamental research.

Chemistry in the Environmental Protection Agency

The EPA has significant R&D programs specifically and properly directed toward currently recognized environmental problems, and many of these programs involve chemistry. This agency assumes a much less active role in fundamental research relevant to its mission as epitomized by its tiny Exploratory Research program. This extramural program is now funded at $16M, less than 0.4 percent of the $4.25B EPA total. The EPA should follow the pattern of other federal mission agencies by defining those areas of research that underlie its mission goals and stimulating the expansion of knowledge in those areas through programs of fundamental research.

Recommendation 11

(a) EPA should increase the percentage of its R&D funds placed in its Exploratory Research program and its commitment to extramural fundamental research relevant to environmental problems of the future.

(b) EPA should encourage fundamental chemical research to clarify reaction pathways open to molecules, atoms, and ions of environmental interest.

(c) EPA should take a prominent role in support of long-range research in analytical chemistry with emphasis on extension of sensitivity limits, increase in detection selectivity, and exploration of new concepts.

(d) EPA should have as a conscious and publicized goal the detection of potentially undesired environmental constituents at concentration levels far below known or expected toxicity limits.

Conclusion

In the next two decades there will be dramatic changes in our basic understanding of chemical change and in our ability to marshal that understanding to accomplish deliberate purpose. The program presented here defines a leadership role for the United States as these advances are achieved. The rewards accompanying such leadership are commensurate with the prominent role of chemistry in addressing society's needs, in ameliorating problems of our technological age, and in sustaining our economic well-being. The costs of falling behind are not tolerable.

CHEMISTRY is a central science
that responds to societal needs.

It is critical in Man's attempt to...
discover new processes

Beauty Is Only Skin Deep

Ever think of going into the gold-brick business? Just take a big hunk of gold and a hacksaw and you've got a good-looking brick with a nice heft. Unfortunately, one such brick and you're talking $140-150,000! There's no room for mark-up. But suppose you get an ordinary brick (wholesale in South Jersey, 17¢!) and just coat the surface with gold—the cost will come down a lot. And you'll have a beautiful brick—well, at least "skin-deep."

So how much would such a surface coating cost? For openers, put a one-atom-thick layer of gold atoms over the entire surface of the brick. Let's see, 2 inches by 4 inches by 8 inches—gold at $320 an ounce—one atom thick—that'll be ... 0.3¢ worth of gold. Wow! There, we've got an attractive product at a total material cost of 17.3¢ (not including packaging).

That's pretty impressive. It means that the outermost layer (the surface) of a $150,000 piece of gold involves so few atoms that they would cost less than a cent. Yet that miniscule fraction of atoms on the surface of a piece of metal controls the chemistry of that piece. For instance, these surface atoms are the ones that determine whether the metal surface acts as a catalyst or not. And catalysts account, one way or another, for about 20 percent of our gross national product.

So what is a catalyst? It's a chemical substance that speeds up a chemical reaction without itself getting into the act (i.e., it is not consumed while doing its thing). A solid catalyst merely furnishes its surface as a meeting place for gaseous molecules. For instance, when a molecule of methanol lands on a rhodium catalyst surface, it usually sticks for a while (becomes adsorbed). Now, if a carbon monoxide molecule happens to arrive, zingo, it reacts with an adsorbed methanol molecule and they leave the surface as acetic acid. When methanol and carbon monoxide meet in the gas phase, they won't even give each other the time of day. But because of the special environment provided by that thin layer of surface atoms on the rhodium catalyst, methanol and carbon monoxide react so rapidly that 500,000 tons of commercial acetic acid are made every year this way! This kind of speed-up might be anywhere from a thousand-fold to a million-fold when things are working.

Because of such successes, chemists care a lot about how these catalytic gold bricks do their job. What actually happens to that thin layer of adsorbed molecules as they come and go on a catalytic metal surface? Unfortunately, that's where the skin-deep principle works against us. If there isn't much on the surface, there isn't much to see.

But nowadays, we have several powerful instruments with which we can learn about the special properties of the skin of a metal. These instruments also let us watch molecules as they lodge on the surfaces of catalysts like platinum and rhodium and many others. We can see how the molecules are chemically changed by the metallic skin to make them more reactive when a suitable reaction partner comes along. So chemists are beginning to understand how to design these catalytic gold bricks to do whatever we want. Right now, every gallon of your gasoline began as a bunch of molecules sure to make your engine knock and then some chemist catalytically converted them into other molecules that make your engine purr. But now we are looking ahead to new energy feedstocks with more sulfur and metallic contaminants that will require much better catalysts so that we can keep your engine purring and the air clean at the same time. We'll do it by learning how those catalytic gold bricks work so we can tailor them to our needs. This is a case where skin-deep beauty really pays off!

CHAPTER III

Control of Chemical Reactions

III-A. New Processes

A prime reason for wishing to understand and control *chemical reactions* is so that we can convert abundant substances into useful substances. When this can be done on an economically significant scale, the reaction (or sequence of reactions) is called a chemical process.

A significant number of employed chemists are engaged in perfecting existing chemical processes and developing new ones. Their past success is attested by the vitality and strength of the U.S. chemical industry. It has manufacturers' shipments totalling $175 billion (see Table A-2), a $12 billion positive international balance of trade (in both 1980 and 1981, see Table A-3) and more than a million employees. The industry makes billions of pounds of organic chemicals at low cost, in high yield, and with minimum waste products. For example, we produce 9.8 billion pounds of synthetic fibers (such as polyesters), 28 billion pounds of plastics (such as polyethylene), and 4.4 billion pounds of synthetic rubber.

Continued competitiveness in this multifaceted industry depends upon readiness to improve existing processes and to introduce new ones. Our current position of world leadership can be attributed to our strength in the field of chemical catalysis. The major role of industrial catalysis is signalled by estimates that 20 percent of the gross national product is generated through the use of

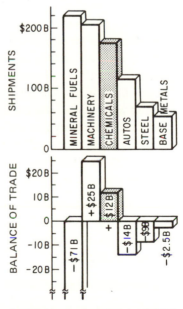

CHEMICALS: SECOND LARGEST POSITIVE TRADE BALANCE

catalytic processes that assist in satisfying such diverse societal needs as food production, energy conversion, defense technologies, environmental protection,

21

and health care. On the horizon, the extensive use of catalysts will tap new energy sources (the subject of Section III-B). Our ability to remain in the forefront of the research frontiers of chemical catalysis will figure strongly in the health of our chemical industry and, hence, in the buoyancy of the U.S. economic condition.

A catalyst accelerates chemical reactions without being consumed. Such accelerations can be as much as 10 orders of magnitude. A selective catalyst can have the same dramatic effect but on only one of many competing reactions. A stereoselective catalyst not only controls the product composition, it also favors a particular molecular shape, often with remarkable effects on the physical properties (such as tensile strength, stiffness, or plasticity) and, for biologically active substances, on the potency. Catalysis can be subdivided according to the physical and chemical nature of the catalytic substance.

• In *heterogeneous catalysis*, the catalyzed reaction occurs at the interface between a metal, metal oxide, or other solid and either a gaseous or liquid mixture of the reactants.

• In *homogeneous catalysis*, reaction occurs in either gas or liquid phase in which both catalyst and reactants are dissolved.

• In *electrocatalysis*, reaction occurs at an electrode surface in contact with a solution but assisted by a flow of current. Electrocatalysis includes the advantages of catalytic rate control, including specificity, and adds the opportunity to inject or extract electrical energy.

• In *photocatalysis*, reaction may take place at an interface (including electrode surfaces) or in homogeneous solution, but in these reactions energy encouragement is provided by absorbed light.

• In *enzyme catalysis*, some characteristics of both heterogeneous and homogeneous catalysis appear. Whether natural or artificial enzymes are considered, large molecular structures are involved that can be seen to provide an "interface" upon which a dissolved reactant molecule can be immobilized, awaiting reaction (as in heterogeneous catalysis). In addition, the structure incorporates at the site of immobilization a suitable chemical environment that facilitates the desired reaction when a suitable reaction partner arrives (as in homogeneous catalysis).

We discuss below the aspects of each of these catalytic situations that are relevant to the development of new chemical processes. Then they will be revisited in Section III-B because of their importance in the development of new energy sources.

Heterogeneous Catalysis

A heterogeneous catalyst is a solid material prepared with large surface area (1-500 m^2/g) upon which a chemical reaction can occur at extremely high rate and selectivity. Some major new commercial processes based on heterogeneous catalyst developments in recent years are shown in Table III-1. The potential

TABLE III-1   New Processes Based on Heterogeneous Catalysis

Feedstocks	Catalyst	Product	Used to Manufacture	1982 U.S. Production (metric tons)[a]
Ethylene	Silver, cesium chloride salts	Ethylene oxide	Polyesters, textiles, lubricants	2,300,000
Propylene, NH_3, O_2	Bismuth molybdates	Acrylonitrile	Plastics, fibers, resins	925,000
Ethylene	Chromium titanium	High-density polyethylene	Molded products	2,200,000
Propylene	Titanium, magnesium oxides	Polypropylene	Plastics, fibers, films	1,600,000

[a] Production by all processes, including the innovative process; U.S. Tariff Commission Report.

economic significance is displayed in the last column, the total U.S. production by all processes.

Surface science is developing rapidly and now gives us experimental access to this two-dimensional reaction domain. Because of the unused bonding capability of the atoms at the surface, chemistry here can be qualitatively different from that of the same reactants brought together in solution or in the gas phase. However, when chemists are able to "see" what molecular structures are on the surface, our knowledge of reactions in conventional settings becomes applicable and opens the door to understanding and control of chemistry in this surface domain. There are five areas of heterogeneous catalysis where this understanding will have major impact on new chemical technologies.

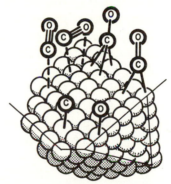

HOW DOES CARBON MONOXIDE
BIND TO A METAL SURFACE?

Molecular Sieve Synthesis and Catalysis

Molecular sieves are natural or synthetic crystalline aluminosilicates containing pores or channels within which chemical reactions can be initiated. They offer unparalleled efficiency both for cracking of petroleum and for conversions such as methanol to gasoline. We need to know better how to synthesize molecular sieves with controlled molecular pore size, and how to determine the elementary reaction steps and intermediates that account for their efficacy.

Metal Catalysis

Finely dispersed transition metals are increasingly coming into use to catalyze hydrocarbon conversions and ammonia synthesis for fertilizers. Other such applications and improved performance will follow from intensive research into the control of surface structures, oxidation states, residence time of reaction intermediates, and resistance to catalyst "poisons" (such as lead and sulfur).

Substitutes for Precious Metal Catalysts

Many of the most effective catalysts are rare metals of limited availability in the United States, including cobalt, manganese, nickel, rhodium, platinum, palladium, and ruthenium. Their strategic value requires a concerted research effort to find more accessible substitutes, such as other transition-metal oxides, carbides, sulfides, and nitrides.

Conversion Catalysts

We must find catalysts to convert abundant substances to useful fuels and industrial feedstocks. These reactions include conversion of atmospheric nitrogen to nitrates, methane to methanol, carbon dioxide to formate, and depolymerization of coal and biomass to useful hydrocarbons.

Catalysts to Improve the Quality of Air and Water

We have many environmental pollution problems for which we need solutions that will match the success of the catalytic converter used in cleaning automobile exhaust gases. To begin, we need catalysts that remove sulfur oxides from smoke plumes, that purify water, and that prevent acid rain.

As we learn more about molecular structures at the solid-gas interface (reactants, intermediates, and products), a better understanding of surface chemical bonding will follow. We can look forward to understanding additives that modify catalyst performance ("promoters" and "poisons"). Then, the challenge of synthesis of the designed catalyst can be addressed. All this fundamental knowledge will underlie and facilitate the development of new and more selective heterogeneous catalysts.

Homogeneous Catalysis

Homogeneous catalysts are soluble and active in a liquid reaction medium. Often they are complex, metal-containing molecules whose structures can be modified to tune reactivity in desired directions to achieve high selectivities. In this respect, homogeneous catalysts can be superior to heterogeneous ones. The largest industrial-scale process using homogeneous catalysis is the partial oxidation of para-xylene to terephthalic acid with U.S. production of 6.2 billion pounds in 1981. The process uses salts of cobalt and manganese dissolved in acetic acid at 215°C as the catalyst system. Most of the product ends up copolymerized with ethylene glycol to give us polyester clothing, tire cord, soda bottles, and a host of other useful articles. The strength of the chemical industry in the United States has been repeatedly enhanced by the introduction of new processes based upon homoge-

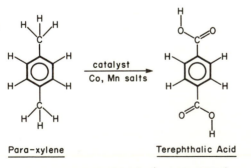

Para-xylene   Terephthalic Acid

U.S. PRODUCTION (1981), $2.3 BILLION!

TABLE III-2   New Processes Based on Homogeneous Catalysis

Feedstocks	Catalyst[a]	Product	Used to Manufacture	Start-up Date	1982 U.S. Production (metric tons)
Propylene, oxidizer	Mo^{VI} complexes	Propylene oxide	Polyurethanes (foams) Polyesters (plastics)	1969	303,000
Methanol, CO	$[Rh(CO)_2I_2]^-$	Acetic acid	Vinyl acetate (coatings) Polyvinyl alcohol	1970	495,000
Butadiene, HCN	$Ni(L_1)_4$	Adiponitrile	Nylon (fibers, plastics)	1971	220,000
α-Olefins	$RhH(C))(L_2)_3$	Aldehydes	Plasticizers Lubricants	1976	300,000-350,000
Ethylene	$Ni(L_3)_2$	α-Olefins	Detergents	1977	150,000-200,000
CO, H_2 (from coal)	$[Rh(CO)_2I_2]^-$	Acetic anhydride	Cellulose acetate (films)	1983	[225,000, Capacity]

[a] L = Ligand; L_1 = Triaryl Phosphite, L_2 = PPh_3, L_3 = $OOCCH_2PPh_2$, Ph = C_6H_5.

neous catalysts. Table III-2 lists six such processes, whose 1982 production figures were valued at over $1 billion.

An important branch of homogeneous catalysis has developed from research in organometallic chemistry. For example, in the second reaction in Table III-2, rhodium dicarbonyl diiodide catalyzes the commercial production of acetic acid from methanol and carbon monoxide. With this catalyst present, the reaction economically gives more than 99 percent preference for acetic acid over other products. Almost a billion pounds of acetic acid is so produced, a large part of which is used to manufacture such polymeric materials as vinyl acetate coatings and polyvinyl alcohol polymers.

There are three areas of homogeneous catalysis where increased understanding has potential for major impact on new chemical technologies.

Activation of Inert Molecules

Several relatively inert molecules are enticing as reaction feedstocks because of their abundance, including nitrogen, carbon monoxide, carbon dioxide, and methane. One way to facilitate their use might be through homogeneous organometallic catalysis, and quite promising examples are beginning to appear. For example, soluble compounds of tungsten and molybdenum with molecular nitrogen have been prepared and induced to produce ammonia under mild conditions. The carbon-hydrogen bonds in normally unreactive hydrocarbons have been split by organorhodium, organorhenium, and organoiridium complexes. Hope for build-up of complex molecules from one-carbon molecules, such as carbon monoxide and carbon dioxide, is stimulated by recent demonstrations of carbon-carbon bond formation at metal centers bound in soluble metal-organic molecules. Synthesis of compounds with multiple bonds between carbon and metal atoms has had major impact in clarifying the catalytic interconversion (metathesis) of olefins. While there is much to learn, the stakes are high and the odds favor success.

Metal Cluster Chemistry

An adventurous frontier of catalysis involves the expanding capability of chemists to synthesize molecules built around several metal atoms in proximity. Many of these "metal cluster" compounds consist of several metal atoms bound to each other in the "core" of the molecule with carbon monoxide molecules chemically attached on the periphery. These metal carbonyls have formulas $M_x(CO)_y$, and x can be made very large. The world's record as of this writing is a platinum compound with $x = 38$, $Pt_{38}(CO)_{44}^{2-}$.

At the same time, very low temperature techniques are revealing the structures and chemistry of small aggregates containing only metal ions or atoms ("naked clusters"). In still another direction, cubical units of four metal

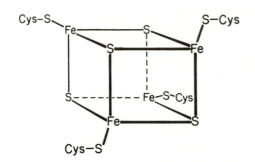

THE BIOLOGICAL ENZYME FERRODOXIN: AN
IRON-SULFUR "CUBANE" STRUCTURE

atoms and four sulfur atoms are now known for iron, nickel, tungsten, zinc, cobalt, manganese, and chromium. This "cubane" structure, which involves three metal-sulfur bonds to each metal atom, has its own characteristic chemistry. This is demonstrated by the iron example, which proves to be a functional unit in the ferrodoxin iron proteins that catalyze electron transfer reactions in biological systems.

These cluster compounds, bound or "naked," furnish a natural bridge between homogeneous catalysis and bulk metal, heterogeneous catalysis. What makes it intriguing is that many of the metals that are most active as heterogeneous catalysts also form cluster compounds (e.g., rhodium, platinum, osmium, ruthenium, and iridium). Now the chemistry of these elements can be studied as a function of cluster size. There is much to be gained from better understanding because all the elements mentioned above are derived from imported strategic mineral ores.

Stereoselective Catalysts

Another frontier full of promise involves the development of homogeneous stereoselective catalysts. Many biological molecules can have either of two geometric structures connected by mirror-image (chiral) relationships, and generally only one of these structures is functionally useful in the biological system. If a complex molecule has seven such chiral carbon atoms and a synthetic process produces all the mirror-image structures in equal amounts, there would be $2^7 = 128$ structures, 127 of which might have no activity or, worse, might have some undesired effect. Thus, the ability to synthesize preferentially at every chiral center the desired structure with the desired geometry is essential.

Immense strides are being made here. For example, L-dopa, a particular mirror-image structure of an amino acid that has revolutionized the treatment of Parkinson's disease, has been made using an asymmetric addition of hydrogen to a carbon-carbon double bond. The catalyst is a soluble rhodium phosphine catalyst that gives 96 percent of the correct structure. Stereospecific oxidations can also be carried out. The recent invention of a titanium catalyst to add, in a specific geom-

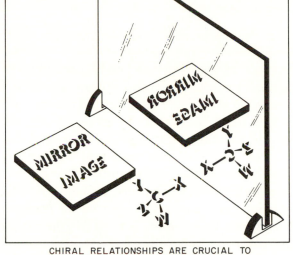

CHIRAL RELATIONSHIPS ARE CRUCIAL TO BIOLOGICAL FUNCTION

etry, an oxygen atom across a carbon-carbon double bond has lowered 10-fold the price of the synthetic sex attractant of the gypsy moth. Despite these successes, the basic factors that produce stereochemical control are not completely understood. Mechanistic studies are needed, and the potential rewards are great.

Future advances in homogeneous catalysis depend upon easy access to the modern instrumental techniques such as X-rays, high-field nuclear magnetic resonance,

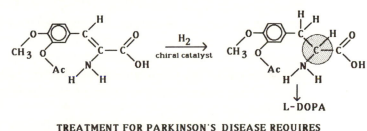

TREATMENT FOR PARKINSON'S DISEASE REQUIRES THE CORRECT CHIRAL STRUCTURE

electron-spin resonance, mass spectrometry, and computational facilities. Breadth of knowledge is also especially important because work at the interfaces of organic, inorganic, and physical chemistry is involved.

Photocatalysis and Electrocatalysis

Significant advances have recently been made in the study and control of chemistry taking place at the interfaces of liquid solutions and electrochemical electrode surfaces. In some applications, absorption of light by a semiconductor electrode initiates the chemistry. Whether light is involved or not, i.e., photocatalysis versus electrocatalysis, this rapidly moving field depends upon our knowledge of homogeneous catalysis, heterogeneous catalysis, and semiconductor behavior.

Photocatalysis

An electrochemical cell can be built with one or both electrodes made of semiconductor materials that absorb incident light. In such a cell, the light absorbed by the electrode can be used to promote catalytic oxidation-reduction chemistry at the electrode-solution interface. The same sort of chemistry can be induced in solutions containing suspensions of semiconductor materials but now at the particle-solution interface. Such oxidation-reduction chemistry has significant scientific interest and, without doubt, practical importance as well. For example, photodestruction of toxic waste material, such as cyanide, has been demonstrated at titanium dioxide surfaces. A more popularized and conceivably feasible concept is that such photocatalytic chemistry, driven by solar energy, could give a process for producing massive amounts of hydrogen and oxygen from water. It is an intriguing prospect: to convert from diminishing, polluting petroleum fuels to a renewable fuel—hydrogen—that burns to water and that is made from water using energy from the Sun.

Electrocatalysis

Apart from light-initiated processes, electrode surfaces with catalytic activity offer a new domain for chemical synthesis. In a field with a long heritage, recent developments have shown that electrode surfaces can be chemically tailored to promote particular reactions. For example, electrocatalytic control of electron flow opens new synthetic pathways that require one-electron transfer in preference to two. Furthermore, this research area has benefitted from techniques used by the semiconductor industry, such as chemical-vapor deposition, by coupling them with imaginative synthetic chemical techniques for surface modification.

An example is the electrocatalyst family developed for use in chlorine generation in chlor-alkali cells. A successful case is based upon a thin layer of ruthenium dioxide—the catalyst—deposited on a base-metal electrode. This electrocatalyst has dramatically improved energy efficiency and reduced cell maintenance in the chlor-alkali industry, an industry representing billions of dollars in sales. The cumulative savings are enormous because this crucial industry consumes up to 3 percent of all electric power produced in the United States.

Chemistry at the Solid/Liquid Interface

Before the technological potentialities of any of the above can be realized, we must have a much better understanding of the nature of chemistry at the semiconductor/liquid interface. Most of the extraordinary instrumentation so far developed for surface science studies is applicable only at solid/vacuum interfaces. We need comparable capability at the solid/liquid boundary, and we will gain it from fundamental research in solid state chemistry, electrochemistry, surface analysis, and surface spectroscopy. There is already reason for optimism. The surprising discovery of the million-fold intensification involved in the surface-enhanced Raman effect provides a technique with applicability yet to be determined. Perhaps even more promising is the demonstration of surface-enhanced second harmonic generation. This method, which depends upon the intrinsic asymmetry at a phase boundary, has become possible because of the high intensity of laser light sources. It may have general applicability and, because pulsed lasers are used, temporal (kinetic) measurements can be expected.

The potential gains from these areas are considerable. We need to know how to catalyze multielectron transfer reactions at an electrode surface. That is the chemistry required, for example, to photogenerate a liquid fuel like methanol from carbon dioxide and water. Multi-electron transfer catalytic electrodes for oxygen reduction in electrochemical cells would find a welcoming home in the fuel cell industry.

It is also likely that research on semiconductor electrode surface modification will reflect beneficially on the field of electronics. Thus, the integrated circuit technology based upon gallium-arsenide may depend upon control of its surface chemistry. Already scientists concerned with photoresist/chemical etching techniques are recognizing the importance of the chemistry involved in surface modification, as shown by the active pursuit of "anisotropic chemical etching."

In summary, our evolving understanding of the electrode/solution interface, buttressed by concepts based on semiconductor electrodes and the development of new methods for modifying electrode surfaces, has opened novel approaches to both photocatalysis and electrocatalysis. Future advances will benefit synergistically from progress in heterogeneous and homogeneous catalysis, increased understanding of mass and charge transport within the electrode surface layers, and continued development of experimental methods and theoretical models for the interface.

Artificial-Enzyme Catalysis

The most striking benefit of our expanding knowledge of reaction pathways and the analytical capacity of modern instrumentation has been the development of our ability to deal with molecular systems of extreme complexity. With the synthetic chemist's prowess and such diagnostic instruments as nuclear magnetic resonance, X-ray spectroscopy, and mass spectroscopy, we can now synthesize and control the structure of molecules that approach biological complexity. This control includes the ability to fix the molecular shape, even extending to the mirror-image properties so crucial to biological function.

There is no application of these capabilities more intriguing than that of coupling them with our growing knowledge of catalysis in an attempt to synthesize artificial enzymes. In Nature, enzymes are the biological catalysts that accelerate a wide variety of chemical reactions at the modest temperatures at which living organisms can survive. An appropriate enzyme selects from a system with many components a single reactant molecule and transforms it to a single product with prescribed chiral geometry.

Without catalysts, many simple reactions are extremely slow under ambient conditions. Raising the temperature speeds things up, but at risk of a variety of possible undesired outcomes, such as acceleration of unwanted reactions, destruction of delicate products, and waste of energy. Hence, there are compelling reasons to develop synthetic catalysts that work like enzymes. First, natural enzymes do not exist for most of the chemical reactions in which we have interest. In the manufacture of polymers, synthetic fibers, medicinal compounds, and many industrial chemicals, very few of the reactions used could be catalyzed by naturally occurring enzymes; even where there are natural enzymes, their properties are not ideal for chemical manufacture. Enzymes are proteins, sensitive substances that are easily denatured and destroyed. In industries that do use enzymes, major effort is devoted to modifying them to make them more stable.

Controlled Molecular Topography and Designed Catalysts

We have a pretty good idea of how enzymes work. Nature contrives a molecular surface suited to a specific reactant. This surface attracts from a mixture the unique molecular type desired and immobilizes it in a distinct shape that facilitates reaction. When the reaction partner arrives, the scene is set for the desired reaction to take place in the desired geometry.

Organic chemists who have taken up this challenge are making notable progress. Without special control, large molecules usually have exclusively convex surfaces (ball-like shapes). So a first step has been to learn to synthesize large molecules with concave surfaces, after which the concave surfaces could be shaped to accommodate a desired reactant. Cyclodextrins, which are toroidal in shape, provide examples. The crown ethers, developed over the last 15 years, have a quite different surface topography. For instance, 18-crown-6 consists of twelve carbon atoms and six oxygen atoms evenly spaced in a cyclic arrangement. In the presence of potassium ions, the ether assumes a crown-like structure in which the six oxygen atoms point toward and bind a potassium ion. Lithium and sodium ions are too small, and rubidium ions too large, to fit in the crown-shaped cavity; so this ether preferentially extracts potassium ions from a mixture. More ornate examples now exist. Chiral binaphthyl units can be coupled into cylindrical or egg-shaped cavities. With benzene rings, enforced cavities have been made with the shapes of bowls, pots, saucers, and vases.

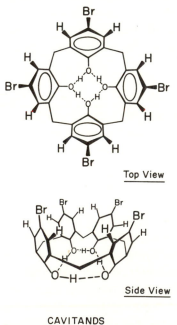

Top View

Side View

CAVITANDS
WHAT SHAPE DO YOU NEED?

We are clearly moving toward the next step, which is to build into these shaped cavities a catalytic binding site, such as a transition metal complex that is already known to have catalytic activity in solution. The earliest successes are likely to be patterned after natural enzymes, but there is no doubt that, in time, artificial, enzyme-like catalysts will not be limited to what we find already known in nature.

Biomimetic Enzymes

A short-cut approach to improved catalysis is to pattern artificial enzymes closely after natural enzymes—sometimes called "biomimetic chemistry." For example, mimics have been prepared for the enzymes that biologically synthesize amino acids. Artificial enzymes that incorporate the important catalytic groups of a natural enzyme, such as vitamin B-6, can show good selectivity and even the correct chirality in the product. Mimics have been prepared for several of the common enzymes involved in the digestion of proteins, and substances that catalyze the cleavage of RNA have been synthesized based upon the catalytic groups found in the enzyme ribonuclease. Mimics have also been synthesized that imitate the class of enzymes called cytochromes P-450, which are involved in many biological oxidations, and the oxygen carrier hemoglobin. In addition, mimics have been prepared for biological membranes and for those molecules that carry substances through membranes. These have potential applications in the construction of organized systems to perform selective absorption and detection, as in living cells. It is important for the United States to build on its early lead in this field. Although most of the work mentioned above has been done in the United States, the Japanese have also become quite active and have specifically targeted "biomimetic chemistry" as an area of special opportunity. Research on synthetic organic chemistry develops novel methods to construct the required molecule and elaborates new kinds of structures. The study of detailed reaction mechanisms in organic and biological chemistry permits a rational approach to catalyst design. It is an area ripe for development, and it deserves encouragement as a part of this program in chemical catalysis.

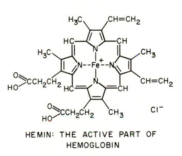

HEMIN: THE ACTIVE PART OF HEMOGLOBIN

Conclusion

A significant share of our economy is built upon the chemical industry. The long-range health of this critical industry will depend upon our ability to innovate, developing new processes that increase energy and cost efficiency, and creating new products for new markets, all the while enhancing our protection of the environment. Today's basic research in all facets of catalysis will provide the source of such innovation. It will also produce the cadre of young scientists working at the frontiers of knowledge with the state-of-the art instrumental skills needed to recognize and implement the potentialities. Research in catalysis, viewed in the broad sense presented here, is one of the research fields of chemistry that deserves high priority.

CHEMISTRY is a central science that responds to societal needs.

It is critical in Man's attempt to...

tap new sources of energy

A Lithium-Powered Heart

The cardiac pacemaker is a modern miracle of science that many of us take for granted—but not a person who owns one! These pacemakers operate on battery power, and the demands put on the tiny batteries that generate it are awesome! They must start the human machine every morning *without fail*, and the human lights and radio are running all the time. Yet many, many people are adding healthy years to life by betting on the chemical reactions that occur in these batteries to generate—day in, day out—the electric current that drives their pacemakers.

These batteries have special requirements because they must be implanted in a human body. They must be rugged and leakproof, have long life and minimal weight, and, of course, they must be nontoxic. The first batteries used in pacemakers had a lifespan of only 2 years, and the periodic operations required for replacement meant additional risk and stress for the patient.

Chemists began to tackle this problem, and research efforts in electrochemistry uncovered lithium metal, a new substance with the potential to give long life to batteries. Unfortunately, lithium is highly reactive—it burns in air and reacts with water to produce flammable hydrogen gas. If lithium were to be used, it would be necessary to discover new, nonaqueous electrolyte systems.

Electrolytes are substances that dissolve in water to form conducting solutions. They dissolve to produce ions, particles carrying electrical charge. The movement of these charges carries the current as the battery's chemistry releases its stored energy. Conventional batteries that draw on the chemical energy of zinc and mercuric oxide depend upon aqueous electrolytes. So the problem for the chemists to solve was defined—to design a battery that would operate without water.

Extensive investigations into new solvents and new materials for use in high energy, long-life batteries eventually led to the discovery of a solid electrolyte for use with lithium metal. The solid electrolyte is iodine, and the lithium-iodine battery was born for biomedical applications. These revolutionary batteries are currently in use, and they have an impressive lifespan of 10 years! The benefits to those who must depend upon cardiac pacemakers are incalculable.

The lithium-iodine battery is not the end of the story. It is a vast improvement over its predecessors and extremely useful in pacemakers, but it has a lower power than would be optimum for other uses. On the horizon is the need for new, higher-power batteries for use in other implantable organs like artificial kidneys and hearts. But further electrochemical research will undoubtedly provide the answer. It has in the past, and it will again.

III-B.   More Energy

This country's economic development is tied to the growth of its use of energy. For six decades, the Industrial Revolution was fueled primarily by coal. Then, petroleum energy use caught up with coal in 1948. Meanwhile, throughout the 20th century, the 3-fold increase in population has been accompanied by a 10-fold growth in energy use in all its forms. As we look ahead, there can be no doubt that the nation's wealth and quality of life will be strongly linked to continued access to energy in large amounts.

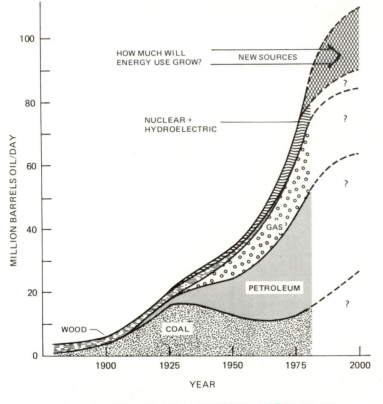

U.S. ENERGY USE: NEW SOURCES ARE NEEDED

Every proposed scenario for energy consumption over the next four decades projects the need to optimize access to every energy source at our disposal. This need is made more urgent as we face the inevitable depletion of liquid fossil fuels because there will also be stiffening constraints imposed by the desire to protect our environment. In this setting, *chemistry will continue to be the central scientific discipline in meeting the nation's energy requirements*. How chemistry has served us in the recent past and its potential role over the next 30 years will be considered for the following important energy sources and emerging alternatives:

- Petroleum
- Natural Gas
- Coal, Lignite, Peat
- Shale Oil, Tar Sands
- Biomass
- Solar
- Nuclear Fission
- Nuclear Fusion
- Conservation

Petroleum

Petroleum use has increased steeply, worldwide: as much petroleum was taken from the ground between 1968 and 1978 as was produced in the preceding 110 years. The significance of the increase is accentuated by the complex chemical processing required to convert the raw natural product into chemical forms that meet the demands of modern, high-compression engines. Refinement of the crude oil begins with distillation for separation by boiling range. Hydro-treating may be needed to remove sulfur and to upgrade feedstock product quality. Then, by catalytic cracking, the large molecules are fragmented into lower boiling molecules. Alternatively, catalytic reforming can convert the molecular structures to higher octane forms. All this is carried out on a gargantuan scale with perilously inflammable substances.

Chemical catalysis has made this miracle of process engineering possible. Table III-3 lists four important catalytic processes recently introduced during a

TABLE III-3 Heterogeneous Catalysis in the Petroleum Industry

Feedstocks	Catalyst	Product	Used for
C_{16}-C_{24} oils	Zeolite molecular sieves (aluminosilicates)	C_7-C_9 alkanes, alkenes	"Cracking" to high-octane fuels
C_7-C_9 unbranched hydrocarbons	Platinum-rhenium/ platinum-iridium	Aromatics, other hydrocarbons	"Reforming" to high-octane fuels
CO, NO, NO_2	Platinum/palladium/ rhodium	CO_2, N_2	Auto exhaust cleanup
CH_3OH	Zeolite molecular sieves (aluminosilicates)	C_7-C_9 branched hydrocarbons, aromatics	Gasoline production

period when environmental concerns dictated the reduction of noxious byproducts and development of high-octane, lead-free gasoline. The need for new discoveries is even greater today as we turn to lower grade petroleum feedstocks with higher sulfur content, with higher molecular weights (Alaskan oils), and with catalyst-poisoning constituents (e.g., vanadium and nickel in California off-shore oils).

Challenging research opportunities for chemists and chemical engineers lie in such key areas as *recovery* (getting more oil from the known deposits), *refining* (converting the crude oil into the most useful chemical form), and *combustion* (getting the most energy from the finished fuel).

Recovery

About 4000 billions of barrels of oil have been discovered, worldwide, with about 12 percent of it in the United States. *Most of that oil, however, is not recoverable by presently known extraction methods. Primary recovery*, based upon natural pressure, typically can recover no more than 10 to 30 percent of the oil from its natural reservoir, a complex structure of porous rock. *Secondary recovery*, in which water, gas, or steam injection is used to revitalize the deposit, can raise the recovery efficiency; but even then, only about 35 percent of the known U.S. oil deposits are classified as recoverable, and of that, more than 80 percent has already been extracted and consumed.

Tertiary recovery requires new chemistry and new methods to gain access to the rest of this valuable resource. Surfactants (detergents) and solution poly-

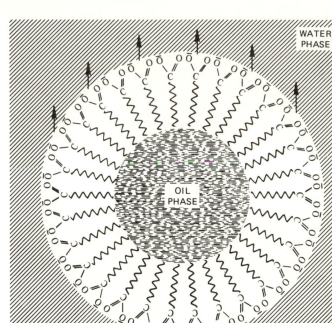

WATER PHASE

OIL PHASE

WATER PHASE

DETERGENT MICELLES AROUND OIL DROPLETS CARRY THEM TO THE SURFACE

mers can be used to lower interfacial tension between oil and water and reduce capillary pressure. Micellar-polymer, caustic, and microemulsion flooding are some of the *enhanced oil recovery* methods under development or on the drawing boards. Fundamental questions of transport phenomena, phase behavior, viscosity, interfacial tension, and influence of electrolytes on surfactants must be better understood. There are difficult problems to be faced; but if recovery could be made feasible, it would have enormous economic significance because it would permit us to tap the remaining 350 billions of barrels of U.S. oil already discovered but currently beyond economic reach.

Refining

The oil most easily removed by primary and secondary recovery also has the most desirable composition. As these best fractions become depleted, we must learn to refine heavier crude oils (higher molecular weights) with lower hydrogen content and more undesirable contaminants, such as sulfur, nitrogen, and organometallic compounds. A new generation of catalysts may be needed to escape the poisoning effects of some of these contaminants. Thus, vanadium seems to be carried by porphyrin complexes into molecular sieve-zeolite-catalysts where it clogs catalyst pores and blocks catalytic sites. In contrast, nickel contaminants have their own undesired dehydrogenation catalytic activity, which increases the amount of coke, again clogging catalyst pores.

It is likely that future refining techniques will differ markedly from those currently used. Petroleum refining technology is already undergoing an evolution as refineries are being adapted to lower quality feedstocks. Some of the heavier components are being converted through catalytic hydroprocessing and coke-forming operations. Future developments may be based upon combustion of the low-hydrogen and coke components to fuel energy-consuming processes. The least desirable crude components may be gasified to generate hydrogen, a useful reactant in catalytic hydroprocessing. More dramatic departures are to be expected, though their development will follow from new research discoveries in separation techniques, molecular characterization of heavy crudes, high temperature chemistry, and catalysis.

Combustion

The United States annually spends about \$30 billion (10 percent of its GNP) on combustion materials. It seems ironic that there is much remaining to be learned about this chemistry, one of the oldest technologies of mankind dating back to the discovery of fire. The need for more knowledge stems from ever increasing dependence on combustion, from changing fuel compositions, and, most important, from the sudden awareness and concern about the environmental impacts of combustion. In the last 30 years, society has recognized and begun to grapple with the undesired side effects of profligate and careless combustion of fossil fuels. These side effects include smog from nitrogen oxides, acid rain from sulfur impurities, dioxins from inefficient burning of chlorinated compounds, and the almost imponderable long-range problem of the effect of accumulating CO_2 on the global climate.

The combustion process is a tightly coupled system involving fluid flow, transport processes, energy transfer, and chemical kinetics. This complexity is epitomized in the methane-oxygen flame. After 60 years of intensive study, only in the last 3 years has this flame been quantitatively modelled with a satisfactory molecular/free radical mechanism.

Fortunately there is no subarea of chemistry offering greater promise than that of chemical kinetics. Such optimism derives from an array of new, sophisticated instrumental techniques that permits us to address and clarify the fundamental behaviors at work. These impending advances of molecular dynamics will be treated in Section III-D; such advances, as they occur, will be quickly taken up by chemical engineers and translated into higher combustion efficiencies and decreased environmental pollution. As one index of its importance, an increase of only 5 percent in the efficiency with which we combust coal, oil, and gas would be worth \$15 billion per year to the U.S. economy and an immeasurable additional value if it is accompanied by reduction in the growing problems of smog and acid rain.

SOME ACETYLENE REACTIONS IMPORTANT IN GASOLINE COMBUSTION

THERMAL REACTIONS

$$C_2H_2 + M \longrightarrow C_2H + H + M$$
$$+ C_2H_2 \longrightarrow C_4H_3 + H$$
$$+ H + M \longrightarrow C_2H_3 + M$$
$$+ C_2H_3 \longrightarrow C_4H_4 + H$$
$$+ C_2H \longrightarrow C_4H_2 + H$$

COMBUSTION

$$C_2H_2 + O_2 \longrightarrow HCCO + OH$$
$$\longrightarrow$$
$$\longrightarrow HCO + HCO$$
$$+ O \longrightarrow CH_2 + CO$$
$$\longrightarrow HCCO + H$$
$$+ OH + M \longrightarrow C_2H_2OH + M$$

Natural Gas

Natural gas is a mixture of low-molecular-weight hydrocarbons, mostly methane (in North America, typically 60 to 80 percent methane, the rest, ethane, propane, and butane in varying percentages). While it contains some sulfur- and nitrogen-containing impurities, they are removable to give a clean-burning fuel and a versatile chemical feedstock. The ethane and propane can be catalytically converted to ethylene, propylene, and acetylene, all valuable precursors to products needed by our society.

Its ease of transport via pipelines and its desirable qualities for application make natural gas an important resource; its contribution to U.S. energy use has almost doubled since 1960.

The U.S. natural gas reserves are comparable to our petroleum reserves, perhaps somewhat larger. However, again like petroleum, natural gas is limited in amount both worldwide and domestically, and its production will undoubtedly peak one or two decades hence.

Coal

Coal is the most abundant of the fossil fuel energy sources. Estimates of recoverable supplies worldwide indicate 20 to 40 times more coal than crude oil. The contrast is even more dramatic here in the United States where the estimates indicate 50 to 100 times more coal than crude oil. There can be no doubt that dependence on coal must increase during the next two or three decades as petroleum reserves are depleted. Fortunately, this predictable chronology gives us time for the basic research needed to use this valuable resource efficiently and cleanly.

It must be noted, too, that petroleum is not only a fuel, it also provides us with many important fine chemicals and chemical feedstocks. In fact, some people contend that petroleum as a source of other chemicals ought to be classified as "too valuable to burn." Insofar as coal can be economically converted on a massive scale into combustible fuels, we gain the option to "save" petroleum for more sophisticated uses. Then, further ahead, we can foresee that with creative advances in chemistry, coal itself can provide its own array of valuable feedstocks, including some now derived from petroleum.

Coal is a carbonaceous rock containing chemically bound oxygen, sulfur, and nitrogen as well as varying amounts of mineral matter and moisture. As a fuel, it has too low a hydrogen-to-carbon ratio (its H/C ratio is near unity, about

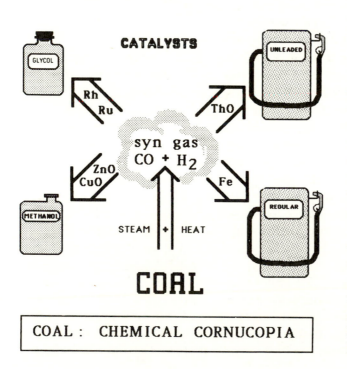

COAL : CHEMICAL CORNUCOPIA

half that of gasoline). For any use of coal more sophisticated than simple combustion, its molecular weight must be reduced, sulfur, nitrogen and mineral matter must be removed, and hydrogen content must be increased. These ends can be approached, either through processes that convert coal to liquid products susceptible to refining (hydroliquefaction), or through conversion to the gaseous form called "syn gas" ("synthesis gas," a mixture of carbon monoxide and hydrogen).

The potentialities of synthesis gas are tantalizingly clear but not as yet economically competitive. Table III-4 lists some of the catalysts that have been found to display product specificity.

TABLE III-4   Catalyst Specificity for Syn Gas Conversion to Useful Products

Catalyst $CO + H_2 \rightarrow$ Product		
Catalyst	Product	Useful for
Nickel	Methane, CH_4	Fuel
Copper/zinc oxide/alumium oxide	Methanol, CH_3OH	Fuels, via zeolite catalysts, chemical feedstock
Iron[a]/cobalt	Straight chain hydrocarbons, $CH_3(CH_2)_N CH_3$, N = 0 to 30	Feedstock for petroleum refineries
Molybdenum/cobalt	Mixed alcohol	Octane booster
Ruthenium complexes (in solution)	C_1 to C_3 oxygenated compounds	Chemical feedstocks
Thorium oxide	Low-molecular-weight branched chains, hydrocarbons	High-octane fuel
Rhodium complexes (in solution)	Ethylene glycol	Polyester feedstock

[a] The catalyst developed by Hans Fischer and Franz Tropsch in the early 1920s.

The details of catalytic conversion of CO and H_2 to particular desired products is an active research area. Equally promising are the potentialities of liquefaction processes, for which more research would clearly be fruitful.

The importance of the processes that can be expected to flow from research on both types of coal conversion was strikingly displayed during World War II. Germany, denied easy access to petroleum, was able to produce 585,000 tons of fuel hydrocarbons from coal. While a good fraction came through gasification combined with cobalt catalysts in Fischer-Tropsch chemistry, the larger share was produced through catalytic liquefaction. In a current situation, the Republic of South Africa now produces 40 percent of its gasoline requirements by similarly converting coal into 1,750,000 tons of hydrocarbons annually (using iron catalysts). Its plants and refineries are literally built on top of extensive coal deposits, and the coal enters the chemical reactors via conveyor belts rising from the mines. These examples do not, however, furnish a general model except under the stress of denied access to petroleum. To impart economic competitiveness to the vast energy resource furnished by coal will surely require advances in catalysis, with specific emphasis on organometallic chemistry and surface chemical science.

Shale Oil and Tar Sands

Shale is a major potential source of liquid hydrocarbons in Colorado, Utah, and Wyoming. In these three states alone, the hydrocarbon content of the sedimentary rock argillaceous dolomite is estimated at 4000 billion barrels. If as much as a third of this enormous reserve could be recovered, it would give us almost 10 times as much fuel as has been removed to date from U.S. oil wells. Complicated new problems of chemistry, geochemistry, and petroleum engineering must be surmounted to reach this end, and a wealth of pertinent research problems must be addressed.

These ancient marine deposits contain varying amounts of kerogen, a mixture of insoluble organic polymers, and smaller amounts of bitumin, a benzene-soluble mixture of organic compounds. Formidable environmental questions (water sources, land reclamation) are raised in the exploitation of shale deposits because a ton of shale may yield only 10 to 40 gallons of crude oil. The kerogen must be heated to about 500°C to be decomposed and produce oil (65 to 70 percent), gas (10 to 15 percent), and coke (15 to 20 percent). To avoid environmental damage, underground thermal processing has been tried.

Shale oil has a favorably high H/C ratio—about 1.5—but it also contains undesired organic nitrogen and sulfur compounds that must be removed. Arsenic compounds can also present a special problem. Crude shale oil obtained by destructive distillation at 500°C has to be subsequently upgraded through centrifugation, filtration, and hydrogenation (to reduce nitrogen and sulfur content) before entering existing petroleum refineries. New extraction and upgrading processes are needed. Chemical kinetics, catalysis research, selective extraction, and selective absorption present directions worthy of study.

In Utah, sands are found impregnated with dense, viscous petroleum. Such *tar sand* deposits are now known in amounts equivalent to about 25 billion barrels of petroleum. Problems analogous to those discussed for oil shales must be confronted, particularly the environmental aspects. Because of the latter, practical use of this potential energy reserve may depend upon whether the rather complicated chemical conversions needed can be handled in situ, i.e., underground. Kinetics of combustion, heat and mass transfer, and multiphase flow in porous media are relevant research areas.

Biomass

An estimated 500 to 800 million tons of methane (equivalent to about 4 to 7 million barrels of oil and with H/C = 4!) are released annually into the atmosphere through bacterial action that takes place in the absence of oxygen. The obvious possibility of applying such anaerobic digestion to methane production from garbage, agricultural by-products, or other wastes is obstructed by the slowness of the process and by its great sensitivity to solution acidity. A detailed understanding of the chemical mechanism of methane production and of the biochemistry of the organisms involved could suggest strategies for overcoming the problems. Concerning the former, the reduction of carbon dioxide is now believed to occur in a succession of enzyme-catalyzed, two-electron steps. Nickel plays a key role in the active enzyme, but neither its coordination state nor its specific action are known. Research on both synthesis and catalytic activity of metal organic compounds, artificial enzymes, and natural enzymes should help us assess the potentiality of biomass as a source of hydrocarbon fuels or chemical feedstocks. The appeal of this possibility is considerably enhanced by the prospect of extracting useful energy from garbage and sewage disposal.

A particularly appealing aspect of biomass as a major fuel source relates to the atmospheric carbon dioxide content. Because carbon dioxide, CO_2, is transparent to visible light but absorbs infrared light, it lets most of the normal solar radiation reach the ground while intercepting infrared light which the cooler earth's surface radiates. Thus CO_2 "traps" the solar energy, tending to warm up the atmosphere (the "greenhouse" effect). The problem we face is that measurements throughout the century indicate that the amount of CO_2 in the atmosphere is rising, which raises concern that in time the atmospheric temperature might rise enough to melt the polar ice caps (an average rise of only 5° might be sufficient).

It is likely that most of the atmospheric carbon dioxide increase over the last 60 years has resulted from combustion of fossil fuels. To arrest this trend, we should be seeking new energy sources that do not release CO_2. Solar energy is such an alternative. Less widely recognized, however, is that new biomass is an ongoing solar energy use that does not exacerbate the CO_2 problem. While combustion of new biomass does produce CO_2, its carbon content was all recently extracted from the atmospheric CO_2 reservoir during growth of the biomass. Hence there is no *net* change in the CO_2 balance.

As mentioned above, this desirable concept can be put into practice only after research progress points to economically viable chemical processes for massive conversions of biomass to combustible substances. Further, there are trade-offs to be considered, such as partial diversion of agricultural land use from food to biomass production. With the prospects afforded by genetic engineering, even this conflict may be diminished or eliminated. Food and energy-producing biomass may be optimized in the same plant. Perhaps, as well, plants can be genetically "engineered" that tend to stabilize carbon dioxide by growing more efficiently when carbon dioxide availability goes up. We should be pursuing the necessary research avenues more aggressively than we are at present.

Solar Energy

By far the most important natural process for use of solar energy is photosynthesis—the process by which green plants use the energy of sunlight to synthesize organic (carbon) compounds from carbon dioxide and water, with the concomitant evolution of molecular oxygen. To be able to replicate this process in the laboratory would clearly be a major triumph with dramatic implications.

Despite much progress in understanding photosynthesis, we are still far from this goal.

The basic path from carbon dioxide to carbohydrate was traced in the 1950s. Since then, further insight has been gained, particularly into the initial events in photosynthesis, by means of new developments in magnetic resonance spectrometry and laser techniques.

The solar spectrum that drives photosynthesis places about two-thirds of the radiant energy in the red and near-infrared spectral regions. Understanding the way nature manages to carry out photochemistry with these low-energy photons is one of the keys to understanding (and mimicking) photosynthesis. Current-day explanations are generally based upon the so called "Z scheme" in which the energy of one near-infrared photon initiates a series of electron transfer reactions (oxidation-reduction steps). While each of these steps necessarily expends some of the absorbed

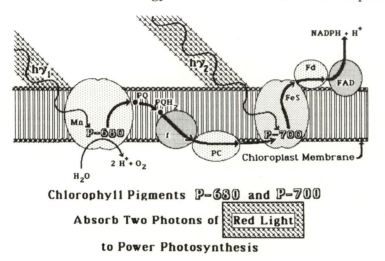

Chlorophyll Pigments P-680 and P-700

Absorb Two Photons of Red Light

to Power Photosynthesis

energy, a fraction is stored through the energy-consuming production of adenosine triphosphate (ATP). Further, the chemistry is set up for the absorption of a second infrared photon to produce still more ATP and to initiate reduction of atmospheric CO_2. This sequence of events gives the "feedstocks" from which the cellular factory manufactures its high energy carbohydrate products. This factory is run by the energy stored in ATP.

Thus natural photosynthesis is energized by near-infrared light through production of energy-storing intermediate substances with long enough lifetimes to await arrival of a second near-infrared photon. The second photon "stands on the shoulders" of the first so that their combined energy is adequate for making and breaking the conventional chemical bonds in the organic molecules of which plants are made.

Several of the steps in this sequence take place in much less than a millionth of a second, at rates too fast to measure only 15 years ago. Now we have picosecond laser and nanosecond electron-spin-resonance spectroscopic techniques with which to probe each successive reaction on its own characteristic time scale. Hence we are in a period of rapid progress in clarifying the chemistry of the photosynthetic process.

This type of spectroscopic study reveals photosynthesis to be a complex process involving cooperative interaction of many chlorophyll molecules. Aggregation of chlorophyll molecules with each other and with proteins has been

probed by infrared spectroscopy and by proton and ^{13}C
nuclear magnetic resonance
(NMR). With the higher magnetic field now becoming
available for NMR, vital new
information on chlorophyll
behavior and the molecular
architecture of in vivo chlorophyll can be expected. Structural studies of the photosynthetic membranes in which
chlorophyll is imbedded will
be further advanced by the
application of small-angle
neutron scattering. Electron

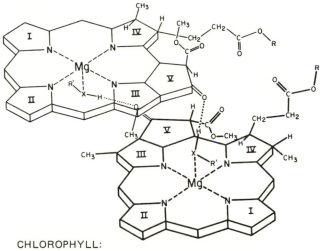

CHLOROPHYLL:
PACKING GEOMETRY AFFECTS ITS FUNCTION

paramagnetic resonance experiments have shown that rapid ejection or transfer
of an electron from chlorophyll (within nanoseconds after the light absorption)
leaves an unpaired electron shared by two chlorophyll molecules. This observation has led to the idea that the photoreaction center consists of a pair of
parallel chlorophyll rings held in close proximity by hydrogen bonding between
amino acid groups.

Another promising approach to using solar energy is the direct conversion of
sunlight to electrical or chemical energy with the aid of electrochemical devices.
Recent advances in electrochemistry have brought us closer to practical realization of this possibility, and there is much opportunity for further research. In
a photoelectrochemical cell, one or both electrodes are made of light-absorbing
semiconductors. The light absorption results in oxidation-reduction chemistry
at the electrode-electrolyte interface and, hence, current flow in the external
circuit. Alternatively, with suitable control, the ultimate products of the
oxidation-reduction chemistry can be hydrogen and oxygen. Elucidation of the
thermodynamics and kinetics of light-induced processes at interfaces has, over
the past decade, led to an order-of-magnitude increase in efficiency of conversion
from light to electrical energy (from 1 percent to better than 10 percent).
Development of thin, polycrystalline semiconductor films with high conversion
efficiencies to replace the expensive single crystals currently used has been
another important achievement. For example, with thin cadmium-selenide-
telluride films, efficiencies of nearly 10 percent have been reported. Improved
understanding of those aspects of surface chemistry and structure that limit
photoelectrode performance will depend on the application of the most powerful
new tools of surface science. Equally important will be basic research on new
materials, including surface coatings of polymers, oxides, noble metals, etc. Of
particular significance will be better understanding and catalysis of multi-
electron transfer reactions.

Nuclear Energy

At the same time that physicists and chemists gave us the atomic bomb, they offered mankind atomic energy, a new source of energy with seemingly unlimited capacity. However, the optimum role of nuclear energy in man's energy future is clouded by long-term risks that are difficult to assess. Whatever course society ultimately chooses, the minimization of its attendant risks will rely heavily upon the ingenuity of chemists and chemical engineers.

Indeed, chemical research is essential to practically all phases of nuclear energy generation and the subsequent management of radioactive waste. To begin with, geochemistry plays a lead role in locating uranium ore deposits. Then, chemical separations are centrally important in the nuclear fuel cycle—from concentration steps at the uranium mill, through reactor fuel manufacture, to the highly automated remote-control reprocessing of fuel elements if we decide to separate uranium and plutonium from fission products. Similarly, radioactive waste management is largely based upon chemistry and geochemistry. If these wastes are to be stored underground, we must find appropriately stable, leach-resistant matrices, we must develop more efficient separations of particularly hazardous radioactive elements (e.g., the actinides that pose the major health hazard after a few hundred years), and we must understand fully the geochemistry of potential waste storage sites. If temporary, recoverable containers are used, the problem shifts to corrosion chemistry under intense irradiation. Next, our analytical techniques must be made more sensitive for a variety of applications that extend from exploring for new uranium deposits to environmental monitoring at trace levels that would help reveal potential problems before real hazard has developed. Finally, we must extend our understanding of the unfamiliar chemistry that would accompany a catastrophic reactor accident. We must have useful estimates of release rates for fission products from a decomposing ceramic in the presence of high pressure ($\sim$150 atmospheres), high temperature ($\sim$3000 K) steam, and an intense radiation field.

The use of nuclear reactors to generate energy is plainly a controversial and emotionally charged issue. Nevertheless, the scientific setting must be fully understood so that political choices can be made among well-defined and well-informed options. It would be unwise to curtail the research efforts that will define these options more clearly when so much can depend upon the confidence with which costs and benefits can be assessed.

Fusion Energy

In fusion reactors, erosion of the internal surfaces determines to a large extent the impurities injected into the plasma. Wall materials are subjected to high temperature gradients, unipolar arcing, neutron damage, and aggressive ion/surface interactions—all of which remove surface layers by chemical and physical processes. Studies of materials suitable for reactor components have been initiated with preliminary experiments on coated refractories. These studies use testing techniques that simulate some aspect of the plasma environment but do not reproduce the total environment. Understanding high temperature physical and chemical reactions, including synergistic effects, at the interface between the plasma and the reactor components, is essential to informed selection of materials and, undoubtedly, to the practical use of fusion energy.

Conclusion

Nothing is more critical to the long-term health of our technological society than continued access to abundant and clean sources of energy. Fundamental changes in these sources are clearly ahead as world petroleum production peaks near the end of this century and begins its inevitable decline. In every one of the foreseeable alternatives, developments are needed in which chemistry and chemical engineering play a dominant role. The fundamental nature of the needed advances dictates an immediate commitment to a broad research program in chemistry. The program will exploit the powerful array of new instrumental methods that permit us (1) to study chemical reactions on surfaces (heterogeneous catalysis); (2) to advance our knowledge of molecular dynamics (combustion); (3) to understand absorption of light and chemical storage of its energy (photosynthesis, photochemistry, photoelectrochemistry); and (4) to deal with the environmental and waste management dimensions of the new energy technologies that will evolve. Fortunately, chemistry is poised to respond to these challenges. Society must declare its commitment to provide the encouragement that will attract bright young people to these tasks and to marshall the resources needed to accomplish them.

CHEMISTRY is a central science
that responds to societal needs.

It is critical in Man's attempt to...
develop new materials

Stone Age, Iron Age, Polymer Age

There was a time when everything from arrowheads to armchairs was made from stones. Other features of those good old days were air-conditioned caves and char-broiled saber-toothed tiger steaks (if you caught him instead of the other way around). Fortunately, this age ended when someone discovered how to reduce iron oxide to metallic iron using coke (carbon) as the reducing agent. That all happened several thousand years ago, so the caveperson chemist who got the patent rights to the iron age wasn't educated at MIT or the University of Chicago. But this chemical discovery profoundly changed the way people lived. It led to all sorts of new products like swords and plowshares and the inner-spring mattress. Can you imagine how those stone-agers would have reacted the first time they put on a suit of armor, or went up the Eiffel Tower, or took the train to Chattanooga? Well, brace yourself, because chemists are at it again! This time, we're about to enter the Polymer Age.

You may think we're already there, with your polyester shirt, polyethylene milk bottle, and polyvinylchloride suitcase. We walk on polypropylene carpets, sit on polystyrene furniture, ride on polyisoprene tires, and feed our personal computers a steady diet of polyvinylacetate floppy disks. In just the last 40 years, the volume of polymers produced in the United States has grown 100-fold and, since 1980, actually exceeds the volume of iron we produce. But the best is yet to come.

The structural materials with which we have been building bridges since even before the one to Brooklyn, and automobiles since the Model T, would seem to be the last stronghold of the iron age (pun intended). Would anyone dare to suggest that polymers could compete on this sacred ground? Well, no one perhaps except chemists. Right now, there's talk of an all-plastic automobile, and you're already flying in commercial airliners with substantial structural elements made of composite polymers. One of these, poly(para-phenylene terephthalamide), has a tensile strength slightly higher than that of steel. But where this polymer really scores is in applications where the strength-to-weight ratio matters a lot, as it does in airplanes. Even with its cumbersome name, this polymer has a strength-to-weight ratio six-fold higher than steel! To appreciate this advantage, you should know that a 1-pound reduction in the structural weight of an airplane reduces its take-off weight by 10 pounds (counting the fuel to lift the pound and the fuel to lift the extra fuel). No wonder this polymer, under the trade name Kevlar®, is used to build tail sections for the biggest airliners. Oh, and bullet-proof vests, too.

So what about this all-plastic automobile? Of course, weight reduction is the name of the game in trying to build fuel-efficient cars. Already there are automobile driveshafts made of polymers strengthened with stiff fibers, and similar composites are used for leaf springs (oops, there goes the inner-spring mattress!). Right now, U.S. cars contain about 500 pounds of plastics if you count, as well, the rubber and paint and sealants and lubricants and upholstery.

But what about the engine and the electrical system? What will we do about these in this allegedly all-polymer car? Gee, I'm glad you asked. . . .

III-C. New Products and Materials

Webster: *Material.* noun   *The substance or substances out of which a thing is constructed.*

Chemistry. noun   *The science that deals with the composition, properties, and changes of properties of substances.*

Expectations are universally high for advances in the materials sciences. What is a *material?* Webster's definition includes all the substances from which one might construct autos and airplanes, bridges and buildings, dishes and doors, hoses and hose, raincoats and radios, spacecraft and sewer pipe, tires and transistors, windows and walls, shirts, sheets, and shoes. That sweep of application is reason enough for the high hopes scientists have for finding new substances and new ways to tailor their properties to better fit our changing needs.

Chemists clearly have a role here because chemistry is the central science for understanding and controlling the composition, structure, and properties of substances. When tailoring a substance to a need, the chemist's particular talent for synthesis and control of composition helps define this role. By no means does that exclude other disciplines. To make this point, we need only mention the remarkable advances made in solid state physics over the last three decades characterizing and developing semiconductor materials. The fields of ceramics and metallurgy, too, have provided substances to meet special needs, from heat shields to tank armor. Equally important are the contributions of engineers in the processing and fabrication of the products we wish to use. There is probably no scientific frontier that is more interdisciplinary.

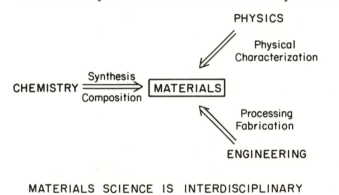

MATERIALS SCIENCE IS INTERDISCIPLINARY

The following analysis will focus on the rich opportunities for chemists to advance materials science to benefit mankind. However, realization of these opportunities will often depend upon synergistic interaction with other scientists in the materials science community.

Plastics and Polymers

We find natural polymeric materials all around us—in proteins and cellulose, for example. But chemists probably learned most about how to make polymers through their attempts to imitate nature in synthesizing natural rubber. Today, chemists have designed so many polymers for so many purposes that it is difficult to picture a modern society without their benefits. Their importance is dramatically displayed in the 100-fold growth of U.S. production of plastics over the last 40 years. Its production, expressed on a volume basis, now exceeds that of steel, whose growth has barely doubled over the same period. The economic implications of these comparisons are self-evident. Furthermore, production of plastics continues upward. New uses are already on the horizon to guarantee a rich future for polymers, a future that will derive from continued research in chemistry.

Polymer chemistry has many dimensions, and chemists are increasingly able to manipulate and control them. Judicious choice of reaction conditions (such as temperature, pressure, polymerization initiator, concentration, solvent, and emulsifiers) and reactant (monomer) struc-

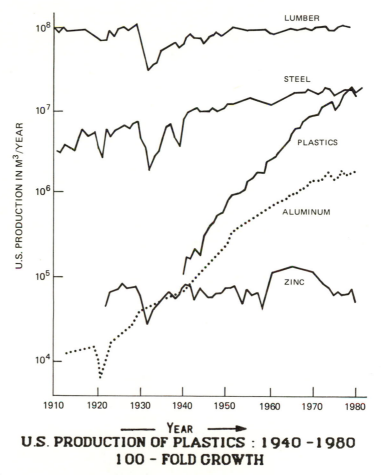

U.S. PRODUCTION OF PLASTICS : 1940 –1980
100 – FOLD GROWTH

tures can determine the average and spread of chain length (molecular weight), extent of chain branching, cross-linking between polymer strands, and, through emplanted functional units, the physical and chemical properties of the final polymer. Sophisticated analytical methods have been developed to relate molecular structure to macroscopic properties. Recent additions to this arsenal include field flow fractionation, size exclusion chromatography, and high-molecular-weight mass spectrometry.

By clever orchestration of these factors, chemists can design a polymer with tailored properties to build in plasticity or hardness, tensile strength, flexibility, or elasticity, thermal softening or thermal stability, chemical inertness or solubility, attraction or repulsion of solvents (wetting properties), permeability to water, responsiveness to light (photodegradability), responsiveness to organisms (biodegradability), viscosity variability under flow (thixotropy), or optical anisotropy. All these possibilities account for the continuing growth of plastics production and their increasing ubiquity in the things we use, wear, sit upon, ride in, eat from, and otherwise find in our everyday environment.

Polymers as Structural Materials

The potentiality of polymers as structural materials is expressed vividly in the hundreds of commercial airplanes flying today that have substantial structural elements made of a composite material made up in part by the light-weight, ultrastrong organic polymer with the trade name, Kevlar, poly(para-phenylene terephthalamide).

The Lear jet, built largely of polymer composites, is a more publicized case. More down to earth, the efforts directed toward an all-plastic/ceramic automobile show the high expectations for polymers' capacity to reduce weight, eliminate corrosion, and lower cost.

In the past, differences in mechanical properties of polymers were discussed in empirical and heuristic ways. Nowadays, theoretical approaches are based upon the primary molecular data and fundamental principles of chemical bonding and conformational structure. The elasticity in the polymer chain direction can now be calculated from bond lengths, bond angles, and the experimental deformation force constants derived from infrared spectroscopic measurements. The resulting progress is evidenced in Table III-5 which compares demonstrated tensile strengths of two organic polymer fibers to both aluminum alloy and drawn steel. In what really matters, strength per unit weight, the two polymers significantly outperform both of the conventional structural metals.

Further developments will

A FEW SIMPLE POLYMERS SHOW THAT POLYMERS CAN BE TAILORED TO NEED

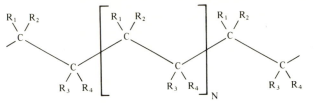

R_1, R_2, R_3, R_4	Name	Product	U.S. Production (tons/year, 1982)
H,H,H,H	Polyethylene	Plastic bags; bottles; toys	5,700,000
F,F,F,F	Polytetrafluoro-ethylene	Cooking utensils; insulation (e.g. Teflon®)	
H,H,H,CH_3	Polypropylene	Carpeting (indoor, outdoor); bottles	1,600,000
H,H,H,Cl	Polyvinyl chloride	Plastic wrap; phonograph records; garden hose; indoor plumbing	2,430,000
H,H,H,C_6H_5	Polystyrene	Insulation; furniture	2,326,000
H,H,H,CN	Polyacrylonitrile	Yarns; fabrics; wigs (e.g. Orlon®, Acrilon®)	920,000
H,H,H,$OCOCH_3$	Polyvinyl acetate	Adhesives; paints; textile coatings; floppy disks	500,000
H,H,Cl,Cl	Polyvinylidine chloride	Food wrap (e.g. Saran®)	
H,H,CH_3,$COOCH_3$	Polymethyl nethacrylate	Glass substitute; bowling balls; paint (e.g. Lucite®, Plexiglas®)	

surely flow from continued research. It is already known,
for example, that the elasticity of a zig-zag polymer chain
can be far higher than that of
a helical structure. Calculations predict that fully oriented polyethylene will be
inherently stiffer than polypropylene, if its properties
can be preserved in the processing steps. In fact, the
strength-to-weight ratio

TABLE III-5   Polymer Fibers Compete as
Structural Materials

	Tensile Strength[a]	Tensile Strength per Unit Weight[a]
Alumium alloy	(1.0)	(1.0)
Steel (drawn)	5.0	1.7
Poly(p-phenylene terephthalamide)[b]	5.4	10.0
Polyethylene	5.8	15.0

[a] Relative to aluminum alloy.
[b] Kevlar®

shown for polyethylene in Table III-5, 10-fold better than steel, is 5 times less
than is theoretically possible. Research is needed to tell us how to exploit these
possibilities. The impact of such research advances will be significantly felt in
our international economic and strategic posture.

Liquid Crystals and Polymer Liquid Crystals

Though known for over a century, liquid crystals flared into prominence only
a decade ago. Today, liquid-crystal display (LCD) devices provide the basis for
an industry second in dollar volume only to cathode ray tubes in the world
market of display technology. No rival matches LCD's in low power consumption for small area displays.

Liquid crystals are organic substances synthesized to possess geometric
and/or polar characteristics that will encourage one- or two-dimensional order.
Because at least one dimension remains disordered, the substance remains fluid
and appears to be a liquid. However, the optical properties reflect the order on
the molecular level. Long slender molecules with skeletal rigidity tend to
become aligned, like logs floating down a river (such one-dimensional order is
called a "nematic phase"). More complex shapes, such as large but flat
molecules, can form layered structures, like the successive sheets in a piece of
plywood (such two-dimension order is called a "smectic phase"). The actual
behavior is determined by a subtle balance between the effects of molecular
shape and electrical charge distribution as the molecule interacts with its local
environment. The balance can often be significantly affected by a small electric
field, which provides a ready means of switching from one optical behavior to
another (e.g., from transparent to opaque).

Plainly, design of liquid crystals is grist for a chemist's mill. Whether to
promote basic understanding or to meet an envisaged use, the chemist's ability
to synthesize new molecules, of spherical, rod-like, or disc-like shape with
prescribed functional groups placed as desired, figures importantly in the
advances already seen and those sure to appear in the future. In fact, one of the
most promising frontiers of liquid-crystal chemistry is the application of this

knowledge to polymerization processes. Coupling the molecular ordering of a nematic liquid with polymerization chemistry permits the order to be built into the polymer, with dramatic effects on physical (and optical) properties. It is just this control that lies behind the production of fibers of exceptionally high tensile strength, which, because of their better strength-to-weight ratio, can replace steel in products ranging from airframe construction to bulletproof vests.

Block Polymers and Self-Organized Solids

Another fascinating area of research that is destined to lead to entirely new types of materials is connected with block polymers. Their concept is based upon recently expanded theories that amorphous polymers of suitable structure will "self-organize" into a continuous medium in which are lodged "microdomains." The microdomains might be spheres or alternating layers or rods in a continuous matrix.

A "triblock" polymer has a segment of one polymer $\overline{B}$ sandwiched between a segment of a different polymer, $\overline{A}$. The resulting material, $\overline{A}$-$\overline{B}$-$\overline{A}$, has the properties of A at its extremities and the properties of B at the middle.

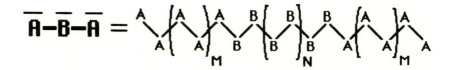

If B and A are chemically designed to be incompatible, the dominant polymer will try to reject the other. The chemical paranoia thus set up can cause the A molecule ends of a polymer $\overline{A}$-$\overline{B}$-$\overline{A}$ to curl up into a ball to minimize contact with B. The result is a polymer in which spheres of A molecules are found dispersed fairly regularly in a continuous matrix of B molecules.

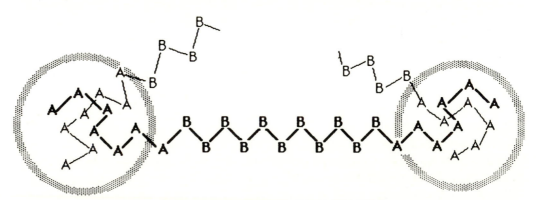

The potentialities of such molecular design are vividly shown by comparing the tensile strengths of the two types of triblock polymers that can be made from butadiene (B) and styrene (A). With $\overline{B}$ chains containing 1400 B molecules and

$\overline{A}$ chains with 250 A molecules, the triblock polymer $\overline{A}$-$\overline{B}$-$\overline{A}$ has a useful tensile strength (about 30 MPa). If the polymers are hooked together in the reverse triblock arrangement, $\overline{B}$-$\overline{A}$-$\overline{B}$, the polymer is a viscous liquid, showing no real tensile strength at all. The first of these two, $\overline{A}$-$\overline{B}$-$\overline{A}$, can be shaped to desired form at high temperature. On cooling to room temperature, it becomes rigid and behaves like a cross-linked rubber. However, unlike conventional rubber, the $\overline{A}$-$\overline{B}$-$\overline{A}$ block polymer can be warmed again and reshaped. Such "thermoplastic" behavior has many functional applications.

This is only the beginning, however. The ability of block polymers to self-organize into microdomains of 10 to 100 Å size and of different shapes (spheres, rods, planes) is sure to provide new materials with hitherto unknown combinations of properties. The microdomains can impart orientational preferences (anisotropic behavior) in mechanical, optical, electrical, magnetic, and flow properties. As research advances give us control of these various dimensions, new applications, new devices, and possibly new industries will be seen.

Photoresists and Chemical Etching

Microelectronics is increasingly dependent upon compressing intricate electrical circuitry ("integrated circuits") onto extremely small semiconducting wafers ("silicon chips"). Demagnification of a carefully drawn circuit diagram coupled with some sort of photographic transfer is a favored technique. Consequently, the fabrication of these complex circuit devices depends critically on the use of thin films (less than .01 microns) of radiation-sensitive polymers called *photoresists*.

In a typical use, the photoresist is placed on top of an equally thin layer of insulating silica (SiO_2), which, in turn, covers the silicon whose conductive properties will determine the electrical functions of the chip. The photoresist film is exposed to the sharply focussed image of a desired circuit using a wavelength of light that will either cross-link (to strengthen) or degrade (to weaken) the polymers. Then a suitable solvent dissolves away the uncross-linked (or degraded) parts of the polymer film. This step exposes the SiO_2 layer below in the pattern of the circuit. Next, the exposed SiO_2 is etched away by more aggressive chemical agents, to which the photoresist polymer must be impervious. Finally, the silicon substrate lies exposed in a faithful reproduction of the original circuit with a density of electrical elements approaching a million per square millimeter.

Older processes used visible light for the photo-cross-linking, drawing upon familiar photographic experience. However, the insatiable desire to place ever more circuit information on a single chip brought the process to a point where diffraction effects at the mask features became limiting. The diffraction effects can be reduced by using shorter wavelength radiation, and chemists are now at work developing new organic polymers sensitive to exposure to electron beams, X-rays, and short wavelength ultraviolet light.

Of course, the photoresist image must still survive the succession of etching steps. Fluid etchants must not swell the mask, and the photoresist mask must remain intact during the subsequent etching of the SiO_2. The current trend is to use chemically reactive gas plasmas (the emitting gas in a fluorescent tube is a "gas-plasma") to etch the exposed SiO_2 surface. It is difficult to design polymers with the necessary combination of chemical and physical properties for use in this technology. Yet they are essential for the manufacture of the next generation of memory chips that will appear in the latter half of this decade and that are expected to carry one-half billion elements (information "bits") per chip. New types of polymers are needed to obtain the optimum high thermal stability, dimensional stability, and easy processing. Hence, economic competitiveness in the microcircuit industry will depend heavily on continued advances in polymer chemistry.

Novel Optical Materials

Optical Fibers

Just as the vacuum tube has been replaced by the transistor in modern electronics, copper wires are being replaced by hair-like silica fibers to transmit telephone conversations and digital data from one place to another. Instead of a pulse of electrons in a copper wire, a pulse of light is sent through the transparent fiber to convey a bit of information. The critical development that made this optical technology possible was the production of highly transparent silica fibers through a new process known as chemical vapor deposition (CVD). Essentially, a silicon compound is burned in an oxygen stream to create a "soot" of pure silica that is deposited inside a glass tube. The tube and its silica deposit are drawn out to produce a glass-coated silica fiber about one-tenth the diameter of a human hair. The CVD process made it possible in less than a decade to reduce fiber light-losses from 20 Db/km to .2 Db/km.

Fibers that are even more transparent may result from a new class of materials, the fluoride glasses. In contrast to traditional glasses, which are mixtures of metal oxides, fluoride glasses are mixtures of metal fluorides, such as ternary glasses derived from ZrF_4, LaF_3, and BaF_2. Although many practical problems remain to be resolved, the new glasses would, in principle, permit transmission of an optical signal across the Pacific Ocean without any relay stations.

Optical Switches

In addition to chemistry's role in development of new materials and processes for optical fibers, it also plays a major part in synthesis of materials for "active" optical devices. These are devices to switch, amplify, and store light signals just as silicon-based devices manipulate electrical signals. Current optical devices are based on lithium niobate and gallium aluminum arsenide, which are spin-offs from the electronics industry, but there is great potential for new materials with unusual optical properties. Chiral organic molecules, liquid crystals, and polyacetylenes can display desirable optical effects greater than those of lithium niobate. The potentials for discovery and practical applications in this field are especially high.

Novel Electrical Conductors

Semiconductors

The modern age of solids was launched during the 1950s by brilliant advances of solid state physicists as they developed deep understanding of pure semiconductor materials. There were early challenges to chemists, too, as it became clear that elemental silicon and germanium were needed in single crystal form with impurity levels as low as one part per 100 million. Thereafter, comparably interesting behaviors were found in compounds of two elements, one from the third group of the Periodic Table (gallium, indium) and one from the fifth group (phosphorus, arsenic, antimony). These "III-V" compounds are typified by the mixed semiconductors, indium antimonide, which has for 15 years provided one of the most sensitive detectors known for near-infrared light. Lately, much attention has been given to single crystals of the III-V compound gallium-arsenide grown on single crystal substrates of indium phosphide, another III-V compound. The resulting structures may have as many as half-a-dozen layers of controlled Ga/As ratio, impurity composition ("doping"), and thickness (micron or less). This class of materials forms the basis for lasers and laser display devices (LED's) for long-wavelength optical communications.

As the range of materials used in semiconductor technologies has broadened, more and more chemists have joined the physicists in such work. This upswing of the chemist's participation was encouraged by the startling discovery that amorphous silicon can also demonstrate semiconductor behavior. Because the prevailing and extremely successful textbook theory of semiconductor behavior is based upon the properties of perfectly ordered solids, such amorphous semiconductors were neither predicted nor comfortably described by theory. Language more familiar to chemists than to physicists has come into use (e.g., "dangling bonds").

We are on the verge of a new era in the solid state field, one in which physicists will continue their important role in characterizing new solids, but in which chemists will now play an increasingly important role. The reason is that entirely new families of electrically conducting solids are now being discovered—families susceptible to a chemist's ability to control local structures and molecular properties. As will be seen, some of these new families are inorganic solids and some are organics.

Conducting Stacks

The field of organic conductors had its beginning in the late 1960s to early 1970s with the synthesis of charge-transfer complexes formed by the reaction of

CONVENTIONAL MATERIALS | NOVEL CONDUCTORS

CONDUCTIVITY (ohm^{-1} cm^{-1})

10^6 — SILVER, COPPER

10^4 — BISMUTH MERCURY

10^2 — INDIUM ANTIMONIDE

1

10^{-2} — GERMANIUM

10^{-4}

10^{-6} — SILICON

10^{-8} — SODIUM CHLORIDE

10^{-10} — IODINE

GLASS

10^{-12}

10^{-14} — DIAMOND

10^{-16} — SULFUR

QUARTZ

10^{-18}

PARAFFIN

METALS

$(SN)_x$

TTF · TCNQ

SEMICONDUCTORS

INSULATORS

·AsF$_5$

·I$_2$

·Br$_2$

trans

POLYACETYLENE

cis

POLYACETYLENE
AN INSULATOR BECOMES A METAL

compounds such as tetra-thiafulvalene (TTF) with tetracyanoquinodimethane (TCNQ). Both of these molecules are flat, and in their mixed crystal they are found alternately stacked like poker chips. The interaction between two neighbor molecules is a familiar one to chemists—a "charge-transfer" complex is formed. Such an interaction always includes an electron donor, a molecule from which electrons are readily removed, and an electron acceptor, a molecule that has a high electron affinity. These two roles are filled, respectively, by TTF and TCNQ. The surprise is that this charge transfer between two neighbors in the crystalline stack provides a mechanism for current flow up and down the stack, the length of the crystal. When detailed study showed that the charge-transfer crystal, when cooled to 60 K, conducted electricity as well as copper at room temperature the excitement grew.

The bright future for conducting stacks has recently been assured by the imaginative synthesis of polymeric conductors based on charge transfer interactions. Large, flat molecules again furnish the elements of the conducting stack (metallomacrocycles). However, the clever innovation lies in lacing them together with a string of covalently bound oxygen atoms. The fact that this chemically designed molecule is, indeed, an electrical conductor is quite a breakthrough. Plainly, the metal atom and the peripheral groups in the flat metallomacrocycle can be modified in great variety. These units can then be connected by an intervening atom chosen to give the desired spacing. The result is a polymer in which carefully chosen macrocycles are held in a molecular stacking that is rigidly enforced and designed to fit the desired function.

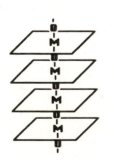

PHTHALOCYANINES
LINKED IN A
"CONDUCTING STACK"

Organic Conductors

Polyacetylene is one of the simplest organic polymers. It has a carbon skeleton of alternating single and double bonds. Chemists call this bonding situation "conjugation," which means that electric charge has special mobility along the skeletal chain. Nevertheless, it came as a surprise when, half-a-dozen years ago, the unusual electrical properties of these polymers were discovered. When exposed to suitable chemical agents such as bromine, iodine, and arsenic pentafluoride (which physicists call "dopants"), such polymers assume metallic lustre and display electrical conductivities higher than those of many metals (though not yet as high as copper). Structural studies have since shown that the electrical conductivity requires molecular structure control (the *trans*-form has electrical behavior different from that of the *cis*-form). The most amazing—and perhaps the most promising—aspect of the polyacetylene polymers is that they can display electrical conductivity over a range of 14 orders of magnitude, depending upon the skeletal structure (*cis* or *trans*) and the chemical exposure selected.

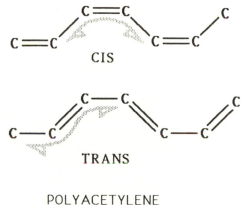

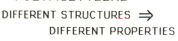

POLYACETYLENE
DIFFERENT STRUCTURES ⟹
DIFFERENT PROPERTIES

Plainly, the gates are open now, and other conducting polymers are already appearing. Thus, the polymer poly(para-phenylene) has been shown to become a conductor on suitable chemical exposure. Next came poly(paraphenylene sulfide) and poly-pyrrole. Now, the artistry of the organic chemist can be brought to bear in combining electrical conductivity with the other manifold benefits of polymers, such as structural strength, thermoplasticity, and flexibility. Semiconductors and transistors became possible when it was shown that polyacetylene could be electrochemically "doped" to either a *p*- or *n*-semiconductor. Because response to light can be designed to match the solar spectrum, these polymers give us hope for cheap organic photovoltaic cells with which to convert solar energy to electricity. Extensive research is in progress to develop lightweight, high power density, rechargeable batteries with polymeric electrodes.

Superconductors

Another discovery as significant as polyacetylene was the synthesis of pure, single crystals of the inorganic polymer, poly(sulfur nitride), $(SN)_x$. This material not only showed metallic conductivity, it was found to become superconducting at about .3 K. It was the first covalent polymer with metallic conductivity (preceding polyacetylene by 4 or 5 years) and also the first covalent polymer composed of nonmetals to show superconductivity. It liberated the thinking of solid state scientists about candidates for electrical behavior as the search proceeded for new superconductors with high transition temperatures.

The potential power of chemistry in furthering developments here is suggested by the conducting stack compound mentioned earlier involving tetrathiafulvalene (TTF). Chemists have now synthesized the analogous compound in which the sulfur atom in each TTF molecule is simply replaced by a selenium atom. Like TTF, this selenium analogue also forms conducting salts but now displaying superconductivity at much higher temperatures than poly (sulfur nitride), $(SN)_x$. It is suggestive and significant that this substitution of selenium for sulfur can have such profound effect on conduction.

Inorganic compounds involving three elements are also under systematic study, and materials with relatively high superconducting temperatures have been discovered among the family of ternary compounds known as Cheverel phases. An example is $PbMo_6S_8$, which can remain superconducting in the presence of magnetic fields of several thousand gauss. This is a crucial property because construction of compact, high-field magnets is one of the most important applications of superconductors. The cagestructure nature of the Mo_6S_8 unit in the Cheverel phases might be a key structural factor in their electrical and magnetic properties. Such systematic investigations will undoubtedly lead to new directions for research in superconductors. In pursuing these new directions, synthetic inorganic chemistry will be in a central position.

Solid State Ionic Conductors

Solid materials with ionic structures are now known with ionic charge mobilities approaching those in liquids. Investigations of such materials over the last decade have already led to their use in memory devices, display devices, chemical sensors, and as electrolytes and electrodes in batteries. Thus, sodium beta-alumina provides the conducting solid electrolyte in the sodium/sulfur battery.

Normally an ionic solid-like sodium chloride has fixed composition and is an electrical insulator. The new solid electrolytes are produced through deliberate manipulations of crystal defects and deviations from integer chemical formulas (nonstoichiometry). The mobile charge carriers might be small ions like lithium ion or hydrogen ion in a crystal lattice that facilitates charge migration. Thus, substances with layered molecular structures—graphite is a familiar example—provide versatile crystal hosts for such behavior. Charge insertion between the weakly bound layers, called *intercalation*, places them in a two-dimensional zone where mobility can be exceptionally high. Many such layered structures are known, so significant opportunities for new discoveries lie ahead.

In a practical application of ionic conduction, zirconium dioxide is used as a sensing element in the oxygen analyzer of an automobile emission control system. The electrical conductivity of this solid changes with the oxygen content of the exhaust gases.

And Other Things

By no means has our discussion of novel conductors been all-inclusive. Here are additional research areas of promise.

Acentric materials (materials with directional properties, such as ferroelectrics and pyroelectrics) are under active development; they include a wide variety of ionic crystals, semiconductors, and organic molecular crystals. Both electrical and optical applications are foreseen: optical memory devices, display devices, capacitors for use over wide temperature ranges, piezoelectric transducers, pyroelectric detectors (for fire alarm systems and infrared imaging), nonlinear optics (second harmonic generation, optical mixing, and paramagnetic oscillation), and integrated optics. To cite an example, the polymer of vinylidene chloride—$(CH_2CCl_2)n$—is piezoelectric and has found use in sonar detectors and microphones.

Filamentary composites are solids containing metallic filaments of small and controlled diameter (.1 to .005 microns in diameter). The physical characteristics of such compounds, including electrical properties, inhibit striking dependence on the size and uniformity of dispersion of the filaments.

Conducting glasses, both metallic and semiconducting, can be prepared by rapidly freezing a liquid, condensing gases on a very cold surface, or ion-implanting in ordinary solids. Thus, amorphous, semiconducting silicon can be prepared by rapidly condensing the products from a glow discharge through gaseous silane, SiH_4. The performance of the low-cost solar cells made of such material depends critically upon hydrogen impurities chemically bound to the interstitial "dangling bonds" of the silicon atoms randomly lodged in the amorphous solid. Also, inorganic nonmetallic glasses are important for optical fiber communication and for packaging solid state circuits.

Materials for Extreme Conditions

Many areas of modern technology are limited in performance by the available materials of construction. Jet engines, automobile engines, nuclear reactors, magnetohydro-dynamic generators, and spacecraft heat shields provide contemporary examples. The hoped-for fusion reactor lies ahead. Engine performance provides a convincing case. Any thermal engine, be it steam, conventional internal combustion, jet, or rocket engine, becomes more powerful and more efficient if the working temperature can be increased. Hence, new materials that extend working temperatures to higher ranges have real economic importance.

New Synthetic Techniques

There are a number of promising synthetic techniques for producing new refractory materials. Among them are ion implantation, combustion synthesis, levitation melting, molecular-beam epitaxy, and plasma-assisted chemical vapor deposition. Most recently, laser technology has provided unusual synthetic approaches. A high-power, pulsed laser beam focused on a solid surface can locally create a very high temperature (up to 10,000 K) for a very short time (less than 100 nanoseconds). Such a transient high temperature pulse can cause significant chemical and physical changes, modifying the surface, forming surface alloys, and promoting specific chemical reactions when coupled with vapor deposition. All these techniques share the ability to form thermodynamically metastable compounds with special properties "frozen in." (Diamond is an example. This expensive gemstone, valued for its sparkling beauty and extreme hardness, is thermodynamically unstable with respect to graphite under normal conditions.)

Some Examples—Real and Projected

Two examples of "exotic" high temperature materials recently developed are silicon nitride, Si_3N_4, and tungsten silicide, WSi_2, both of technological importance in the semiconductor industry. The first, Si_3N_4, can be an effective insulating layer even at thicknesses below .2 microns. The second, WSi_2, is a low-resistance connecting link in microcircuits. Plasma deposition synthetic techniques allow sufficient control to permit these high temperature materials to be deposited upon a less refractory substrate held at much lower temperatures (usually below 700 K). Thus the temperature-resistant material can be deposited without detracting from the desired electrical properties of the substrate.

Polymer precursors offer another promising route to new, "high-tech" ceramics. Preformed silicon-containing polymers, on pyrolysis, form silicon carbide and silicon nitride solids with the predetermined complex shapes. These and other recent advances in the synthesis and fabrication of ceramics make it reasonable to anticipate the future construction of an all-ceramic internal combustion engine.

Conclusion

The next two decades will bring many changes in the materials we use, the materials in which we are clothed, housed, transported, the materials of our daily lives. New industries will be founded—just as polymers led to synthetic fabrics, as phosphors led to television, and as semiconductors led to computers. Metals will be used more deliberately and sparingly as tailored materials outperform them in many of their traditional functions. It is the potentiality for tailoring that points to the increasing role for chemists in this interdisciplinary field. Ultimately the control of the properties of any material depends upon understanding its composition, bonding, and geometry at the atomic/molecular level—the chemist's home territory. What we can do with this understanding then depends on what we can make—and synthesis is again the chemist's bag. That is why industries dependent upon use of new materials are looking for bright young chemists to add to their scientific staffs. That is why more chemists are being attracted to research in the materials sciences. The chemist's talents are not the only ones needed, but they are among the essential ones.

CHEMISTRY is a central science
that responds to societal needs.

It is critical in Man's attempt to...
discover new processes

The Time It Takes to Wag a Tail

When your pet dog sniffs a bone, instantly his tail begins to wag. But it must take *some* time for the northernmost canine extremity to send the news all the way south where enthusiasm can be registered! How long does it take for that delicious aroma to lead to the happy response at the other end? Chemists are now asking the questions much like this about their pet molecules! If one end of a molecule is excited, how long does it take for the other end to share in the excitement? That time may determine whether the excitation will result in a chemical reaction in the part of the molecule where the energy was injected, somewhere else, or nowhere at all.

For the canine experiment, we need a hungry dog, a quick hand with the bone, and a quick eye to read the stopwatch. For molecules, it's much harder. Only within the last few years has it been possible to measure the rate of energy movement within a molecule. But chemists now have pulsed lasers giving bursts of light with durations as short as a millionth of a millionth of a second (a "picosecond"). Comparing a chemical change that takes place in 1 picosecond to a 1-second tail-wag delay involves the same speed-up as a 10-second instant replay of all historical events since the pyramids were built.

The alkyl benzenes provide an example. Each of these molecules has a rigid benzene ring at one end and a flexible alkyl group at the other. At room temperature, this flexible "tail" vibrates and bends under thermal exci-

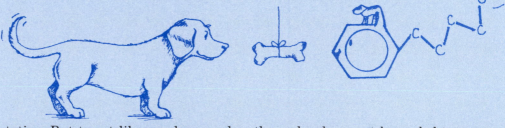

tation. But to act like our hungry dog, the molecules must be cooled to cryogenic temperatures, while avoiding condensation. Supersonic jet expansion makes this possible. When a gas mixture flows through a jet nozzle into a high vacuum, the molecules can be cooled almost to absolute zero. An alkyl benzene molecule carried along in such a stream loses all its vibrational energy, thus relaxing the molecular tail. Then, the cold molecules intersect a brief pulse of light with color that is absorbed by the benzene ring. With careful "color-tuning," extra vibrational energy can be placed in the head without any vibrational excitation in the tail. Then we must watch the molecule to see how long it takes for the tail to wag. Fluorescence lets us do this.

When a molecule in a vacuum absorbs light, the only way it can get rid of the energy is to re-emit light. Such fluorescence can be recorded with a fast-response detection system to give a spectrum that carries a tell-tale pattern showing where the extra energy was at the instant the light was emitted. Those molecules that happen to emit right away after excitation show the molecular head vibrating and the tail still cold. Those that emit later have an emission spectrum that shows that the tail is wagging. In this way, we have learned that the time it takes for the alkyl benzene tail to begin to wag depends on how long the tail is. Surprisingly, the longer the alkyl, the faster the movement out of the ring. The result shows what determines energy flow within molecules (the "density of states"). Such information might one day clarify combustion and help us make fine chemicals out of coal.

62

III-D. Intellectual Frontiers

A substantial array of benefits has been shown to flow from and depend upon chemistry. Subsequent chapters will amplify this theme. All these rewards derive ultimately from our ability to control chemical change, a control made possible by our understanding of chemical reactivity. That is the foundation upon which chemistry is built.

Fortunately, this is a time of special opportunity for intellectual advances that will greatly strengthen this foundation. *The opportunity derives from our developing ability to probe the elemental steps of chemical change and to deal with extreme molecular complexity.* Powerful new instrumental techniques are a crucial dimension. They account for the recent acceleration of progress that gives chemistry unusual promise. Three of these intellectual frontiers of particular promise will be explored here: molecular dynamics, some aspects of chemical catalysis, and reaction pathways.

Molecular Dynamics

Molecular Dynamics encompasses the theoretical and experimental exploration of:

i. the energetics, structures, and reactivities of equilibrium molecular species

ii. the detailed mechanisms by which such equilibrium species change from one set of structures to another.

The theoretical foundation for all chemical behavior resides in quantum mechanics. Though this has been known for half a century, most of the predictive benefit to be derived has been out of reach because of mathematical intractability. Experimental progress on equilibrium molecular species has been rapid and counts as one of the successful enterprises in chemistry of the last three decades. It undergirds the remarkable advances in chemists' ability to control molecular compositions and configurations and, hence, chemical properties. There is no more convincing evidence of this prowess than the single datum that chemists have prepared and characterized more than eight million compounds, 95 percent of them since 1965. In contrast, our advance on the temporal aspects of chemical change has been sporadic and limited by experimental bounds set by transient events too fast to be observed.

Now a new era has begun. Chemical theory, in the hands of a brilliant cadre of chemical theorists and supported by the power of modern computers, has emerged from heuristic empiricism. At the same time, we have at last a battery of new experimental techniques that has opened the way to detailed mapping of the temporal dimension of chemical change. *Over the next three decades we will see advances in our understandings of chemical kinetics that will match the advances in molecular structures over the last three decades.*

Fast Chemical Processes in Real Time

Most crucial to these advances is the capability to identify and characterize intervening molecular species that participate in the train of events between the mixing of reactants and the formation of final products. Fifteen years ago, we were limited to tracking those transient molecules that persisted as long as a millionth of a second. The many interesting studies on this time scale only whetted chemical appetites because it became clear that a whole world of processes took place too rapidly to sense at that limit. Nowhere was that more apparent than in the centuries-old desire to understand combustion, perhaps the most important reaction type known to man.

Lasers have spectacularly expanded these experimental horizons over the last decade. One of their novel capabilities is to provide short duration light pulses with which to probe chemical processes that occur in less than a millionth of a second down to another million-fold (from a microsecond, 10^{-6} sec, to a picosecond, 10^{-12} sec). At the state-of-the-art, physicists are learning how to shorten these pulses even more; pulses as short as .01 picoseconds (10 femtoseconds) have been measured and kinetic studies are just beginning in the .1 picosecond range. At one-tenth of a picosecond, frequency accuracy is limited to about 50 cm^{-1} by a fundamental physical principle—the "Uncertainty Principle." This implies that *chemists can now interrogate a reacting mixture on a time scale short compared to the lifetime of any transient molecular species that can be said to have an identifiable vibrational signature.*

The exploitation of this remarkable capability has only just begun. At this time there are probably fewer than 500 pulsed and tunable dye lasers being used for nanosecond spectroscopy throughout the world. There may be fewer than two dozen laboratories studying chemical reactions in the 10-1000-picosecond time domain. Already a host of exciting types of investigation have been demonstrated, a number of them opening entirely new fields. Study of transient species—free radicals, electronically excited molecules, intermediates in photosynthetic processes, vibrationally excited molecules—goes beyond detection and characterization. It now includes quantitative measurements of time behavior, such as reaction rates, energy relaxation rates, reactivity, and mobility. Such capabilities foretell a decade of striking advances in our understanding of the factors that control rates of chemical reactions.

For example, when benzophenone in ethanol solution absorbs light at 316-nm wavelength, it reemits at two longer wavelengths, near 410 and 450 nm. The active emission processes are definitively clarified when 10-picosecond light pulses are used for excitation (at 366 nm) and the emission is collected with attention to time scale. "Prompt" emission is seen at 410 nm with intensity that diminishes with a 50-picosecond half-life. This corresponds to prompt reemission of the light absorbed in the singlet excitation of the n, II* state, S_1. It occurs at slightly longer wavelength because of vibrational deactivation that takes place too rapidly to measure, i.e., in less than 10 picoseconds. Weaker emission at 410 nm continues, however, with a half-life four orders of magnitude slower, i.e., in about 1 microsecond. This "delayed" emission can be attributed to the transfer of some of the S_1 excitation to the lower-lying triplet state T_1 followed by thermal reexcitation to the S_1 state. Then the emission at still longer wavelengths, 450 nm, is due to direct emission from T_1 to the ground state, S_0. All this is verified by its temperature dependence. At lowered temperatures, the delayed fluorescence disappears, and the 450-nm phosphorescence becomes much brighter and diminishes with a much longer half-life, about a millisecond.

Thus the temporal measurements verify the interpretation and give us quantitative information about the speed of the various processes. The vibrational deactivation with S_1 occurs in less than 10 picoseconds. Then the singlet-triplet transfer occurs with about a 50-picosecond lifetime since it regulates the intensity of the "prompt" emission. The delayed emission reveals the S_1 S_0 radiative lifetime, in agreement with expectation based on absorption coefficient. Finally, the phosphorescence decay at low temperature measures the lifetime of the triplet state, whether by T_1 S_0 "forbidden" radiation or by radiationless relaxation processes. Here we see clarified a set of processes that have

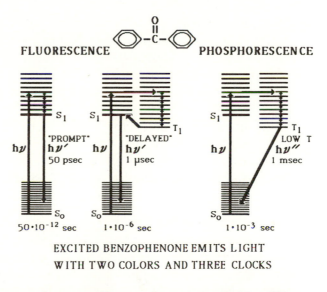

EXCITED BENZOPHENONE EMITS LIGHT
WITH TWO COLORS AND THREE CLOCKS

characteristic times from 50 picoseconds to a millisecond, a range of 100 million. All these types of energy movement are active in natural photosynthesis.

There are many other types of laser-based, real-time studies of rapid chemical reactions now being made, including chemical isomerizations, proton-transfers, and photodissociations. Some of the phenomena to follow also depend upon use of short-pulse laser excitation, molecular beams, fast-response electronic circuits, and computer-controlled data acquisition and interpretation. Such instrumentation has opened new frontiers of chemistry.

Energy Transfer and Movement

In all chemical changes, the pathways for energy movement are determining factors. Competition among these pathways, including energy dissipation, determines the product yields, the product state distributions, and the rate at which reaction proceeds. This competition is influential in stable flame fronts (as in bunsen burners, jet engines, and rocket engines), explosions, shock waves, and photochemical processes.

The collisional transfers of vibrational energy between and within molecules have long been recognized as key processes in determining kinetic behavior. Yet progress has been slow because of limited experimental access to the phenomena. Now a variety of techniques—almost all based on laser methods—has opened the way to providing critical data relevant to the pathways and rates of energy flow. These data, in turn, furnish a basis for the testing and development of useful theory. As much has been learned about vibrational energy movement in the last 15 years as was learned in the preceding half-century.

As tuned lasers became available, they were used to excite selectively particular modes in a molecule. Then, a variety of detection schemes revealed subsequent transfers of that energy into other degrees of freedom, either of the same molecule in absence of collisions or of the molecule and its collision partner, if collisions occur. Propensity rules are emerging that govern the probability of particular pathways. Nanosecond and picosecond excitation, often combined with fluorescence detection, are giving quantitative rate constants for these extremely fast processes.

A clear-cut example is provided by recent studies of the alkyl benzenes, C_6H_5-$(CH_2)_n CH_3$ with n from 1 to 6. This molecule has a structure like that of a pollywog, where n determines the length of its tail. First, the molecule is cooled almost to 0 K by gas expansion through a supersonic jet. Then tuned-laser excitation permits deposition of prescribed amounts of vibrational energy in one end of the cold molecule (in the head of the polywog) under conditions in which the molecule has no collisions with other molecules. When this energy is reradiated (fluorescence), it has a spectral signature that characterizes its vibrational excitation at the instant of radiation. Since this light emission is a time-dependent process, it permits us to monitor the movement of energy from the locus of excitation into the rest of the molecule. This movement in absence of collisions is called *Intramolecule Vibrational Redistribution* (*IVR*). Light emitted in the first few picoseconds shows that the energy has not yet left the benzene unit where it was absorbed. The time scale for appearance of vibrational excitation in the alkyl tail de-

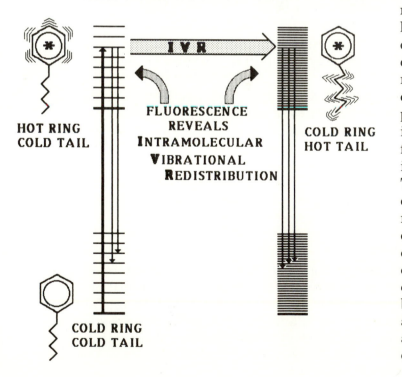

HOT RING
COLD TAIL

IVR

FLUORESCENCE
REVEALS
INTRAMOLECULAR
VIBRATIONAL
REDISTRIBUTION

COLD RING
HOT TAIL

COLD RING
COLD TAIL

pends upon the tail length. For $n = 4$, vibrational energy moves out into the tail in 2 to 100 picoseconds. In contrast, for $n = 1$, (ethylbenzene), it takes much longer, probably 100 nanoseconds or more. Thus, we have direct evidence about the factors that determine *IVR* energy movement in an isolated molecule. This technique is called laser-induced fluorescence.

Of course, a reaction between two molecules requires that they come close together, so chemists must also know about energy transfer caused when molecules collide. Some experiments successfully explore these processes with vibrational excitation using a short-pulse laser and time-resolved infrared fluorescence measurements. In another type of experiment, the highly reactive formyl radical HCO can be produced from formaldehyde with a 12-nanosecond pulse of ultraviolet radiation at 308 nm. Then a second laser tuned to a suitable HCO absorption reveals the presence of HCO, its vibrational state, and its lifetime. In the presence of various collision partners, such lifetime data show collision efficiencies for both vibrational deactivation and reaction.

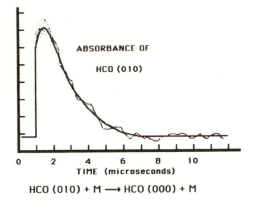

ABSORBANCE OF

HCO (010)

HCO (010) + M $\longrightarrow$ HCO (000) + M

VIBRATIONAL DEACTIVATION MEASURED IN REAL TIME

The detailed understandings to be gained are shown by the different behaviors observed with the two diatomic collision partners N_2 and NO. Vibrational deactivation of the bending motion of HCO required about 1500 collisions with N_2 but only about 10 collisions with NO! This two-order-of-magnitude increase in collision efficiency is made even more intriguing because reaction between HCO and NO takes place as well. Surprisingly, the results show that the reaction is *slower* if HCO is vibrationally excited than if it is not! The unexpected outcome is reasonably interpreted in terms of a long-lived collision complex. These elegant experiments display the power of modern spectroscopic techniques in clarifying rapid and competing chemical processes.

State-to-State Chemistry

When two gaseous reactants A and B are mixed and observed to react and form products, C and D, the outcome is a statistical one. The encounters between A and B include all the possible energy contents, specific types of excitation, and orientational geometries at the moment of collision. Not all of these collisions are favorable for reaction—most collisions have too little energy, or the energy is in the wrong place, or the collision is at an awkward geometry. If we are to understand in all detail the factors that permit chemical reactions to occur, we would like to control the energy content of each reactant, i.e., control the "state" of each reactant. Then we could systematically vary the amount and type of energy available to determine specific reaction probability. Finally, we would like to see how the available energy is lodged in the products. Such an experiment is called a "state-to-state" study of reaction dynamics, and 20 years ago it was beyond all reach. Now, with modern instrumentation, chemists are realizing this goal.

The earliest efforts, based upon chemiluminescence, revealed a part of the picture: the energy distribution among the products. For example, the reaction products from a gaseous hydrogen atom and a chlorine molecule emit infrared light. Spectral analysis shows that much of the energy of this heat-releasing reaction is initially lodged in vibration of the hydrogen chloride product (39 percent). This led directly to the demonstration of the first chemical laser—a laser that derived its energy from the hydrogen/chlorine explosion. Chemical lasers then joined chemiluminescence as a means for determining in a detailed way the energy distribution among the products in quite a variety of gaseous reactions. Through the principle of microscopic reversibility, these findings are equally informative about the important degrees of freedom—the ones that need to be energetically excited—to cause the reverse energy-consuming reaction.

CHEMICAL LASERS REVEAL THE PRODUCT ENERGY DISTRIBUTION

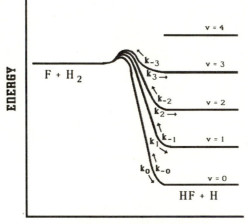

These beginnings led to the discovery of dozens of chemical lasers, including two sufficiently powerful to be considered for initiation of nuclear fusion and for military use (the I* and HF lasers). New concepts based on information theoretic considerations were developed, giving us a new basis for describing these nonstatistical behaviors—the "surprisal" method. The data encouraged ab initio and trajectory calculations to investigate the detailed shape of the reaction surfaces.

"Molecular beams" move even closer toward "state-to-state" investigations. In such experiments, reactants meet at such low pressures—10^{-10} atmospheres—that each reactant molecule has at most one collisional opportunity to react, and the products have none. These sophisticated instruments depend upon ultrahigh vacuum equipment, high-intensity supersonic beam sources, sensitive mass spectrometers for detectors, and electronic timing circuitry for time-of-flight measurements. It has become possible to select the energy state of each reactant molecule and to measure both reaction probability and energy distribution in the products. We are nearing complete state-to-state measurements.

For example, a current study has elucidated a key reaction in the combustion of ethylene. The beam experiments show that the initial reaction of oxygen atoms with ethylene produces the unexpected transient molecule CH_2CHO. With this starting point, theoretical calculations have confirmed that a hydrogen atom can be knocked out of an ethylene molecule by an oxygen atom more readily than it can be moved about within the molecule. This combustion example illustrates the intimate detail with which we can now hope to understand chemical reactions.

Now tunable lasers at ultraviolet frequencies (including vacuum ultraviolet) are being coupled with these molecular beam (collision-free) reactors. They are used to produce exotic molecules usually only found in flames, furnaces, and explosions, such as radicals, refractory atoms, and short-lived excited states. Supersonic jets are used to cool large molecules to almost zero Kelvin, removing the spectral complexity of such a molecule at normal temperatures.

Despite the difficulty and cost of molecular beam experiments, the "state-to-state" information is of crucial relevance to many of the fundamental questions of molecular dynamics and to practical problems of combustion. The molecular beam technique will increase in importance as the sophisticated equipment becomes more generally available.

Multiphoton and Multiple Photon Excitation

Photochemistry has traditionally been concerned with the consequences of absorption of a single photon by an atom or a molecule. This fruitful field accounts for the energy storage in photosynthesis, the ultimate source of all life on this planet. Photochemistry furnishes new routes in organic synthesis and, through photodissociation, provides a variety of transient molecules that play critical roles in flames and as intermediates in reactions.

Now lasers give us optical powers 10,000 times higher at a given frequency than even the largest flashlamps built in the prelaser era. Clearly these devices do not simply extend the properties of conventional light sources, they open doors to new processes as molecules interact with such intense photon fields. As an obvious example, the simultaneous absorption of two photons depends on the square of the photon flux; if we intensify the light source by a factor of 10,000, the two-photon absorption will be enhanced relative to one-photon absorption by four orders of magnitude. When two visible or ultraviolet photons are absorbed, molecular states can be prepared that cannot be reached with a single photon (e.g., states whose wave functions have a center of symmetry and Rydberg states placed just below the ionization limit). Furthermore, the total energy absorbed can be enough to produce ions. This opens a new avenue to the chemistry of ions, a field of rapidly rising interest because of the discovery of interstellar ion-molecule reactions and because ions are major species in the plasmas (glow discharges) of nuclear fusion.

Applications are multiplying as more chemists are able to purchase the high power lasers and as their ease of operation is improved. Multiphoton ionization has been used to detect specific molecules in difficult environments, such as in molecular beams and in flames. Thus the smog constituent nitric oxide, NO, can be easily measured in a flame by counting the ions produced by a laser probe so carefully tuned that only the desired molecule, NO, can absorb. Atomic species can be detected at almost the one-atom level. A multiphoton ionization source in a mass spectrometer enhances selectivity, again because the laser can be tuned to resonance with only a single molecule in a mixture. In quite a different application, a laser focussed on even such refractory metals as tungsten can produce gaseous metal atoms. When this is done in the throat of a supersonic jet expanding into a vacuum, the atoms form clusters of controlled size in the range of 2 to 200 atoms. Immediate interest lies in the spectroscopy and chemistry of these clusters because they bridge the gap between the gaseous and the metallic state. The major impact will be in heterogeneous catalysis because the chemistry of such clusters is dominated by their surface reactivity.

Coherent Raman spectroscopy depends upon the cube of the optical power. In conventional Raman effect, photons of one frequency produce scattered light at a different frequency and leave behind the energy difference in vibrational excitation of the scattering molecule. With extremely high intensities, so many molecules are left excited that they begin to participate in the scattering in a coherent way. This causes a huge enhancement of intensity (as large as a million-fold) and the same sort of collimated beam emission that characterizes the initial laser beam. Equally important, the effect preferentially highlights vibrations localized in the molecular group responsible for interaction with the radiation. Hence the coherent Raman effect can be used to study complex biological molecules like rhodopsin, which plays an essential role in human vision.

However, the most spectacular instance of multiphoton excitation came with the development of extremely high power CO_2 infrared lasers. One of the most surprising scientific discoveries of the 1970s was that an isolated molecule whose vibrational absorptions are in near resonance with the laser frequency could absorb not two or three, but dozens and dozens of photons. In a time short compared to collision times, so many photons can be absorbed that chemical bonds can be ruptured solely with vibrational excitation. This unprecedented and unpredicted behavior is usually called *multiple photon* excitation to distinguish it from two-photon (multiphoton) excitation.

This behavior has already added substantially to our understanding of infrared radiation, and it helped trigger a host of studies on internal energy flow within excited polyatomic molecules. Many uni-

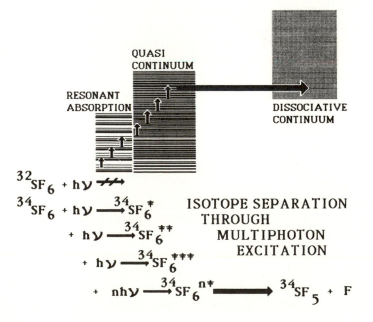

molecular decompositions and rearrangements have been initiated without involvement of higher electronic states using multiple photon excitation followed by laser-induced fluorescence for product detection. However, the practical importance of this new phenomenon may transcend in importance the new fundamental insights it provides. Infrared absorption depends upon vibrational movements whose resonant frequencies are quite sensitive to atomic mass. Consequently, the tuned laser can be used to dissociate only those molecules containing particular isotopes, leaving behind the others—a new method for isotope separation. For example, deuterium is present at .02 percent abundance in natural hydrogen. Yet, by multiple photon excitation, this tiny percentage can be extracted using the freon, trifluoromethane, CF_3H. The process has been shown to have a 10,000-fold preference for exciting CF_3D over CF_3H. This could be of considerable importance because "heavy water," D_2O, is used in large quantity in some nuclear reactors.

Even more significant is sulfur isotope separation through excitation of sulfur hexafluoride, SF_6. This gaseous compound gave the first convincing evidence that multiple photon excitation really occurred so rapidly that collisional energy transfer could be avoided. The successful use of SF_6 for sulfur isotope separation could have heavy implications for human history. The gaseous substance that has always been used in the laborious uranium isotope separation processes is uranium hexafluoride, UF_6. Because UF_6 and SF_6 have identical molecular structures, they have similar vibrational patterns. Thus multiple photon excitation might offer a new and simpler approach to isolation of the uranium isotopes that undergo nuclear fission. It depends, of course, upon finding a sufficiently powerful and efficient laser at the lower frequencies absorbed by UF_6. It will bring more general access to the critical ingredients of nuclear energy and nuclear bombs. It is sobering that Soviet chemists were among the leaders in this work with SF_6 at a time when few U.S. chemists had the resources to purchase the large lasers needed for such fundamental research experimentation.

Mode-Selective Chemistry

With high power, sharply tunable lasers, it is possible to excite one particular degree of freedom for many molecules in a bulk sample. As long as this situation persists, such molecules react as if this degree of freedom is at a very high temperature while all the rest of the molecular degrees of freedom are cold. The chemistry of such molecules has the potential to reveal the importance of that particular degree of freedom in facilitating reaction. To extract this valuable information, energy redistribution and relaxation must be brought under control, and this frontier is being explored.

Because molecular collisions are needed for bimolecular reactions, one of the crucial aspects of mode-selective chemistry is the competition between reaction when a collision occurs and the collision-induced randomization of the mode-specific excitation. For that reason, energy transfer under collisions has already been extensively investigated, and it remains one of the most active research questions in chemistry today. Propensity rules are now coming into focus, and understanding of vibrational energy transfer among polyatomic molecules—both experimentally and theoretically—is advancing rapidly.

Both unimolecular reactions and molecular beam studies of bimolecular reactions escape this problem. Unimolecular reactions involve only one molecule, so collisions are not required. At sufficiently low pressures, reactivity enhancement under selective excitation can be studied. The beam experiments sidestep the problem by giving each excited molecule only one chance for collision and by noticing only reactive collisions. Nevertheless, mode-selective reactions are not readily coming from such experiments. Apparently the problem is that intramolecular vibrational redistribution takes place even without collisions. This problem is of such basic importance to molecular dynamics that it will be one of the most important study topics for the next decade. Picosecond lasers will play a key role.

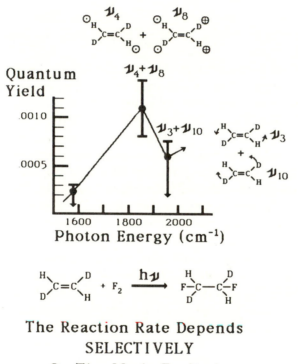

**The Reaction Rate Depends
SELECTIVELY
On The Mode Excited**

There is some evidence for mode-selective bimolecular chemistry in solid inert-gas environments, where the cryogenic situation holds the reactive molecules immobilized in a "sustained, cold collision" with rotational movement quenched. In gas phase experiments, search for conditions under which nonstatistical behavior can be perceived (non-RRKM) is an active research area. It is already known that the density of states close in energy to that of the excited mode is important and that rotational degrees of freedom play a role (through Coriolis coupling). These clues may indicate that supersonic jet reactant cooling in molecular beam experiments will be productive. In any event, as intramolecular vibrational redistribution becomes more well understood, the potential for mode-selective chemistry will become clear.

Ab Initio Calculations of Reaction Surfaces

With today's computers, the structure and stability of any molecular compound with up to three first-row atoms (carbon, nitrogen, oxygen, fluorine) plus various numbers of hydrogen atoms can be calculated almost to the best accuracy available through experiment. This capability opens to the chemist many situations not readily accessible to experimental measurement. Short-lived reaction intermediates, excited states, and even saddle points of reaction can now be understood, at least for small polyatomic molecules. In a major advance, we can now calculate the forces on all the atoms during their reorganization from reactant to product molecule geometries.

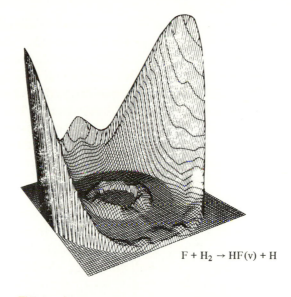

$$F + H_2 \rightarrow HF(v) + H$$

THEORETICALLY CALCULATED PRODUCT SCATTERING ANGLES AND VIBRATIONAL DISTRIBUTION

One example so studied is the reaction of fluorine atoms with molecular hydrogen. This reaction is of great practical importance because it drives one of the most powerful of all chemical lasers (the HF chemical laser). It is of theoretical importance because so much is known experimentally about the product energy distribution that the $F + H_2$ reaction has become a prototype to test and develop our understandings. The entire energy surface on which this reaction proceeds has been mapped with the best available mathematical techniques. Consequently, we know the height of the energy hill to be surmounted, its early placement as reactants approach each other, and the precise energy contours thereafter as the reactants move to closest approach and then separate as excited products. This surface contains the explanation for the efficiency of this laser.

A second case is the key acetylene combustion reaction involving hydroxyl radi-

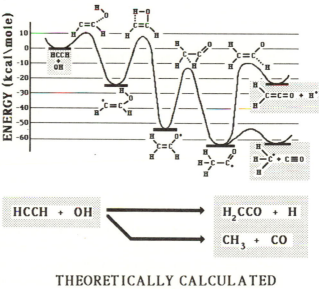

THEORETICALLY CALCULATED
COURSE OF AN
ACETYLENE COMBUSTION REACTION

cals and acetylene. Experimental evidence is found for ketene and hydrogen atoms—one set of products—and also for methyl and carbon monoxide—a second plausible set. Ab initio calculations fill in substantially the intervening sequence of events. After addition across the double bond with an 11 kcal/mole activation energy, hydrogen migration takes place. The calculations show that, at this point, branching takes place. The detailed information advances our understanding of this important combustion reaction and shows how significant ab initio calculations have become in chemistry.

Theorists now aspire to extend their calculations to compounds involving elements deeper in the Periodic Table. These are important chemical species in catalysis, isotope separation, organic conductors, and biological mechanisms. For tractability, it is still essential to separate within the wave function the part due to the inner (core) electrons from that due to the outermost (valence) electrons. Thus, in mercury, with 80 electrons, the quantum mechanical description of the outermost 12 electrons is carried out in the presence of a "pseudopotential" that aims to reproduce the effect of the inner 68 electrons. Agreement between such "effective potential" calculations and *tour de force* all-electron calculations provide encouraging evidence of accuracy.

The problem is complicated even further for elements beyond the lanthanides in the Periodic Table because relativistic effects for interatomic potential curves become increasingly important. It is now believed that the chemical properties of gold, mercury, and thallium are all markedly influenced by these relativistic terms. By no means is this an esoteric nicety. Thus the common Hg_2^{+2} aqueous ion and the dominance of UO_2^{+2} in the solution chemistry of uranium both depend significantly on relativistic effects.

Currently, relativistic calculations for molecules with only one or two heavy atoms are feasible, but for larger molecules, such as metalcontaining biological molecules, only the largest existing computers are adequate. The field will be inhibited until theoretical chemists gain access to such machines.

Theory of Reactions

The rapid accumulation of detailed experimental information about chemical reactions presages a corresponding blossoming of the applicable theory. Theoretical understanding of radiationless transitions, curve crossing, predissociation behavior, energy redistribution, and intermolecular energy transfer is beginning to develop. In addition, recent theoretical developments are providing new insight into the dynamics of reactive collisions. There has been renewed interest in deducing reaction path Hamiltonians for molecular dissociations, isomerizations, and reactive collisions. Gradient techniques in electronic structure calculations can now reveal reaction paths and provide force constants for vibrational motion normal to the reaction path. State-to-state isomerization rates can be computed from action integrals drawn from classical trajectories. Semiclassical quantization of classical trajectories has led to excellent predictions of threshold and resonance energies.

The most active advances in theories of solution reactions have been connected with electron transfer reactions. These important reactions are relevant to biological oxidation-reduction reactions, photosynthesis, electrochemical processes, and solar energy conversion at electrodes. There has been fruitful interaction between theory and experiment that has now been extended to the transfer of other particles, such as H^-, CH_3, and H^+. Rotational isomerizations in simple liquids can now be treated because of advances in the statistical mechanical theory of the liquid state. Further developments in nonlinear dynamics now permit theoretical understanding of the fascinating "oscillating" chemical reactions. Hence, we can mimic biological oscillating (cyclic) reactions and understand steady-state behaviors in engineering-scale processes.

These theoretical advances will have impact on and support a number of neighboring disciplines. For example, atmospheric and planetary chemistry, hydrocarbon combustion, the development of high-power gas lasers (including excimer lasers), chemical processing, and photochemical reactions will all benefit from better theoretical models. Bulk reactions can be understood and controlled only with microscopic understanding of the dynamical details, including energy transfer processes. Chemical theory is moving rapidly on all these fronts.

New Reaction Pathways

A manifestation of our increasing understanding and control of chemical reactivity is the rapid advance now taking place in devising new reaction pathways in synthetic chemistry. The progress presents a high leverage opportunity because it provides the foundation for future development of new products and new processes.

Again powerful instrumental techniques play a central role. The rapid and definitive identification of reaction products, in both composition and structure, accounts for the speed with which synthetic chemists are able to test and develop their synthetic strategies. The use of X-ray structure determination has become an essential technique. The nuclear magnetic resonance and the mass spectra reveal the presence and the local chemical environment of every atom. The X-ray crystal structure reveals the complete molecular structure: the interatomic distances, bond angles, and even mirror-image relationships when present. Spectroscopic techniques, as well, have been essential to progress in the rapidly developing area of organometallic chemistry. The visible and infrared spectra of transition metal complexes reveal electronic configurations and bonding, the foundation for clarifying mechanisms for ligand substitution and electron transfer processes.

Organic Chemistry

Organic chemistry today involves three areas of concern. First there is the study of isolation, characterization, and structural determination of substances from nature. New natural products are thus identified—alkaloids and terpenes from plants, antibiotics from microorganisms and fungi, peptides and polynucleotides from animal and human sources. Success here is strongly coupled to major developments in other disciplines. For example, chromatography permits purification and characterization of a substance present in only trace amounts from a complex mixture of similar compounds. Thus workers in pheromone chemistry regularly fractionate microgram amounts of these biologically potent molecules. The next challenge lies in determination of composition, gross structure, and three-dimensional stereostructure. Here nuclear magnetic resonance, mass spectroscopy, and X-ray crystallography fill essential roles. Using proton NMR, only 100 nanograms of a substance will provide crucial information about the number and types of molecular linkages. With only 100-picogram amounts, mass spectrometry supplements by furnishing precise molecular weights up to 13,000 and, through the fragmentation patterns, providing revealing clues to substructures. Then, if 10 micrograms or more of a crystalline material become available, every sterochemical nuance of structure is displayed through X-ray spectroscopy.

Physical organic chemistry is the second major area; it seeks to relate changes in physical, chemical, and spectroscopic behavior of organic compounds to changes in molecular structure. It grapples with the detailed pathways by which reactants become products—it infers what transient species or structures intervene and determines how the reaction path is influenced by solvent environment, catalysts, temperature, pH, etc. It provides a theoretical framework with which to predict behavior and probable viable synthetic routes toward materials not yet known. Physical organic understandings intellectually undergird the logic and practice of both structure determination and synthesis.

Synthesis, the third area, is a process of inventive strategy. Two contemporary challenges it faces are to supplement availability of useful natural products and to synthesize new and useful substances not found in nature. Thus thousands of pounds of ascorbic acid (vitamin C) are synthesized annually at purities suitable for human consumption so that society can have an ample supply of this healthful substance. Smaller amounts of 5-fluorouracil, an artificial drug extremely effective in curbing certain skin cancers, are synthesized for prescription medicinal use.

Meeting such challenges has required a creative evolution of the process and philosophy of organic synthesis. Only a few decades ago, synthetic strategies were based on clever choices from an array of already known reactions. Like moves in a chess match, the range of feasible reactions was defined in advance. With the development of mechanistic reasoning, it has now become possible to invent new reactions for applicability to specific synthetic goals. Because of the success of this reasoning process, which combines analogy, deduction, and a priori conception, organic synthesis has unprecedented power.

At the same time, there has been an imaginative and fruitful expansion in the settings in which reactions are conducted. An example is solid phase peptide

synthesis in which amino acids are added sequentially to
produce a desired peptide, all
carried out under covalent attachment to an insoluble polymer substrate. Such polymer-
bound peptide synthesis is
already being applied to synthesis of important hormones
and bioregulatory peptide
substances (see p. 172). A
quite different dimension now
being exploited is pressure.
Equilibrium can be shifted to
favor products with specially
compact structures, and activation barriers can some-
times be affected to speed up
selectively a desired process.
A step in the synthesis of
alkavinone, used in the syn-

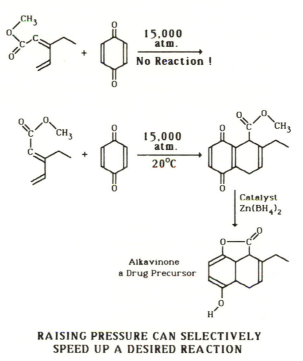

**RAISING PRESSURE CAN SELECTIVELY
SPEED UP A DESIRED REACTION**

thesis of certain drugs, provides an example. At 15,000 atmospheres and room
temperature, quinone will react with the conjugated butadiene ester of the
correct structure to form the desired bicyclic ester. This process completely
avoids undesired alternative structures that would be obtained if high temperature were used instead of high pressure as the control variable. A third
dimension discussed later in this chapter is the use of "tuned photochemistry"
in which selectivity can be increased by use of lasers to induce photochemical
reactions.

Striking developments have occurred in the use of catalysis to reach new
synthetic goals. In a major advance over traditionalist views, synthetic chemists
now search for new reactants over the entire sweep of the Periodic Table.
Notable successes have been registered in the discovery of metal catalysts that
achieve quite exact transformations. Palladium and molybdenum catalysts, for
example, are able to activate with surgical precision one particular bond in a
complex structure.

Nowhere has progress had more far-reaching significance than in our growing
ability to control molecular complexities in the third dimension. This frontier,
stereochemistry, can be divided into issues of topology and "handedness" (i.e.,
"relative" and "absolute" stereochemistry). The production of a particular
molecular topology already requires artful control of spatial relationships as
reaction proceeds. However, this control does not usually differentiate between
spatial relationships that differ only in a mirror image sense (i.e., in chirality).
Thus an elegant pair of Italian gloves uses the same sort of patterns for the left

as for the right glove. When right- and left-handed molecular structures are possible, most chemical reactions will produce a mixture of the two.

Of course, a left-handed glove will not fit a right hand, so it cannot serve the function of a right-handed glove. It is the same in the function of biologically important natural products where this "handedness" aspect of molecular structure assumes critical importance. Biological molecules must, of course, have proper topological conformation (relative stereochemistry); but, for them to be functional, nature also insists upon a particular handedness (absolute stereochemistry). A molecular "right-handed" glove can play a crucial role in a biological reaction while its "left-handed" counterpart will be totally impotent or, worse, may introduce undesired chemistry.

Though stereochemistry has been recognized for almost a century, major advances have been made within the last decade. In one technique, an auxiliary molecular fragment of defined handedness is attached to a reactant. This "chiral auxiliary," properly placed, can govern the handedness of products derived from that reactant. The auxiliary is then removed from the product and reused in another cycle. Synthesis of stereospecific propionates for biological precursor reactants provides an example.

Even more exciting is the use of asymmetric (chiral) catalysts to direct the handedness of the products. This obviates need for embedding and then later disengaging the chiral guiding element within one of the reactants. Thus highly effective asymmetric oxidation-reduction catalysts have recently appeared. Asymmetric reduction is now a key step in the industrial synthesis of the important anti-Parkinsonian agent L-dopa. More generally applicable has been the devel-

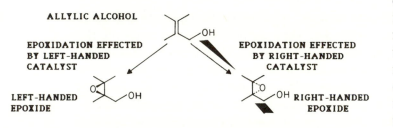

ALLYLIC ALCOHOL

EPOXIDATION EFFECTED BY LEFT-HANDED CATALYST

EPOXIDATION EFFECTED BY RIGHT-HANDED CATALYST

LEFT-HANDED EPOXIDE

RIGHT-HANDED EPOXIDE

NOW THE CATALYST CAN FIX THE DESIRED "HANDEDNESS" OF THE PRODUCT

opment of asymmetric epoxidation through asymmetric catalysis. When an oxygen atom is inserted equally into either face of a carbon-carbon double bond to produce an epoxide, two mirror image-related products result. With inexpensive and recyclable chiral catalysts, it is now possible to prepare uniquely whichever one of these two steroisomers is needed. The resulting stereospecific epoxide can be used in many synthetic pathways, carrying along and preserving the left/right specificity. In a major application, all the naturally occurring six-carbon sugars have been synthesized with nature's preferred handedness.

Many specific examples could be cited to demonstrate the significance of the new frontiers of organic synthesis. Thus the prostoglandins have biological activities that have such extensive applicability in medicine that they may play a central role in therapeutic strategies a decade hence. The biosynthetically related leukotrienes may have a similar role, specifically including a new approach to the control of asthma. The availability of modified prostoglandins and leukotrienes for biological scrutiny and testing is an easily identifiable triumph of synthetic organic chemistry.

Equally far-reaching accomplishments are connected with the synthesis of safe compounds for population control, such as the 19-nor-steroids and 18-homosteroids. The modified cephalosporin and thienamycin antibiotics help meet the challenge of increasingly sophisticated microorganisms. The roles of Aldomet® in antihypertension, procardia in antierythmia, and Tagamet® as an anti-ulcer medication display the creative confluence of organic synthesis and biology. An impressive example from the world of large-volume commodity chemicals is provided by the sophisticated monomer needed to manufacture the promising structural plastic Ultem®.

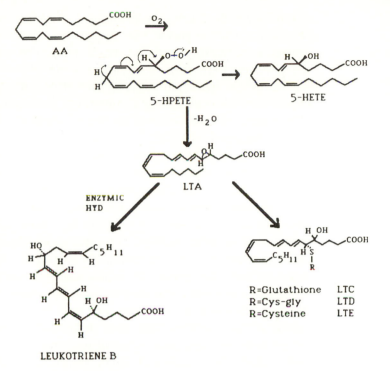

BIOSYNTHESIS OF LEUKOTRIENES

The continuance and acceleration of these advances can be foreseen. Within the next few years we shall see efficient, asymmetric catalysis of carbon-carbon bond formation. Catalysts will be developed for cleaving unactivated carbon-carbon bonds. New strategies for synthesis will be devised. Such advances will be incorporated into the production of new medicinals (e.g., an anticholestimic or antitumor drug), new agrochemicals (e.g., fully safe and biodegradable fungicides), new structural plastics (e.g., an inexpensive structural polymer stable to 400°C). They will result from creative collaboration of the three branches of organic chemistry: isolation-structure determination, physical-organic chemistry, and synthesis, all working in tandem with the cognate disciplines physical, inorganic and, computational chemistry, biochemistry, and biology.

Inorganic Chemistry

There is great intellectual ferment now in inorganic chemistry, much of it at the interfaces with sister disciplines: organometallic chemistry, bioinorganic chemistry, solid state chemistry, biogeochemistry, and other overlapping fields as yet unnamed. The same instrumental array that is so effective in organic chemistry is applicable, making new problems amenable to study in every area of science that involves the inorganic elements. Deeper insights have been gained concerning the structures of molecules and materials, the reactivities of new species, and the possible uses of new compounds and new materials. Geochemists are exploring the role of organic substances in sedimentary ore deposition. Thus inorganic chemistry is entering a revolutionary period; some of the important discoveries of the next decade will be found at the boundary areas just being touched today.

For example, there is uncommon interest in bioinorganic chemistry, stimulated by the growing awareness of the crucial roles played by inorganic elements in biological systems. Living things, far from being totally organic, depend sensitively on metal ions distributed across the Periodic Table in such essential life processes as transport and consumption of oxygen, absorption and conversion of solar energy, communication through electrical signals between cells, establishment of osmotic discontinuities across membranes, and subtle roles in enzyme action. This has led to a surge of research activity in the inorganic chemistry of biological systems. Many problems, both structural and dynamic, are being attacked. How does an organism or plant build its components so as to carry out the chemical reactions necessary to life? What structures surround the metal atoms, and how do these structures enable the metal atoms to react with such exquisite sensitivity to changes in pH and oxygen pressure, and to electron donors and acceptors? Can we understand the mechanisms of the reactions and recreate the steps by which the transformations take place? Can we create simple model systems that mimic the complicated biological systems while preserving the functionality of the metal? What is the minimal model system that will accomplish in vitro what the biological system does in vivo?

Answers to these significant structural questions are being sought by spectroscopists, synthetic chemists, and crystallographers around the world who want to learn how Nature has solved these extremely complicated chemical problems. These scientists are joined by those studying reaction dynamics in these systems, seeking to describe the details of electron transfer through protein systems, energy transfer and utilization in cells, electrical signal transfer through nerves and across gaps, and molecular recognition at all levels. Every one of these processes involves inorganic chemistry and materials, most often metal atoms with organic ligands, and the tools of the physical inorganic chemist have worked well in opening up this new field of chemistry. Significant major challenges await tomorrow's chemists in their attempts to reach a complete understanding of the processes and structures involved in respiration and energy use by plants and animals. Thus bioinorganic chemistry is a major frontier of inorganic chemistry.

A second new frontier is clearly visible at the intersection of solid state chemistry and inorganic chemistry. Using the tools of both the inorganic chemist and the solid state scientist, we are making progress in understanding the reaction chemistry of surfaces, specifically inorganic surfaces. New, more accurate descriptions of the structure of a surface are available, and diffraction techniques plus ultrasensitive spectroscopic measurements now tell us how and where a chemical species is attached to such a surface. This knowledge is vital to catalyst design but is also applicable in semiconductor and electronic chip fabrication. Our abilities to understand the nature of a surface species and a substrate-surface bond will be reflected in improved catalytic processes of all kinds and in smaller, cheaper, more efficient electronic devices. The synthesis of new materials and the development of processes for the control of microstructure are at the heart of much of the scientific and technological progress of the last 40 years; the full understanding of the structure and bonding in these materials, at the atomic level, will be a significant challenge of the next 40.

There are a number of specific needs in this area that can only be met if we achieve such an understanding. Composite structures are needed in several fields: multilayer ceramic substrates for interconnections between semiconductor chips and new compositionally modulated layered structures are now being fabricated, their designs based on experience and guesswork. The rational synthesis of these materials will be a significant challenge to the inorganic chemist of the next decade. Another new class of materials of considerable interest comprises the ultrafine filamentary composites. The unique microstructure of these metallic composites, which contain an extremely dense uniform dispersion of very small filaments (50-1000-Å thick) leads to dramatic changes in material properties as compared to conventional composites. The physical properties of ultrafine filamentary composites exhibit striking size effects not predictable by the rules of mixtures, some related to the composite microgeometry and others due to extremely high interfacial and dislocation density. Some of these anomalies are synergistic in nature, the mere presence of one phase affecting the properties of the adjacent phase. The challenge for the future will be to obtain a full understanding of all these material interactions so as to be able to design and synthesize new materials with properties to order.

Bridging the gap now between solid state chemistry and the chemistry of simple substances in solution is the field of metal cluster chemistry. The field has grown from a subfield of organo-metallic chemistry—itself an interface between traditional areas—to a discipline of its own. In the process of developing, a variety of questions have been left unanswered that will become some of the frontier areas of inorganic chemistry in the decades ahead. First, is metal cluster chemistry really a bridge between single atoms and solid metals? How big must a cluster be before it exhibits some of the bulk properties of the metal? Perhaps the clusters—now known up to one containing 38 platinum

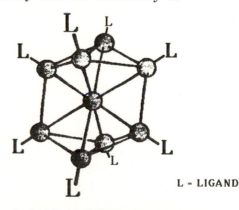

L = LIGAND

A GOLD CLUSTER COMPOUND

atoms in cubic close packing—are simply a different phase in themselves and should be studied as such. Second, how can the detailed electronic structures of these metal cluster complexes be described? Until these questions are answered the highly creative synthetic chemistry in the field will remain semiempirical. As we gain real insight into the electronic structures of clusters, progress will accelerate toward understanding and controlling their reaction mechanisms. Because the outcome may have significant bearing on the advance of the field of catalysis, a heavy investment in fundamental research in the area is called for.

Many cluster complexes can be made and studied in the gas phase as well as in solution or as solids. They can be prepared and studied spectroscopically in cryogenic matrices and under molecular beam conditions using supersonic jet cooling. The latter techniques have provided a wealth of information about the so-called "van der Waals" molecules, including molecular geometry, vibrational amplitudes, dipole moments, and ease of energy movement from one part of the complex to another. Such studies, and studies of even simpler molecules, lead to two

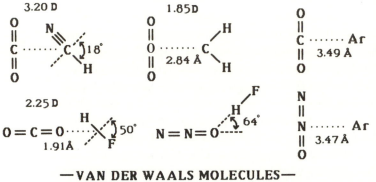

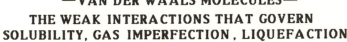

—VAN DER WAALS MOLECULES—
THE WEAK INTERACTIONS THAT GOVERN
SOLUBILITY, GAS IMPERFECTION, LIQUEFACTION

kinds of information: the energetics of bonding and bond-breaking within molecules, and the nature of weak interactions between molecules and ions. Here there should be progress in the coming years on both the experimental and theoretical sides. Better techniques for laser excitation of complex inorganic ions can lead to more precise definition of the energy input to a system; the subsequent reaction can be studied to identify the bond that broke, for example, and precisely what its energy content was. Information like this is crucial to the development of detailed theories of reaction rates and prediction of reaction pathways. Further studies should be made of the anisotropy of nonbonding interactions, in both gas and condensed phases. These forces need to be understood to explain such phenomena as condensation, critical behavior, solvation, and surface attraction.

Perhaps the most explored interface area, one of the richest in reward and still rich in potential, is organometallic chemistry. Here is a discipline that has developed its own literature and that promises, in the decades ahead, more surprises and more satisfaction as workers attempt to correlate facts and to apply rational design principles. The molecule-makers of the field have had a highly synergistic interaction with structural chemists, who, by spectroscopic and diffraction techniques, are unraveling many unexpected bonding patterns and structural motifs. The key to further progress is to understand the reaction mechanisms of these molecules. Through the design of new ligand environments and unusual oxidation states for the metal, organometallic chemists have prepared some remarkable compounds, which exhibit selective reactivity toward molecules previously thought too inert to participate in useful chemical transformations. For example, the activation of the carbon-hydrogen bonds of saturated aliphatic hydrocarbons has recently been achieved by several research groups. Low-valent rhodium or iridium compounds with tertiary phosphine or carbonyl and pentamethylcyclopentadienyl ligands oxidatively add the C-H bonds of hydrocarbons such as methane and cyclopropane, whose C-H bond energies exceed 100 kcal/mol^{-1}. The challenge now is to couple this important new reaction with other well established transformations such as olefin or CO insertion and hydrogenation, so that new catalytic reactions may be developed that use saturated hydrocarbons directly. The direct conversion of methane to ethanol could have a tremendous impact on the world energy situation, and the realization of such a catalytic process seems closer than ever before.

A key to understanding these new types of chemical reactivity and their application, for example, in the design of new, more efficient catalytic processes, or in the synthesis of fine chemicals and new types of polymers, is the elucidation of reaction mechanisms. The primary steps of a chemical reaction (bond formation, bond breaking, atom or electron transfer, etc.) can be studied by examining intermediates, if they can be isolated, or by applying one or more of the many powerful new techniques that are available to the chemist. In particular, two-dimensional NMR can reveal some of the most intimate details of a reaction; fast-scanning spectrophotometers aid the study of moderately fast reactions, and variable-temperature NMR studies are indispensable for probing equilibrium situations. In fact, the entire array of tools of the physical organic chemist is now being used in the study of the reactions of organometallic compounds with results as surprising and as useful as when they were first applied in organic chemistry.

The chemistry of the main group elements—those to the right of the Periodic Table—has in the past largely been explored abroad. This situation is rapidly changing as exciting new developments are now appearing in the United States. For example, the discoveries of compounds involving double bonds between silicon atoms, phosphorus atoms, and arsenic atoms open an essentially new area of main group chemistry. There has also been success with inorganic polymers involving phosphorus-nitrogen linkages. There is even a polystyrene analog with a silicon-silicon polymeric backbone.

A new subfield is being developed in oxidation chemistry. Classical oxidation systems are hard to study, but new metal-based oxidizing systems that allow careful control of the reaction promise to provide chemoselective, regioselective, and

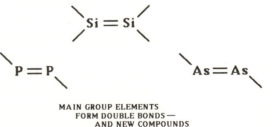

MAIN GROUP ELEMENTS
FORM DOUBLE BONDS—
AND NEW COMPOUNDS

stereospecific oxidations. Ultimately, new methods for activating molecular oxygen to perform these oxidations must be sought; it is likely that these will involve metal species. New tools for characterization of these compounds are being developed—^{17}O and metal nuclide NMR, chiral supports for chromatographic analysis—that will help the experimentalist establish the conceptual framework of the field. Already a metal-containing, highly enantioselective system for the epoxidation of prochiral allylic alcohols has been discovered and assimilated into the organic chemist's battery of synthetic techniques.

Electrochemistry of inorganic materials has recently increased in importance. Electrochemists and inorganic chemists working together have designed inorganic molecules that can catalyze the four-electron reduction of dioxygen to water at nearly reversible potentials. The new catalysts are absorbed on the surface of electrodes rather than dissolved in solution, a significant advantage in reducing the quantity of catalyst needed and facilitating its separation from the product. They should lead to the development of more efficient fuel cells. Further advances in sophisticated analytical techniques, such as hydrodynamically modulated rotating disk voltammetry and digital simulation, promise more applications in the future.

Many of the new experimental developments will eventually come from more complex systems. The major future opportunities appear to lie in the chemistry of metal clusters, reactions that take place on solid surfaces, and reactions in ordered media, such as matrices and micelles. An important need exists for the development of stereoselective synthesis techniques. Despite several demonstrations of this effect, the basic factors producing stereochemical control are still not well understood. Similarly, organometallic photochemistry offers great possibilities for future growth. The photochemical generation of reactive species and catalysts is in its infancy, but it shows great promise. Finally, one can note that most organometallic compounds studied to date have been diamagnetic, but the presence of unpaired electrons in outer orbitals should have a marked influence on reactivity and should open new catalytic pathways for exploration.

Selective Pathways in Organic Synthesis

Selectivity is the key challenge to the organic chemist—to make a precise structural change in a single desired product molecule. The different intrinsic reactivity in each bond type must be recognized (*chemoselectivity*), reactants must be brought together in proper orientation (*regioselectivity*), and the desired three-dimensional spatial relations must be obtained (*stereoselectivity*). The degree to which this type of control can be achieved is shown in the synthesis of the substance adamantane $C_{10}H_{14}$. This novel molecule resembles in structure a 10-atom "chip" off a diamond crystal. In a *tour de force*, it was finally produced in a many-step process in only 2.4 percent yield. Recent research in polycyclic hydrocarbon synthesis now gives adamantane in one step in 75 percent yield. Then a surprise practical payoff came when it was discovered that adding a single amine substituent to adamantane gave adamantine (l-amino-adamantane), which proved to be an antiviral agent, a prophylactic drug for influenza, and a drug to combat Parkinson's disease.

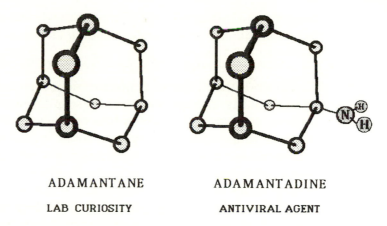

ADAMANTANE

LAB CURIOSITY

ADAMANTADINE

ANTIVIRAL AGENT

Cycloaddition to make five-membered rings becomes important for a diverse array of applications ranging from novel electrical conductors to pharmaceuticals (e.g., antibiotics and anticancer compounds). The catalytic rhodium catalyst ring closure to form a critical precursor to thienamycine is an example. In this case, the five-membered ring contains a nitrogen atom. The final product proves to be a relative to penicillin and an important drug in the battle against infectious diseases.

At another extreme, large ring compounds have been exceptionally difficult to synthesize. Their structures are complicated by functionally crucial left/right handed structural geometries ("chiral" centers). Their wide-ranging biological properties—from pleasant fragrances for perfumes to anti-fungal,

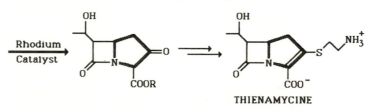

CATALYTIC CLOSURE OF FIVE-MEMBERED RINGS

THIENAMYCINE

anti-tumor, and antibiotic activities—make large ring synthesis an interesting challenge. An example is erythromycin, $C_{37}H_{68}O_{12}N$, which, even after the desired atomic hookup is found, can be shaped into 262,144 different structures derived from the many possible ways to couple the right- and left-handedness at chiral centers ($2^{18} = 262,144$). Twenty-five years ago, this compound was judged to be "hopelessly" complex by R. B. Woodward, who won the Nobel Prize for synthesizing molecules as complex as quinine and vitamin B_{12}. Today we can aspire to such a goal, in part because of the development of specially designed templates that bring together the terminal atoms of a 14-atom chain to form a 14-membered ring. This provides the structural framework of erythromycin,

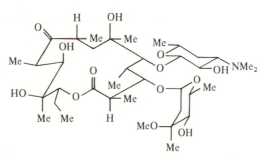

ERYTHROMYCIN
ONCE CONSIDERED "HOPELESSLY COMPLEX"

and it has already resulted in the synthesis of a number of constituents of musk and contributed to our understanding of smell.

Crossing Inorganic/Organic Boundaries

The traditional line of demarcation between organic and inorganic chemists has virtually disappeared as the list of fascinating metal organic compounds continues to grow. The ubiquitous appearance of these compounds in biological systems underscores the importance of encouraging cross-boundary research. Furthermore, research in developing new inorganic substances has provided a surprising dividend in their frequent applicability in organic synthesis.

The latter situation is illustrated by the borohydrides. The cohesive picture we have, at last, for this strange boron/hydrogen family was not possible before their study by X-ray crystallography, infrared and NMR spectroscopy, and molecular orbital theory. Now borohydrides are widely used as selective, mild reducing agents in organic synthesis. Silicon and transition metal organometallic compounds give other examples. Silicon compounds, for example, are used to fold an extended molecular reactant precisely as needed to synthesize the molecule cortisone. Now this valuable therapeutic agent can be made in fewer than 20 steps at a yield 1000 times higher than was achieved in the earlier, 50-step process.

Cortisone

Prednisone

LESS ARTHRITIC PAIN, SMALLER DOSES

Cortisone is well known in the treatment of arthritis. Unfortunately, experience showed that relief could be temporary and that continued use had undesired side effects. These developments made the new silicon-mediated synthetic routes all the more valuable. A variety of cortisone derivatives were prepared and tested for therapeutic effectiveness. One such product, prednisone, is more effective than cortisone, even when used in much smaller doses, with the result that side effects are much diminished.

Because organometallic species are vital intermediates in most metal-mediated organic reactions, it has been important to establish how they make and break carbon-to-metal bonds rapidly, selectively, and with stereospecificity. Oxidation-reduction forms an important basis for such understanding. Organometallics are electron-rich, hence susceptible to oxidation by both inorganic oxidants and organic electron acceptors in solution and at electrode surfaces.

Important theoretical developments have accelerated progress here. Electron transfer theories from inorganic chemistry and charge-transfer views on organic systems have been unified to provide a basis for predicting oxidation-reduction reaction rates. Fine tuning of the steric and electronic properties of organic ligands allows electron transfer mechanisms to be placed within a spectrum of mechanisms connected with proximity of the reactant approach at the time of electron transfer. The extremes are called "outer-sphere" and "inner-sphere" mechanisms.

Transition states with little penetration of coordination spheres of uncharged oxidant (A) and reductant (D) are then insensitive to steric effects, and electron transfer theory sucessfully describes reaction rates. Configurational changes of the electron donor (D) as it releases its electron to become D^+ may then contribute importantly to the energy barrier to electron transfer. An example is the change that occurs as the tetrahedral tetralkyl tin reagent releases an electron and changes to trigonal pyramidal geometry.

"Outer Sphere" Transition State for Electron Transfer

A much larger number of reactions involve significant interpenetration of the coordination spheres, such as additions to alkenes, substitution in aromatics, Diels-Alder ring closures, and bond cleavages. While calculations of ion pair interactions are less feasible at such close approach, charge-transfer spectral absorption bands provide a valuable diagnostic tool for recognizing inner-sphere electron transfer reactions and then for predicting reliably their reaction rates.

This unified understanding will continue to be extremely fruitful because it bears directly on important catalytic processes, including a number with commercial importance. Striking examples include the cobalt-catalyzed oxidation of para-xylene to terephthalic acid (see Section III-A, p. 24), the catalytic oxidation of cyclohexane to adipic acid for nylon production, and the radical chain processes for ligand substitution of metal carbonyls to aid us in synthetic use of carbon monoxide ("syn-gas" from coal).

"Inner Sphere" Transition State for Electron Transfer

Pathways Using Light as a Reagent

Another promising chemical pathway is connected with the use of photons in chemical synthesis. Many natural products and complex molecules of medicinal importance involve high energy ("strained") molecular structures. In traditional synthetic procedures, the aggressive reagents needed to force molecular reagents into these uncomfortable geometries tend to threaten the fragile product. Photochemistry has been remarkably successful in circumventing this difficulty.

The reason for this success is that absorption of light can change the chemistry of a molecule dramatically. After excitation, familiar atoms can have unexpected ideas about what constitutes a comfortable bond angle; functional groups can have drastically different reactivities; acid dissociation constants can change by 5 to 10 orders of magnitude; ease of oxidation-reduction can be drastically altered; and stable structures can be made reactive. The energy absorbed by the molecule puts its chemistry on a high energy "hypersurface" whose reactive terrain can be nothing like the ground state surface below, the one that chemists know so well. Though much imaginative synthetic photochemistry has been performed in the last 10 or 15 years, the field is still opening.

Many examples can be given to illustrate the potentialities. Most dramatic are those that involve cyclic structures that require unusual ("strained") bond angles around carbon. Thus, rings containing three or four carbon atoms are relatively unstable and, hence, difficult to synthesize; they were long sought just because they were chemical oddities. Now we know that many biologically active molecules or their synthetic precursors contain such "strained" rings as essential structural elements, so their synthesis has assumed great practical importance. These unusual, energy-rich structures are natural targets for photon-assisted synthesis. The photon provides extra energy, and it places the reaction on a "hypersurface" where unconventional bond angles can be the preferred geometry. Using these principles, chemists have made many molecules of bizarre structure. Aptly named *cubane* is an example: eight carbon atoms are placed symmetrically at the corners of a perfect cube. Once formed, the molecule is surprisingly unreactive. *Propellane* also involves eight carbon atoms, now in a structure made up of three squares sharing a side. Even more amazing is the family of *tetrahedranes* whose central structural element looks like a three-sided pyramid. Each corner carbon atom is simultaneously bound to three others at 60° angles to form four interlinked three-membered rings.

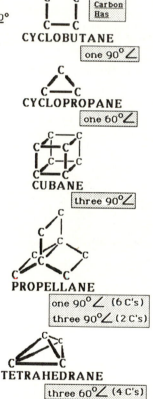

As mentioned above, these photochemical syntheses have proved to be much more than an intellectual chemical chess game. All these syntheses store energy in chemical bonds (the reactions are endothermic). The energy can be recovered later for its own use or to facilitate subsequent synthetic steps to form other desired, energy-rich molecules. Among the important biological molecules already prepared photochemically are the alkaloid atisine, several mycine antibiotics, and precursors of vitamin D_3.

To exploit the new domain offered by light-assisted pathways, chemists need to become as familiar with the energy topography of the multidimensional reaction "hypersurfaces" as they are with the "ground" reaction surfaces upon which stable molecules react. Lasers will be a powerful aid in this exploration. Already it is known that a 1 percent change in the wavelength for the exciting light (from 3025 to 3000 Å) can double the yield in synthesis of provitamin D_3. In the formation of the steroid hormone mentioned above, the combination of wavelength control (3000 Å) and low temperature ($-21°C$) can quadruple the product yield. As tunable and intense ultra-

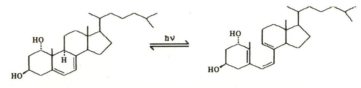

1 *a*-Hydroxyprevitamin D_3 1 *a*-Hydroxyprovitamin D_3

TUNED LASER IRRADIATION DOUBLES THE EFFICIENCY OF THIS STEP TOWARD VITAMIN-D_3

violet lasers become available to synthetic chemists, the reactive surface topography can be systematically mapped and then exploited to move selectively on that surface toward the desired products.

Novel Solids

The synthesis of solid materials tailored to need has traditionally been a fairly empirical branch of chemistry. Symptomatically, this has led to specialist communities, each with highly developed expertise in connection with a particular class of materials such as glasses, ceramics, alloys, polymers, or refractory materials. Now we are seeing a broader resurgence of interest in the chemistry and properties of novel solids. Advances in both experimental techniques and chemical understandings are permitting more systematic strategies that actively draw upon the established principles of chemical thermodynamics, chemical kinetics, chemical bonding, and molecular structure. Increasingly, chemists are joining and expanding the specialist communities mentioned above to address a variety of important societal needs.

A number of examples that have been discussed in a practical context in Section III-C are appropriately identified with emerging intellectual frontiers. For example, there is an intrinsic spatial (stereo) control associated with chemistry in the solid state. Spectacular use of this control is embodied in the zeolite catalyst structures. These alumino-silicate solids can now be synthesized with cavities and channels deliberately contrived to accommodate reactants and products of particular shapes. Guest molecules that slip comfortably into these channels can be held in favored conformations as reactants bring about desired chemical changes. The result is that molecules selected by the cavity can react, and they do so in a structurally specific way. Thus the zeolites furnish a prototype for new families of catalysts. Another dimension of this spatial control is expressed in the intuitively appealing "topochemical hypothesis" that postulates minimum atomic motions will accompany reactions in molecular solids. Considerable attention and interest is being directed toward applying this hypothesis to the control of left- or right-handedness (chirality) through reaction in the solid state. Only a few years ago, the first planned synthesis of a polymer was achieved in which each molecular unit was constrained to the same handedness without any source of control except the crystal structure of the starting material (no enzymes!). Epitaxy may also furnish chiral control based on reactions taking place on chiral surfaces, including the natural chiral templates, such as certain micas.

Still another aspect of solid state chemistry is the role of crystal imperfections (defects) in crystal growth and solid state reactivity. Of course, reaction of one molecule with a neighbor in a perfect crystal immediately creates such a defect. While trace-element influence on crystal morphology has been known for decades, only recently has it become possible to control predictably the pattern of crystal growth by deliberate introduction of tiny amounts of a logically selected impurity to create growth-controlling defects. A technological outcome has been the development of 1000-speed color film in which the light-sensitive crystals are grown in a contrived shape. Direct observation of such defects by high-resolution electron microscopy is already being done for inorganic crystals; it may soon be possible at sufficiently low temperatures for organic substances. This would provide a needed bridge from the molecular defect structure to the bulk properties (including reactivity) of organic solids.

In the polymer field, the variety of frontiers has already been displayed in Section III-C, again in the context of application to societal needs. Incentive for advancing these frontiers is strong because of the potentiality for substitution of tailored polymers for scarce, expensive, or inaccessible conventional materials. As structural materials, polymers are already competitive with metals, and techniques for tailoring are developing rapidly using primary molecular data and fundamental principles of chemical bonding and structure. The elasticity of a polymer chain can now be calculated from bond lengths, bond angles, and experimental deformation constants derived from X-ray and infrared spectroscopic measurements. Control of bulk properties of block polymers by inducing microdomain structures offers many prospects. Self-organizing properties can be imparted that encourage the polymer to form spherical, rod-shaped, or planar microdomains of 10 to 100 Å size. Controllable orientational preferences can be expected in mechanical, optical, electrical, magnetic, and flow properties. New materials with hitherto unknown properties will surely result.

III-E. Instrumentation

All our knowledge, both factual and interpretive, is rooted ultimately in our observational and measuring skill. Hence, the advance of science inevitably accelerates when more incisive diagnostic and measuring techniques come on the scene. This is the situation in chemistry today. A ubiquitous theme in our discussions of the impressive opportunities before us has been the crucial role of sophisticated, complex instrumentation in opening new questions to investigation and extending the boundaries of our scientific frontiers. The advance of chemistry and the realization of these opportunities depend upon access to this instrumentation and the support structure needed to operate and maintain it. Current support levels for research in the chemical sciences do not provide such access.

The discussions that follow identify a number of instrumental methods that serve in the everyday arsenal of research chemists. First we focus on capabilities: today's levels, how much they have changed over the last decade or two, and the capabilities that might develop in the next decade. Then costs are examined and compared to available resources.

Lasers

An array of complementary experimental methods has come into existence that makes molecular dynamics one of the most active frontiers of chemistry research. On this frontier, perhaps the highest potential for gain lies in understanding, at last, the factors that control temporal aspects of chemical change. Nothing is more fundamental to our ability to control chemical change. *Lasers*, the most popular of the new techniques, are finding a wide variety of applications that depend upon one or more of the qualities of a laser to deliver light of extremely *high intensity*, extremely *high power*, extremely high *spectral purity*, and/or extremely *short duration*. Generally, laser design is dictated by the one feature among these that is of greatest value to the experiment at hand,

PULSE DURATION		SPECTRAL PURITY
ONE MICROSECOND = .000 001 SECOND	⇄	.000005 cm^{-1}
ONE NANOSECOND = .000 000 001 SECOND	⇄	.005 cm^{-1}
ONE PICOSECOND = .000 000 000 001 SECOND	⇄	5 cm^{-1}
ONE FEMTOSECOND = .000 000 000 000 001 SECOND	⇄	5000 cm^{-1}

PULSE DURATION LIMITS FREQUENCY ACCURACY AND VICE VERSA

and usually at some sacrifice to the others. Some of the trade-off is imposed in a fundamental way by the uncertainty principle, which relates the duration of a light pulse to its spectral purity. Thus, a 1-picosecond light pulse must spread over a frequency range of 5 cm^{-1}. At this band width, most information is lost about molecular rotations of gaseous molecules. Conversely, if a line width of .005 cm^{-1} is needed to discern individual rotational states, then the molecule of interest must be examined by a light pulse at least as long as 1 nanosecond. This deprives us of temporal information about species with shorter lifetimes or about events of shorter duration than the nanosecond probe.

Developments in the Last Decade

There were three crucially important developments in laser technology that took place during the 1970s and which are having great impact on chemistry. First, a wide range of tunable lasers (in particular the dye laser) evolved and became commercially available. Second, the invention of efficient short wavelength lasers (excimers) gave access to ultraviolet wavelengths at high power. The third development was the ability to produce shorter and shorter pulse durations, reaching 1 picosecond and beyond. In 1970 the tunable dye laser did not exist except as a laboratory curiosity. As of the early 1980s, almost every chemistry research laboratory has more than one tunable laser source. Tunable lasers can now be conveniently operated over the wavelength range from 1600 Å in the vacuum ultraviolet to 4 microns in the infrared. Already in the state-of-the-art stage are lasers that extend the wavelength range to beyond 20 microns in the infrared and to less than 1000 Å in the vacuum ultraviolet.

The tunable laser source has opened the fields of nonlinear spectroscopy, including coherent antistokes Raman spectroscopy (CARS), picosecond spectroscopy, saturation absorption spectroscopy, two-photon Doppler-free spectroscopy, multiphoton-ionization spectroscopy, laser magnetic resonance spectroscopy, and many other important variations of known spectroscopic techniques. These spectroscopic techniques in turn have led to a broader understanding of all aspects of chemical reactions.

Developments to Come

In the next generation of tunable source development, we shall see computer-controlled coherent sources with narrow linewidth, higher peak powers, and subpicosecond duration. The wavelength range will extend over the 1000 Å to 50 microns spectral range. The basic tunable laser system cost may rise to the range $100,000 to $200,000 as the capability continues to evolve.

A new frontier is soft X-ray (XUV) sources for spectroscopy, surface studies, microscopy, and lithography. Here the laser may play an important future role as a source of incoherent soft X-rays via the laser-produced plasma and coherent soft X-rays via the free electron laser (FEL) and nonlinear mixing techniques. The laser-produced plasma source should provide about the same average power output in a laboratory as is available from current synchrotron sources,

TABLE III-6   List of Laser Types and Their Cost

Type	Wavelength Range (microns)	Cost ($)
1. Continuous wave ion laser	Discrete visible lines	45K depending on power
2. Continuous wave pumped solid state	1.064 (most common)	45K depending on accessories
3. Pulsed solid state	1.064, 532, .355, .266, .73-.79, .37-.40	45K 75K
4. Excimer (pulsed)	.193, .222, .248, .308, .351	40K
5. Color center laser	1.4-1.6 and 2.3-3.3	25K pumped with 1 or 2
6. Continuous wave dye laser	.4 to .1	10K pumped with 1
7. Pulsed dye laser	.35 to .95 or second harmonic down to .26	30K pumped with 3, 4, or 12
8. TEA CO_2	Near 10	25K
9. Molecular gas, cw or pulsed	Regions from 2 to 11, depending on gas.	30K
10. Semiconductor diode	.8 to .30	1-20K depending on line-width and tuning
11. Flashlamp excited dye	.34 to .78	20K
12. Pulsed metal vapor	.51, .58, .628	45K
13. High-resolution ring dye laser	.4 to .8	50K pumped with 1
14. Mode locking accessory for short pulse applications	—	20K addition to 1, 2, 3, or 8

although it may not compete with undulator-equipped synchrotrons. However, the laser plasma source will be priced at one-tenth the synchrotron beam line cost. The free electron laser is an outstanding new development in tunable lasers. As discussed later in this section, these devices currently operate in the IR but will soon be extended into the UV and vacuum ultraviolet regions. Finally, a combination of excimer lasers, dye lasers, and nonlinear mixing techniques will be used to generate coherent soft X-rays in an intensity range intermediate to the free electron laser and the synchrotron, but at a cost considerably less than either. The mixing techniques have already been demonstrated in research laboratories. Optical coatings, filters, mirrors, and spectrometers are all evolving for use in the 10-30 eV soft X-ray spectral region. Although affordable and portable commercial systems may be several years away, there is a significant application for them in X-ray lithography for ultra small integrated circuit fabrication.

Costs and Applications

Table III-6 lists many different types of lasers, their wavelength ranges, and rough costs at present. It is important to note that most of the more powerful lasers have only discrete output wavelengths and are most useful in the study of solid materials, which usually have broad absorption features. For most chemical applications, tunable sources are critically important, and these lasers are often excited with a powerful monochromatic laser. The cost listed in Table III-6 is for the laser only and does not include detector, measurement electronics, optics, specialized support equipment (e.g., data acquisition), and other items that may be necessary to perform an experiment. These ancillary pieces of equipment will add at least $20K to $40K to the laser cost. Consequently, the cost of equipping a laboratory with tunable sources over a wide spectral range with both pulsed and continuous capability can easily exceed $250K. These are often delicate instruments that are not readily shared, so dedicated use is required. Their impact on chemistry already extends over a wide range of research applications (see Table III-7). Ready access to the optimum laser system is essential for work at many of today's most exciting research frontiers.

Table III-7 lists the most common uses of these different types of lasers in chemical research and applied problems. The last column refers to the type of laser used in these experiments (as numbered in Table III-6).

Computers

The use of computers by chemists has paralleled the revolutionary computer development of the last three decades. The magnitude of the growth is typified

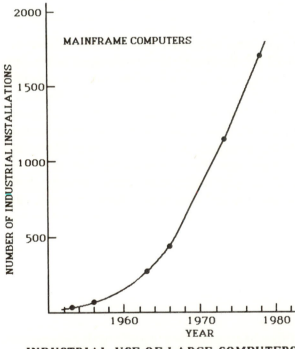

INDUSTRIAL USE OF LARGE COMPUTERS

by the number of industrial installations of the largest IBM computers, for which data are available over this period. In the mid-1950s, there were 20 or 30 such machines (IBM 701s). By the mid-1960s, the much more powerful 7094 and 360 systems numbered about 350. Today, there are perhaps 1700 industrial installations of IBM 3033s. This numerical growth has been accompanied by an increase in computer power that has taxed the field's supply of superlatives. We shall use only a bit of this jargon, as approximately defined in Table III-8.

The extent to which chemistry has benefitted by the growth of computing speeds is well illustrated by comparing two landmark calculations. The first ab initio self-consistent field methods for polyatomic molecules appeared in the early 1960s, and study of the internal rotation barrier in ethane was of special importance. In that work, a minimum basis set of 16 functions was employed.

TABLE III-7 Research Areas Utilizing the Laser

Area	Relative Number of Users	Application	Laser Used (see Table III-6)
A. Subpicosecond kinetics	Very few	Vibrational relaxation in condensed phase	Passively mode-locked dye laser—1, 6
		Fast semiconductor decay	Amplifier—3, 7
B. Several picosecond kinetics	Few	Fast electronic state relaxation	High rep. rate { Mode-locked pump—1 or 2 ; Synchronously pumped dye laser—6, 14 }
		Decay of coherent processes in the condensed phase	High power { Mode-locked Solid state—3, 14 }
C. Nanosecond	Many	Lifetimes of excited states	Visible—3 or 4, 7
		Characterization of fast reactions	IR—8
D. Microsecond kinetics	Many	Gas phase decay processes; nonthermal chemical reactions	Visible—11 ; IR—8 or 9
E. Photochemistry	Many	UV or visible photolysis	4 or 11
F. Isotope separation	Few	Pure element isolation	4 or 12, 7
G. Materials science	Many	Controlled melting and crystallization	1, 3, or 8
H. Microprobe analysis	Few	Source for mass spectrometer or atomic emission	3
I. Raman spectroscopy	Very many	Routine sample characterization and analysis	1 optionally 6
J. Atomic absorption/fluorescence	Few	Trace element analysis	1, 6
K. Combustion diagnostics	Few	Probing reaction chambers	3, 7
L. Atmospheric gas sampling	Many	Monitoring industrial processes	10
M. Ultrahigh resolution spectroscopy	Few	Linewidth measurement; excitation of single quantum states in the gas phase	Visible—1, 6, 13 ; IR—10
N. Tunable cw spectroscopy	Very many	Condensed phase absorption and fluorescence excitation	1, 6
O. High power experiments	Many	Saturation of transitions	Visible—3 or 4, 7 ; IR—8 or 9
P. Generation of extreme frequencies	Few	Frequency conversion stimulated Raman scattering or frequency sum/difference	Visible—3 or 4, 7, 8 ; IR range—.03 to 300 m
Q. Cells sorting	Many	Discrimination based on fluorescent tags	1
R. Cellular bleaching	Few	Photochemistry within microscopic structures	1, 6
S. Nonlinear spectroscopy	Few	Saturation spectroscopy; CARS and related methods	3 or 4, 7

TABLE III-8   Relative Computing Speeds of Computer Levels

Computing	Example	Relative Speed
Superminicomputers	DEC VAX 11/780	(1)
Mainframes	IBM 3033	10-15
Supercomputers	CRAY 1S	80-120

This can be contrasted with a recent study of decamethyl ferrocene, which involved 501 basis functions. Because such studies require computing effort proportional to the fourth power of the number of basis functions, the decamethyl ferrocene computation involves $(501/16)^4$ or 1 million times more computation than the prototype ethane problem!

Superminicomputers

This level of computer has become a workhorse in chemistry. Instruments like the DEC VAX 11/780 are comparable to the largest mainframe computers available in the late sixties. They have revolutionized computing in chemistry because of their substantial capacity, high speed, and lower cost, which is now in the range of $300K to $600K.

The last 20 years have also seen three important development phases in the use of computers in chemical experiments. In the first, the *computerization* phase, advances in both hardware and software greatly enhanced data acquisition. Then an *automation* phase increased the possibilities for experiment control through real-time monitoring of critical parameters. Finally, a *"knowledge engineering"* phase ushered in an era in which computers perform high-level tasks in interpreting collected information.

An excellent example is the Fast Fourier Transform algorithm, which permits us to record spectral data in the time domain and then to transform the results to the frequency domain. Because this allows detection of quite weak signals, the algorithm is now routinely used to record ^{13}C NMR signals and to transform infrared interferograms. This is accomplished by building into the instrument a dedicated computer of adequate capability and speed. Because of the success of these instruments, the Fourier transform algorithm is now being incorporated into electrochemical, microwave, ion cyclotron resonance, dielectric, and solid state NMR equipment.

Now, microprocessors have come down sufficiently in cost to motivate chemists and instrument designers to integrate them into their scientific instruments. Such microprocessor-based equipment can monitor data from several sensors simultaneously to provide a multidimensional perspective that is difficult to obtain otherwise. Research examples include excitation-emission fluorescence and mass spectrometry, and practical applications include Computerized Axial Tomography (CAT) and NMR imaging as diagnostic tools in medicine.

Despite their capability, superminicomputers are barely practical for the larger chemical computations because of long turn-around times (e.g., many days of continuous computing). However, addition of an attached processor greatly enhances computational speed, while retaining the convenience of the local superminicomputer but with a price/performance ratio better than those of many large mainframe computers by several-fold.

Mainframe and Supercomputers

Even so, the potential for some computation in chemistry can be met only with the greater capacity and capability of the largest scientific computers (Cray/M and X-MP or CYBER 205) coupled with specialized resources, such as software libraries and graphics systems. This is true most notably for ab initio electronic structure studies.

The entire development of ab initio electronic structure studies has been closely linked with parallel developments of computer hardware and software to facilitate manipulation of massive amounts of high-precision numbers. In some cases, computational quantum chemists have interacted closely with hardware manufacturers in the area of design and performance standards. For example, the Hitachi vector processor was designed in consultation with quantum chemists at the Institute for Molecular Science in Okazaki, Japan. In its April 1984 report, the Task Force on Large Scale Computing of the Committee on Science (ComSci) of the American Chemical Society recommended that "*. . . the ACS take initiative to establish interaction between the scientists who are users of large-scale computation and the designers of new supercomputers.*"

Another area that would be stimulated by increased access to supercomputers is computational biochemistry. Most dynamical simulation procedures applicable to biological molecules require energy solutions for the simultaneous motions of many atoms. A conventional 100-picosecond molecular dynamics simulation of a small protein in water would require about 100 hours on a DEC VAX 11/780 or 10 hours on an IBM 3033. Calculations of the rate constant for a simple activated process require a sequence of dynamical simulations to determine the free energy barrier and additional simulations to determine the nonequilibrium contributions; times required can now reach 1000 hours on a DEC VAX 11/780. More complicated processes or longer simulations become impossible without extensive access to supercomputers.

Costs

It is plain that computers have already exerted a strong and beneficial impact on chemistry and that this will continue. At present, the progress that can be made using computers in chemistry is limited exclusively by lack of resources. *Existing* computers at all levels could increase enormously the research productivity of chemists if they had access to the computing equipment of the appropriate capability (whether dedicated, locally shared, or networked) and to the support infrastructure needed for cost-effective use of that capability. For chemistry, the problem is less the need for a next-generation development than

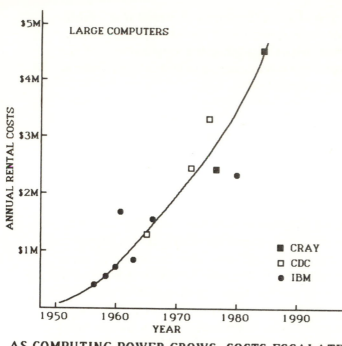

AS COMPUTING POWER GROWS, COSTS ESCALATE

it is for ability to use, whenever applicable, the computational capabilities that already exist.

Molecular Beams

When the NRC report *Chemistry: Opportunities and Needs* was written in 1965, the powerful crossed molecular beam studies on reaction dynamics relied entirely on the surface ionization method for the detection of scattered products, and systems investigated were limited to those containing alkali metals. The situation has changed drastically over the past 17 years. The development of universally applicable crossed molecular beam systems and high-intensity beam sources has made this method a powerful experimental tool for the investigation of elementary chemical reactions, energy transfer processes, and intermolecular potentials.

Capabilities

A typical, crossed molecular beam apparatus can contain as many as eight differentially pumped regions provided by various high-speed and ultrahigh vacuum pumping equipment. It may be necessary to maintain a pressure differential of 14 orders of magnitude, from 1 atm of pressure behind the nozzle of the molecular beam source to 10^{-11} torr at the innermost ionization chamber of the detector. What is glibly called the detector is likely to be an extremely sensitive, ultrahigh-vacuum electron-bombardment mass spectrometer detector with which to measure the velocity and angular distributions of products. With optimum design, an angular resolution better than $1°$ and velocity resolution better than 3 percent can be achieved for scattering processes that provide a steady state concentration of scattered molecules of less than 100 molecules/sec ($\sim 10^{-15}$ torr) in the ionization region of the detector chamber. With such sensitivity and versatility, many new experiements become possible. For example, by replacing one of the beams by a high power laser, molecular beam systems are now giving new kinds of information on the dynamics and mechanism of primary photochemical processes.

In the past 5 years, molecular beam experiments have played a crucial role in advancing our fundamental understandings of elementary chemical reactions at the microscopic level. The advances provide deeper insights with which to build our explanations of macroscopic chemical phenomena from the information gathered in microscopic experiments. In view of this success, more than 10 new advanced crossed molecular beam systems have been constructed abroad in the last 5 years, in Germany, France, England, Japan, Italy, Australia, and other countries. China and Taiwan are contemplating building comparable molecular beam laboratories in the coming years. But the high cost and the complexity of setting up and operating a crossed molecular beam apparatus have limited the general availability of this powerful tool in chemistry communities.

Costs

A state-of-the-art crossed molecular beam apparatus equipped with high-intensity beam sources and data acquisition electronics will cost $350K to construct and $40K/year to maintain. If a tunable laser is also used for the excitation of reagent atoms or molecules to specific quantum states, an additional $100K will be needed. In addition, auxiliary general supporting equipment costing in the neighborhood of $100K will generally be needed in a molecular beam laboratory.

Thus about half-a-million dollars in equipment funds is needed to establish a new, state-of-the-art, molecular beam laboratory. Such an amount has become almost beyond reach in the United States, particularly for scientists in academic institutions. Only two new crossed molecular beam systems equipped to measure angular and velocity distributions of products have been constructed in the United States during the past 5 years. If the current trend were to continue for another decade, we would certainly fall significantly behind other countries in this area of research.

As the experimental sophistication of crossed molecular beams methods continues to increase, a broader range of investigations come within reach. Laser technology is playing a more important role. Thus we can expect crossed molecular beam techniques to have great impact on chemistry provided resources are made available to exploit the potentialities.

Synchrotron Light Sources

Existing Characteristics of Synchrotron Sources

The most intense, currently available source of tunable radiation in the extreme ultraviolet and X-ray region is synchrotron radiation, which is produced when energetic electrons are deflected in a magnetic field. Current capabilities and future needs for synchrotron radiation were recently reviewed by the NAS/NRC Major Materials Facilities Committee. As described in detail in their 1984 report, the principal current use of tunable synchrotron radiation

TABLE III-9   U.S. Synchrotron Light Sources

Facility Name (Location)	Year[a]	Beam Energy (GeV)	Critical Energy (keV)	Spectral Brilliance[f]
Dedicated				
Tantalus (U. Wisconsin)	1968	0.24	0.05	$4 \cdot 10^{10}$
Surf II (NBS)	1974	0.28	0.06	$5 \cdot 10^{11}$
NSLS (Brookhaven, N.Y.)	1981	0.75	0.5	$3 \cdot 10^{13}$
NSLS (Brookhaven, N.Y.)	[b]	2.5	5.0	$1 \cdot 10^{14}$
Aladdin (U. Wisconsin)	[b,c]	0.75	0.45	$(2 \cdot 10^{13})$
"Hard X-ray" ring	[d]	6	10	$(1 \cdot 10^{18})^{e}$
"Soft X-ray" ring	[d]	1-2	0.010	$(3 \cdot 10^{18})^{e}$
Parasitic				
SPEAR (Stanford U., Calif.)	1974	3-4	5	$6 \cdot 10^{12}$
CESR (Cornell U., N.Y.)	1980	5.5	11.5	$5 \cdot 10^{12}$

[a] Year first experiments were conducted.

[b] Not yet operational.

[c] Construction interrupted.

[d] Proposed, NRC Report "Major Facilities for Materials Research and Related Disciplines," D. E. Eastman and F. Seitz (1984).

[e] Proposed brilliance using undulator insertion devices.

[f] Spectral brilliance is the number of photons per square millimeter per square radian per unit bandwidth.

falls in the photon energy range of 1 to 100 keV as provided at several, dedicated facilities and as a parasitic activity at a few high energy particle-physics accelerator facilities here and abroad. Table III-9 shows that in the United States, sychrotron radiation is currently in research use at three dedicated synchrotron laboratories and parasitically at two particle-physics accelerator laboratories. By comparison, there are in foreign countries seven dedicated synchrotrons operating (in France, Germany, Great Britain, Japan (three), and the Soviet Union) and five under design or construction.

Over the past decade, there have been important advances as attention has turned from synchrotrons as accelerators (with radiation seen as an undesired energy dissipation) toward synchrotrons as sources of light. Insertion devices were designed to place sharp bends in the electron trajectories to increase the radiative properties (bends, "wigglers," or "undulators"). These devices show potential for intensity increases by several powers of 10.

Such a quantum jump in brightness will surely lead to new types of experiments. For many chemical applications, the intensity will be of particular importance if the design specifications attempt to optimize radiation in the vacuum ultraviolet spectral region rather than regard it as a parasitic use. It is important to note that the pulsed nature of synchrotron radiation (tens of picosecond pulse durations) and its high repetition rate (10^{8}-10^{9} pulses per second) can be of particular value in chemical kinetic investigations if the wavelength range is appropriate.

Applications of Synchrotron Sources in Chemistry

Scientific use of synchrotron radiation in the United States has been building. There were some 210 individual users in 1976, and the number had grown to about 600 by 1982. Statistics are not available on the fraction of these users who would identify themselves as chemists, but the number is not negligible. A recent estimate at the NSLS facility indicated that less than 20 percent of the research was placed in chemistry. The range of problems under study at our synchrotron light sources is illustrated in the examples below.

Extended X-ray Absorption Fine Structure (EXAFS) has been one of the more fruitful applications of synchrotron radiation to solid substances. When one of an atom's inner-shell electrons is excited above its X-ray edge energy, the atom emits light that is diffracted by neighboring atoms. The result is a diffraction pattern that contains information about the interatomic spacings of these neighbors. Much attention has been directed toward crystal structures of inorganic solids, some of it seeking information on oxidation state when other methods are not definitive. Because heavy atoms are most readily detected, EXAFS has been usefully employed to learn the immediate chemical environment of transition metal atoms as they occur in biologically important molecules, including manganese in chlorophyll. The method is also applicable to dilute species (as low as one part in 10^4-10^5) using fluorescence intensity as a function of incident photon energy. Applicability to surface corrosion studies can be achieved through measurement of photon-induced desorption. Time-resolved EXAFS is also feasible through the use of dispersive techniques in which the entire absorption spectrum is measured simultaneously.

As synchrotron intensities are increased, photoelectron emission intensity can be measured instead of absorption coefficient. A promising development in this area is called Angle Resolved Photoemission Extended Fine Structure (ARPEFS). The diffraction patterns so obtained are sensitive to bond distances and bond angles of atoms located beyond the closest neighbors. Still another possible application of brighter synchrotron X-ray sources would be time-resolved X-ray scattering. Time dependence of pulsed-laser surface damage (annealing) could be measured in real time. Time-resolved, small angle scattering experiments on muscles have already shown changes in repeat distances as muscles undergo contraction and relaxation.

Synchrotron Radiation Costs

The costs of synchrotron radiation are highly varied because such facilities range from relatively small, in-house facilities to large, user facilities. However, the recently proposed hard X-ray (optimum, 1.2 Å wavelength) 6-GeV synchrotron light source (which would find some limited use in chemical applications) has been priced at about $160M for construction, including its proposed 10 insertion devices and associated beam lines. A European counterpart proposal considering a 5-GeV storage ring has an estimated construction cost of $200M. Softer X-ray synchrotron light sources, for which there may be more general chemical applicability, might cost in the range $60M to $80M.

At the storage rings at the University of Wisconsin and at the Brookhaven NSLS—both designed specifically as radiation sources—once the synchrotron is in place, the additional cost for a new, dedicated beam line falls in the range $.8M to $1.5M. Of course, once built, such an installation requires and warrants a substantial, continued annual investment for operation and maintenance. For example, the 1985 operating budget at NSLS is about $15M.

Free Electron Lasers

When a beam of electrons with velocities near the speed of light moves through a static, periodically alternating magnetic field (a "wiggler"), light is emitted in the direction of electron beam propagation. The wavelength of the light is determined by the period of the wiggler field and the energy of the electrons. This provides a "gain medium" that, if placed between the mirrors of a conventional laser, can emit coherent laser light. Such a device is called a free electron laser (FEL).

Potential Capabilities

Experience to date indicates that high-efficiency, wavelength tunability and high average and peak power will all be forthcoming over a wavelength range

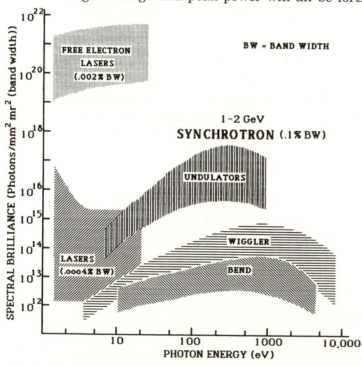

extending from microwave frequencies through the infrared and visible to the vacuum ultraviolet spectral ranges. If the hopes and expectations of the most enthusiastic FEL proponents are realized, average brightnesses several powers of 10 greater than those provided by conventional tunable lasers or synchrotron sources may be possible, particularly in the ultraviolet. Furthermore, short wavelength performance may be extended beyond the limit of present mirror reflectivity, e.g., to the 10- to 30-eV range, either with multilayer mirrors now under development, or with "single pass" high-gain FEL's that do not use mirrors.

DESIGN GOALS ARE AMBITIOUS – AND PROMISING

Possible Costs

The optimum design (and cost) may vary greatly, depending upon the wavelength to be produced. Theoretical estimates of energy efficiency range up to 20 percent for linear accelerator-driven FEL'S, a performance most readily achieved in the microwave and infrared spectral regions. Such devices, which might cost from $10M to $30M, have proposed performance characteristics of 30-picosecond pulse duration and peak powers comparable to those of laboratory CO_2 lasers (tens of megawatts peak power). An FEL with approximately these characteristics has already been operated at Los Alamos National Laboratory. It is based on a linear accelerator 2 or 3 meters long to produce electron energies of 10 to 25 MeV. The device provides a train of pulses of tunable infrared radiation—currently in the 9- to 11-micron range—with 30-picosecond pulses, peak power of 5 megawatts, 50-nanosecond spacing between pulses, and a pulse train duration of 80 microseconds once a second. Such performance extended over the mid-infrared spectral region (4 to 50 microns) would open the way to many novel applications in chemistry. Examples are vibrational relaxation, multiphoton excitation, nonlinear processes in the infrared region, fast chemical kinetics, infrared study of adsorbed molecules, and light-catalyzed chemical reactions. As the wavelength is moved through the visible and toward the ultraviolet, not only the electron energy, but also the current density of the electron beam must be raised. Some researchers (but not all) feel that the current density needs are best met by the larger (and more costly) storage rings like those proposed for use as synchrotron light sources. In fact, free electron laser emission has been demonstrated at visible wavelengths making use of existing storage rings not initially designed for FEL use. It seems likely that a synchrotron-type storage ring with electron energies in the range of .5-1.5 GeV could provide an effective electron beam gain medium for FEL use. At this energy range, the synchrotron could be suitable both as a soft X-ray source and as a tunable FEL source. If designed with the FEL use as a primary application, extremely high brightness might be achieved in the ultraviolet and vacuum ultraviolet spectral ranges. Such a synchrotron might cost between $30 and $80M. Again, a variety of novel chemical applications could be explored in photochemistry and fast chemical kinetics, as well as multiple photon and other nonlinear processes. Instrument developers should be aware that most of these applications could be productively pursued in the visible and normal ultraviolet spectral ranges.

CHEMISTRY is a central science
that responds to societal needs.

It is critical in Man's attempt to...
feed the world's population

Whipping a Wicked Weed

The plant *Striga asiatica* is one of the most devastating destroyers of grain crops in the world. This wicked weed restricts the food supply of more than 400 million people in Asia and Africa. It is a parasite that nourishes itself by latching onto and draining the vitality of a nearby grain plant. The results are stunted grain, a meager harvest, and hungry people.

Basic research on *Striga asiatica* by chemists and biologists has revealed one of the plant world's incredible host-parasite adaptations. The parasite seed lies in wait until it detects the proximity of the host plant by using an uncanny chemical radar. The give-away is provided by specific chemical compounds exuded by the host. *Striga asiatica* can recognize the exuded compounds and use them to trigger its own growth cycle. Then the parasite has an independent growth period of 4 days, during which it must locate the nearby host.

Researchers trying to solve the mystery of this recognition system faced formidable obstacles; they were seeking unknown, complex molecules produced only in tiny amounts. But, by extending the sensitivity of the most modern instruments, chemists have been able to deduce the chemical structures of these host-recognition substances, even though the agricultural scientist could accumulate the active chemicals in amounts no larger than a few bits of dust (a few micrograms). One method used, nuclear magnetic resonance (NMR), depends upon the fact that the nuclei of many atoms have magnetic fields that respond measurably to the presence of other such nuclei nearby. Thus precise NMR measurements reveal molecular ge-

ometries, even of ornate molecules. A second, equally sophisticated approach is high-resolution mass spectrometry. In a high vacuum, molecules are given an electric charge, then accelerated with a known energy. By measuring the velocities at which these molecules and fragments from them are traveling (or their curved paths in magnetic fields), chemists can measure the masses and decide the atomic groupings present. These are critical clues to the molecular identities.

Now, the complex host-recognition (xenogistic) substances have been identified and their detailed structures are known. With this information in hand, we may be able to beat this wicked weed at its own game. Chemists can now synthesize the substances and give agricultural scientists enough material for field tests designed to trick the parasite into beginning its 4-day growth cycle. It will die out never having found its host. A few days later, grain can be planted safely.

With this success for guidance, similar host-parasite relationships are being sought— and found—here in the United States. In addition to grains, bean crops have similar parasite enemies. Thus in collaboration with agricultural and biological scientists, chemists play a crucial role in our efforts to increase the world's food supply and eliminate hunger.

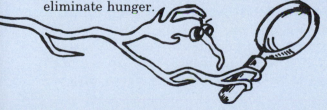

CHAPTER IV

Dealing with Molecular Complexity

IV-A. More Food

Agriculture, discovered 12,000 years ago, was the beginning of man's attempt to enhance survival by increasing food supply. The human population at that time was about 15 million, but agriculture helped it rise to 250 million 2000 years ago. By 1650, it had doubled to 500 million. But then, it took only 200 years, until 1850, for the world population to double again, to 1 billion. Eighty years later, in 1930, the 2 billion level was passed. The acceleration has not abated: by 1975, the number of humans to be fed had reached 5 billion. If the growth were to continue at the 1975 level of 2 percent, the world population in 2015 will be about 10 billion. While the rate of natural increase in population is starting to slow worldwide (Table IV-1), with the industrial countries adding only 80 million up to the year 2000, this is not the case for Africa. Population growth there has been accelerating at an alarming pace.

In 1983, about 20 million human beings starved to death—about .5 percent of the world's population. Moreover, an additional 500 million are severely malnourished. Estimates indicate that by the end of the century, the number of severely undernourished will reach 650 million.

TABLE IV-1 Population Growth Rate, 1960-1980

Area	Annual Increase (%)		Change (%)
	1960-1965	1975-1980	
World	1.99	1.81	− 9.0
Industrialized	1.19	0.67	−43.7
Asia	2.06	1.37	−33.5
Developing	2.35	2.21	− 6.0
Latin America	2.77	2.66	− 4.0
Africa	2.49	2.91	+16.9

SOURCE: W. P. Mauldi (1980); *Science* 209, 148-157.

Plainly one of the major and increasing problems facing the human race will be providing itself with adequate food and nourishment and, ultimately, limiting its own population growth. And whose problem is this? In the most elemental way, it is the problem of those who are hungry, those who are undernourished, those who are least able to change the course of events on more than a personal and momentary scale. But human hunger is also the problem, indeed, the *responsibility*, of those who *can* affect the course of events. Any attempt to fulfill that responsibility will surely need the options that can come from science, and among the sciences that can generate options, chemistry is seen to be one of the foremost. It can do so, first, by increasing food supply and, second, by providing safe aids to voluntary limitation of population growth (see Section IV-B, p. 138).

Food production cannot be significantly increased simply by cultivating new land. In most countries, the arable land is already in use. In the heavily populated, developing countries, expansion of cultivated areas requires huge capital investments and endangers the local ecology and wildlife. To increase the world food supply, we need improvements in food production, food preservation, conservation of soil nutrients, water, and fuel, and better use of solar energy through photosynthesis. Such improvements are coming through science, and, in each of them, chemistry plays a central role by providing increasingly detailed clarification of the chemistry of biological life cycles and better understandings at the molecular level of the factors that must be controlled. These factors include hormones, pheromones, self-defense structures, and nutrients, both for our animal and plant food crops and for their natural enemies. At the same time, undesired side effects of any measures we pursue must be monitored and minimized.

In the last analysis, we can address these problems best by understanding living systems. An example is provided by pest control, an essential element of efficient food production. Currently, most agrochemical activity is connected with biocidal chemicals. But our purpose is to *control* insect pests, not exterminate them, because we have had ample warnings in the past about the reverberations that may accompany profound ecological disturbances. Understanding the biochemistry of the organisms opens the way to limiting what the pests will do in ways that can be sustained indefinitely. Increasingly, such fundamental questions about biological systems have become questions about molecular structures and chemical reactions.

The active and opening opportunities for chemistry in our attempts to expand the world food supply are vividly displayed through the examples below.

Plant Hormones and Growth Regulators

Growth regulators are compounds that in small concentrations regulate the physiology of plants and animals. They include natural compounds produced within the organism (endogenous substances) and also some natural products that come from the environment (exogenous substances). However, many analog compounds have been synthesized and shown to function as growth regulators. They are usually patterned after natural prototypes, and some of them possess comparable effectiveness while avoiding certain undesired side effects. The endogenous chemicals that are ubiquitously present in plants or animals and that exert regulatory actions are called hormones (e.g., growth hormones and sex hormones). A hormone can be said to be a chemical message sent between cells. However, this definition is becoming less clear in view of recent characterizations of new types of physiologically active compounds. The so-called plant hormones include growth substances (e.g., auxins, gibberellins, and cytokinins) and growth inhibitors (e.g., abscisic acid and ethylene) that seem to be structurally unrelated. The brassinolides, a family of recently discovered steroidal growth substances, are attracting attention as possible new plant hormones. The naturally occurring plant-growth regulators fall into two broad classes: (i) "factors," which are compounds produced in minute quantities that show high activity in a species-specific manner and that have a role in the maintenance of the plant's life cycle; and (ii) "secondary metabolites," which are compounds produced in larger quantities that function as growth regulators but with no recognized specific activity related to the life cycle of the host plant.

Whether they are hormones, factors, secondary metabolites, or synthetic analogs, these growth regulators are surely of immense social (and economic) importance for the world's future because they influence every phase of plant development. Unfortunately, even though we know the structures of many plant growth regulators, there is little insight concerning the molecular basis for their activity. Since chemical interactions and reactions are involved, chemistry must play a central and indispensable role in the development of this insight.

Typical growth regulators are listed to display the variety of molecular structures developed by nature for these functions. Establishing these structures is an essential step toward understanding, and thus controlling, the growth processes they regulate.

Indoleacetic Acid (IAA), an Auxin (1)

This compound, the first plant hormone to be characterized, promotes plant

INDOLE ACETIC ACID
(IAA)

growth and rooting of cuttings. It also induces formation of callus (a state in which cells are not differentiated) and parthenocarpy (asexual reproduction). The synthesis of numerous IAA analogs led to the first commercial herbicide, 2,4-dichlorophenoxyacetic acid, or 2,4-D.

Gibberelic Acid (GA) (2)

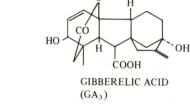

GIBBERELIC ACID
(GA₃)

Since the landmark discovery of gibberellins as secondary metabolites of the fungus *Gibberella fujikuroi* (the causal agent of bakanae disease in rice in which shoots are elongated), more than 65 GA's have been characterized from plant and lower organisms. Commercially produced by large-scale cultures of *G. fujikuroi*, GA$_3$ has extensive use in agriculture. Its applications range from inducing formation of flower buds to growing seedless grapes and manufacturing malt in the beer industry.

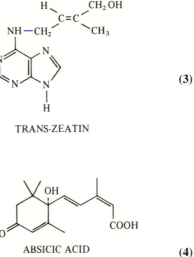

Cytokinins (3)

The first cytokinin was isolated as a compound that enhances cell division in callus cultures. Many analogs, including *trans*-zeatin, have since been isolated from DNA, transfer RNA, and other sources, and quite a number have been synthesized. They promote cell division, enhance flowering and seed germination, and inhibit aging.

TRANS-ZEATIN   (3)

Absicic Acid (ABA) (4)

ABA was isolated as the growth-inhibitory hormone that promotes dropping of cotton fruit, induces dormancy of tree buds, stimulates flower

ABSICIC ACID
(ABA)   (4)

and fruit drop in yellow lupin, and regulates the opening of stoma. ABA has recently been isolated from microorganisms, opening up the possibility for large-scale fermentation.

Ethylene (5)

This simple gas has been found to function as a hormone by enhancing fruit ripening, leafdrop, and germination as well as growth of root and seedling. Hence a substance that generates

ETHYLENE   (5)

ethylene above pH 4 is used widely as a fruit ripener. It is suggested that ethylene modulates the action of the growth hormones auxin, GA, and cytokinin. In addition, many other compounds are known that are not themselves hormones but that possess bioactivity of a regulatory type.

Strigol (1972) (6)

The seeds of witchweed (*Striga*) lie dormant in the soil for years and will only germinate when a particular chemical substance is released by the root of a host plant. The parasitic weed then

STRIGOL (1972)   (6)

attaches itself to the root. The active substance, strigol, has recently been isolated from the root exudate of the cotton plant, and its structure identified. Now it has been synthesized. Strigol and its synthetic analogs are proving effective in the germination of these parasitic weeds in the absence of the host plant.

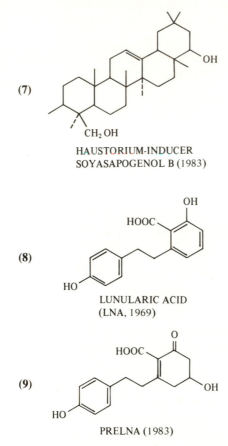

(7)

HAUSTORIUM-INDUCER
SOYASAPOGENOL B (1983)

(8)

LUNULARIC ACID
(LNA, 1969)

(9)

PRELNA (1983)

Haustorium-Inducing Factor, Soyasapogenol-B (1983) (7)

The parasitic angiosperm *Agalinis purpurea* develops a specialized organ, the haustorium that attaches itself to the host. The differentiation of this haustorium depends on specific molecular signals produced by the host root. Such a factor has been isolated from a *Leguminosae* root directed by haustorium-inducing activity. A new NMR method together with other spectral data showed its structure to be none other than (7), i.e., the revised structure (1982) of the common triterpene soyasapogenol-B.

Lunularic Acid (LNA) and preLNA (1983) (8) and (9)

An endogenous growth inhibitor of liverworts and algae, LNA appears to be the lower plant equivalent of absicic acid, (4), the growth inhibitory hormone of higher plants. Although still early in its development, the technique of plant cell culture promises to produce new and commercially important secondary metabolites. Recently, this technique has been used for isolating reactive intermediates. For example, preLNA, the reactive biosynthetic intermediate of LNA, has been extracted from suspension-cultured cells of a liverwort.

G2 Factor or Trigonelline (1978) (10)

Plants have cells containing nuclei (eukaryotic cells), and they proliferate according to a four-step cycle that begins with cell division (mitosis). Then there is a stage called "gap 1" or G1 during which DNA is not being replicated. Next,

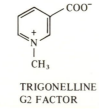

(10)

TRIGONELLINE
G2 FACTOR

synthesis takes place, S, to double the DNA content, followed by a pause called "gap 2" or G2. Then the cycle repeats. The first regulatory compound characterized is one that arrests the cell cycle predominantly at the G2 stage (hence, "G2 factor"). The cotyledons of 150,000 garden pea seedlings gave only one-quarter of a milligram of the hygroscopic G2 factor. By a combination of advanced spectroscopic techniques the active compound was shown to be *N*-methylnicotinic acid, a substance already isolated and synthesized a century ago. Since it is known that the legume cortex cells are mainly in G2 when nodules leading to nitrogen fixation are formed, better understanding of the role of (10) is of particular importance.

Glycinoeclepin A (1984) **(11)**

Nematodes are tiny worms that inflict huge damage on such crops as soybean and potato. The nematode eggs can rest dormant in the soil for many years until the root of a nearby host plant releases a substance that will promote hatching. The first such hatching initiator was elucidated recently. During a span of 17 years, a total area corresponding to 500 football fields was cultivated with soybeans to give 1.5 mg of the active sub-

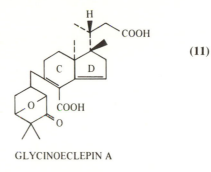

(11)

GLYCINOECLEPIN A

stance, glycinoeclepin A, which has the unusual structure **(11)**. It induces hatching of nemotode eggs at a dilution level of around 10^{-12}. Synthetic analogs clearly have great potentiality for agricultural use.

Hundreds of natural plant products are now known to exert growth regulatory activity of one sort or another. These compounds represent a surprising range of structural types. Recognition of these structures is the first step toward their systematic use to increase the world's food supply. We are only at the beginning of this important process.

Insect Hormones and Growth Regulators

Crop yields are made capricious and food supplies are limited by insect populations that prey upon food-bearing plants. The ability to understand and control these natural enemies provides another dimension by which the world's food supply can be increased. The desire to reduce malnourishment and starvation across the globe is not incompatible with the strong element of environmental concern in our society. Pests can be controlled without being exterminated. Furthermore, with the sensitivity of detection methods constantly improving, we can be assured that measures to achieve such controls can be monitored to give ample early warning of unexpected side effects. Certainly knowledge of the basic chemistry involved in the growth and increase of insect populations should be extended to provide options that may or may not be needed to preserve human lives. We must know what these options are.

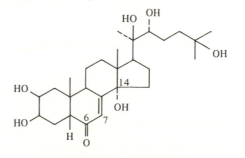

20-HYDROXYECDYSONE INSECT
AND CRUSTACEAN MOLTING
HORMONE (1965, 1966)

(12)

Molting Hormones (MH)

Two types of hormones are directly involved in the metamorphosis of insects—the molting hormones and juvenile hormones. The molting hormones cause insects to shed their skins. The representative MH is 20-hydroxyecdysone (12). Nine milligrams of this complex substance were extracted from 1 ton of silkworm pupae. It was also shown to be the active molting hormone of crustaceans when 2 milligrams were isolated from 1 ton of crayfish waste. Immediately following the structural determination of MH, it was discovered that (12), as well as other closely related steroids with the 14-hydroxy-7-en-6-one system (ecdysteroids), are widely distributed in plants. Approximately 50 such steroids with insect MH activity have been identified since the first isolation of ponasterone A (13) in 1966. They are probably produced by the plant as defense substances because force feeding to insects induces a variety of deleterious effects including insecticidal activity.

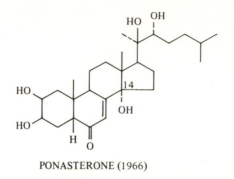

(13)

PONASTERONE (1966)

Juvenile Hormone (JH)

These hormones tend to keep insects in the juvenile state. The first JH (14) was identified in 1967 using .3 mg of sample isolated from a *Lepidoptera*. Several JH analogs are now known, the most universal being JH-III (1973) with three methyl groups on carbons 3, 7, and 11. Their importance has stimulated syntheses of thousands of related compounds, which culminated in methoprene (15). This biodegradable compound mimics the natural hormone, and hence insects cannot readily become resistant; it is widely used as a larvicide for fleas, flies, and mosquitoes. Because it produces oversized larvae and pupae by prolonging the juvenile stage in silkworm, it has been widely used in China to increase their silk production by 10 percent.

20-HYDROXYECDYSONE INSECT AND CRUSTACEAN MOLTING HORMONE (1965, 1966)

(14)

JUVENILE HORMONE JH-I (1967)

(15)

METHOPRENE

Anti-Juvenile Hormones

These are substances, natural or synthetic, that somehow interfere with normal juvenile development. Systematic screening of plants has led to identification of a number of compounds with anti-JH activities, the precocenes (16). Certain insects undergo precocious metamorphosis into diminutive sterile

adults when treated with precocenes. Another
synthetic anti-JH is (17), which contains the
-CH_2F group instead of a -CH_3 group in meva-
lonic lactone, the common precursor to all ter-
penoid compounds including cholesterol, MH, and
JH.

(16)

PRECOCENES R=H
AND OMe (1976)

(17)

FLUOROMEVALONIC
LACTONE (1980)

Peptide Hormones

Studies are under way on the peptide hormones
that control quiescent periods in the growth of
immature species (diapause) and hatching of larvae (eclosion). The work is exceptionally challenging because of the minute quantities that
must be handled. A neuro-
secretory hormone that releases stored glycerides for
energy consumption upon insect (locust) flight, the adipokinetic hormone (AKH) (18),

GLU-LEU-ASN-PHE-THR-PRO-ASN-TRP-GLY-
THR-NH_2 (ADIPOKINETIC HORMONE 1976)

(18)

GLU-VAL-ASN-PHE-SER-PRO-ASN-TRP-NH_2
PERIPLANETIN CC-1 (1984)

(19)

was identified in 1976. Recently, two peptides, including (19), involved in the
release of sugars as an energy source have been characterized from the
cockroach.

Natural Defense Compounds: Antifeedants

Plants produce and store a number of chemical substances used in defense
against insects, bacteria,
fungi, and viruses. One category of such defense sub-
stances is made up of chemical compounds that interfere
with feeding. Many antifeed-
ants have been characterized
and they include phenols,
(20), quinones, nitrogen het-
erocycles, alkaloids, and ter-
penoids. Among these, azadirachtin (21) is probably the
most potent antifeedant iso-
lated to date. Found in the seeds of the common folk medicinal trees, the neem

GLU-LEU-THR-PHE-THR-PRO-ASN-TRP-NH_2
PERIPLANETIN CC-2 (1984)

(20)

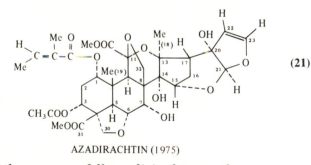

(21)

AZADIRACHTIN (1975)

tree *Azadirachta indica* and the closely related *Melia azadarach.*, azadirachtin
affects a variety of pest insects. An amount of only 2 ng/cm^2 (2×10^{-9} g/cm^2) is
sufficient to stop the desert locust from eating. Although (21) is far too complex
for commercial synthesis, it might be possible to isolate it in useful amounts
from cultivated trees. It is known that (21) has no acute toxicity because twigs

from the neem tree have been commonly used for brushing teeth, its leaves are used as an antimalarial agent, and the fruit has been a favorite food of birds.

The simple terpene warburganal (**22**), synthesized by several research groups,

(22)

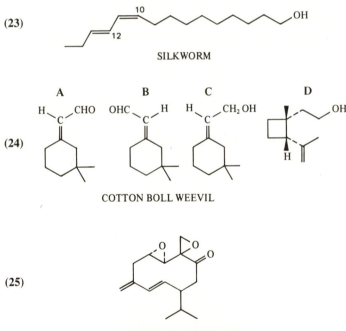

WARBURGANAL

seems to be specifically active against the African army worm. An insect kept for 30 minutes on corn leaves sprayed with warburganal will permanently lose its ability to feed. The plant from which warburganal has been isolated is also commonly used as a spice in East Africa and therefore cannot have acute oral toxicity. Practically all antifeed ants are isolated from plants that are resistant to insect attack. While no antifeedant has yet been developed commercially, they offer an intriguing avenue for integrated control of insect pests.

Insect Pheromones

Pheromones, such as insect sex attractants, are chemical compounds released by an organism that selectively induce response by another individual of the same species. Pheromones function as communication signals in mating, alarm,

(23)

SILKWORM

(24)

COTTON BOLL WEEVIL

(25)

AMERICAN COCKROACH

territorial display, raiding, building initiation, nest mate recognition, and marking. They have attracted great interest in recent years as a means to monitor and perhaps control insect pests.

The first insect pheromone to be identified was from the female silkworm (1959), which was shown to be an unbranched C_{16} alcohol containing two double bonds, structure (**23**). Since then, hundreds of pheromones have been identified, including those for most major agricultural and forest pests. The isolation and full identification always involve handling extremely minute quantities.

Characterization of the four pheromones for cotton boll weevil pheromones (**24 A-D**) required over 4 million weevils and 25 pounds of fecal material. The structure of the sex excitant of the American cockroach (**25**) took more than 30 years to be clarified; it required processing of 75,000 virgin females, which finally gave .2 mg and .02 mg of two compounds. Because of the complexity of the structure, however, full identification had to wait for a successful synthesis (1979). In some cases insect pheromones are specific mixtures of *cis/trans* double bond isomers or enantiomers (mirror images), as is the case of the *Ips pini* beetle pheromone, which is a 35:65 mixture of (**26 A,B**). A newly reported sex pheromone released by the female azuki bean weevil (erectin) is a synergistic mixture of hy-

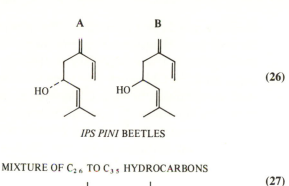

IPS PINI BEETLES (26)

MIXTURE OF C_{26} TO C_{35} HYDROCARBONS

AND

AZUKI BEAN WEEVIL (27)

drocarbons and acid (27) that induces the male to prepare for and try to copulate with any object that has been dosed with the mixture.

Numerous microscale collection and analytical methods, such as ultrasensitive capillary chromatography and special mass spectrometric methods, had to be developed to cope with the micro-quantities. It is now possible to extract a single female moth gland, strip out the intestines of a single beetle, or collect airborne pheromone directly on glass wool and analyze the emitted pheromone of an individual insect. One of the most important developments in this area is the electroantennogram technique, which has made it possible to carry out neurophysiological assays with a single sensillum of an olfactory antenna hair. These meticulous techniques have permitted clarification of many biosynthetic and genetic aspects of pheromone production. They will enable us to investigate more difficult and, as yet, unrecognized pheromones used by social insects and by higher animals.

In addition to natural pheromones, chemists continue to synthesize artificial pheromones, some of which specifically modify the olfactory signal pattern perceived by the central nervous system and others that covalently interact at the antennal active sites to disrupt further processes.

Pheromone-baited traps have been used worldwide to monitor and survey pest populations. They assist in precise timing of insecticide application, thus reducing the amount of spray, and in trapping applications. For example, more than 1 million traps have been deployed for the past 4 years in the Norweigan and Swedish forests, resulting in spruce bark beetle captures of 4 billion a year. Another commercial use is pheromone distribution throughout an area to confuse the insects. In 1982, formulated pheromone from commercial companies in the United States was used on 130,000 acres of cotton to control pink bollworms, 2000 acres of artichokes to control plume moths, and 6000 acres of tomato to fight pinworms. Pheromones are also combined with microorganisms to keep insects from attacking stored products.

The history of expectations concerning application of pheromone research to society's needs is instructive. The simplistic view of chemical communication derived from the pioneering case of the silkworm moth created overly optimistic assumptions. The complexity of other systems subsequently studied conversely suggested that pheromones were too complex to be useful. It is clear now that such pessimistic views are likewise quite unjustified. Despite renewed interest, however, the absolute level of research activity is still small. Many questions of basic chemistry and biology remain to be answered before we can define the economic advantages to be won. In the long run, it is clear that research on pheromones will yield useful benefits to agriculture and to health.

Pesticides

Pesticides—insecticides, herbicides, and fungicides—are essential to our attempts to improve food and fiber production and to control insect-transmitted diseases in humans and livestock. Although major changes have recently occurred in pesticide use, environmental concerns make it increasingly difficult to introduce better pesticides into practical use in this country. The time and cost of developing a new compound currently runs about 10 years and $30M. More than 10,000 new compounds normally have to be synthesized and tested before a single acceptably safe, hence marketable, pesticide is found.

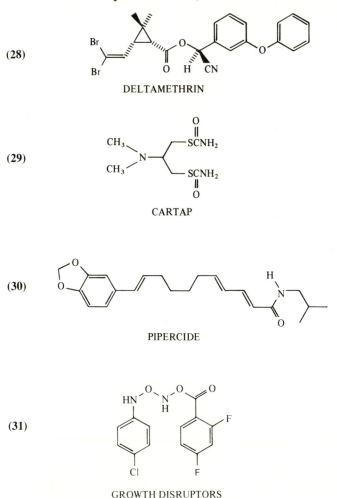

(28) DELTAMETHRIN

(29) CARTAP

(30) PIPERCIDE

(31) GROWTH DISRUPTORS

Insecticides

Most potent insecticides discovered recently are modeled on natural products and act on the nervous system. They include deltamethrin **(28)** based on the pyrethrins of chrysanthemum flowers, cartap **(29)** modeled on a marine worm toxin, analogs of the isobutylamide pipercide **(30)** still undergoing evaluation, and avermectin, which is a dihydro derivative of a complex macrocyclic lactone produced by the microorganism Actinomycete. Chemical synthesis and testing programs have led to other novel structures that act as nerve poisons, inhibitors of chitin synthesis, and growth disruptors (e.g., (31)). This increasing diversity of insecticide classes has helped in pest control despite expanding resistance thresholds of the pests.

Herbicides

Highly novel structures derived through chemical synthesis have provided a variety of new herbicides in recent years. Some function as pre-emergence weed-controlling agents, such as the butylates (32). Others, e.g., atrazine (33), inhibit photosynthesis. Still others interfere with seed germination or block chlorophyll formation. Herbicide resistance in weeds is an increasingly important problem. Genetic research currently directed toward improved crop tolerance suggests transferring to the crop the gene that makes the weed resistant to the same herbicide.

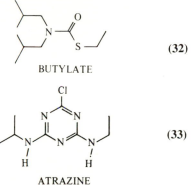

BUTYLATE (32)

ATRAZINE (33)

Fungicides

Major advances have been made in systemic fungicides and antibiotics to control fungal and bacterial plant pathogens. The systemic fungicides can act by inhibiting succinic dehydrogenase, the mode of action of oxycarboxin (34), by retarding RNA synthesis, the action of triadimefon (35), or blocking synthesis of ergosterol. Some fungicides, the benzimidazoles (36), exert a dual action, i.e., half of the molecule blocks cell division while the other inhibits the enzyme involved in epidermis formation (cutinase). Some antifungal antibiotics inhibit synthesis of cell walls (chitin). Many of these newer fungicides are very selective and act upon specific targets, which unfortunately allow the fungi to develop bypasses around the block so that they rapidly become resistant. New fungicides are therefore needed, not only for those of high selectivity and potency due to specific action, but also for hitting multiple targets where resistance is less likely to appear quickly.

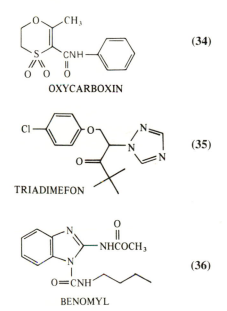

OXYCARBOXIN (34)

TRIADIMEFON (35)

BENOMYL (36)

Special Techniques

Specialized techniques, instrumentation, and facilities are required to address the multidisciplinary problems encountered in pesticide chemistry. The quantities and circumstances of pesticide use on crops are restricted so that they will be free of hazardous residues. An increasing number of pesticide-

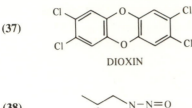

(37)

DIOXIN

(38)

DIPROPYLNITROSAMINE

derived residues—the parent compound, impurities, metabolites, and photoproducts—are being evaluated quantitatively for safety levels. Some hazardous impurities have been placed under strict analytical control, such as tetrachlorodibenzodioxin (37), an impurity in 2,4,5-T, and nitrosamines (38) that occur in some other useful herbicides. The multidisciplinary aspects of pesticide research have important implications in training and cooperative programs. Specialties are becoming less distinct; increased cooperation is required on a local, national, and international basis between industrial, government, and university scientists.

Research into pesticide chemistry provides farmers and public health officials with safe and effective means to control pests. The research permits replacement of compounds of high acute toxicity or with unfavorable long-term effects (DDT, carcinogens, mutagens, teratogens, or delayed neurotoxins) with better and environmentally safe pesticides. It also increases the availability and use of selective and biodegradable compounds. Because pest control problems are complex, multifaceted, and of extreme importance to society's well-being, long-term commitments to pesticide research are necessary.

Fixation of Nitrogen and Photosynthesis

All of our food supply ultimately depends upon the growth of plants. Hence, a fundamental aspect of increasing the world's food supply is to deepen our knowledge of plant chemistry. Because of special promise, two frontiers deserve special mention—nitrogen fixation and photosynthesis.

Nitrogen Fixation

Nitrogen is a crucial element in the chemistry of all living systems and a limiting agent in food production. It is drawn from the soil by plants, and replenishment of the soil's nitrogen content is a primary concern in agriculture. It accounts for the centuries-old practice of crop rotation and figures importantly in the choice and amounts of fertilizers. Ironically, nitrogen is abundantly available—air is 80 percent nitrogen—but present in the elemental form that is difficult to convert into useful compounds. Plants have learned to carry out this important chemistry; we'd like to know just how they do it.

Certain bacteria and algae are able to reduce atmospheric nitrogen to ammonia (nitrogen fixation), which is then converted into amino acids, proteins, and other nitrogeneous compounds by plants. A rather diverse group of organisms has the capability of reducing nitrogen. In addition to the symbiotic system in the *Rhizobium*/leguminous plant association, about 170 species of nonleguminous plants fix nitrogen in association with actinomycetes in root nodules. Many free-living bacteria also fix nitrogen.

Nitrogen fixation involves an enzyme complex called nitrogenase, which consists of two proteins. One protein (dinitrogenase) has a molecular weight of approximately 220,000. It contains 2 molybdenum atoms and about 32 atoms each of iron and acid-labile sulfur atoms, and it is made up of 4 subunits. The other protein (dinitrogenase reductase) is made up of 2 identical subunits of 29,000 molecular weight, each containing 4 iron and 4 acid-labile sulfur atoms.

For nitrogen fixation to occur, a strong reductant reduces the dinitrogenase reductase, which in turn reduces the dinitrogenase. Then, the reduced dinitrogenase converts nitrogen into ammonia. The sequence of events in these reductions, as well as the enzyme structures, have been partially resolved by spectroscopic and purification techniques, but many crucial aspects such as the roles of metals in the catalytic processes are not understood. Not only can nitrogenase reduce nitrogen, it can also reduce a variety of other substrates, including cyanide, acetylene, proton, cyclopropene, and azide. Studies with these model substrates will contribute greatly to the elucidation of this very complex biological process. Equally important are the rapid developments in synthesis of novel metal-organic compounds, a number of which have shown promise as homogeneous catalysts for nitrogen fixation.

On another active frontier, the current emphasis on research in biotechnology guarantees that genetic studies will be brought to bear on nitrogen fixation by plants. The efficiency of the nitrogenase system may possibly be increased by combining genetic manipulation with our understanding of the relevant reaction mechanisms. A more adventurous goal would be the transfer of legumous nitrogen fixation to other food-bearing plants so that they become self-fertilizing. Other approaches in which recombinant DNA techniques might be effective include control of plant senescence to extend their period of nitrogen fixation, development of more efficient strains of symbiotic bacteria, and exploitation of inadequately used nitrogen-fixing organisms, such as the blue-green algae.

Photosynthesis

Currently, the only practical method for fixing solar energy on a very large scale is photosynthesis. It is the process in nature by which green plants, algae, and photosynthetic bacteria use the energy from sunlight to convert carbon dioxide and water into organic compounds, some of which are stored in the plants to provide energy for nonphotosynthetic forms of life. Although 10^{11} tons of carbon are annually converted into organic compounds by photosynthesis, the total amount of the earth's stored energy in the form of hydrocarbons is decreasing, and the atmospheric carbon dioxide is increasing. These changes are a direct result of man's profligate energy consumption. Elucidation of the photosynthetic mechanism becomes increasingly important. Two hundred years of study of photosynthesis has clarified many facets of this extraordinarily complex set of phenomena, but some of the most important aspects are still puzzling. Science is still far from replicating natural photosynthesis in the laboratory to produce an abiotic photosynthetic system.

Chlorophyll is an essential agent in the primary events of natural photosynthesis. The majority of chlorophyll molecules are used to absorb light energy (photons), which is then transferred to a few special chlorophyll molecules bound to a protein complex. These chlorophyll-protein complexes play a central role in photosynthetic electron transfer processes, and they are being studied extensively; one has been crystallized and studied by X-ray techniques. The light-absorption and energy transfer processes, which occur in the time range of picoseconds (10^{-12} seconds) to nanoseconds (10^{-9} seconds) can be studied by modern laser spectroscopic methods. It is thought that two chlorophyll molecules are held in close proximity by the central magnesium atoms and two molecules of a bridging agent, such as water or the amino groups contained in proteins. In fact, models in which two chlorophyll molecules are linked together have been prepared by organic synthesis. The newly developed spectroscopic methods coupled with model studies are greatly increasing our understanding of how photosynthetic organisms make use of solar energy. This will inevitably increase our access to and use of solar energy, which will profoundly affect the everyday life of mankind in ways we cannot yet foretell.

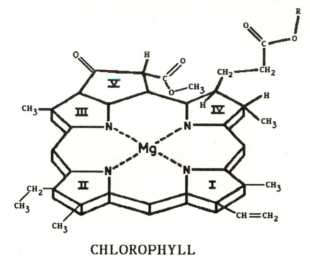

CHLOROPHYLL

Food from the Sea

Seventy-one percent of the Earth's surface is covered by water, so more than two-thirds of the solar energy potenially available for photosynthesis is absorbed in our oceans and seas. Yet, on a global scale, food from the waters has not been as important as that from terrestrial sources. Of the total of 3.3 billion tons of food harvested in 1975, only 2 percent came from the ocean and inland waters. Moreover, the harvest of fish, mollusks, and crustaceans has leveled off in recent years. Significant advances can be made, for example, in aquaculture technology and in the cultivation of algae, fish, and crustaceans. Knowledge of the chemistry of biological life cycles in marine species is an important requirement for such advances.

Isolation and Characterization Techniques of Bioactive Molecules

The advances discussed above are the more remarkable in view of the tiny amount of quite complex molecular compounds that must be isolated and identified. The techniques and concepts dealing with the bioassay, purification, structure determination, syntheses, and mode of function, of naturally occurring bioactive molecules and analogs are undergoing revolutionary improvements that open up entirely new frontiers for chemical research.

Dramatic improvements in isolation techniques, mostly in chromatography and electrophoresis, have made it possible to separate compounds that occur in minuscule amounts. Some isolations deal with invisible amounts, quantities in the range of a thousandth of a millionth of 1 gram (nanogram, 10^{-9} g). Moreover, some compounds are sensitive to oxygen, moisture, or light, or have only a fleeting existence. Successful separations of the cleavage products of proteins and nucleic acids, i.e., amino acids, peptides, and nucleotides, were indeed a major factor responsible for the launching of genetic engineering. While a successful purification may take years of frustrating endeavor, it is often the mandatory first step that permits the studies needed to explain a biological behavior on a concrete molecular structure basis. Of course, we also need an assay to tell whether and how much of the substance of interest has been isolated. For biologically active molecules, these assays are often biological; here again novel concepts for assays are enabling chemists to work effectively with tiny amounts of material.

Of the modern spectroscopic methods, probably nuclear magnetic resonance (NMR) has had the widest impact on all branches of chemical, biochemical, and biological sciences. Mass spectrometry has also made dramatic progress so that molecular weights of nonvolatile material up to 23,000 are measurable; if the compound is known, as little as 10^{-13} g is sufficient for detection under favorable conditions. The classical methods of infrared and Raman spectroscopy have been revolutionized by Fourier transform, time-resolved, and subtractive techniques, while diffractive methods (X-ray, neutron, electron microscope) can now clarify structures and shapes of nonrigid biopolymers, including flexible proteins. Circular dichroism, a powerful method that so far has attracted less attention than it deserves, can clarify three-dimensional shapes and mirror image characteristics of molecules. While these instruments are expensive and their maintenance is not routine, they play on essential role in the advancement of science relevant to food production and in the maintenance of our international competitiveness in this crucial field.

Conclusion

Food supply and efficient use of energy are rapidly emerging as dominant concerns for the world's future. The theme "more food" requires understanding of the basic principles that govern nature so that practical applications can follow. The traditional disciplinary classifications of biology, chemistry, biochemistry, physics, physiology, and medicine are becoming less distinct, and collaborative effort among scientists with broad and overlapping interests is becoming common as research moves into topics dealing with the nature of life.

In these cross-disciplinary collaborations, chemists have an essential role because they have the clearest concepts of structures and shapes of molecules, of their reactivities, and of how to synthesize molecules of biological importance. Thus chemistry will play a central role in the search for options that will help us feed and limit the world's population in the decades ahead. Chemistry must have adequate resources with which to fulfill its potentiality.

CHEMISTRY is a central science
that responds to societal needs.

It is critical in Man's attempt to...
improve health and conquer disease

R$_x$-Snake Bite

High blood pressure, anyone? Maybe you'd like a dose of snake venom? Yes, it's true! Hypertension sufferers may find their future treatment coming from this unlikely source—and from sustained research in chemistry and physiology.

This story began 30 years ago when scientists discovered the chemical mechanism by which blood pressure is elevated in humans. Chemical techniques isolated two closely related substances, angiotensin I and angiotensin II. In the human body chemistry, II is produced from I with the help of a specific enzyme, "angiotensin-converting enzyme" (ACE). Though I has no physiologic effect, its reaction produced *angiotensin II*, the most potent blood pressure-elevating substance known. Thus I provides a reservoir from which II can be made as needed to maintain a normal blood pressure level, a conversion controlled by the enzyme ACE.

It is no surprise that there is also a substance provided by Nature to lower blood pressure—this substance is called *bradykinin*, which, along with angiotensin II, seems to complete the control mechanism. To raise pressure when it is too low, make some angiotensin II using ACE. To lower blood pressure when it is too high, a dash of bradykinin will do the trick.

During the 1960s, a group of Brazilian scientists were bent upon learning how a deadly snake like the South American pit viper manages to immobilize its prey. It was recognized that this snake's venom contained some substances that could cause the victim's blood pressure to drop precipitously. Biochemical research showed that these snake substances were acting by stimulating bradykinin, so they were named "bradykinin potentiating factors" (BPF). Again, chemists did their part by purifying BPF from the pit viper venom and identifying several compounds that carried the activity. Chemical analysis showed them to be specific peptides.

The next chapter in this story began when ACE had been purified and characterized. That opened the door to understanding how the snake venom BPF did its work. Some of the peptides in BPF block ACE to interfere with the production of angiotensin II. Then, as a bit of a surprise, it was discovered that ACE derived part of its control function from an ability to inactivate bradykinin. Realizing this, the canny pit viper provides some peptides in its venom to protect bradykinin from inactivation! Thus these BPF peptides deprive the body of its ability to use ACE, either to raise blood pressure by producing angiotensin II or to moderate the lowering action of its own control substance, bradykinin.

With this understanding, teams of biologists and chemists recently began a systematic attack on hypertension, one of the most insidious causes of death in our stressful world. They synthesized a series of peptides modeled on those found in snake venom but designed for therapeutic use. Success came with the synthesis of the compound captopril. It acts as an ACE inhibitor, and clinical trials have amply demonstrated its ability to lower abnormally high blood pressure. No wonder that the medical profession has great expectations for ACE enzyme inhibitors in the treatment of our hypertensive population.

124

IV-B. Better Health

Introduction

Chemistry in the next decade will contribute to the solution of some of contemporary biology's most important problems. All life processes are regulated by interactions between macromolecules, including enzymes, nucleic acids, and receptors, and a host of molecules of diverse structural types, representing hormones, neurotransmitters, neuromodulators, and trace elements. Ultimately, our ability to control complex biological events will depend upon understanding at the molecular level, so chemistry is in a position to make important contributions to physiology and medicine.

The following discussions illustrate how advances in chemical knowledge and technology have led to the discovery of new and improved therapeutic agents in recent years and indicate where rapid progress can be anticipated in the future.

Investment of the additional funds required to exploit our opportunities fully will pay dividends in terms of the nation's health and, through exports, its economic well-being. Failure to act will allow competitors abroad to reap the benefits of past achievements. Perhaps already foreshadowing this likelihood is the significant increase in the Investigational New Drug applications (INDs) recently filed in this country, which involve compounds first synthesized abroad.

Notable Scientific Advances During the Last 15 Years

One of the most significant changes in new drug discovery during the last 15 years is the trend toward the replacement of random screening by more rational, mechanism-based approaches. Remarkable progress has been made in understanding how chemical reactions control and regulate biological processes. The discovery and characterization of chemical messengers and the specific binding sites or receptors through which their action is expressed was achieved largely through the use of such chemical and physiochemical techniques as radioimmunoassays, radioligand displacement assays, gel electrophoresis, high-performance liquid chromatography (HPLC), NMR, and mass spectroscopy. The discovery of agents that selectively block or mimic the effects of these messengers has provided therapeutically useful compounds, but, more important, it has forged an understanding of the relation between drug effect and mechanism of action. Medicinal chemists have thus successfully corrected metabolic imbalances often found in disease states.

Significant advances have been made in enzyme inhibitor design. Enzymes are potent and specific catalysts. They promote most of the chemical transformations of life, including the production of the chemical messengers that regulate physiological processes: hormones, neurotransmitters, and neuromodulators. In the past, enzyme inhibitors were discovered by random screening or by modification of known active structures. Now, however, our understanding of the mechanisms of many enzymes is at a molecular level, as a result of advances in chemistry. Particularly important have been structure determinations through computer-aided high-resolution X-ray crystallography. With such structural knowledge at hand, the chemist can design enzyme inhibitors far more effectively. The joining of our knowledge of the mechanisms by which enzymes accelerate chemical reactions with our knowledge about tertiary structures of proteins has led to effective strategies for designing enzyme inhibitors. One such strategy derives from the concept that enzymes act by specifically stabilizing a transitory form of the substrate molecule. Compounds that mimic such structures but cannot be converted to other products can be potent inhibitors of the enzyme. Suicide or mechanism-based inhibitors represent a second approach. The enzyme itself converts the inhibitor into a chemically reactive species that permanently inactivates the enzyme. Such inhibitors can have high specificity. To illustrate their successful use in therapy, enzyme inhibitors have been designed and found to be effective in treatment of hypertension, atherosclerosis, and asthma, as discussed elsewhere in this report.

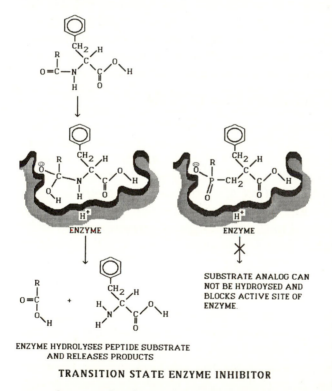

ENZYME HYDROLYSES PEPTIDE SUBSTRATE
AND RELEASES PRODUCTS

TRANSITION STATE ENZYME INHIBITOR

Another rapidly advancing research field with clinical relevance concerns the so-called "receptors," which, like enzymes, are macromolecules. As the first step in the action of virtually all known hormones and neurotransmitters as well as many drugs, these protein macromolecules recognize and bind biologically active molecules. After receptors have been activated by their particular hormones or other agonists, specific biological processes are initiated.

Until recently, receptors were studied only indirectly. Various compounds were tested for their ability to either stimulate or inhibit a biological process. Deductions were then made about the structural features required to fit a given receptor. Over the last 10 to 15 years, more powerful approaches have been developed using radioactive molecules that allow a more facile evaluation of the structural requirements for receptor binding. Moreover, new biochemical techniques have made it possible in several cases to isolate and characterize receptor molecules by physiochemical means. Two types of agents may bind to receptors. *Agonists* include naturally occurring hormones and neurotransmitters as well as the drugs generated by chemists that trigger a biological response. *Antagonists*, on the other hand, are compounds that bind to a receptor without producing a response but prevent the agonist from binding and fulfilling its biological mission.

Receptors are usually characterized by the hormones or neutrotransmitters that trigger them. However, some chemical messengers can bind to more than a single receptor type and thus mediate different types of biological actions. For example, histamine mediates allergic reactions by binding to a receptor designated H_1 and promotes gastric acid secretion by activating what is called the H_2-receptor. Norepinephrine, the chemical messenger for the adrenergic nervous system, has been shown to bind to at least four subtypes of receptors mediating different types of biological responses via different pathways. With their proven value in treating cardiovascular disease, cancer, disorders of the central nervous system, endocrine disorders, and the like, compounds that act as specific antagonists can be seen to be among the most important drugs that chemists have provided to clinicians.

Increasingly sophisticated chemical technology is constantly being developed to allow the investigation of physiological systems whose function and mechanisms have hitherto been unknown. In many cases, it has been possible to identify the biochemical abnormalities that produce diseases for which there has been no treatment, thus setting the stage for the discovery of effective therapeutic agents. Minute amounts of biologically active compounds can now be isolated from complex mixtures in sufficient purity for structure elucidation by advanced spectroscopic techniques. Analytical techniques have been developed to permit determination of the nucleotide sequence of genes and the structures of the biologically important proteins derived from them.

A few applications of advances in chemical technology to the development of specific new therapeutic agents are illustrated in the following section.

Antibiotic Research

Antibacterials Before World War II, sulfonamides were the only effective antibacterial agents available. During and after World War II, antibiotic research had a major impact in decreasing morbidity and mortality in both humans and animals.

During the period 1945 to 1965, penicillins came into large-scale use and the cephalosporins were discovered. The tetracyclines, chloramphenicol, erythomycin, and aminoglycosides were being used to treat infectious diseases. In addition to antibiotics obtained by fermentation, synthetic antibacterial agents, such as nalidixic acid and nitrofurans, were also being discovered. Thus chemistry was already playing a critical role in both the isolation and structure determination of life-saving drugs from natural sources and the synthesis of antibiotics not found in nature. During the past 20 years, major efforts have been made to improve the spectrum, potency, and safety of the antibiotics available to the clinician. This has involved the discovery of new fermentation products, chemical modifications of less-than-optimal natural products (semisynthesis), and the introduction by synthesis of new structural types. The newer semisynthetic penicillins include agents that are not only active against common Gram-negative bacteria, but are also effective against the *pseudo-monal* organisms, which are increasing problems in the hospital environment. The early cephalosporins have been successfully modified to provide compounds possessing remarkably broad spectra and high potencies combined with increased safety. Biochemical insights have also facilitated discovery of superior antibiotics through the design and application of new screening techniques. All of these refinements have been extremely valuable in medical practice; they were achieved by chemists working in close collaboration with biologists.

Much of the effort in antibiotic research has concentrated on the problem of resistance development, especially in the hospital environment. We recognize two types of resistance problems. In one type, certain bacteria can gain the ability to produce enzymes that inactivate the antibiotic. Progress has been made in the design and synthesis of antibiotics that are resistant to these bacterial enzymes. Alternatively, antibiotics have been combined with inhibitors of the inactivating enzymes. In the other type problem, bacteria can become resistant to antibiotics by preventing the antibacterial agent's penetration of the bacterial cell. Here again, advances have been made by both semisynthetic modification and the discovery of new agents. Finally, compounds with better pharmacodynamic properties have been synthesized; some of these are orally active or longer acting, properties that can reduce the cost of therapy.

Although enormous progress has been made, the search must continue for the antibiotic that combines complete safety with effectiveness at comparable dose against all bacteria, aerobes and anaerobes, Gram-positive and Gram-negative, in part because concerns about resistance development remain.

Antifungals   The treatment of fungal infections has made modest gains during the past decade, but they have been less dramatic than those connected with infections of bacterial origin. The widespread use of ketoconazole and related imidazoles in the treatment of dermatomycoses and candidosis has demonstrated the clinical opportunities for antifungal agents. The search for systematic fungicidal agents is likely to be intensified in the years ahead.

Antivirals   Recent advances in the discovery of *antiviral* agents deserve special mention. While antiviral chemotherapy is in its infancy compared with antibacterial therapy, breakthroughs are being made. Acyclovir, discussed below, is an example.

Viruses, the smallest of the infectious organisms, do not contain much genetic information, and they manifest only a few unique biochemical steps that are attractive targets for a chemotherapeutic agent. Instead, viruses take over the host metabolism in order to survive and multiply. This means, unfortunately, that most of the steps in viral biology are identical, or closely similar to those of the mammalian host. Viruses are, therefore, difficult to attack by chemotherapy. To discover a *safe*

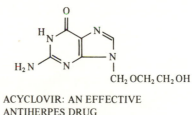

ACYCLOVIR: AN EFFECTIVE
ANTIHERPES DRUG

chemotherapeutic agent, it is necessary to identify a biochemical pathway that is unique to the virus-infected cell. Viral DNA polymerases represent such a target. These enzymes are involved in the synthesis of viral nucleic acids. Examples of compounds that function as viral polymerase inhibitors are known, but these compounds are suitable only for topical use. The antiherpes drug, acyclovir, is effective topically and after oral or intravenous administration. Its relative safety is due to the fact that it is ignored by cellular enzymes under normal conditions. However, certain *viral* enzymes can convert acyclovir to a form that the cellular enzymes can use to produce the active drug, which then acts on the viral polymerase to inhibit DNA synthesis. Biochemists and organic chemists, working hand-in-hand with virologists, have achieved this important advance.

Chemistry also plays an important role in the development of vaccines against viruses. Isolation of an antigen, a substance that stimulates production of an antibody, requires chemical isolation techniques; an example is the so-called Australian surface antigen of hepatitis B. Then, when recombinant DNA techniques are employed to generate the antigen, organic chemists again play a role. Recent developments have suggested that smaller peptides, designed and synthesized by the organic chemist, may also become important in viral vaccine development.

Cardiovascular Disease

Cardiovascular disease is currently the major cause of death in the United States. Therefore, hypertension and hyperchloresterolemia, two important risk factors, have been the subject of extensive research. In this report we will be able to refer only to selected developments.

Hypertension   Death rates for coronary heart disease in the United States fell 20.7 percent between 1968 and 1978. Improvements in the control of moderate and severe hypertension have undoubtedly contributed to this decline. The earliest drugs had such serious side effects that they were used only when blood pressure was elevated to life-threatening levels, but several types of antihypertensive agents that have few adverse effects are now used extensively for the treatment of mild and moderate hypertension.

A breakthrough in the therapy for hypertension occurred 30 years ago when medicinal chemists synthesized the thiazide diuretics. This class of drug still retains great importance in first-line therapy, and it is used in combinations

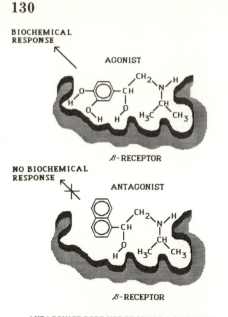

BIOCHEMICAL RESPONSE

AGONIST

β-RECEPTOR

NO BIOCHEMICAL RESPONSE

ANTAGONIST

β-RECEPTOR

ANTAGONIST DOES NOT PRODUCE A RESPONSE BUT BINDS TO RECEPTOR AND BLOCKS ACCESS OF AGONIST

TWO TYPES OF DRUG BINDING TO RECEPTORS

with other antihypertensive drugs for the treatment of nearly all types of hypertension.

While the cause of essential hypertension remains unknown, it has long been recognized that the adrenergic nervous system through its chemical messenger, norepinephrine, plays a major role in regulating blood pressure and cardiac function. Over the years chemists have supplied clinicians with many useful antihypertensive agents that modify the activity of the adrenergic system. α-methyldopa, tremendously valuable in the treatment of hypertension, is known to act within the central nervous system via an adrenergic receptor. The recognition that norepinephrine acts on several different subtypes of receptors has allowed the design of compounds that lower blood pressure by different pharmacological mechanisms. For example, compounds that block the action of norepinephrine on what are called the β-adrenergic blocking agents are now the most widely used antihypertensive drugs. They are also effective therapeutic agents for angina and arrhythmias. Importantly, two of them, timolol and propranolol, have also been shown to reduce the risk of mortality and the recurrence of myocardial infarction after an initial heart attack. (It is worth mentioning that timolol has also become the primary treatment for glaucoma). The identification of further subclasses of β-adrenergic receptors has led to the synthesis of newer β-blocking agents with improved specificity of action that results in fewer side effects.

Two other classes of antihypertensive compounds include the calcium channel blockers, of importance also in the treatment of angina and stroke, and the so-called angiotensin-converting enzyme inhibitors, typified by captopril, a breakthrough achievement in rational drug design, and by enalapril. They also show much promise for the treatment of heart failure.

Very recently, chemists from several laboratories working with biologists have discovered, identified, and synthesized a group of peptides released in the heart. These peptides have been named atrial natriuretic factors. Their biological properties are now being investigated to determine their potential for developing new therapeutic agents. We already know that these compounds possess diuretic and natriuretic activity, that they serve as vasorelaxants, and that they lower blood pressure.

Atherosclerosis The second major cardiovascular risk factor is hypercholesterolemia, an inappropriately high level of chloresterol. An intensive search has been under way for many years for safe and effective drugs that will lower plasma chloresterol levels to the normal range by either inhibiting the synthesis or promoting the metabolism of chloresterol. An exciting new enzyme inhibitor approach to the treatment of hyperchloresterolemia via inhibitors of HMGCoA reductase is mentioned elsewhere in this report. It promises to provide for the first time effective treatment for the disease. It also elegantly displays both enzyme inhibitor and receptor-related intervention in disease.

Heart Failure   In spite of serious side effects, steroid glycosides like digitalis have remained a mainstay in the management of heart failure for the last two centuries. To find less toxic agents that improve the contractility of a depressed myocardium, mechanisms other than inhibition of the digitalis-sensitive sarcolemmal enzyme (sodium potassium ATPase) have been investigated. Stimulation of contractility through enhanced cyclic AMP (cAMP) levels has been the most thoroughly investigated of the alternative mechanisms. An increase in intracellular cAMP levels can be accomplished through direct activation of the β-receptor with agents such as prenalterol, dopamine, and dobutamine, or indirectly with agents such as caffeine and theophylline, which inhibit the enzyme phosphodiesterase (PDE), an enzyme that inactivates cAMP. New promising agents, exemplified by milrinone and amrinone, which selectively inhibit the enzyme PDE-III, are being introduced into therapy.

Within the last 10 years, the traditional treatment of congestive heart failure using digitalis and diuretics has been supplemented or, in some instances, replaced by vasodilators. These drugs have no direct cardiac action but increase left ventricular performance by affecting the peripheral vasculature. New vasodilators, such as the above-mentioned captopril and enalapril alone or in combination with recently developed inotropic agents, can be expected to have significant impact on the management of congestive heart failure over the next decade.

Arrhythmia   Two of today's widely used antiarrhythmic drugs, quinidine and digitalis, trace their origins back over 200 years. Since the 18th century, quinidine and digitalis have been used to treat the potentially lethal condition characterized by abnormal cardiac rhythm.

As our basic understanding of the disease state has improved over the past decade, the concepts of antiarrhythmic therapy have also undergone synergistic changes. As the mechanism of action of both old and new agents is becoming clear, drugs are now divided into groups defined by electrophysiologic classification. Drugs that inactivate the sodium channel (examples are quinidine, procainamide, lidocaine), inhibit sympathetic activity (propranolol, timolol), prolong the action potential (amiodarone), or depress the calcium channel (verapamil) form the base for contemporary antiarrhythmic therapy. This grouping aids in providing a more rational approach to therapy. Although the ideal agent still does not exist, progress continues to be made. Our ability to control sympathetic activity will particularly benefit from better understanding at the molecular level.

Drugs Affecting the Central Nervous System (CNS)

The cost of direct care for mental illness is estimated to be 15 percent of our total national health care expenditure. Although approximately 2½ percent of our population receive treatment for mental or emotional disorders each year, it is likely that the proportion of the population actually in need of care is quite a bit greater. Antidepressants and tranquilizers have enabled men and women to live useful lives who would not otherwise have functioned effectively. Further, these drugs have reduced the cost of the medical care required by those suffering from mental disorders.

Clinical observation, rather than mechanism-based drug design, was a major factor in the discovery of many early useful antipsychotics, antidepressants, and anxiolytics. Subsequent advances resulted when chemists synthesized compounds with more desirable therapeutic characteristics. More recently, chemists working with neurobiologists have begun to define biochemical mechanisms by which these drugs may exert their therapeutic effect. As a consequence, alternative approaches for achieving therapeutic effects in psychosis, depression, and anxiety are now emerging. Expectations are high that these novel agents will provide important improvements in therapy.

The opiate analgesics, typified by morphine, are among the most important centrally acting drugs. The ideal analgesic has not been found, but the use of morphine has been largely supplanted by synthetic drugs with fewer side effects and reduced likelihood of addiction. Drugs useful in the treatment of illicit opiate abuse are also now available. Ten years ago, two peptides with actions similar to morphine, the enkephalins, were isolated from the brain, chemically characterized, and synthesized. The discovery had a profound impact on CNS research. A number of different types of opiate receptors can now be distinguished while synthetic compounds with selective activities can be expected to lead to improved analgesics.

A biochemical approach to CNS therapy is typified by treatment for Parkinson's disease. The known deficiency of dopamine in this disease is corrected by oral administration of its biochemical precursor levodopa, which, unlike dopamine, can gain access to the brain where it is converted to the neurotransmitter by the enzyme dopa decarboxylase. A further advance was achieved when chemists combined levodopa with carbidopa. Carbidopa prevents the unwanted metabolism of levodopa outside the brain, thus allowing the active agent to be formed only where it is wanted, within the brain. Side effects are minimized.

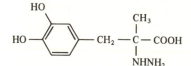

S-CARBIDOPA FACILITATES L-DOPA TREATMENT OF PARKINSON'S DISEASE

During the past decade, there has been a remarkable change in our understanding of the process of chemical signalling within the mammalian CNS. Some eight or nine monoamine and amino acid neurotransmitter candidates were known 10 years ago, but now 40 or more small peptides whose chemical structures have been determined can be added to the list. Each of these compounds has a potential messenger function. The opportunities for important advances in therapy through interdisciplinary chemical and biological research are enormous.

Diabetes

More than 10 million Americans have diabetes mellitus, and the number is increasing annually by about 6 percent. Diabetes is the third leading cause of death and the leading cause of blindness in the United States.

In diabetes, the body fails to secrete an adequate amount of insulin for proper glucose metabolism and/or does not make proper use of that which is secreted. For the insulin-dependent diabetic (10 percent of the total), insulin replacement therapy has been used for 60 years. Recently, important advances in supporting this type of therapy were achieved. The production of *human* insulin in bacteria using recombinant DNA techniques has been shown to be commercially feasible. In addition, chemists have been successful in achieving the large-scale chemical conversion of porcine into human insulin. Thus, diabetics are no longer restricted to the use of animal insulin. However, the complications of diabetes, including blindness, atherosclerosis, and nephropathy, remain a major problem. Exciting novel approaches to treatment of diabetes are receiving the attention of chemists, biologists, and clinicians. We have reason to expect significant advances in the control of diabetes and its complications during this decade. Chemical research is also expected to contribute significantly to the treatment of other endocrine disorders.

Cancer Research

The group of diseases collectively known as cancer is second only to cardio-vascular disease in the number of deaths that result in the United States, where cancer will strike one out of four persons alive today. It is gratifying that cancer research has entered a fruitful phase. Chemistry played a critical role in bringing about past advances and must continue to be an essential component if we are to capitalize on them. The advances can be conveniently divided into those dealing with our understanding of carcinogenesis and those relating to cancer chemotherapy.

Carcinogenesis The discovery in the 1930s that organic compounds can act as carcinogens in experimental animals led eventually to the finding of many diverse compounds with the ability to induce cancer in many tissues of mice, rats, and other mammals. Today, some naturally occurring and some synthetic chemicals in the environment are suspected of being capable of causing cancer in humans, and interest in the detection of these agents and in their mechanisms of action has increased greatly.

Several salient features of chemical carcinogens and carcinogenesis by these agents were established before 1965. As new carcinogens were discovered, covalent binding in vivo of several different chemical carcinogens to cellular macromolecules (proteins, RNA, DNA) was demonstrated and correlated with the carcinogenic process. The findings set the stage for much further research.

The majority of known chemical carcinogens are actually "procarcinogens," i.e., they must be metabolically activated to chemically reactive molecules

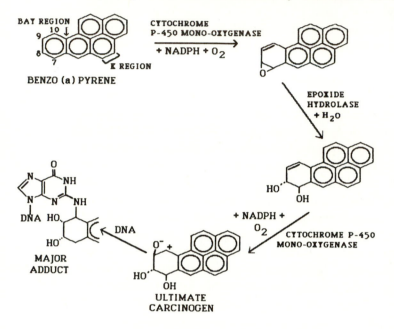

ENZYMATIC REACTIONS OF CARCINOGENESIS

known as ultimate carcinogens. It is the ultimate carcinogens that react with the nucleic acids and proteins in cells to alter their normal functions in cell growth. The major enzyme systems metabolizing pro-carcinogens have been identified and studied.

The chemical basis for the reactions forming carcinogen-DNA adducts is well understood, but the specific involvement of these adducts in the induction of cancer in animals has not been demonstrated. However, reactive metabolites of chemical carcinogens do produce mutagenic effects in both bacterial and animal cells. There is qualitative correlation of mutagenicity and carcinogenicity for many, but not all, classes of compounds, providing useful information for the organic chemist. Thus, a wide variety of compounds have been found to inhibit the actions of chemical carcinogens.

Perhaps the most promising and certainly the most dramatic recent development in cancer research is the recognition that certain genes in normal cells are closely tied to the development of malignancy. Importantly, these genes resemble or are identical to genes (oncogenes) from certain viruses that transform normal cells to malignant ones. Organic chemistry can determine (1) the nucleotide sequence of the normal gene and of the oncogene, and (2) the amino acid sequence of the proteins derived from these genes. A single nucleotide change in a gene derived from bladder, colon, or lung cells can replace a particular amino acid by another in the gene product and thereby make an otherwise normal cell malignant. The striking achievement implicit in this discovery is that we now understand *on a molecular basis* the difference between the protein of a normal and a malignant cell, at least for some transformations. Many laboratories are analyzing genes from human tumors that resemble genes from viruses capable of causing tumors in animals. The sequence of the cloned bladder carcinoma oncogene has been related both to viral oncogenes and to the normal bladder genes. That we can know that a single amino acid replacement in a protein can mean the difference between a healthy and a malignant cell is a striking example of the power of modern chemical techniques. Chemists are also in a promising position to investigate, for example, possible effects of amino acid changes on the conformation of a protein. These results remind us that a single amino acid change in hemoglobin has been known for some time to lead to sickle cell anemia and that the underlying chemistry is reasonably well understood.

Even more recently, close similarities have been discovered between oncogenes and other genes encoding endogenous growth factors. Their biochemical properties have given clues as to possible biochemical mechanisms that control cell growth.

Overall, these developments will result in new rational approaches to therapy.

Chemotherapy Compounds used for the treatment of cancer originally were toxic substances isolated from natural sources or of synthetic origin. The role of the medicinal chemist has been to design and synthesize potential new drugs with improved therapeutic index and/or a novel mode of action. Many new and clinically important antitumor agents have been isolated from microbial sources in the last 15 years, and their chemical structure has been determined. In a number of classes of these compounds, it has been possible to prepare semisynthetic derivatives with diminished toxic side effects. Also, a number of these antibiotics interact with DNA in the malignant cell by interleaving in the helical DNA coils, a process called "intercalation." This mechanism has furnished a model for the design of new synthetic compounds now in clinical trial.

The synthesis of derivatives of the first synthetic anticancer agent called nitrogen mustard, which acts by alkylation of DNA, has in the past yielded more selective drugs, such as cytoxan and, more recently, agents for prostate cancer. Synthetic analogs of natural substances that disrupt normal metabolic processes, known as "antimetabolites," include some of the most widely used anticancer drugs. Compounds with high electron affinity have been found to sensitize hypoxic tumor cells to radiation, and misonidazole has been used clinically to increase the effectiveness of radiotherapy. The discovery that platinum electrodes release a toxic substance led to the isolation of cisplatin and the synthesis of analogs as a new class of highly beneficial antitumor agents.

About 40 anticancer agents have proven to be clinically useful. The most significant breakthroughs in treatment have resulted from combination therapy. For example, in 1963 advanced Hodgkins's disease in adults was incurable, but today 81 percent of patients enter complete remission with combination therapy. Complete remission can also be achieved in 97 percent of children with acute lymphocytic leukemia and in 60–70 percent of patients with testicular

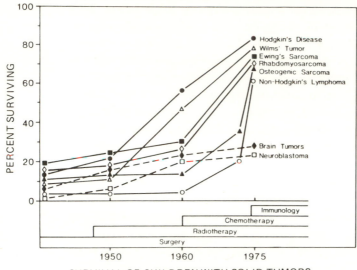

PERCENT SURVIVING

- ● Hodgkin's Disease
- △ Wilms' Tumor
- ■ Ewing's Sarcoma
- ◇ Rhabdomyosarcoma
- ▲ Osteogenic Sarcoma
- ○ Non-Hodgkin's Lymphoma
- ◆ Brain Tumors
- □ Neuroblastoma

Immunology
Chemotherapy
Radiotherapy
Surgery

SURVIVAL OF CHILDREN WITH SOLID TUMORS

cancer. Over the last 30 years, the greatest progress in chemotherapy has been made in the treatment of cancer in children. For several tumor types, the percentage survival for children so afflicted has risen from below 20 percent to above 60 percent.

There remains a pressing need for more effective and less toxic anticancer drugs, in particular for slow-growing solid tumors, lung cancer, and brain tumors. New approaches are being developed for the design of more effective drugs based on the mechanisms of action of known agents and new methods for transport of drugs into cells. Differences between the surfaces of normal and tumor cells being discovered by immunologists and cell biologists may provide new directions for drug design. Chemists will play a critical role in the discovery of drugs that can stimulate the host's immune response.

Gastrointestinal Drugs

In the United States there are 22.4 million visits to physicians annually for gastrointestinal disorders, and many more people treat themselves with over-the-counter products. One of the major problems in this area is the peptic ulcer, which has been the main target for therapeutic intervention and the one in which major inroads have been made. Duodenal ulcers, which are the most prevalent form, are associated with increased rates of gastric acid and pepsin secretion and are susceptible to treatment with agents that neutralize or reduce gastric acid secretion.

The major advance toward controlling acid secretion stemmed from the discovery that the histamine receptors regulating gastric secretion were different from those affected by the classical antihistamines used in allergies. This realization led to the design and synthesis of drugs specifically for the histamine receptors of the acid-secreting cells. The era of histamine H_2-receptor antagonists opened with the discovery of burimamide and developed through metiamide to the clinically useful agent cimetidine, a breakthrough in drug discovery. Today about three-quarters of all peptic ulcer patients receive H_2-receptor antagonists. Cimetidine has served as the standard lead-

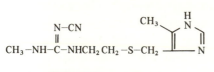

CIMETIDINE
CONTROLS PEPTIC ULCERS

ing the way to the development of even more potent and more selective agents, such as ranitidine and famotidine, and resulting in a reduced incidence of side effects.

Inflammatory and Immunological Diseases and Defense Systems

Inflammatory and immuological diseases are major medical problems. Chronic and degenerative inflammatory disorders, such as arthritis, affect 7 percent of the total population. The isolation, characterization, and partial synthesis of cortisone in the 1940s enabled clinicians to make the dramatic discovery of its potent anti-inflammatory effect. This era was followed by the discovery of a family of nonsteroidal anti-inflammatory/analgesic drugs, typified by indomethacin, which are in wide use today. Although these drugs were developed as anti-inflammatory agents, a number of them are more effective analgesic agents than aspirin and are widely used in controlling various types of moderate pain. The biochemical mechanism of action of these compounds, like that of aspirin, has been shown to be inhibition of the enzyme cyclooxygenase. The anti-inflammatory steroids and the cyclooxygenase inhibitors have provided enormous medical benefits, but they do not arrest the progress of diseases such as rheumatoid arthritis. There is, therefore, still an urgent need to develop effective therapy that can modify the course of the disease without undesired side effects. Advances in the biochemistry and cell biology of inflammation, coupled with the identification of mediators and cell surface receptors involved in the complex inflammation process, have indicated new research directions. The recognition that many inflammatory diseases represent disorders of the immune system has been particularly important. Chemistry provides the opportunity for us to understand the chemical basis of these events. Monoclonal antibody technologies open the way to more precise diagnosis and the monitoring of disease progression. Chemistry is crucial not only to generating the synthetic immunogens required for the production of monoclonal antibodies, but also for the discovery of completely new classes of anti-inflammatory agents that may be expected to modulate immune responses. A cyclic peptide, cyclosporin, isolated from natural sources, was found to be an immunosuppressant and has produced dramatic results in reducing rejection after organ transplants.

In the last 20 years much has been learned about the *molecular* mechanisms of activation and regulation of the so-called plasma complement system. This group of enzymes and other proteins plays a key role in the molecular process whereby our body decides that a foreign organism is present and through which it coordinates the response of cells and molecules to that foreign organism. These advances, combined with the advances in enzyme inhibitor design, may make feasible the design of a new class of anti-inflammatory agents. Chemists have also made major contributions to our understanding of the nature of antibody molecules, first demonstrating that they are proteins, and then actually determining their chemical structure and that of the genes that code for these proteins. From this has emerged a recognition of nature's design of these molecules. They have a "variable region," which specifically binds to the foreign substance against which the antibody is directed, and a "constant region," which determines the biological mechanism of removal of the foreign substance. This recognition opens promising new research avenues.

Advances in Fertility Control and Fertility Induction

Our understanding of the human reproductive cycle moved ahead rapidly as we became able to determine the chemical structures of the steroid hormones of reproduction and to connect their release to the presence of hormones and neurotransmitters secreted by the hypothalamus and pituitary gland. It then became possible to influence normal physiology and pathophysiology to achieve fertility control and, more recently, fertility induction.

Orally absorbable estrogens and progestins, or their analogs, have been used as contraceptives with enormous impact on population control worldwide. However, multiple side effects, including thrombophlebitis, migraine headache, stroke, and myocardial infarction, have been associated with their use. In the last several years, preclinical and clinical attention has been devoted to reducing the doses of estrogen and progestin and to optimizing the ratio of the two to achieve oral contraception with minimal side effects. The effort will probably result in decreasing the risk of breast cancer or endometrial carcinoma of the uterus, although the contribution of oral contraceptives to inducing these neoplasms appears minimal.

Hormone antagonists of the sex steroids have proven useful in inducing fertility. Clomiphene blocks estrogen receptors in the hypothalamus and in the pituitary gland. When administered with appropriate timing in the reproductive cycle in women, this agent interferes with the normal feedback inhibition of estrogen on hypothalamic secretion of releasing hormones and on the gonadotropins secreted by the pituitary gland. Interference results in the desired hormonal surge by the hypothalamus and pituitary gland, often causing ovulation and subsequent fertility.

The peptide hormone, gonadotropin-releasing hormone (GnRH) (which is secreted by the hypothalamus) has been isolated, chemically characterized, and synthesized. It normally stimulates the pituitary gland to secrete glycoprotein hormones, the gonadotropins, luteinizing hormone (LH), and follicle-stimulating hormone (FSH). Many analogs of the 10-amino acid polypeptide GnRH have been chemically synthesized, and their pharmacologic effects have been evaluated. The thrust of the early work was to develop hormone antagonists that might be used in fertility control. Certain side effects have decreased enthusiasm for use of these analogs in contraception, but they remain of interest and are receiving attention for treating sex-hormone-dependent cancers. Dramatic medical successes have been achieved using analogs of GnRH of enhanced potency. These compounds have been used in patients who have congenital absence of GnRH, a rare disorder. An analog of GnRH is administered using sophisticated small pumps that are worn by the patient, and the drug is administered in a pulsatile fashion to mimic its normal secretion pattern by the hypothalamus. Patients in their twenties who have never undergone puberty can be brought through all the successive endocrinological stages of puberty and then, successfully, brought to fertility. This combination of impressive drug design with advanced drug delivery systems is an indication of future advances in the reproductive field. The nonpulsative administration of potent GnRH analogs, in contrast, is now known to lead to desensitization of the pituitary and thus to inhibition of reproductive function.

Finally, there are major new directions that should also result in important therapeutic advances. Preliminary evidence from several laboratories indicates that we will soon know the molecular structure of inhibin, the key hormone involved in regulating sperm production. Synthetic variation of this structure should enable the medicinal chemist to develop male contraceptives. It is envisioned that this kind of endocrine manipulation should have fewer side effects than the use of oral contraceptives in females. Next, the role of the brain in regulating reproductive function has been observed for a long time. Factors such as stress, exercise, and depression are known to alter or abolish menstrual cycles in adult women or delay the onset of puberty in prepubescent adolescents. Structures of the neurotransmitters that influence hormonal secretion by the hypothalamus are now being elucidated. Brain peptides such as the endorphins, opiate analogs, and peptide analogs of the endorphins and enkephalins may prove useful in restoring normal menstrual cycles to women athletes and normal reproductive function to women who suffer from anorexia nervosa. It can be hoped that the next decade will see great impact from chemical design of hormone analogs on treatment of sexual and reproductive dysfunction resulting from psychological disorders, another major health problem.

Vitamins

Throughout mankind's history, vitamin deficiencies have been a major cause of death. However, the existence of these essential dietary ingredients was first recognized in the 18th century when it was found that small amounts of citrus fruit, which provides vitamin C, could prevent scurvy on long sea voyages.

Many of these compounds have been isolated and identified. They act as coenzymes or cofactors, which are necessary for the functioning of many enzymes. A few of the advances and discoveries that have been made in this area are described below.

The isolation and characterization of vitamin B_{12} as the dietary component required to prevent fatal pernicious anemia was reported in 1948. Determination of its molecular structure in 1956 by X-ray crystallographic and chemical studies showed it to be by far the most complex of any of the vitamins. Its synthesis in 1976 was a landmark of organic chemistry. There have been major advances in our understanding of the functions and mechanisms of action of the coenzyme forms of vitamin B_{12}, but it can be expected that additional roles remain to be discovered.

Considerable progress has been made in the understanding of the flavins, of which riboflavin, vitamin B_2, is an example. The flavins in various forms act as coenzymes for oxidation-reduction systems, which are required for normal metabolic processes. Over 100 flavoproteins are now known. It is of interest that a modified flavin has recently been discovered to be a coenzyme in methane-producing bacteria, which may be of future interest in the development of methane as an energy source.

It has long been known that vitamin D is required for the prevention of rickets. By the use of advanced chemical and spectroscopic techniques, it has now been shown that vitamin D is actually a prohormone. It is metabolized in the body to a highly potent dihydroxy derivative, which regulates absorption of calcium from the diet, reabsorption in the kidney, and metabolism of calcium in bone. It is not yet understood how the vitamin D hormone carries out its functions, but research is in progress. The metabolite has been synthesized and shown to be effective in the treatment of a number of bone diseases. Trials are in progress to evaluate its usefulness in osteoporosis. New functions of vitamin D hormones will undoubtedly be discovered, now that the compound is available for research.

Biochemists have greatly advanced our understanding of vitamin K's mechanism of action. Vitamin K is required as a coenzyme for the production of three or four proteins that help blood to clot. We need continued biochemical studies to clarify how vitamin K brings about the modification of clotting proteins and to elucidate how these modified proteins function in various sites in the body.

For some time, we have known that a vitamin A derivative is required for the recording of light as it strikes the eye. However, vitamin A is now recognized to play an essential role also in the growth of higher animals. It also plays an important role in the development of bone, spermatogenesis in the male, and placental development in the female. Vitamin A must be converted into several related compounds before it can satisfy all these functions, and much progress has been made in elucidation of the chemical changes involved. For example, it appears to be converted to retinoic acids for function in epithe-

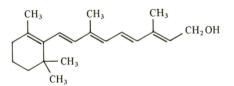

VITAMIN A: ESSENTIAL TO VISION AND GROWTH

lial tissues, and some of these acids and synthetic analogs are useful in the treatment of skin disorders such as acne, psoriasis, and ichthyosis. Another important development is the observation that vitamin A compounds can retard some chemical carcinogenesis.

Conclusion

It is tempting to speculate in which disease categories the most dramatic discoveries will occur during this decade, even though breakthroughs are rarely predictable. Nevertheless, it is likely that new directions in receptor-related research will have an impact on drug discovery in cardiovascular diseases, especially atherosclerosis and hypertension, as well as on endocrine diseases like diabetes. Recent research with oncogenes has begun to provide an understanding on the molecular level of certain human cancers. These observations, which are certain to be exploited intensively, have opened promising new frontiers for drug discovery in cancer research. Progress in our ability to regulate the immune system should open up new approaches to the treatment of chronic inflammatory diseases, such as arthritis. Developments in neurobiology should lead to new CNS active drugs. Finally, the discovery of new enzyme inhibitors and of hormone and neurotransmitter antagonists will certainly lead to the discovery of important new drugs in several categories, including among others, asthma and infectious diseases. Recent advances in our understanding of new second messengers related to phosphatidylinositol and of tyrosine kinases, and other kinases, are likely to have major applications in therapy.

CHEMISTRY is a central science
that responds to societal needs.

It is critical in Man's attempt to...
improve health and conquer disease

A Pac-Man for Cholesterol

Since the 1960s we've known that high levels of cholesterol correlate with heart ailments, the major cause of death in the United States. What we need is a Pac-Man to chomp up the cholesterol in the blood and reduce "hardening" of the arteries that carry blood from the heart (atherosclerosis). Now a lowly fungus—not unlike the famous mold, penicillium—may have shown us one.

A normally functioning human cell uses a dual system for meeting its cholesterol needs. First, the cell has its own factory to manufacture cholesterol. In addition, the cell's exterior has a number of lipoprotein receptors that can grab onto cholesterol-containing lipoproteins as they pass by in the bloodstream and pull them inside. The cell fixes the number of these Pac-Man-like receptors so that just the right amount of imported cholesterol is added to the factory-made product. If the inner cell cholesterol level falls too low, more receptors are added to extract more from the blood stream.

There's an idea! If the cell's cholesterol factory could be slowed down, would the cell produce more receptors to make up the difference from the blood stream supply? A chance to test this scenario came when a biochemist discovered that certain fungi produced something that inhibited cholesterol synthesis. Chemists joined in the plot, purified the effective compound, determined its structure, and named it COMPACTIN. Knowing this structure, chemists were able to synthesize close relatives of compactin that are even more potent. Chemical tests with these new chemicals indicate that the scheme works as planned. The inhibitor slows down the cellular cholesterol factory, the cell produces more lipoprotein receptors, and the blood cholesterol level drops.

The importance of this advance is shown by the fact that the average person with double the normal blood level of cholesterol can expect to live only 45 to 50 years. For the few unlucky people with triple the

normal amount, life expectancy drops to 30 or 35 years. To complicate matters, 1 in 500 Americans has the genetic disease *familial hypercholesterolemia* (FH). Victims of FH don't produce enough receptors at their cell surfaces, so lipoproteins accumulate in the blood and eventually cause heart attacks. Thus clinical researchers are excited to find that the new cholesterol-inhibitors work with FH patients, bringing the blood levels of cholesterol all the way down to the normal level. Much research remains, but these moldy chemicals offer immediate hope to FH sufferers and, in the future, to all people with abnormally high blood cholesterol.

IV-C.   Biotechnologies

Introduction

The use of microorganisms to produce desirable products is not a recent concept. The fermentation of sugars in grapes to make wine, the fermentation of starch to leaven bread, and the conversion of milk into cheese are technologies that go back many centuries. During modern history, however, the developing sciences of microbiology and chemistry have determined the chemical nature of these processes and enabled the refinement and control of nature's biotechnology.

More recently, man's knowledge has expanded to where biology has begun to be understood in chemical terms—on the molecular level. This development is the result of progress in various of the classical sciences, including organic chemistry, microbiology, and biochemistry and continuing with their fusion into the modern discipline of molecular biology with its subset of recombinant DNA technology.

We now have a basic understanding of the structural and functional relationship between the molecules and macromolecules (large molecules) within biological systems. Hence, manipulation of their chemical structures, both within and outside of living organisms, has led to improved processes and new products with impact upon various aspects of modern life. Many key steps in the development of biotechnology were made by chemists. The elucidation of the chemical structures of DNA (deoxyribonucleic acid), RNA (ribonucleic acid), and protein and their biological relationship is a milestone concept at the very heart of biotechnology.

Through X-ray crystallographic studies, DNA was shown to be a double-stranded molecule with each strand consisting of chains of four basic molecular units called nucleotides (A, C, G, and T). Each of these molecular units is a particular heterocyclic amine whose structures are shown in the next chapter. For the purpose here, it will suffice to note that these units form hydrogen bonds in complementary pairs (A to T and C to G) to hold DNA in its helical structure. At the same time, their sequence carries the DNA's genetic information.

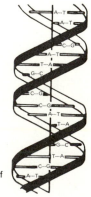

A schematic diagram of the DNA double helix.

A three-dimensional representation of the DNA double helix.

Base pairs

Sugar-phosphate backbone

The DNA macromolecules were shown to contain the information necessary for the function of the cells. One of these two DNA strands is copied into RNA, a complementary chain also consisting of four heterocyclic amine nucleotides, A, C, G, and U (U is chemically similar to the T found in DNA). Some of the RNA is "messenger RNA " (mRNA), the information-carrying link between the gene DNA and the desired protein. The information is expressed in a genetic code, a "language" in which the mRNA chains specify the structure of a protein in a three-nucleotide "word." Each such word specifies 1 of the 20 amino acid building blocks out of which a desired protein chain is to be constructed, as represented below:

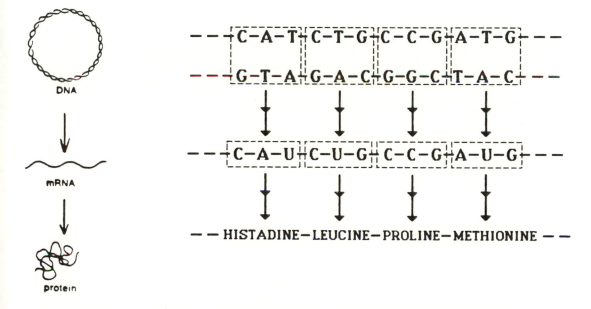

In addition, chemistry provided the methods for determining the sequence of amino acids in the polypeptide (strings of amino acids linked by chemical bonds) chains of proteins, a development crucial to the correlation of structure with specific function. Chemists also learned how to assemble amino acids in a desired sequence so as to create directly polypeptides and even small proteins that were identical in structure and, in some cases, also in function to those that were isolated from natural biological sources.

More recently, the development of rapid chemical means for sequencing single-stranded DNA was a breakthrough of profound importance because the primary structure of a gene could now be ascertained. Ironically, the sequencing at the gene level is more readily executed than that of the encoded protein and has immensely expanded our knowledge of protein structures.

Of equal importance and at the very heart of biotechnology has been the successful elaboration of simple, rapid, chemical strategies for gene synthesis. Two useful chemical methods have been developed: the first is based on the activation of the phosphoryl moiety for ester formation by dehydrating agents; the second employs the nucleophilic properties of a phosphoramidite intermediate to form the desired 5'-3' linkage. The latter, in particular, has been adapted to a solid state support, thus permitting the routine synthesis of oligonucleotides of chain lengths approaching 50 base pairs. The construction of probe molecules essential for clone selection via strand hydridization and of oligonucleotide mutagenesis is now a facile preparative exercise.

The aforementioned developments in chemistry were tremendous advances in our ability to understand biological molecules in chemical terms. Without these advances, biotechnology as it exists today would not be possible.

Recombinant DNA Technologies

Recombinant DNA technology is a recent discipline whose roots reside in the fusion of nucleic acid chemistry, protein chemistry, microbiology, genetics, and biochemistry. Further development in the field will depend upon developments in all of its parent disciplines. Genetic engineering consists of ways to purify and identify genetic material (DNA) from one source, tailor it for insertion into a new host organism, and isolate a colony of cells containing the desired genes.

The micromanipulation of DNA was made possible by the discovery by molecular biologists of restriction enzymes (a class of proteins) that catalyze the cutting of DNA at specific nucleotide sequences, and ligation enzymes that can catalyze the splicing together of DNA in a a defined orientation. For example, a restriction enzyme called Bam H1 recognizes the pallindromic double-stranded sequence, GGATCC, and cuts between the two G moeities to create fragments as follows:

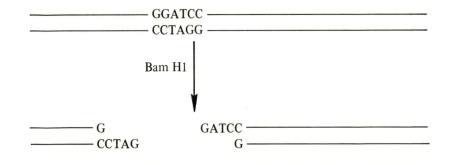

The enzyme, DNA Ligase, can take fragments like those created above and join them together to form a single continuous duplex chain as follows:

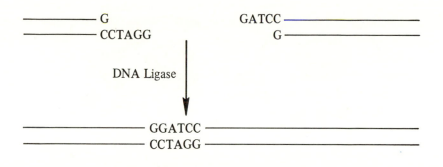

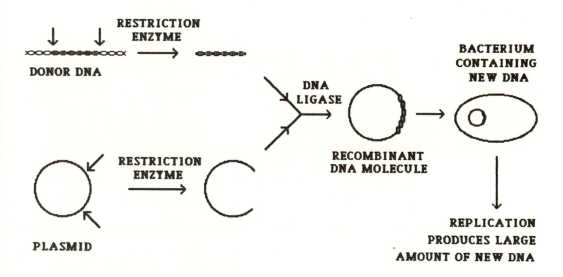

Through the excision and isolation of a segment of DNA from one source and its joining to a DNA segment from another source, the restructuring of DNA to create recombinant DNA can be achieved:

   Many fragments generated in the above manner contain entire genes or multiple genes. These fragments can be inserted into plasmids—rings of DNA that can autonomously replicate within bacterial cells. If the construction contains the proper molecular signals, they can direct the synthesis of mRNA and, subsequently, protein. The genetically engineered bacteria can then be grown as colonies of identical bacteria (clones), all of which will then produce the protein for which the synthesis information was encoded by the original DNA fragment.

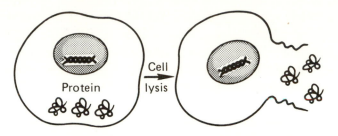

Numerous analytical techniques have been developed to identify particular DNA fragments, including those containing specific genes. Separations technology has been developed to isolate such DNA fragments. Other analytical techniques have been developed to identify the genetically engineered cells in which the desired DNA has been introduced as well as those within which the DNA (through the intermediary mRNA) is directing the synthesis of proteins. Once again, the isolation of the protein molecules requires the application of separations technology. Thus the application of chemical techniques to biological systems is the key thread of recombinant DNA technology.

Biotechnology Applied to Medicine

In addition to the development of clones containing isolated fragments of DNA, various genes have been chemically synthesized, cloned, and utilized to direct the synthesis of a desired protein via recombinant DNA technology. For example, insulin (a hormone) is a protein used for the treatment of diabetes. The gene that led to the production of human insulin was synthesized by chemists in 1978 and was engineered into a plasmid, which was introduced into the common bacterium, *E. coli*. Another example is human growth hormone, a protein that is a sequence of 191 amino acids. A gene encoding the protein was created through the fusion of some naturally isolated DNA with some chemically synthesized DNA. This protein was expressed in *E. coli* in 1979, and it is now in clinical trials as a potential medication for dwarfism and similar conditions caused by a deficiency of this hormone.

The production of a hormone is not the only type of protein for which recombinant DNA technology is useful. Classical vaccines developed to protect against viral infections are often isolated from natural sources. They can be killed or attenuated viruses, or portions of viruses. The DNA for the protein found on the surface of a particular virus can be cloned and produced via recombinant DNA technology. This leads to a safer vaccine because the DNA and the proteins associated with the disease symptoms caused by the virus are not present in the clone, thereby creating a vaccine that cannot accidently cause the disease or be contaminated by other viruses. For example, the classical vaccine for protection from hepatitis B virus is isolated from blood and therefore presents the risk of contamination with other blood-borne diseases such as AIDS. Through recombinant DNA techniques, the gene encoding the protein from the surface of the hepatitis B virus has been cloned. The protein, currently being produced in recombinant yeast, is in clinical trials as a vaccine.

These examples illustrate the great power of recombinant DNA technology to synthesize, on a potentially large scale, valuable protein materials that would be difficult or prohibitively expensive to produce by other means. They represent the combined efforts of chemists, biologists, and other scientists and are a prime example of the interdependence of the different disciplines. The potential of recombinant DNA technology, however, has only been scratched. The chemically prepared DNA sequences can be used to screen genomic libraries to locate genetic defects that may indicate the subject's sensitivity to the appearance of disease. Importantly, the correction of genetic diseases through the replacement or augmentation of defective genes with genes specifying normal proteins is forseeable. Perhaps the most important contribution that recombinant DNA technology can make is through the expansion of knowledge in the regulation of genes within cells. Toward that end, this knowledge was recently used, with encouraging results, in a clinical setting to attempt to express, in adults, long-silent fetal globin genes for the purpose of overcoming some genetic blood diseases.

A naturally occurring molecule that is found to have useful biological activity is often not the one that becomes a pharmaceutical. For reasons of economy, suppression of undesirable side effects, duration of action, and the need to develop a stable formulation, fragments, or analogs of the natural product may be more useful than the product itself. Recombinant DNA techniques can produce these modified products. Polypeptide hormones have many types of useful biological activity, but they suffer from the disadvantages of not being orally active and of having short duration of action. Further progress in the chemical modification of proteins may correct these drawbacks. Often a protein produced using recombinant DNA technology requires modification before its biological activity can be realized. This was true for the insulin described earlier. Chemical modification of the insulin protein produced in *E. coli* led to a biologically active hormone.

Alternatively, the desirable pharmaceutical may be a compound that is inhibitory or antagonistic to the biological activity of a naturally occuring biomolecule. In this case, recombinant DNA technology can provide an abundant source of the biomolecule, which can be screened against a multitude of chemically (or biotechnologically) synthesized compounds to develop a useful pharmaceutical. Advanced biochemical and chemical technology, therefore, can generate initial leads to active structures and can provide intermediates and methods for synthesis of the ultimate pharmaceutical.

Bioengineering

An increasingly important part of modern medicine is the development of safe and effective methods for delivering drugs and developing materials or assemblies that can replace failed human parts. This involves chemical development as well as engineering. Examples include cardiac pacemakers, heart valves (and now artificial hearts), tendon replacements, and heart-lung and kidney dialysis machines. Fluorocarbon chemical emulsions and serum fractions such as albumin and factor VIII (recently reported to be produced by recombinant DNA technology) are increasingly promising as blood substitutes, especially as the hazards from the use of whole blood products become more apparent. Thin membranes used as artificial skin and cultured epithelial cells promise major therapeutic advances in burn treatment. Materials for tooth implants and bone replacement are being developed. Implantable insulin pumps may be able to control the serious complications that sometimes attend present methods for the treatment of insulin-responsive diabetes. In the longer term, it may become possible to implant genetically engineered cells that will provide treatment for genetic and hormonal deficiencies.

Biocatalysis

The proteins that act as catalysts in biochemical reactions—enzymes—are the focus of yet another union of biotechnology and chemistry. A catalyst accelerates the chemical process of conversion of one substance into another.

The ability of recombinant DNA technology to control the synthesis of enzymes will surely extend the application of the microbe as a biocatalyst. First, it will be possible to produce almost any enzyme found in nature inexpensively; the economic barrier to biocatalysis will be at least lowered. Second, and more exciting, is the prospect of refining present techniques for preparing biocatalysts that currently do not exist in nature through synthesis of the appropriate DNA sequence and subsequent production of the novel protein whose synthesis it directs. X-ray crystallographic techniques have provided the chemist with detailed understanding of the three-dimensional structure of some enzymes. Further chemical research to increase the understanding of the relationship between the chemical structure and catalytic activity of enzymes will be needed before rational design of such biologically produced synthetic biocatalysts can be achieved. Recent developments in biocatalysis have come about largely through the technology of enzyme immobilization on a solid support, whereby the stability of an enzyme is increased and the enzyme can be more

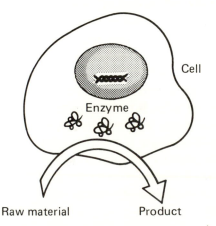

Cell

Enzyme

Raw material   Product

readily separated from the reaction products. It is therefore able to covert more material to the desired product per quantity of enzyme and, at the same time, immobilization helps to simplify the purification of the product. One example of this technology is the use of the immobilized enzyme, penicillin acylase, to con vert the naturally occuring antibiotic penicillin G into 6-aminopenicillanic acid (6-APA). This compound is then used to prepare the clinically effective semi-synthetic penicillins by chemical addition of specific chains of atoms at the amino nitrogen (N) atom in place of the chain, which is specifically removed by the acylase enzyme.

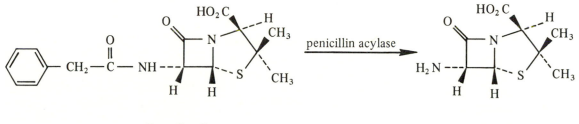

Penicillin G   6-Aminopenicillanic acid

In another example, corn starch can be enzymatically converted to glucose. An immobilized enzyme, glucose isomerase, is then used to convert some of the glucose to the sweeter fructose. Over 2 million metric tons of this high-fructose corn syrup are produced annually in the United States.

Immobilization technology does not necessarily require the isolation of a particular enzyme. Whole cells containing the enzyme can be immobilized on a solid matrix. For example, whole cells of the bacterium *E. coli* have been immobilized and used to catalyze the chemical conversion of fumaric acid and ammonia into one of the building blocks of proteins, the amine acid, aspartic acid. In addition, immobilized yeast cells can be used in the fermentation production of alcohol (ethanol). This process has been demonstrated industrially in a large pilot plant facility. No discussion of biocatalysis would be complete without addressing the renewable resource of biomass. At this point, a relatively small amount of the total available biomass in the United States is converted into useful chemicals through biotechnology. There is increasing interest in biomass conversion because the fossil sources of raw materials are ultimately limited. The potential volume of cellulosic materials that could be converted into industrial chemicals, however, is large. Large-scale conversion of biomass into industrial chemicals requires a relatively constant, low-cost source of biomass. From a technical point of view, molasses, starch from corn or wheat, and sugar are well suited for fermentation. They are readily converted into glucose, and microorganisms are known for converting glucose into many useful chemical products. These starting materials, however, are needed for food and are subject to wide fluctuations in price and supply depending upon crop success and trade policies.

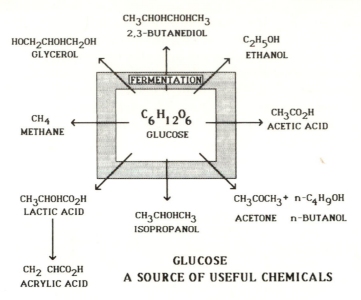

**GLUCOSE
A SOURCE OF USEFUL CHEMICALS**

The potential biomass available from agricultural and forestry residues is estimated to be 10-fold greater than the aforementioned sources, and it is also less subject to the fluctuations of both price and availability. Unfortunately, it is composed principally of lignocellulose (lignin, cellulose, and hemicellulose). Lignin resists biocatalytic degradation and physically interferes with the fermentation of the cellulosic materials. Accordingly, lignocellulose biomass must be chemically pretreated to remove the lignin. Except for use as a combustible fuel, no large-scale uses for lignin have been developed, and it often becomes a waste. Biocatalysis of these abundant sources of biomass is therefore dependent upon further development in the chemical modification of the raw materials to produce substrates suitable for the action of biological systems.

Conclusion

Over the past two decades, progress in the development of biotechnology has been dramatic. It is now possible to program living cells to generate products ranging from relatively simple molecules to complex proteins. We have only begun to realize the immense potential of recombinant DNA technology as a means of obtaining protein materials that were previously very costly or unobtainable in appreciable quantities. Biocatalysts have already established themselves in the large-scale production of various industrial chemicals. Continued progress in biotechnology will require cooperative efforts as well as individual advances in several disciplines, including chemistry, chemical engineering, molecular biology, microbiology, and cell biology. The United States currently has a strong world position in biotechnology, but if that position is to be maintained, vigorous research and development must continue in all the sciences that have an impact on biotechnology.

CHEMISTRY is a central science
that responds to societal needs.

It is critical in Man's attempt to...
feed the world's population

Jack and the Soybean Stalk

Perhaps a modern explanation for the amazing size of Jack's fairytale beanstalk can be found in *brassinolide*. This remarkable chemical is an extremely effective plant hormone that can double the growth of food plants, by both cell elongation and cell division. Only recently have chemists been able to isolate, identify, and then synthesize this valuable substance so that it can be used to increase the world's food supply.

Plant hormones have already revolutionized agriculture. They allow us to coerce cotton plants to release their cotton balls at harvest time, command fruit trees to cling to their fruit, induce Christmas trees to keep their needles, and order stored potatoes not to sprout. *Brassinolide* now can add to this list, and it is active in quantities of less than one-billionth of an ounce!

Chemists play a crucial role along the long and arduous research road from discovery to use of a new plant hormone. For example, *brassinolide* is found in minute quantities in the pollen of the rape plant (*Brassica rapus* L.). To isolate enough chemical to study, researchers laboriously collected pollen brushed off the legs of bees who had been cavorting in the rape plants. From 500 pounds of pollen so gathered, chemists were able to extract only 15 milligrams of *brassinolide*, an amount as small as a grain of sand. From this they were able to grow a single tiny crystal, so that a chemical crystallographer could analyze the molecular structure with X-ray diffraction. Just as X-rays penetrate an arm to reveal broken bones, they penetrate a crystal and reveal the geometrical arrangement of the atoms in *brassinolide*. The chemists were surprised to discover an unprecedented seven-atom ring within the molecule, a feature that must be essential to the function of this beneficial compound. With this key information, synthetic chemists have now made several close relatives of *brassinolide*, and agricultural scientists are evaluating them in greenhouse production of potatoes, soybeans, and other vegetables.

This advance involved the knowhow and interaction of plant and insect physiologists, organic chemists, and chemical crystallographers from many different laboratories. It shows that mental effort is as good as magic beans.

Maybe better, Jack!

IV-D.   Intellectual Frontiers

As detailed in earlier sections of this chapter, natural products are enormously useful in meeting society's needs. These chemical substances include regulators of plants and insect growth, agents for communication among insects, pesticides, antibiotics, vitamins, drugs for cardiovascular and central nervous system diseases, and anticarcinogens. As we develop their potential for societal benefit, chemistry becomes the key science at every stage: natural products must be detected, chemically isolated, structurally characterized, and synthesized as a final proof of structure. Chemical synthesis may also be critical in providing key natural products in amounts adequate for biological testing and subsequent practical use.

Chemical synthesis may also improve upon what nature has provided. Many natural products have fascinating biological properties even though they are not optimal for our needs. For example, thienamycin has excellent antibiotic properties, but the molecule is unstable and therefore unsuitable for use in human medicine. A synthetic chemical modification has provided a stable molecule that promises much as an agent for combatting infectious disease. Thus, synthetic chemists have been able to follow a lead provided by a natural product to design and prepare a new molecule with even more useful biological and chemical properties.

As was emphasized in the discussion of biotechnology, our understanding of macromolecules has provided new insights into their function in biological systems. The new insights have come from structural studies, synthetic modifications, increased understanding of the relationship between structure and function, and the techniques of molecular genetics. This work too has been profoundly chemical, and chemists will continue to contribute as these insights are translated into useful products for societal needs.

Synthesis and Biosynthesis

The development of modern organic synthetic techniques has provided access to molecules not formerly available to us, including, now, complex molecules of biological systems. Synthesis of both peptides and nucleic acids of substantial size—molecules widely useful in molecular biology and biotechnology—has become routine.

In complementary advances, our ability to understand and modify the synthetic processes of living organisms has progressed. Understanding step-by-step how a microorganism puts a molecule together may permit us to alter the nature of the final product in useful ways or to identify those enzymes involved along the pathway. Identification of key enzymes may, through the techniques of molecular biology, permit us to amplify their expression and, consequently, to increase the yield of a fermentation product.

Examples of this growing power in synthetic and biosynthetic chemistry follow.

Chemical Synthesis: Research and Discovery Horizons

Over the past 150 years, organic synthesis has moved ahead through about seven distinct levels of sophistication and power. Every 20 years or so, new advances move the field to a new level of capability at which it can solve problems beyond reach in the preceding period. This evolutionary history has reached another such point of rapid advance, a point characterized by new heights of sophistication in problem-solving and by penetration of other disciplines. The borderlines between organic chemistry and medicine and between organic chemistry and biochemistry have faded just as they have between biochemistry and biology.

Currently, the number of high-quality academic synthetic research groups greatly exceeds that of the 1960s, the result of striking discoveries being made and a reflection of the field's attractiveness to bright young scientists. We see before us a most promising era of organic synthesis. The methodology of chemical synthesis will include new synthetic operations, more elegant strategies, and reagents and catalysts of greater selectivity. Improved methods for the purification and isolation of organic substances, such as affinity chromatography and higher performance liquid chromatography, will greatly speed research in synthesis and hence make it possible to solve more complex problems. Continued advances in physical, instrumental, and computational methods for determination of exact structure (e.g., X-ray crystallography, nuclear magnetic resonance spectroscopy, mass spectrometry) will facilitate discovery and identification of many new and synthetically interesting biologically active molecules. Together, these developments will culminate in an understanding of how bioactive molecules function.

Because many of the chemical elements are still unexplored in regard to their application to organic synthesis, much important chemistry remains to be discovered. Only recently, for example, investigation of the chemistry of the abundant element silicon has been pursued with most impressive results. Numerous new synthetic reactions and reagents have emerged within just the past decade. Beyond any doubt the broadening of synthetic organic chemistry through the periodic table of the elements will produce dramatic advances in synthetic methodology for many years to come.

The computer looms large in the future of synthetic organic chemistry. Organic structures can be communicated to and from computers graphically in the chemist's natural language of two- or three-dimensional formulas. Organic chemical data can now be stored and retrieved in vast amounts with great efficiency and convenience. In time, this will prove to be an enormously important tool of synthetic organic chemists. Computers will be used not only for computation but also for a variety of other problem-solving tasks and for interactive teaching. Computer-assisted modeling and synthetic analysis will be a commonplace tool of chemistry.

Synthetic organic chemists will increasingly devise new chemical structures as synthetic bioactive agents. These synthetic molecules will function as activators or inhibitors of enzymatic or receptor function and will extend the range of chemical bioregulation. The synthetic chemist will also contribute substantially to the identification of new biologically important substances that occur in only trace amounts. These compounds can then be synthesized to make them available in amounts adequate for biological and medical research.

As the sophistication of synthetic organic chemistry advances, striking innovation in chemical catalysis can be foreseen. Organometallic catalysis will continue as a large and active branch of chemistry heavily involving synthesis. The era of synthetic enzyme-like organic catalysts, long a vague hope for the future, will emerge in the years to come: on the one hand, starting from chemically modified polypeptides or polynucleotides of modest size (20th century versions of the primeval enzymes), and, on the other hand, based on completely nonprotein structural types.

Synthesis of Natural Products

Over the last two decades, the multi-stage, total synthesis of natural products has consistently advanced to new levels of molecular complexity. Chemists are now addressing the major challenge of organic chemistry: the synthesis of only one desired conformation of a mirror image pair, i.e., selective synthesis of a particular chiral center. Progress here is redefining research frontiers and opening new targets to effective attack.

The structure determination and synthesis of the polyether antibiotics offers a prime example. Monensin, produced by a strain of *Streptomyces cinnamonensis*, is perhaps the best known example from among a group of about 50 naturally occurring polyether antibiotics. Three polyether antibiotics— monensin, lasalocid, and salinomycin—are currently in use for control of infectious parasitic disease in the poultry industry (coccidiosis); monensin has an American market of about $50M annually.

Monensin presents a formidable challenge to synthetic chemists: 17 asymmetric centers are present on the backbone of 26 carbon atoms, which means that, in principle, 131,072 different stereoisomers exist for the antibiotic. The total number of isomers for monensin will be infinite when constitutional isomers are counted. Thus, to achieve the total synthesis of monensin, it is essential to have a high degree of stereo-selectivity (selective synthesis of a diastereomer) and regio-selectivity (site-selective reaction of a functional group).

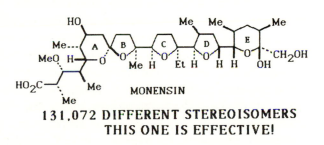

131,072 DIFFERENT STEREOISOMERS THIS ONE IS EFFECTIVE!

The successful total synthesis of monensin and its structural relatives (lasalocid, salinomycin, and narasin) involved revolutionary and trend-setting breakthroughs. Until these achievements, it was uncertain whether a stereo- and regio-controlled reaction could effectively be realized in flexible acyclic molecules. Encouraged by these results, chemists have now extended this approach to ansamycin antibiotics and carbohydrate syntheses. However, the most dramatic developments have been made in the chemistry of *palytoxin*.

Palytoxin, a toxic substance isolated from marine soft corals of the genus *Palythoa*, is one of the most poisonous substances known: intravenous injection

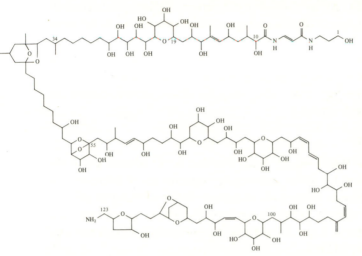

PALYTOXIN

into a rabbit of only .025 micrograms can be lethal (LD50). Pioneering investigations by organic chemists in Japan and Hawaii led to suggestions for the gross structure of palytoxin that indicated the uniqueness of its structural complexity and molecular size. When synthetic chemists set their sights on the total synthesis of palytoxin, they were turning a new page in the history of organic chemistry.

This monster molecule contains 128 carbon atoms, 64 of which are asymmetric centers. These centers, coupled with the seven skeletal double bonds, give palytoxin over two sextillion stereoisomers $(2,000,000,000,000,000,000,000 = 2 \times 10^{21})$! The gross structure had tentatively established the stereo-geometry of 13 of the centers, leaving 51 yet to be learned. Hence the first step toward synthesis was to establish the stereochemistry of palytoxin.

Though the desired final product was in hand (in tiny amounts), an intricate strategy was needed because X-ray analysis could not be applied—palytoxin has not been obtained in crystalline form. Furthermore, NMR is not conclusive, because palytoxin is structurally too complex. However, organic synthesis was up to the task thanks to experience gained with the polyether antibiotics.

The strategy employed began with careful degradation of palytoxin to break it, chemically, into more manageable fragments. The degradation had to be gentle, so that each fragment would retain the stereochemistry it has in the parent molecule. Then, each fragment was synthesized from known optically active reagents in its various isomers to find which one matched the natural product fragment. The process required that 20 key degradation products be synthesized, each in its various stereoisomeric forms, to identify the natural structure.

The success of this *tour de force* has built a critical foundation for further investigations on palytoxin, including total synthesis and conformational analysis. These are essential steps toward understanding why this natural molecule is so dreadfully toxic. It has also raised the sights of synthetic organic chemists everywhere.

Biosynthesis of Natural Products

Natural products have for many years played a central role in the development of organic chemistry, as a vehicle for the evolution of mechanistic and structural theory, as targets for new synthetic methodology and strategy, and as substrates for the development of powerful instrumental and spectroscopic tools. A continuing stimulus to this growth has been the fact that a significant proportion of the most widely used agents in human medicine for the relief of pain and treatment of disease are of natural origin, including morphine (**1**) (alkaloid), penicillin (**2**) and cephalosporin antibiotics (-lactams), erythromycin (**3**) (macrolide), and tetracyclines (aromatic polyketide). Speculation about the biogenesis or biological formation of natural products has itself contributed significantly to the development of structural, mechanistic, and synthetic theory. Only recently has it become possible to put many

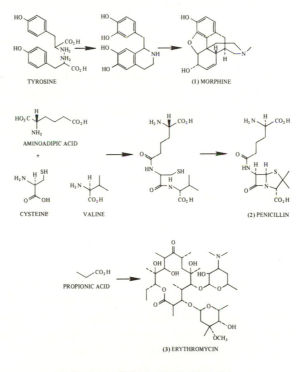

NATURAL PRODUCTS POINT TO
NEW SYNTHETIC PATHWAYS

of these original biosynthetic notions to experimental test so that the broad outlines of many biosynthetic pathways could be reasonably well understood. Moreover, recent developments in molecular biology, particularly the use of recombinant DNA techniques, now hold out the promise of a future technological leap in the field of natural products biosynthesis that may make it possible to manipulate the biosynthetic pathways themselves. For many years the field of biosynthesis has been led by the Swiss, United States, and British Schools and over the last 10 years an even more vigorous effort has developed in the United States. It is not unrealistic to expect that over the next decade American scientists will emerge as the pacesetters in this area.

Today it is possible to rationalize the origins of the vast majority of naturally occurring organic substances. With radioisotopic tracers and stable isotope nuclear magnetic resonance methods, we have gained a firm experimental base for the widely accepted precursor—product relationships between the simple starting compounds of metabolism (acetate, amino acids, and carbohydrates) and the seemingly endless variety of organic natural products. Over the last several years, the study of natural products biosynthesis has entered a new and extremely promising phase. Rather than working almost exclusively with intact cells or whole organisms, an increasing number of investigators have begun to turn their attention to the individual enzymes of secondary metabolic pathways. Besides avoiding the traditional problems caused by permeability barriers and competing metabolic pathways, cell-free investigations bring all the techniques of modern enzymology to bear on establishing the detailed mechanisms of key biosynthetic transformations. It is becoming possible to establish the sequence in which bonds are made and broken, to delineate the key ground state intermediates that characterize a given transformation, and to establish the types of reactive species—cations, anions, radicals—that are responsible for the reactions observed. We can now, for the first time, confront directly the central transformations that lie at the heart of biogenetic theory. Among the most notable achievements resulting from the use of cell-free systems during the last 10 years have been important advances in the understanding of the formation of penicillin and cephalosporin antibiotics, the detailed mapping of many of the key steps in the biosynthesis of indole alkaloids, and the exploration of the marvelously elaborate pathway by which the pigments of life—porphyrins (heme), chlorophyll, and corrins (vitamin B_{12})—are formed.

The major experimental tool for biosynthetic investigations has been the use of isotopic tracers of the common elements—carbon (^{13}C, ^{14}C), hydrogen (^{2}H, ^{3}H), nitrogen (^{15}N), and oxygen (^{17}O). The development of stable isotope nuclear magnetic resonance and the availability of high-resolution NMR spectrometers have revolutionized the study of biosynthetic systems by obviating the need for extensive chemical degradations to locate sites of isotopic labeling. As a result, the time required for a single biosynthetic experiment has been dramatically shortened, in some cases from years to a matter of days. Moreover, the use of sophisticated multiple-label techniques, based on spin-spin couplings or minute isotope effects, has made possible experiments that were almost inconceivable using conventional radioisotopic tracers. For example, the combination of stable isotope NMR and multinuclear labeling can be used to detect the making and breaking of carbon-carbon and carbon-heteroatom bonds and to distinguish between inter- and intramolecular structural reorganizations. A fruitful application of NMR techniques has been the elucidation of the biosynthetic pathways leading to potent fungal toxins, such as aflatoxins and trichothecin derivatives, whose role as dangerous contaminants of grain and other foodstuffs poses major public health problems.

Recombinant DNA technology provides another set of potentially powerful new tools for the study of biosynthetic pathways. The polyether monensin and the antibiotic erythromycin, both discussed above, provide excellent examples. These two substances are structurally and stereochemically among the most complex natural products. Beyond the basic building blocks for each antibiotic (the simple substances acetate, propionate, and butyrate), little is known about the details of the pathways by which these polyoxygenated, branched-chain fatty acids are assembled. Recent advances in the understanding of *Streptomyces* genetics, along with the development of promising cloning vectors for these organisms, have now made it more possible to unravel biosynthetic pathways at the genetic level. We should now be able to address the question of the genetic basis of structural and biogenetic regularities among diverse groups of related natural products. Industrial microbiologists have traditionally achieved dramatic increases in antibiotic yield by the empirical process of strain selection and adjustment of fermentation medium. Parallel advances in molecular genetics and in the understanding of biosynthetic mechanisms may soon make it possible to improve product yields on a rational basis and to engineer superior microorganisms and antibiotics.

The field of biosynthetic inquiry has roots in our earliest curiosity about the nature and origin of pigments, flavors, medicines, and toxins produced by nature. Now, drawing on the combined tools of synthetic chemistry, spectroscopy, enzymology, and molecular biology, the biosynthetic investigator can probe the most subtle details of the intricate pathways nature has evolved to do organic chemistry.

The Chemical Synthesis of DNA

The information needed to generate a living organism from a single fertilized egg is encoded in molecules of deoxyribonucleic acid (DNA). DNA is a chain-like molecule, composed of a string of sugar-phosphate ester links. Attached to each link is a nitrogen-rich structure called a base (a heterocyclic amine). Four such bases are found in DNA—adenosine, thymine, cytosine, and guanine (abbreviated, A, T, C, and G). Adenosine and thymine have geometrically fixed and complementary capacities to form two hydrogen bonds to each other, while cytosine and guanine match in a similar complementary way to form three hydrogen bonds (cytosine to guanine). Two sugar-phosphate strings can, then, intertwine into the famous double-helix structure, the covalent skeletons being held together by much weaker hydrogen bonds. Because of the matching characteristics, however, this helix can form only if the sequence of bases on the first string is perfectly complementary to the sequence on the second string.

Thus, the sugar-phosphate units, each with an attached base (A, T, C, or G), furnish labeled building blocks, called "nucleotides," from which a macromolecule can be formed. By inserting them with the base labels in some specific order, the bases impart information to the macromolecule. This information can be copied to produce a duplicate DNA molecule through enzymatic synthesis, each strand of the DNA serving as a sequence guide for its complementary

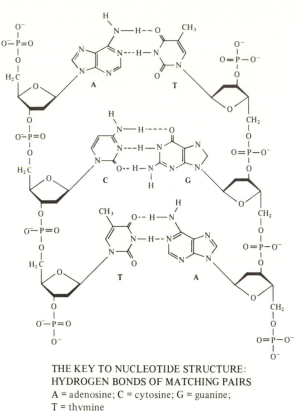

THE KEY TO NUCLEOTIDE STRUCTURE:
HYDROGEN BONDS OF MATCHING PAIRS
A = adenosine; C = cytosine; G = guanine;
T = thymine

strand. The reading process involves making and breaking complementary hydrogen bonds which, because of the low bond energies, can be done without breaking the much stronger sugar-phosphate covalent bonds. Thus, the genetic coding in DNA and its reproduction are accomplished through a delicate orchestration of chemical bond energies and molecular structures. The first chemical synthesis of a gene, accomplished about 15 years ago, required many person-years of effort. The remarkable (and continuing) progress since then permits synthesis of a gene of comparable size by a single researcher in 2 weeks. There have been a number of syntheses of the gene for insulin in industrial laboratories and a noteworthy synthesis of the gene for interferon in the United Kingdom. Each of these products shows promise for major medical and commercial value. The recent synthesis of the gene for the enzyme ribonuclease was designed to facilitate subsequent altering of the gene, thereby making possible efforts to change deliberately the physical and chemical properties of this protein.

Much progress is still needed. The yields of individual steps in DNA synthesis are still too low to permit routine synthesis of long molecules of DNA. State-of-the-art methods now can prepare gene fragments over 100 base pairs long, but we would like to deal with fragments 10 or 100 times longer yet. Chemical methods are only slowly being applied in molecular biological laboratories, primarily because the synthetic skills needed to apply them are only rarely found in these laboratories. Costs for commercial custom syntheses of DNA molecules are coming down, but they can still exceed $200 per nucleotide. Commercial machines for synthesizing DNA have only begun to meet the standards of durability and dependability needed.

Meanwhile, appetites are being whetted by the exciting examples that are appearing. Synthetic oligonucleotides have been used to clone medically valuable proteins, such as Factor 8 (a blood fraction used in the treatment of hemophilia), and commercially important proteins, such as renin (used in the manufacture of cheese). The next decade will see continued efforts to alter the structure of enzymes to make them more useful in industry, to alter the structure of proteins and peptides to make new pharmaceuticals, and to uncover new knowledge concerning genetic regulation and human disease. In all these efforts, chemical methods for the synthesis of DNA will play a crucial role.

Structures of Macromolecules

The structures of the giant molecules of living systems—the proteins and nucleic acids—offer challenges just like those encountered for smaller natural products. We must first know which atoms are bonded to which in order to describe the covalent molecular structure, and then we must learn how the chains of these large polymers are spatially configured. The latter question is of great interest because the biological properties of the proteins and nucleic acids are intimately connected to their three-dimensional structures.

Protein and Peptide Conformation

Life depends on the interplay of the two classes of large molecules, nucleic acids (DNA and RNA) and proteins. The genetic endowment of an organism is stored in its DNA and expressed through its RNA. DNA serves as both a template for the formation of identical copies of itself for the next generation and as the blueprint for the formation of proteins, the executors of nearly all biological processes. The other nucleic acid, RNA, is the intermediary in protein formation according to instructions given by DNA. Proteins are large molecules made up of 20 amino acid building blocks linked in deliberate sequence by amide (peptide) bonds. The relationship between DNA sequence and protein sequence, called the genetic code, is direct and simple: three particular bases in DNA specify one particular amino acid in a protein.

Proteins Carry Out an Astonishing Range of Biological Functions   Nearly all chemical reactions in organisms are catalyzed by specific proteins called enzymes. The breakdown of foods to generate energy and the synthesis of new cell structures involve thousands of chemical reactions that are made possible by protein catalysis. Proteins also serve as carriers—as exemplified by hemoglobin, which transports oxygen from the lungs to the tissues. Muscle contraction and movements within cells depend on the interplay of protein molecules designed to generate coordinated motion. Another group of protein molecules, called antibodies, protects us from foreign substances such as viruses, bacteria, and cells from other organisms. The operation of our nervous system depends on proteins that detect, transmit, and amplify stimuli. Proteins also serve as hormones that control cell growth and integrate the activities of different cells.

Proteins Have Complex Three-Dimensional Shapes   Chemical research of the past two decades has revealed that proteins have highly intricate three-dimensional forms that are critical for these diverse and essential biological functions.

A protein chain consisting of hundreds of linked amino acids spontaneously assumes a three-dimensional architecture (called a conformation) determined by its particular amino acid sequence. For example, collagen, a protein that gives tensile strength to skin and bone, has the shape of a rod. Antibodies are Y-shaped molecules with niches that recognize foreign substances and trigger subsequent reactions for their efficient disposal. Enzymes have clefts called active sites that bring reactants together and facilitate the formation of new chemical bonds between them. Thus proteins have defined conformations that are at the heart of their biological roles. Major advances have been made in viewing protein conformation. X-rays, neutron and electron beams, and other probes enable us to "see" proteins magnified more than a million times and to discern their inner workings.

Proteins Are Highly Dynamic   Chemical studies of the past decade have also shown that proteins are highly dynamic molecules. Proteins change their shape while performing their functions. For example, light changes the conformation of rhodopsin, a protein in the retina, as the first step in vision. This structural change occurs in less than a billionth of a second. Such rapid changes in protein molecules can now be detected by using pulsed lasers. Another fruitful approach to the elucidation of protein dynamics involves cooling a protein to very low temperatures so that individual steps in its action are slowed down to permit more leisurely study.

Recurring Themes in Protein Structure and Mechanism   Even the simplest cells contain more than five thousand kinds of proteins. Yet, we are finding that protein diversity is not limitless; structural and mechanistic motifs seen in one protein frequently recur in others. For example, there is a close relationship between the enzymes thrombin (for blood clotting) and chymotrypsin (for digestion). Moreover, the structures of many proteins have been conserved over long evolutionary periods. There is surprisingly little difference, for example, between human and mouse hemoglobins. Enzymatic mechanisms used in simple organisms are employed with little modification in complex ones. This enhances the value of the growing store of information concerning protein conformation, dynamics, and mechanism as a basis for understanding physiological and pathological processes. This knowledge is now being used to unravel disease mechanisms, devise new diagnostic tests, and develop novel drugs and therapeutic strategies.

Protein Conformational Studies Are Beginning to Show at the Molecular Level How Biological Functions Are Accomplished   For example, we now have detailed understanding of how peptide (amide) bonds are hydrolyzed by a number of enzymes that utilize different amino acids and metal atoms in their active sites. Studies of chymotrypsin and trypsin have shed light on how proteins are converted from an inactive precursor form to an active form by the cleavage of specific peptide bonds. We also know how the activity of enzymes can be switched off by the binding of specific protein or peptide inhibitors. X-ray crystallographic studies have given valuable information about the architecture of antibody molecules, a factor that must be involved as they recognize specific foreign molecules.

Important advances have also been made in elucidation of the structure of assemblies of proteins and nucleic acids. The molecular architecture of several viruses is now known. The structure of tobacco mosaic virus has revealed how it is assembled from RNA and identical protein subunits. A different principle of virus construction is displayed by tomato bushy stunt virus, which exhibits icosahedral symmetry. Another noteworthy accomplishment is the determination of the mode of binding of histone proteins to DNA in chromatin. This structure gives insight into how the very long DNA thread is packaged within the confines of the cell nucleus.

New methods have been devised for reconstructing three-dimensional images of biological structures from a series of two-dimensional electron micrographs. These image-reconstruction methods have given the first views of protein molecules in biological membranes. Three important structures have been solved at low resolution: an energy-transducing proton pump, membrane-bound ribosomes, and intracellular channels. These structures reveal how protein chains are constructed to transverse a biological membrane. They also provide insight as to how energy from light can be used by a cell to generate ATP.

Many Challenges Facing Chemists in the Field of Peptide and Protein Conformation Are Ripe for Solution   For example, we would like to be able to predict the conformation of a protein from its amino acid sequence. Theoretical approaches will play a role here because the prediction of the entire three-dimensional architecture of a protein by calculations using high-speed, large-memory computers is an aspiration that will someday become a reality. Next, we would like to direct bacteria and yeast to synthesize a wide variety of proteins so that we can learn the relationship between amino acid sequence and protein conformation. This is on the horizon because genes can now be modified in a systematic way by using recombinant DNA technology. Then we need to know much more about how proteins recognize specific sites on DNA and alter their biological state. The knowledge will provide insight into how organisms develop and will serve as a basis for modifying patterns of gene expression in disease states.

Finally, we want to learn how peptides interact with receptor proteins to produce physiological changes in organisms. For example, the body produces endorphins, a series of peptides that act as opiates. How the binding of these peptides to cell-surface proteins leads to profound changes in mood and consciousness is one facet of neurochemistry that must be understood as we unravel the intricacies of brain function.

Structural Studies on Dihydrofolate Reductases and Their Inhibitors

Dihydrofolate reductase (DHFR) is an enzyme present in all living creatures, from bacteria to mammals. The integrity of its function is necessary to the continuing synthesis of new DNA in proliferating cell lines.

Quite some time ago, it was noticed that feeding of folic acid actually promoted the growth of induced tumors in laboratory animals. Hoping to find an antagonist that would block and reverse this effect (an "antifolate"), investigators set about synthesizing and testing many chemical analogs of folic acid. This shotgun approach paid off with the discovery of aminopterin and later of methotrexate. Amazingly, the essential difference between these compounds and folate itself was simply the substitution of folate's 4-hydroxyl group by a 4-amino group.

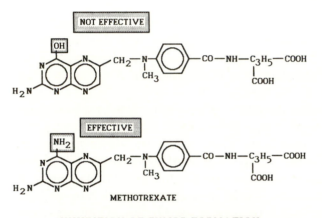

INHIBITION OF TUMOR FORMATION
LITTLE CHANGES CAN MATTER A LOT

Thereafter it was determined that methotrexate acts by inhibiting the enzyme DHFR. In fact, the enzyme binds methotrexate so strongly that inhibition is essentially quantitative and irreversible. Today, methotrexate is in widespread and effective clinical use for treatment of childhood lukemia, choriocarcinoma, osteogenic sarcoma, and Hodgkin's disease.

Meanwhile, more distant analogs of folic acid were synthesized and tested in great number, including the substituted 2,4-diaminopyrimidines. This program led to the discovery of the antibacterial agent trimetho and the antiprotozoal agent primethamine, among others. All these antifolates also act by inhibiting DHFR, in some cases with sharp species-selectivity. For example, trimethoprim has about 100,000 times greater affinity for bacterial (*E. coli*) DHFR than for the vertebrate enzyme—which is why it can be used as an antibiotic.

A decade ago, study of several DHFRs by X-ray crystallographic methods was initiated to illuminate the molecular-structural basis for their action and point the way toward a rational, structurally based approach to drug design. Furthermore, DHFR, as a relatively small (159 to 189 amino acid residues) monomeric enzyme, provides an excellent model for studying how such enzymes contrive to catalyze hydride transfer to and from the otherwise rather unreactive nicotinamide nucleotides. Biochemists who study metabolic pathways have long recognized that the nicotinamide nucleotides, NADH and NADPH, serve as a kind of universal oxidationreduction currency, a medium of exchange for electrons in biological reactions.

The X-ray crystallographic approach has begun to bear fruit. So far, the structures of DHFRs from three widely differing species, namely the two bacteria *E. coli* and *L. casei*, and the chicken (representative of vertebrates), have been determined. Moreover, these enzyme structures have been examined as they appear when various combinations and permutations of cofactor, substrate, and inhibitors are bound to them.

The most carefully determined *E. coli* enzyme structure contains bound methotrexate, and the *L. casei* structure contains both methotrexate and NADPH. The two structures have now been extensively refined at high resolution. Additionally, refined at medium resolution is a crystal structure of the *E. coli* enzyme containing bound trimethoprim, and a preliminary structure for a ternary complex of the *E. coli* enzyme containing both trimethoprim and NADPH is available.

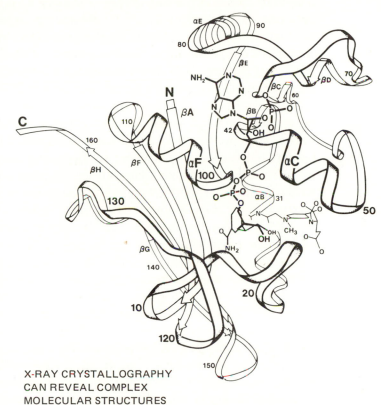

X-RAY CRYSTALLOGRAPHY
CAN REVEAL COMPLEX
MOLECULAR STRUCTURES

The most striking feature seen on comparing DHFR molecules from the different species is the close similarity in their overall foldings. Clearly the molecular structure of the enzyme was highly conserved during the course of evolution, even though only about 25 percent of the amino acid sequence remained unaltered (80 percent among the vertebrates, however).

These structural studies are beginning to reveal the detailed interactions that cause methotrexate (and the other inhibitors) to be so strongly bound and hence so effective. Methotrexate has a heterocyclic ring (a pteridine ring) in an inverted position that happens to fit in the enzyme's binding pocket while placing its quite basic nitrogen atom in an optimum locale for hydrogen bond formation to the enzyme. In the case of NADPH, again careful examination of the stereochemical aspects of its placement suggests that they optimize hydrogen bonding in a fashion that facilitates hydride transfer an insight that brings us close to understanding this enzymatic mechanism.

Frontiers in the Chemistry of Genetic Material

In higher organisms (including humans), the percent of DNA nucleotides that actually specify the sequence of amino acids in proteins is estimated to be about 5 percent. What is the role of the remaining 95 percent? Recently, it has become apparent that another type of information expressed in a sequence of DNA nucleotides codes for alternative conformations that the DNA can adopt. Hence comprehending the nature of the conformational changes that both DNA and RNA can undergo and developing an understanding of the chemical basis for these changes (including relative stabilities) are important frontiers.

Conformational changes are brought about by relatively free rotational movements around single bonds. In cyclic structures, such rotations tend to pucker the ring into nonplanar conformations. While there is usually an energy barrier between two (or three) energetically comfortable structures resulting from such rotation (conformers), the barrier can be small so that transfer between these structures can be relatively facile at room temperature. In sharp distinction to stereoisomers, the conformation a molecule takes can be determined by secondary interactions, it may change in response to environment, and two or more conformers can be present in dynamic equilibrium.

The recent availability of chemically synthesized oligonucleotides has made it possible to address conformational questions with X-ray diffraction analysis of single crystals. This is a great forward step in our ability to discern with some accuracy the details of conformational changes and the effect of nucleotide sequence on those conformations. Previously, investigations had been largely confined to X-ray studies of oriented DNA fibers, whose diffraction patterns did not provide the resolution necessary to reveal conformational changes. Currently, the rate of growth of conformational information based on single-crystal X-ray diffraction studies is rapid, as it is commonplace now to have crystals of DNA fragments 10 to 20 pairs in size. Within the next few years, it will be possible to extend such studies to single crystals of DNA molecules containing 50 to 100 base pairs.

The growing power of nuclear magnetic resonance analyses of the nucleic acids has been directed toward the same oligonucleotide fragments that have been studied by X-ray analysis. The correlation and complementation of the two techniques is most impressive. Similar NMR studies have been carried out on transfer RNA molecules that contain 75 to 90 nucleotides. We can anticipate a rapid growth in the experimental base with which we can refine present understanding of conformational roles.

Of the important variables that lead to conformational flexibility in the nucleic acids, the first is the pucker of the furanose ring common to both DNA and RNA. A number of different conformations can be assumed by the ring, but the most prominent is called the C2′ *endo* conformation. It has been considered to be characteristic of DNA nucleotides, while the C3′ *endo* conformation was more frequently found in ribonucleotides. We must learn more about the energy barriers between these two conformations; it is now thought that the deoxynucleotides can more easily adopt different conformations with a lower energy barrier between them than is found for ribonucleotides. In the three-dimensional structure of yeast phenylalanine transfer RNA, which has 76 nucleotides, the majority were found to adopt the C3′ *endo* conformations. This has a significant effect on the spacing of certain phosphate groups whose phosphate-phosphate distance is close to 6.7 Å in the C2′ *endo* conformation and less than 5.6 Å in the C3′ *endo* conformation. Thus changes in sugar pucker make the polynucleotide backbone elastic, so that it can accommodate different conformations. We need to know those conformations more precisely, how easily they can interconvert, and how they affect biological function.

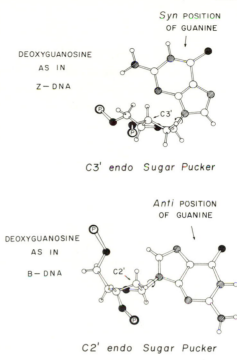

SUBTLE DIFFERENCES MATTER

For almost 30 years, DNA has been known to adopt two different right-handed conformations, A and B-DNA. The A conformation is one in which all the deoxynucleotides have the C3′ *endo* conformation, while in B-DNA all the nucleotides have the C2′ *endo* conformation. However, this simple classification into possible right-handed conformations has now been modified considerably as a result of single-crystal X-ray diffraction analyses. For example, structure analysis of certain sequences reveals alternations C3′ *endo* and C2′ *endo* conformations with alternating phosphate distances. We must investigate whether this offers a sequence-specific recognition element for proteins that interact with DNA.

A recent striking example of conformational changes is presented by the discovery of left-handed conformations. Polynucleotides were synthesized in the laboratory with a deliberate alternation of purine and pyrimidine bases. This molecule adopts a conformation in which the purines take the C3′ *endo* conformation, while the alternating pyrimidines take the C2′ *endo* conformation. This structure is called Z-DNA.

Another important element of variability in the conformation is the adoption of *syn* or *anti* conformations of the base relative to the sugar. Until the discovery of Z-DNA, it was widely assumed that the *anti* conformation with the base lying away from the sugar would be the only one found in natural systems. In the regularly alternating sequences of Z-DNA structures, all the purine residues adopt the *syn* conformation, while the pyrimidines adopt the *anti* conformation. This alternation of *syn* and *anti* joins the sugar conformational changes to result in "flipping over" the base pairs in Z-DNA being relative to their conformations in B-DNA.

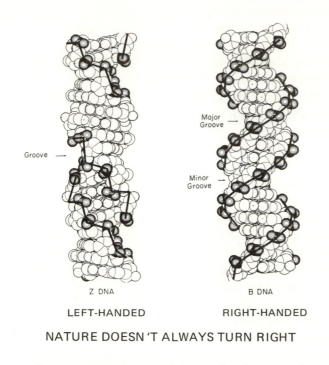

Z DNA   B DNA

LEFT-HANDED   RIGHT-HANDED

NATURE DOESN'T ALWAYS TURN RIGHT

The stacking of the planar purines and pyrimidines is a major energy factor in the stability of the nucleic acid structure, as shown by the fact that the bases are stacked in virtually all the double helical nucleic acids. A striking exception is found in Z-DNA where the stacking between alternate bases depends upon the sequence. In the structure formed with alternating guanine (G) and cytosine (C) residues, pyrimidines on opposite strands are stacked over each other, while the purines are stacked on the oxygen of the sugar of the residue below. It is quite likely that the stacking interactions represent one of the major features determining the conformation of the nucleic acids. Much work, both experimental and theoretical, has to be carried out on stacking interactions before we will understand the particular contributions they make to the conformation of the nucleic acid.

At present, the overall view of the nucleic acids is that they are conformationally active and that the well-known right-handed B-DNA structure is likely to be in equilibrium with a number of other structures, including left-handed Z-DNA. More broadly, our view of the conformational activity of the nucleic acids suggests that the focus of much chemical and biological research will be on the nature of these conformational changes. We need to know more about how they are affected by changes in the environment, modifications in the molecule, or alterations in the nucleotide sequence as these may considerably influence the biological activity of the nucleic acids.

Structure and Function in Biochemistry

Structure determines function. From the simplest arrangements of a few atoms in a small molecule, such as ethyl alcohol, to molecules with the exquisite and varied architectures of proteins, the molecular structure uniquely and unambiguously determines their function as drugs, antibodies, biological catalysts, hormones, transport agents, cell surface receptors, structural elements (bone or cartilage), or muscles that convert chemical energy into work.

The secret of generating many structural variants of a protein is to be able to alter, in a precisely controlled manner, its sequence of amino acids—thereby fixing its three-dimensional structure and its functional properties. This permits a rational approach to the question of how the structure of a protein determines its function.

Today we have procedures that allow us to achieve this objective. Modern molecular biology has taught us how to introduce essentially any piece of DNA into a microorganism and cause therein the synthesis of the protein that its nucleotide sequence encodes. At the same time, modern synthetic organic chemistry has enabled us to synthesize, rapidly and easily, sequences of nucleotides that constitute pieces of genes. These pieces of genes can then be used to alter, in a way precisely specified by the synthetic gene fragment (oligonucleotide), the prescribed sequence of bases in the gene for the parent protein. In this way a modified protein with an altered sequence of amino acids can be generated, and a structure and function never before available can be produced.

This ability is tantamount to creating specific mutants of normal proteins and is formally termed *oligonucleotide directed mutagenesis*. Not only does this lead to proteins with any structure we may desire, but once a single molecule of the gene encoding that protein has been prepared, the protein itself can be produced forever after in microorganisms by the techniques of modern genetic engineering in whatever quantities may be desired.

These techniques focus on the creation of a mutant protein with a predetermined amino acid sequence; such approaches are useful in learning the properties and functions of a protein altered in a prespecified manner. An alternative approach is to generate, by nonspecific mutagenesis, a large number of structural variants, to select those with particular properties, and then to determine the structures of those variants that manifest the desired properties. Such random mutagenesis can be allowed to take place anywhere in the structural gene of interest, or it can be restricted to a particular region to determine the role of a particular domain of the protein.

Advances in synthesis and structure determination of proteins or nucleic acids will have profound effects on progress in these areas. We can presently synthesize oligonuleotides using the phosphite chemistry methodology in a machine at a rate of one base every 5 minutes and at a repetitive yield per base of 98 percent. Improvements here could make the rapid synthesis of entire genes, rather than just oligonucleotides, a routine procedure and thereby greatly facilitate the creation of new proteins.

Chemical and biochemical techniques may also be greatly improved for determining base sequences in nucleic acids and amino acid sequences in proteins. Currently, the gas phase sequenator can reliably determine about 60 residues from the amino terminus of a protein. Use of mass spectrometry or other novel approaches might allow the complete sequence to be established for a protein of several hundred residues by automated techniques. In this respect, chemistry that allows sequence determination from the carboxyl terminus would be of enormous utility.

Gene Structure and RNA Splicing

The abilities to join DNAs from diverse organisms, to isolate DNA segments that encode specific proteins, and to determine the linear nucleotide sequence of long DNA segments have given startling insights into the gene structure of man and other complex organisms. The new knowledge has raised many new questions and opened new areas of research.

To find the DNA segment that contains a single gene within the total genetic material of a human cell is like finding the proverbial needle in the haystack. The sequences that specify any one particular gene are about one millionth of the total genome. The solution to the problem is to use recombinant DNA techniques to distribute fragments of human DNA into well over a milion rapidly dividing bacteria, to grow each bacterium, separately to give a colony of progeny of the single bacterium, and to identify the colony of bacteria containing the gene of interest. The process is called cloning. The rapidly growing bacterial colony produces billions of identical copies of each gene, which can be isolated as a chemically pure substance. DNA segments for well over a hundred different human genes have been so purified to date. A similar number have been isolated from a few other vertebrates, such as the mouse, and a greater number from simpler organisms, such as yeast.

PART OF THE HUMAN β-GLOBIN GENE

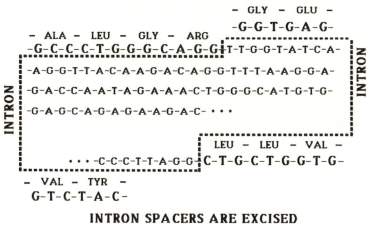

**INTRON SPACERS ARE EXCISED
TO GIVE MESSENGER RNA**

The DNA sequence coding for the globin protein is mosaic in nature with sequences specifying the amino acid sequence of the protein interrupted by sequences that do not specify protein sequence. This is typical in eukaryotic genes—the coding region is interrupted by one or more stretches of noncoding DNA, called "intervening sequences" or "introns." Introns occur in most genes that code for messenger RNA and in some genes that code for transfer and ribosomal RNAs.

In all cases that have been studied, the introns are transcribed along with the adjacent coding sequences as part of a large precursor RNA. The introns are then deleted by a cleavage process termed RNA splicing, which results in a functional RNA molecule with a continuous coding region. For example, there are two introns in the human globin gene. After they have been excised, the resulting messenger RNA is transported from the nucleus to the cytoplasm for translation.

The phenomenon of RNA splicing is common in cells with nuclei, *eukaryotes*, but it is thought to be absent in cells without well-defined nuclei, *prokaryotes*. It is the only major step in gene expression in which eukaryotes and prokaryotes differ profoundly. As such, it is interesting to examine the extent to which RNA splicing is used to provide unique circuits for the regulation of gene expression and the extent to which introns in the gene organization might be responsible for the evolution of eukaryotic genes. Much current work has been directed toward the mechanism of RNA splicing to provide a framework for understanding the role of the process in eukaryotic gene expression.

All introns in genes specifying proteins begin with the dinucleotide :GT and end with the dinucleotide AG: These two invariant dinucleotide sequences are part of a more extended bias in sequence common at the boundaries of introns. These consensus sequences specify, at least in part, the site of the splicing reaction. For example, all mutations known to interfere with RNA splicing either destroy a consensus-type sequence or create a new such sequence at an inappropriate location. The total specificity of the splicing reaction cannot be explained by the simple consensus sequences, because prototype sequences can be found in the middle of long introns. So little is known about the chemistry of splicing that we can only speculate about the nature of the additional specificity.

Specificity in RNA sequence is frequently recognized by a second complementary RNA. For example, during translation, a short consensus sequence near the initiation site of bacterial mRNA is recognized through a complementary sequence on ribosomal RNA. A similar RNA-RNA recognition appears to be involved in splicing of mRNA precursors. In this case, an abundant nuclear RNA, U1, which constitutes part of a ribonucleoprotein particle, recognizes and pairs with sequences in the intron at the 5′ splice site.

The discovery of RNA splicing and introns was startling because previous characterization of bacteria genes had not detected these nonsense sequences in the middle of genes. Introns with the consensus sequence discussed above are common to yeast, insect, plant, and vertebrate genes. In fact, an intron has been mapped to a common position in genes coding for a highly conserved protein, actin, in both plants and mammals. Thus RNA splicing and introns were present in the primitive organism from which both these lineages evolved.

The isolation and sequencing of genes from complex organisms have also led to the identification of signals for gene expression. For genes encoding proteins such as β-globin, the signals controlling transcription are of two types. Sequences immediately before the gene are responsible for both specifying the location and influencing the frequency of initiation of transcription by RNA polymerase. In addition, other sequences mapping at a distance from the gene may also affect transcription frequency. DNA segments that stimulate transcription at promoter sites positioned over distances of 1000 nucleotides have been discovered. These studies and more conventional biochemistry of RNA polymerases will ultimately yield a molecular understanding of gene regulation in complex organisms such as man.

The impact on society of future research on gene structure and expression will be enormously beneficial. Many human diseases are the result of defects in gene expression; using the newly created methodology, we are investigating the nature of these defects. In some cases, a combination of gene replacement therapy and cell culture procedures has the potential to alter the course of such a disease. The nature of the genetic alterations in cancer cells has in part been determined recently, and this may open new avenues to pharmacological treatment of cancer. The process of aging is poorly understood at either the cellular or multicellular level. It is possible that some of the more debilitating aspects of the process are controlled by the activity of a few gene products, so that identification of the functions of those genes may lead to better treatments for aging patients.

Mechanism of Ribonucleic Acid (RNA) Splicing

Removal of an intron from an RNA molecule by splicing requires precise cleavage of the RNA at the intron borders and covalent joining of the flanking sequences. There are bacterial enzymes (endoribonuclease) that can cleave RNA, and an enzyme (RNA ligase) from T4 bacteriophage-infected *E. coli* can join RNA molecules. It has been the source of much excitement that three different mechanisms for RNA splicing have been partially elucidated.

For example, some aspects of the splicing of pre-rRNA in the ciliated protozoan, *Tetrahymena*, have recently been described. The reaction does not proceed by separable breakage (cleavage) and reunion (ligation) steps. Instead, each step is a transesterification reaction (concerted cleavage-ligation). Such reactions are expected to be isoenergetic; the lack of ATP or GTP hydrolysis accompanying the reaction is consistent with this view. The reaction can be considered to be RNA recombination, in the sense that strand breakage, strand switching, and reunion are the essence of recombination.

There has been more general interest in these reactions because they occur in vitro in the absence of any protein. Splicing is as accurate in vitro as in vivo; in both cases, only two of 6600 phosphodiester bonds undergo breakage and reunion. The excised intervening sequence RNA is capable of converting itself into a covalently bound circular form, again via a breakage-reunion (transesterification) mechanism and again in the absence of any other macromolecule.

It should be noted that demonstration of the lack of a protein requirement was made possible by

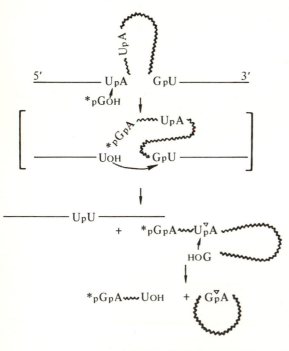

MODELS POINT TO PROBABLE MECHANISTIC STEPS (SQUARE BRACKETS)

recombinant DNA technology. The eukaryotic gene was cloned in a bacterial plasmid and the RNA synthesized using a purified bacterial polymerase, thereby avoiding the possibility that the "purified" RNA contained a trace amount of a *Tetrahymena* splicing enzyme that was responsible for splicing in vitro.

The structure of the RNA molecule somehow lowers the activation energy for specific bond cleavage and reformation events. As such, the RNA may be said to be a catalyst. The mechanism by which the RNA molecule weakens specific phosphodiester linkages and promotes its own recombination must be better understood. At present, there is evidence that a specific binding site for the guanosine nucleophile in proximity to a phosphodiester bond may account for the catalysis, just as many enzymes facilitate reactions by bringing two substrates into a particular spacial arrangement.

It has long been thought that biological catalysis is the realm of proteins. Now that we have a well established example of an RNA-mediated reaction, researchers are looking into the generality of RNA catalysis. There is already strong indication that another large class of RNA splicing reactions—both mRNA and rRNA splicing in the mitochondria of various fungi—follow a similar mechanism. Other candidates for RNA catalysts include the tRNA-processing enzyme RNase P, various small nuclear RNPs, and the ribosome; these all have both RNA and protein components, and it is certainly possible that the RNA is serving more than a structural role. Thus the subject of biological catalysis is gaining added dimension.

Continued study of all the various RNA splicing reactions is certain to lead to a better understanding of structure-function relationships in RNA molecules. The field is currently in its infancy, and it is likely that some new roles for RNA structures will be uncovered. Some RNA molecules may have active sites that bind various ligands and perhaps facilitate the flow of electrons. Some of these new roles for RNA may have an impact beyond the RNA processing field, e.g., in the areas of transcription, translation, recombination, and evolution.

Applications of Oncogenes to the Diagnosis, Therapy, and Prevention of Human Cancer

During the last 15 years, the study of viruses that induce cancer in susceptible hosts (oncogenic viruses) has led to a major change in the framework within which the process of oncogenesis can be studied. The study of the chemical structure of oncogenic viruses has revealed that each virus carries a gene (an oncogene), which is required for the induction of malignancy by that virus. The oncogene encodes a protein whose function is required for the maintenance of the oncogenic state of a cell transformed by such a gene. Approximately 15 to 18 such oncogenes have been identified.

It has now become clear that each viral oncogene has a normal cellular counterpart called a protooncogene. Protooncogenes are present in all vertebrate species and are highly conserved between vertebrate species. The exact biological function of protooncogenes is not known, but the conservation of such genes throughout the vertebrate phylum of the animal kingdom suggests that protooncogenes play an important role in normal cellular processes.

The chemical and functional relationship between protooncogenes and viral oncogenes was the subject of much conjecture before the relaxation of the NIH guidelines governing molecular cloning of DNA. Under the relaxed guidelines, protooncogenes could be molecularly cloned in bacteria and compared chemically and biologically to viral oncogenes. The chemical method for sequencing DNA molecules has been of prime importance in analyzing these cloned genes. Based on the use of controlled, base-specific chemical cleavage reactions to deduce the order of the bases that comprise a specific DNA strand, this procedure is an excellent example of the interplay between DNA chemistry and biology in molecular biological research.

From a variety of studies, it has become clear that certain protooncogenes are capable of being oncogenes if they are linked to a strong transcriptional promoter. In the cases of three different protooncogenes, strong evidence has linked the transcriptional activation of a protooncogene to the malignant transformation of target cells either in vivo, in a case of avian leukemia, or in cell culture in mammalian cells. The experiments indicate that a quantitative increase in a protein coded for by protooncogene can lead to the cancer process. Although this result has been clearly demonstrated in model systems, it is important to realize that, thus far, no clear example of this type of protooncogene activation has been found in human cancers.

A second method by which a protooncogene can be activated has recently been discovered in human cancers. For 15 to 25 percent of human cancers, the DNA of a given cancer can be isolated and introduced into an appropriate mouse cell to induce malignantly transformed cells. The gene(s) in human cancers responsible for such genetic transfer are being cloned and characterized in many different laboratories. The molecular identification of these activated protooncogenes has been made possible by the application of recombinant DNA technology and chemical sequencing methods to the study of cancer biology. Without the untargeted basic biological and chemical research that led to these DNA techniques, goal-oriented cancer research would not have been able to utilize the work on oncogenes to study the causes of human cancers.

The process of human oncogenesis is thought to involve multiple steps in the evolution of a given malignant tumor. The possible role of chemical or physical carcinogens in this multistep process has been widely discussed, as has the possibility that such carcinogens induce tumors via the induction of mutations in DNA. There is now evidence that a single base change in a normal *has* protooncogene can activate the protooncogene to an oncogene, which shows that chemical mutations can indeed cause cancers in man.

Up to now, the diagnosis of the causes of human cancer has not been possible. In cancers with activated oncogenes, we can look ahead to the precise chemical identification of the responsible molecular species. It will then be feasible to develop a rational system of differential cancer diagnosis, allowing clinicians to recognize common casuality of cancers originating in different organs and to distinguish the causes of cancers within a single organ.

The new differential diagnosis of cancer will have a profound effect on the design of therapies for human cancers. Currently, the choice of an effective drug for cancer treatment is based on the ability of the drug to kill all histologically similar tumors originating in a given organ. In the future, it should be possible to choose drugs that act selectively for classes of tumors with a common molecular cause. The treatment of cancer can then evolve into a rational therapeutic discipline and resemble, therapeutically, the field of infectious diseases, in which one chooses an antibiotic to treat an infection caused by a given type of bacterial or viral microorganism. Clearly the field of cancer biology is being dramatically changed by the application of molecular biology and sophisticated DNA chemistry to the problem of the pathogenesis of a cancer cell.

IV-E.   Instrumentation

The chemical identification and synthesis of complex molecules ultimately depends upon chemists' ability to bring about a chemical change and then ascertain the composition and three-dimensional structures of the products. The fact that chemists are now active in the biological arena is strong testimony to the prowess that now exists. It permits us to aspire to understand the chemistry of life processes at the molecular level. This aspiration is within reach because of an array of diagnostic tools invented by physicists and remarkably honed in the hands of chemists to meet the analytical and structural challenges presented by extremely complex molecules. Foremost among these are nuclear magnetic resonance, X-ray diffraction, and mass spectrometry.

Nuclear Magnetic Resonance (NMR)

In the 1950s, physicists began measuring the magnetic properties of nuclei. For this purpose, sensitive techniques were developed to search for the characteristic resonant frequencies to flip the nuclear magnets in a high magnetic field (nuclear magnetic resonance, NMR). Their precision was so great that the physicists discovered, a bit to their dismay, that the measured nuclear resonance frequency depended not only on the magnetic properties of the nucleus, but also upon the chemical environment the nucleus found nearby. Chemists were elated, however, because they saw the method as a new probe of molecular structure to supplement the rapidly developing infrared spectroscopic methods. Instrument developers quickly responded to the many opportunities seen for applications in chemistry. The outcome surpassed the most extravagant dreams. Today, NMR is surely one of the most important diagnostic tools used by chemists. It has had momentous impact in such diverse areas as synthetic chemistry, polymer chemistry, mechanistic chemistry, biochemistry, medicinal chemistry, and even clinical diagnosis.

Capabilities

The bulk of the chemical applications of NMR to date have involved liquid solution samples. The reason is that the averaging effects of random motions in liquids produce sharp spectral features that reveal meaningful nuances of difference in chemical environments. Performance has been limited by the uniformity of the high magnetic fields required, which also limited sample size and sensitivity. Through the 1960s and 1970s, technological developments (including superconducting magnets) permitted steady increases in magnetic field intensity and uniformity. Now a barrage of new developments in other parameters, including Fourier transform methods, high-resolution solid-state techniques, and a variety of pulsed measurments, is opening new dimensions for NMR.

Fourier Transform NMR (FT NMR)   Modern computers make it possible to record data continuously in the time domain and then to transform into the frequency domain the accumulated spectral information (see Section III-E, Computers). This Fourier transform method was first applied in NMR in 1966; because of the better performance it brings, virtually all commercial research instruments now use FT. For example, it permits detection of the ^{13}C isotopically labeled molecules in an organic compound based on the ^{13}C present in nature (1 in 100 carbon atoms is ^{13}C). At the same time, improvements in superconducting magnet technology raised the magnetic field intensity almost 3-fold (from 5 Tesla in 1966 to 12 to 14 Tesla in 1979). Together, those two improvements provided overall increases of about 100 in sensitivity and 10 in resolution. Chemists can now obtain ^{1}H spectra of as little as 5 to 10 micrograms of the anti-Parkinsons' drug L-dopa. Spectra of complex molecules, such as insulin, or of abnormal hemoglobin (e.g., sickle-cell) can be studied. In some proteins, more than 100 individual resonances can be monitored as found in sam-

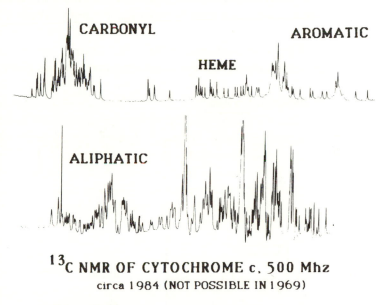

^{13}C NMR OF CYTOCHROME c, 500 Mhz
circa 1984 (NOT POSSIBLE IN 1969)

ples relevant to vision, photosynthesis, and drug-receptor interactions. Such instruments are now essential for research on all new pharmaceuticals, including structural studies of novel anticancer drugs, hormones, and some products of recombinant DNA-technology.

Solid State NMR In the late 1960s, a variety of pulsed NMR experiments were introduced that began a resurgence of interest in obtaining high-resolution NMR spectra of solids. Initially, abundant and sensitive nuclei (^{1}H, ^{19}F) were studied with resolution near 1 part per million. Then, in the period 1972 to 1975, methods were developed in which the sample is rapidly

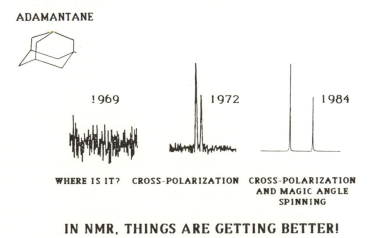

IN NMR, THINGS ARE GETTING BETTER!

spun about a prescribed angle relative to the magnetic field (54.7°, the angle at which the "averaging function," $1-3\cos^2\theta$, equals zero; this angle is called the "magic angle") to provide averaging effects and band sharpening approaching those available for liquids. Today, both organic and inorganic solids can be studied at .01 parts-per-million resolution. Novel applications that have been made to inorganic samples include observations of six-coordinate silicon in silica formed at meteor impact sites and studies of high-tech ceramic materials. Structures in rubbers, plastics, papers, coal, wood, and semiconductors can be examined over wide temperature ranges, from 4 K to 500 K.

Two-Dimensional NMR By means of clever and sophisticated pulsed radiofrequency excitation techniques, it has been shown to be possible to excite normally weak, multiple-quantum transitions, and to record NMR spectra in "two dimensions." In both types of experiments, normally inaccessible spectral information is obtained. In the 2-D case, spectra appear as contour maps in which different types of interaction spread out resonances along two axes. In addition to the characteristic frequency shifts caused by atoms in the immediate neighborhood (e.g., by which we can differentiate CH_2 groups and CH_3 groups), the new dimension reveals more distant interactions. Thus, conformational information can be determined for complex molecules even when single crystals cannot be obtained (so X-ray techniques cannot be used). This is quite crucial for biological molecules because it gives access to conformational information under conditions close to the in vivo conditions in which biological molecules actually function.

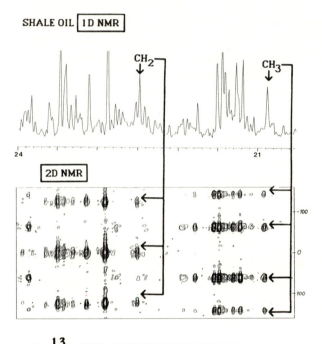

2D ^{13}C NMR GIVES MORE INFORMATION ABOUT COMPLEX COMPOUNDS

Imaging In 1973 the first two-dimensional spatial resolution by NMR was reported by chemists. Today, there exist instruments capable of determining in three dimensions the NMR chemical shifts and nuclear concentrations for objects as large as a human patient. Such NMR scanners, comparable in some respects to X-ray CT scanners, appear to have considerable potential for noninvasive diagnosis of diseases, possibly including multiple sclerosis, muscular distrophy, and malignant tumors. Further increases in field strength should permit real-time imaging, e.g., of a beating heart. In a closely related, but invasive medical application, NMR measurement coils have been surgically placed around intact and functioning animal organs. These have been used to study, for example, metabolism by measuring high-resolution phosphorus, carbon, and sodium NMR spectra in the organ. These remarkable uses of NMR place before us the possibility of studying the chemistry of a living system truly in vivo.

Costs

Resolution and sensitivity of an NMR instrument depend upon the interplay among the parameters associated with magnetic field intensity, sample volume, and field uniformity over that sample volume. As chemists work with increasingly complex molecules, better resolution immediately advances research capabilities as soon as it becomes technologically feasible. This can be seen in the steady rise in the magnetic fields available in commercial NMR instruments (as manifested in the proton NMR frequency, expressed in megahertz, Mhz). Over the last 25 years, the highest field available has increased by a factor of about 1.5 every 5 years or so. However, the resultant higher performance, coupled with other improvements, has exponentially increased the cost of the highest performance machines. Thus the price of commercial NMR instruments has risen from about $35,000 in 1955 to $850,000 in 1985, a few percent per year faster than inflation. The next level of improvement will probably operate at about 750 Mhz, it will be available in 1988 or 1989, and it will cost in the neighborhood of $1.5M.

The critical importance of state-of-the-art NMR instrumentation is reflected in the speed with which it paces the field. Annual sales of

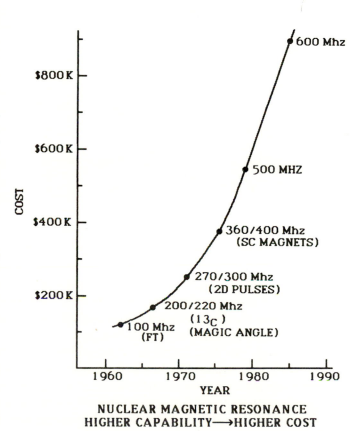

NUCLEAR MAGNETIC RESONANCE
HIGHER CAPABILITY⟶HIGHER COST

NMR instruments now total about $100M. The highest field spectrometers now delivered are 500-Mhz instruments, and they have been available for purchase for only a little over a year. There have been 70 such instruments produced already, many of which are in U.S. industrial laboratories. A number of them are in Europe, Japan, and the Soviet Union. About 14 of them are placed in U.S. academic institutions as multi-user facilities. There are three home-built, individual-user (dedicated) instruments in the United States. Magnet technology will soon permit commercial production of 600-Mhz instruments at a cost of about $850,000. On the horizon, perhaps 3 or 4 years away, are 750-Mhz instruments, and extrapolation of the reliably logarithmic dependence of cost on proton frequency projects a cost of about $1.5M. To be used in a cost-effective way, these state-of-the-art machines must be supported by operating and maintenance funding at about 20 percent of the purchase price per year.

The costs of their NMR instrumentation now represent the major capital expenditure of any research-oriented chemistry department, and their ongoing maintenance and operating costs furnish a major item in departmental budgets. A typical breakdown of capital costs and capabilities for an academic research department among the top 40 is shown in Table IV-2. Thus in 1965, a typical

TABLE IV-2 Past and Projected NMR Capital Needs of Research-Oriented Chemistry Departments

Year	Spectrometer (Mhz)	Cost ($)	Capabilities
1965 (typical)	60	50K	Continuous, proton
	100	100K	Continuous, proton
1984 (typical)	100	150K	Proton, ^{13}C, ^{31}P (FT)
	270-360	300K	Multinuclear (FT)
1986 needs	300	200K	Routine proton, ^{13}C, ^{19}F (FT), graduate, undergraduate instruction
	400	350K	Multinuclear, ^{17}O, ^{103}Rh, ^{183}W
	500	600K	Proton, ^{13}C 2-D (FT), solid state
	600	850K	Multinuclear, 2-D, quadrupolar solids
1990 needs	750-900	1.2-1.7M	All of above (except large sample imaging)

department would be well equipped for about $150K, for that represented the state-of-the-art at that time. In 1984, most research departments typically have about $450K in useable but inadequate NMR instrumentation. The use of NMR in undergraduate instruction is considered essential, even if it must make use of the departmental research instrument(s).

Now, the impressive technological developments of the last 3 or 4 years are causing a qualitative change (e.g., intoduction of 500-Mhz instruments, array processors, data stations, 2-D, and solid state capabilities). Virtually all the top U.S. chemistry departments need substantial funding infusions to remain competitive with many European, Japanese, and Eastern block laboratories. Without such research capability in our own academic institutions, our Ph.D. graduates will not be well prepared to move into well equipped industrial laboratories, and leadership in a number of critical fields will tend to move abroad.

The NMR developments made by chemists have revolutionized many areas of chemistry, and they are exerting profound influences on contiguous research fields in biochemistry, materials research, geochemistry, botany, physiology, and the medical sciences. Thus, the costs of modern NMR instrumentation are high, but the potential rewards are so great that we cannot afford to lose them.

Mass Spectrometry

In a mass spectrometer, a molecule of interest is converted to a gaseous ion, the ion is accelerated to a known kinetic energy with an electric field, and then its mass is measured either by tracking its curved trajectory through a known magnetic field or its time of flight through a fixed distance to the detector. In the first instance, this would seem to give only the most crude diagnostic information—the parent molecular weight. Quite to the contrary, a variety of uses and aspects of mass spectrometry give it remarkable value in identifying the structural subunits that exist in the molecule and their connectivity. The first source of such information is the fragmentation pattern that accompanies the ionization process. Patterns of fragment ions are obtained that become extremely informative when combined with mass spectra of prototype molecules of known structure. Next, the mass spectrometer can be coupled with other "selective filters" that add greatly to the significance of the mass spectrum. These coupling schemes, discussed in Section V-D as a part of Analytical Chemistry, include a variety of methods for vaporizing and ionizing the molecule (see Section V-D, Table V-3) and tandem use with other segregating and/or analytical techniques (see Section V-D, Analytical Chemistry, Combined Techniques). In fact, some scientists contend that where applicable, the coupling of gas chromatographic fractionation followed by mass spectrometric analysis provides the best general purpose, analytical instrument for sensitive work on complex mixtures drawn from chemical, biological, geochemical, environmental, and forensic applications.

Applicability

A basic requirement for mass spectrometry is the formation of ions from the compound of interest. Until recently, this limited applicability to those substances with some volatility within their range of thermal stability. Now, over the last decade, capabilities and applications of mass spectrometry are rapidly widening because of the development of a series of techniques by which ions can be desorbed from a nonvolatile solid sample (see Section V-D, Table V-3). Now molecular weights of 20,000 can be measured, and mass resolution of 1 part in 150,000 is available in commercial instruments. Perhaps 5- to 10-fold higher resolution can be achieved with Fourier transform techniques but only for relatively low-mass ions. Extremely high resolution can be quite useful for low-molecular-weight fragments to distinguish between the masses of one deuterium and two hydrogen atoms (7 parts per 10,000) or between one ^{13}C atom and a ^{12}C plus a hydrogen atom (3 parts per 10,000).

The breadth of applicability is implicit in the statistic that about $200M worth of instruments are purchased each year. Several thousand people in the United States are engaged full-time in using them, more than double the number so employed 15 years ago. The chemical, nuclear, metallurgical, and pharmaceutical industries all make extensive use of mass spectrometry. Environmental regulations (particularly those covering organic compounds in water supplies) are written around mass spectrometry. Established and emerging methods of geochronology and paleobiology are based on this technique. Research applications in chemistry are legion, ranging from routine analysis in synthetic chemistry to beam detection in a molecular beam apparatus.

Still another type of application is based on the laser desorption technique. Because of its sharp focusability, a laser can be used to provide a chemical map of a surface with micron resolving power. This method, called MS ion microprobe, is finding use in semiconductor fabrication, as well as with metallurgical and biological samples.

Sensitivity and Selectivity

An unknown sample can be identified with as little as 10^{-10} grams (100 picograms), while a specific compound with known fragmentation pattern can be detected with as little as 10^{-13} grams (100 femtograms). As a striking example, a .1 mg dose per kilogram body weight of Δ^9-tetrahydrocannabinol (an active drug from marijuana) can be tracked in blood plasma for over a week down to the 10^{-11} grams per milliliter level using combined gas chromatography and tandem mass spectrometry. As an example of specificity, in a simple MS examination of a coal sample containing a small amount of trichlorodibenzodi-

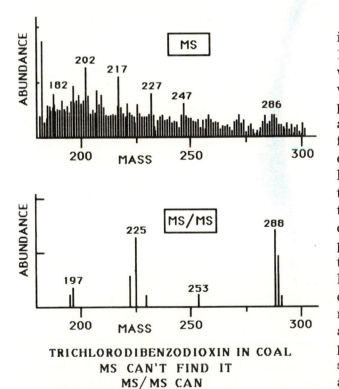

TRICHLORODIBENZODIOXIN IN COAL
MS CAN'T FIND IT
MS/MS CAN

oxin, interference by the great variety of similar compounds in the sample ("chemical noise") can reduce the effective signal to noise to near unity. However, the parent mass of the desired compound (288) can be extracted from this background in a tandem MS/MS apparatus, ionized by collision and analyzed in the second spectrometer to produce a mass spectrum essentially identical to that of the pure compound. In a novel research application, the reactivity effect of solvation on reactivity for gaseous ions can be demonstrated. For example, a methoxide ion has been shown to abstract a proton when it collides with acrylonitrile. However, if the methoxide is solvated with a molecule of methanol, instead of abstraction, simple adduct formation occurs.

Costs

Just as for NMR, costs of mass spectrometers have increased exponentially over the last few decades, but these increasing costs carry with them enormous increases in capability. For example, in 1950 for about $40,000, the best instrument available had a resolution of about 1 part in 300 and a molecular weight limit of 150. Assuming an average inflation of 6 percent over the 30-year period, this translates into a cost of $230K in 1980 dollars. In 1980, the best instrument available cost about $400K, 1.7 times higher than the $230K figure. However, this price increase buys a 500-fold increase in resolution (to 150,000) and a more than 10-fold increase in the mass limit (to 2,000). Along with these obvious performance characteristics, scanning speeds (which have been greatly increased), data processing

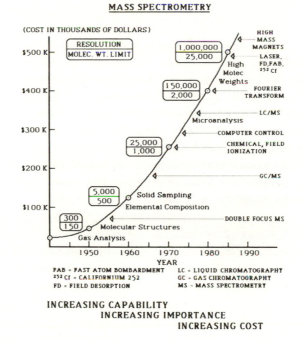

(which has been automated), and coupled use (such as with gas chromatography) have greatly enhanced the power of mass spectrometry.

Again, as for NMR, no first-rate research laboratory (academic or industrial) can operate without modern instrumentation of this type. Not only capital investment but maintenance and operation costs must be included in budgeting plans to ensure the access needed for our research universities to perform their educational role at the Ph.D. level and to maintain world-class research competitiveness in the many fields that depend upon mass spectrometry.

X-Ray Diffraction

The term structure implies the arrangement of atoms in substances. Knowledge of such arrangements elucidates the physical and chemical properties of materials, clarifies reaction mechanisms, and identifies new substances. At present, X-ray diffraction techniques offer the most powerful route to determining these structures for any substance that can be obtained in crystalline form. The most appealing feature of this type of analysis is the unambiguous establishment of the complete structure, whether the crystal be that of a mineral, an alloy, an inorganic, organometallic or organic substance, or a macromolecule of biological origin. It is as close as we can come to "seeing" the atoms in a molecule. It reveals which atoms are attached to which, the geometric arrangement of the atoms, how atoms are moving, and how charges are distributed in a molecule or crystal. Crystals of complicated molecules containing only 10 to 15 micrograms of the material are now being analyzed successfully.

Applications

The X-ray technique has become an integral part of inorganic, metal-organic, and organic synthesis. Whenever an unknown substance can be crystallized, an X-ray structure determination is liable to provide the most informative data available about the identity, molecular structure, and conformation of the molecule. With present computer-automated data interpretation, molecular complexity is not a great obstacle. In fact, the stipulation that the substance must be available in single-crystal form emerges as one of the major limitations to the range of applicability of this powerful technique. When single crystals are available, even the most complex biological molecules can be examined.

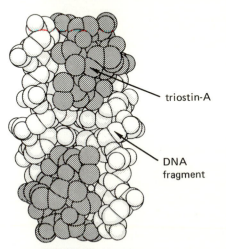

triostin-A

DNA
fragment

X-RAYS SHOW HOW A
DRUG BINDS TO DNA

For example, X-ray structure analysis has become a vital tool for understanding the specific mechanisms for drug action. Such studies of molecular substrates, inhibitors, and antibiotics give information on the geometry and physical specificity of the receptor site and open pathways for improving drug design. An example is the recent elucidation of the binding of triostin A to a DNA hexanucleotide.

In synthetic programs, these methods figure importantly. Many substances that have been isolated from natural products and shown to have potent biological properties, but the molecular formula must be known before progress can be made toward their chemical synthesis. Examples already mentioned in Section IV-A extend from insect pheromones for pest control in agriculture and forestry to growth hormones to increase food, forage, and biomass production. Elucidation of the structures of toxins from poisonous tropical frogs, poisonous sea life, and poisonous mushrooms have provided medical probes for the studies of nerve transmission, ion transport, and antitumor agents. Recently the seeds of *Sesbania drummondii*, a perennial shrub growing in wet fields along the Florida to Texas coastal plain, were found to yield a possible antitumor compound. The most active compound found in the seeds is present at only ½ parts per million so that 1000 pounds of seed provided only milligram quantities. The structure of this molecule, called sesbanimide, was determined by X-ray diffraction of a crystal weighing only 10 micrograms. The analysis displayed a novel tricyclic structure previously unknown in nature or among synthetic organic compounds. Now organic chemists have begun devising synthetic approaches to sesbanimide and analogs.

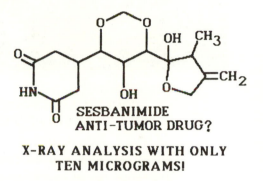

SESBANIMIDE ANTI-TUMOR DRUG?

X-RAY ANALYSIS WITH ONLY TEN MICROGRAMS!

The determination of the precise size and geometry of the cavities in natural zeolite frameworks by crystal structure analysis has provided information for the production of synthetic zeolites with specific pore sizes and shapes. Zeolites are indispensable in catalytic cracking, alkylation, and separation in the fuel industry.

More than 4000 new crystal structures are determined every year at present as compared to about 100 per year 15 years ago. The great increase has been made possible by theoretical advances in structure determination, by the advances in computers and sophisticated computer programs, by modern, automated diffractometers, and, for large biological molecules, molecular graphics units. Some analyses of small molecules can be performed in 1 day by personnel relatively untrained in crystallography. However, the more difficult analyses need specialists in the field and may take months or even years to complete.

Costs

A typical, state-of-the-art, diffractometer currently costs between $300K and $500K, depending upon specialized accessories (e.g., low-temperature, high-temperature, plotting, viewing screens). The more primitive diffractometers of 15 years ago cost about $70K. Today every research-oriented chemistry department requires at least one diffractometer for relatively routine analytical use, and many departments will need another that can be dedicated to advanced research problems.

The potentialities of molecular graphics deserve special mention. For some time, computer-driven graphics programs have been used for modelling and fitting structures to X-ray derived electron-density maps of molecules. However,

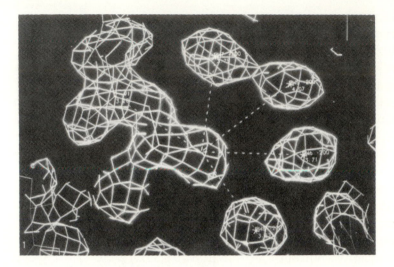

COMPUTER GRAPHICS SHOW
MOLECULAR STRUCTURES IN 3D

in the last few years, new developments have appeared that greatly increase our ability to picture complex molecular arrangements. Computer-automated graphics units have recently become commercially available that present the molecular structure in three dimensions together with the capacity to rotate the molecule slowly and to highlight with color those molecular components of particular interest. Even an untrained eye can perceive three-dimensional spatial relationships that might go unnoticed without these instrumental features. As such capabilities become more widely available, they are sure to be regarded as an essential analytical tool for connecting molecular structure to molecular function, particularly for biological molecules.

The cost of a molecular graphics unit is currently about $80K to $100K, but it cannot be used without access to substantial computing capability (e.g., a VAX computer). However, decreasing computer costs encourage the expectation that in only a few years dedicated computer capacity will become an integral part of a molecular graphics unit at a cost still under $250K.

Neutron Diffraction

Complementary to X-ray diffraction and of increasing importance to structural chemistry is neutron diffraction. Thermal neutrons have wavelengths comparable to atomic spacings in crystal lattices, and their scattering from crystalline materials therefore gives rise to diffraction patterns. The unique advantages of neutrons over X-rays are, first, that their scattering from proteins is of comparable intensity to that from heavier nuclei so that neutron diffraction gives precise information on positions and bonding of hydrogen atoms, and, second, that the neutron has a magnetic moment, so that neutron diffraction can be used to study magnetic structures.

Applications

Among the accomplishments of neutron scattering research in the past decade are the determination of structures and transitions in magnetic superconductors, elucidation of tunneling modes in chemical systems (such as hydrogen trapped by impurities in metals), determination of the spatial organization of macromolecular assemblies such as ribosomes, and the location of hydrogen atoms in the hydrogen bonds that determine protein structures.

In addition to extensions of current techniques to more complex structures, there are enticing opportunities in studies of hydrogen tunneling phenomena, diffusion mechanisms, intercalation compounds, and catalyst behavior. Many of these studies will require higher intensities and better energy resolution than are currently available.

Costs

Improved facilities at existing reactors to meet these requirements, including "guide halls" and cold-neutron instrumentation, have been recommended as a high priority by the NRC committee on "Major Facilities for Materials Research and Related Disciplines." The cost of a neutron diffractometer is approximately $1.5M. Another important development would be improved instrumentation at the Los Alamos National Laboratory pulsed-neutron facility and, eventually, the construction of a higher-intensity pulsed-neutron source, the latter with a probable cost near $250M.

Electron Spin Resonance

While most molecules contain an even number of electrons that occur in pairs, a reaction in which an electron is transferred can generate a species with an "odd" or unpaired electron (e.g., free radicals, radical ions). The unpaired electron gives the molecule unique magnetic properties that allow detection and characterization by the technique of electron spin resonance (ESR). The ESR instrument consists of a strong magnet, microwave equipment (originally based on radar technology), sensitive electronic apparatus, and, frequently, a dedicated computer.

Applicability

Even though molecules with unpaired electrons tend to be reactive, they are important in many chemical and biological processes, usually as transient intermediates. For example, samples of photosynthetic materials give rise to ESR signals when they are irradiated. These signals arise from primary electron-transfer events initiated by the absorption of light by the

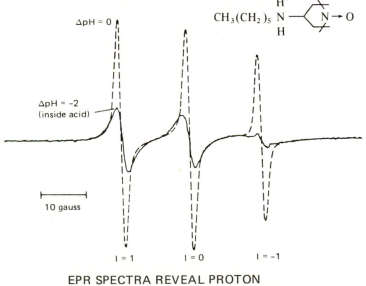

EPR SPECTRA REVEAL PROTON
GRADIENTS ACROSS A CELL MEMBRANE

photosynthetic pigments, and their study has been important in understanding the mechanism of photosynthesis. Organic radicals and radical ions produce a unique ESR spectrum that allows their identification. Moreover the pattern in the spectrum provides information about the electron density distribution in the molecule. The ESR spectrum can also be used to measure the rate of rapid electron transfer reactions. Another important application involves the use of spin labels—molecules whose ESR spectra are exquisitely sensitive to their motion and environment. These can be covalently attached to a target molecule and then used to probe its rotational freedom. Such studies have revealed the fluidity of lipids in biological membranes, the presence of proton gradients or electric fields across membranes, and motion in polymers.

Costs

An ESR spectrometer costs about $200K for state-of-the-art instruments. The earliest ESR spectrometers were developed and manufactured in the United States, but there is currently no U.S. manufacturer, so spectrometers must be purchased from foreign suppliers. Improvements in design, including improved microwave sources, cavities, and detection electronics (e.g., low-noise GaAs FET amplifiers) have given higher sensitivities to allow detection at the parts-per-million level. The application of computer-mediated signal-averaging methods can lead to even better sensitivities. The application of ESR to studies of rapid reactions, e.g., in photosynthesis investigations, requires improvement of the time resolution to the microsecond or nanosecond regime. This is accomplished by increasing the field modulation, by using superheterodyne detection, or by employing pulsed (spin-echo) techniques; such instrumentation is not now commercially available. The combination of electron and nuclear magnetic double resonance (ENDOR) is also possible, and new classes of information will become available with the application of the newer pulsed ESR techniques.

CHEMISTRY is a central science
that responds to societal needs.

It is critical in Man's attempt to...
monitor and protect our environment

Investigating Smog Soup

Air pollution is a visible reminder of the price we sometimes pay for progress. Emissions from thousands of sources pour into the atmosphere a myriad of molecules that react and re-react to form a "smog soup." We are already aware of some of the potential dangers of leaving these processes unstudied and unchecked: respiratory ailments, acid rain, and the greenhouse effect. Surprisingly, you and I are the principal culprits in generating much of this unpleasant brew—everytime we start our cars or switch on our air conditioning or central heating! Transportation, heating, cooling, and lighting account for about two-thirds of U.S. energy use, almost all derived from combustion of petroleum and coal.

Pinpointing cause and effect relationships begins, inevitably, with the identification and measurement of what is up there, tiny molecules at parts-per-billion concentrations in the mixing bowl of the sky. Finding out what substances are there, how they are reacting, where they came from, and what can be done about them are all matters of chemistry. The first two questions require accurate analysis of trace pollutants. Physical and analytical chemists have successfully applied to such detective work their most sensitive techniques. An example is the *Fourier Transform Infrared Spectrometer*. This sophisticated device can look through a mile or so of city air and identify all the chemical substances present and tell us their concentrations down to the parts-per-billion level. Recognizing a substance at such a low concentration is comparable to asking a machine to recognize you in a crowd at a rock concert attended by the entire U.S. population.

How does this superb device work? "Infrared" means light just beyond the red end of the rainbow visible to the human eye. Hence infrared light is invisible, though we can tell it is there by the warmth felt under an infrared lamp. But molecules can "see" infrared light. Every polyatomic molecule absorbs infrared "colors" that are uniquely characteristic of its molecular structure. Thus each molecular substance has an infrared absorption "fingerprint"—different from any other substance. By examining these fingerprints, chemists can identify the molecules that are present.

An example of what can be done is the measurement of formaldehyde and nitric acid as trace constituents in Los Angeles smog. Unequivocal detection, using almost a mile-long path through the polluted air, revealed the growth during the day of these two bad actors and tied their production to photochemical processes initiated by sunlight. Continuing experiments led to detailed characterization of the simultaneous and interacting concentrations of ozone, peroxyacetyl nitrate (PAN), formic acid, formaldehyde, and nitric acid in the atmosphere. These detections removed an obstacle to the complete understanding of how unburned gasoline and oxides of nitrogen leaving our exhaust pipe end up as eye and lung irritants in the atmosphere. This advance doesn't eliminate smog soup, but it is a big step toward that desirable end.

192

CHAPTER V

Chemistry and National Well-Being

V-A. Better Environment

Every society tries to provide itself with adequate food and shelter and a healthful environment. When these elemental needs are assured, attention turns to comfort and convenience. The extent to which all these wishes can be satisfied determines a society's "quality of life." However, choices are usually required because one or another of these needs or wishes is more easily satisfied at the expense of others. Today we find our desires for more abundant consumer goods, energy, and mobility in conflict with maintenance of a healthful environment. A major concern of our times is the protection of our environment in the face of increasing world population, increasing concentration of population (urbanization), and increasing standards of living.

Environmental degradation—with its accompanying threats to health and disruption of ecosystems—is not a new phenomenon. Human disturbance of the environment has been noted from the earliest recorded history. The problem of sewage disposal began with the birth of cities. Long before the 20th century, London was plagued with air pollution from fires used for heating and cooking. An early example of an industrial hygiene problem was the reduced longevity of chimney sweeps attributed retrospectively to cancer arising from prolonged exposure to soot with its trace carcinogen content (polynuclear aromatic hydrocarbons).

There is small consolation, though, in the fact that environmental pollution is not a new invention. The global population burgeons upward, while cities grow even faster. Per capita consumption and energy use continue to increase. Pollution problems are becoming increasingly obvious, and we are recognizing subtle interactions and secondary reverberations that went unnoticed before. A number of environmental disturbances have begun to manifest themselves on a global scale. Occasional industrial accidents, like those at Bhopal and Seveso, remind us that large-scale production of needed consumer products may require handling of large amounts of potentially dangerous precursor substances.

On the positive side, the public awareness has been raised about the importance of maintaining environmental quality. In the United States, a large majority of citizens from across the political spectrum have indicated that they are prepared to pay more for "cleaner" products (e.g., lead-free gasoline) and to pay more taxes to improve their environment. These attitudes are spreading abroad, an essential aspect of containment of the problems more global in scope.

Effective strategies for safeguarding our surroundings require adequate knowledge and understanding. We must be able to answer the following questions:

— What potentially undesirable substances are present in our air, water, soil, and food?

— Where did these substances come from?

— What options are there—alternative products and processes—to alleviate known problems?

— What is the quantitative degree of hazard as a function of the extent of exposure to a given constituent?

— How shall we choose among and implement available options that offer corrective action?

Plainly, chemists play a central role in answering the first three crucial questions. To find out what is around us, we need analytical chemists to apply and develop ever more sensitive and selective analytical techniques. To track pollutants back to their origins, again we look to analytical chemists acting as sleuths, now usually in collaboration with meteorologists, oceanographers, volcanologists, climate dynamicists, biologists, and hydrologists. But finding origins can require detailed chemical understandings of reaction sequences and transformations that intervene between the source and the final noxious or toxic product. Then, developing options calls on the full range of the chemist's arsenal. If the world's mortality rate from malaria is not to be reduced with DDT because of its environmental persistence, what substances can be synthesized that are as effective as DDT in saving lives and spontaneously degradable as well? If we must use lower grade energy sources to satisfy our society's energy needs, what catalysts and new processes can be developed to avoid exacerbating already-existing problems of acid rain and carcinogen release from coal-fired power plants?

Thus our society must assure the health of its chemistry enterprise if it wants earlier warning of emerging environmental degradation, better understandings of the origins of that degradation, and access to a full array of economically feasible options from which to choose solutions. Other disciplines make their own particular contributions, but none plays a more central and essential role than chemistry.

The fourth question, the quantitative degree of the hazard/exposure equation, is the province of the medical profession, toxicologists, and epidemiologists. These scientific disciplines face serious challenges now that society has recognized the inverse relationship between what is taken to be a tolerable risk and the cost to society in attaining it. The medical profession must refine its knowledge of risks associated with such substances as lead in the atmosphere, chloroform in drinking water, radiostrontium in milk, benzene in the workplace, and formaldehyde in the home. A qualitative statement that a certain class of substances might be carcinogenic will no longer suffice. We must be able to weigh risks and costs against benefits that would be lost if use of that class of substances were restricted. We must be able to compare these risks to those already present because of natural background levels. More importantly, society cannot afford to pay the exorbitant cost of eliminating *all* risk, because, as the requested degree of risk approaches zero, the cost escalates toward infinity.

Finally, the choice among options and their implementation moves properly into the public arena. Chemists and scientists in the other relevant disciplines have a secondary, but important, informational responsibility here. Every political decision deserves the best and most objective scientific input available. There is nothing more frustrating to our citizens and our government than to befaced with decisions without the benefit of facts and a usefully predictive scientific knowledge base. Scientists, including chemists, must meet their responsibility to provide the public, the media, and the government with an objective picture expressed in language free of technical jargon to help establish the scientific setting for a given decision and the options that lie before us.

Turning Detection into Protection

All our environmental protection strategies should be founded on realistic hazard thresholds and on our ability to detect a particular offending substance well before its presence reaches that threshold. Chemists must continue to sharpen their analytical skills so that, even at minute concentrations well below the hazard threshold, a given substance can be monitored long before crisis-corrective action is dictated. When this is possible, we see that *detection can be equated to protection*.

Unfortunately, the media, the public, and government agencies have too often equated detection with hazard as a result of the prevalent assumption that a substance that is demonstrably toxic at some particular concentration will be toxic at any concentration. There are innumerable examples to prove that this is not a generally applicable premise. Consider carbon monoxide (CO). This ubiquitous atmospheric constituent becomes dangerously toxic at concentrations exceeding 1000 parts per million and is considered to have adverse health effects for prolonged exposure to concentrations exceeding 10 parts per million. We do not, however, leap to the conclusion that CO must be completely removed from the atmosphere. This would be foolish (and impossible) because we live and thrive in a natural atmosphere that always contains easily detectable CO at about 1 part per million. Clearly, our task is to decide where we should place controls between the known toxicity threshold and the known safe range—as EPA has in fact attempted to do.

In recent trends, the naive "zero-risk" approach is gradually being supplanted by a more sophisticated risk assessment/risk management rationale. In both the assessment and management phases, a major theme is the crucial importance of being able to analyze complex air, water, soil, and biological systems that may contain hundreds of natural chemical compounds. The roles that chemical analysis and monitoring play in protecting and managing our air and water resources are analogous to the role that intelligence-gathering plays in protecting and promoting the nation's public interest in the military, geopolitical, and economic realms. Conclusions regarding causes and effect, sources, movement, and fates of pollutants in crucial issues such as acid deposition, global climatic change, ozone layer destruction, and toxic waste disposal depend upon environmental measurements that must be made with sufficient selectivity and sensitivity. Enormously costly decisions about how to protect and enhance the quality of our air, water, and land resources are sometimes based on environmental "intelligence" that can be grossly inadequate and inaccurate. Crash projects to remedy crises caused by past indiscretions or ineffective strategies that were based on insufficient knowledge have been expensive. A small fraction of the money spent on such a corrective program, if invested in long-term fundamental environmental science and monitoring techniques, can significantly reduce the need for future expensive remedial programs.

THERE ARE 22 DIFFERENT TETRACHLORODIOXINS

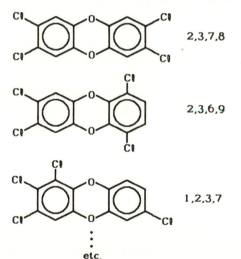

HOW MUCH IS IN THE TOXIC 2,3,7,8 FORM? AN ANALYTICAL CHALLENGE

Increased effectiveness of environmental measurements requires improved surveillance tools. The challenge is to measure trace levels of a particular compound present in a complex mixture containing many innocuous compounds. The principal objectives of research in environmental analysis and monitoring are improved sensitivity, selectivity, separation, sampling, accuracy, speed, and data interpretation. For example, an active research area is connected with separation techniques to allow rapid and unequivocal analysis of complex mixtures of pollutants and pesticides found in toxic wastes, polluted streams and lakes, and biological samples. A success story in analytical selectivity is the development of analytical methods to allow separation and quantitative measurement of each of the 22 individual isomers of tetrachlorodioxin at the parts-per-trillion level.

Research is needed on multi-stage separation and detection methods, such as tandem mass spectrometry. Additional research on developing techniques that exploit the separation powers of selective sorbents, liquid chromatography, supercritical fluid chromatography, field flow fractionation, and parametric pumping will be fruitful. Attention must be given to basic research that will produce selective detectors (based, e.g., on laser-induced fluorescence or on chemiluminescence) that can be used to simplify analysis and minimize interferences that can accompany environmental sampling.

Highly reactive species in the atmosphere cannot be sampled and transported to the laboratory for analysis. Such substances pose special challenges in measurement and will require research aimed at remote sensing techniques capable of measuring them in situ. Past successes include the measurement of formaldehyde and nitric acid in the atmosphere of Los Angeles, during severe smog attacks, by Fourier transform infrared spectroscopy in which absorbance due to these pollutants was measured in situ over a 1-kilometer path. With these experiments it was possible to perform a detailed characterization of the simultaneous concentrations of formaldehyde, formic acid, nitric acid, peroxyacetyl nitrate, and ozone in the ambient air at the part-per-billion level at which these substances are contributors to photochemical smog. Notice that 1 part per billion (1 part of a pollutant in 10^9 parts of air) is a minute concentration, but it is still sufficient to be significant in atmospheric reactions. Differential scanning laser devices based on radar-like technology ("lidar") have been used successfully to measure sulfur dioxide plume profiles downwind of coal-fired power plants at the part-per-million level. Tunable diode lasers are also capable of providing real-time in situ detection of pollutants from internal combustion engines and industrial processes.

Several laser techniques, including linear methods (e.g., absorption, fluorescence), nonlinear methods (e.g., coherent antistokes Raman spectroscopy, optical heterodynes), and double resonance methods (e.g., laser magnetic resonance), need to be examined more extensively. Other spectroscopic methods, such as Fourier transform infrared and photoacoustic spectroscopy, are promising and warrant further study. One goal of such research should be better measurements in the stratosphere and troposphere. Rapid, reliable, accurate, and less-expensive methods are needed for measuring concentrations of trace species, such as OH radicals, that play key roles in atmospheric chemistry.

At the same time that research aimed at more sophisticated measurement technology is conducted, parallel efforts need to be devoted to simpler, less costly *routine* monitoring techniques.

Research directed at fixing the chemical state of environmental constituents (speciation research) is gaining importance because we now recognize that transport mechanisms and toxicities vary markedly with chemical form. Chromium in the hexavalent oxidation state is toxic, while in the trivalent form it is much less so, and, for some living systems, it may be an essential trace element. Arsenic in some forms can move rapidly through aquifers, while other forms are rapidly adsorbed on rock or soil surfaces. Of the 22 distinct structural arrangements of tetrachlorodioxin, the most toxic is three orders of magnitude more toxic (to test animals) than the second most toxic. These examples illustrate the importance of analytical methods that allow identification of chemical form as well as quantity of potential pollutants. Electrochemistry, chromatography, and mass spectrometry are among the powerful tools for speciation studies.

The complexity of environmental problems requires analysis of massive amounts of data. Research is needed to assist in the interpretation and wise use of the accumulated information. Developments in the field of artificial intelligence that use pattern recognition should provide valuable interpretive aid. Recent advances in microprocessors and small computers should be exploited to develop intelligent measuring devices, and attention should be given to better handling, archiving, and dissemination of environmental data.

Ozone in the Stratosphere

The possibility of polluting the stratosphere to the point of partially depleting the protective ozone layer was first raised only about a dozen years ago. This seemingly improbable notion found much scientific support, and it is now one of the best examples of a potentially serious environmental problem of global extent. It is a problem, furthermore, that exemplifies chemistry's central role in its understanding, analysis, and solution.

Why do we need to worry about stratospheric chemistry? Ozone in the stratosphere is the natural filter that absorbs and blocks the Sun's short wavelength ultraviolet radiation that is harmful to life. The air in the stratosphere—a cloudless dry, cold region at altitudes between about 10 to 50 km—mixes slowly in the vertical direction, but rapidly in the horizontal. Consequently, harmful pollutants, once introduced into the stratosphere, might remain there for periods as long as years, and, if so, they will rapidly be distributed around the earth across borders and oceans, making the problem truly global. A large reduction of our ozone shield would result in an increase of potentially dangerous ultraviolet radiation at the earth's surface.

To understand how easily the ozone layer might be perturbed, it is useful to recognize that ozone is actually only a trace constituent of the stratosphere; at its maximum concentration ozone makes up only a few parts per million of the air molecules. If the diffuse ozone layer were concentrated into a thin shell of pure ozone gas surrounding the earth at atmospheric pressure, it would measure only about 3 millimeters (1/8 inch) in thickness. Furthermore, ozone destruction mechanisms are based on chain reactions in which one pollutant molecule may destroy many thousands of ozone molecules before being transported to the lower atmosphere, chemically transformed, and removed by rain.

Chemistry's crucial role in understanding this problem has emerged through the identification and measurement of several ozone-destroying chain processes.

Fifty years ago, the formation of an ozone layer in the midstratosphere was qualitatively described in terms of four chemical and photochemical reactions involving pure oxygen species (O, O_2, and O_3). Today, we know that the rates of at least 150 chemical reactions must be considered in order to approach a quantitative model for simulating the present stratosphere and predicting changes resulting from the introduction of various pollutants. The chemistry begins with absorption of solar ultraviolet radiation by O_2 molecules in the stratosphere. Chemical bond rupture occurs, and ozone, O_3 and oxygen atoms, O, are produced. Then, if nitric oxide, NO, is somehow introduced into the stratosphere, an important chemical chain reaction takes place.

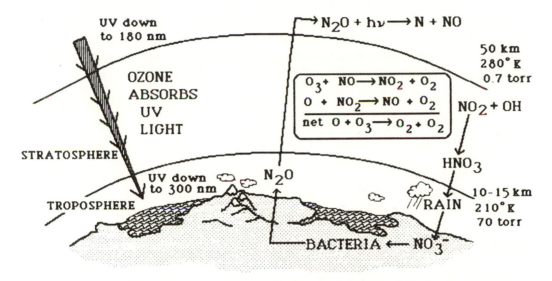

The NO and NO_2 reactions together furnish a true catalytic cycle in which NO and NO_2 are the catalysts. Neither species is consumed, because each is regenerated in a complete cycle. Each cycle has the net effect of destroying one oxygen atom and one ozone molecule (collectively called "odd oxygen"). This catalytic cycle is now believed to be the major mechanism of ozone destruction in the stratosphere. In the natural atmosphere, the oxides of nitrogen are provided by biogenic emissions at the Earth's surface by soil and sea bacteria of nitrous oxide, N_2O. This relatively inert molecule slowly mixes into the stratosphere where it can absorb ultraviolet light and then react to form NO and NO_2.

Of course, oxides of nitrogen directly introduced to the stratosphere are expected to destroy ozone as well, and this was the basis of the first perceived threat to the ozone layer—large fleets of supersonic aircraft flying in the stratosphere and depositing oxides of nitrogen via their engine exhausts. Nuclear explosions also produce copious quantities of oxides of nitrogen, which are carried into the stratosphere by the buoyancy of the hot fireballs. A significant depletion of the ozone layer in the event of a major nuclear war was forecast in a 1975 study by the National Academy of Sciences, although this environmental effect of nuclear war may pale in comparison with the recently suggested potential of a "nuclear winter." Both effects underscore the delicacy of the atmosphere and its sensitivity to chemical transformations.

Then, in 1974, just as the possible impact of stratospheric planes was reaching the analysis stage, concern was raised about other man-made atmospheric pollutants. Halocarbons, such as $CFCl_3$ and CF_2Cl_2 (chlorofluoromethanes, or CFMs), had become popular as spray-can propellants and refrigerant fluids, mainly because of their chemical inertness. The absence of reactivity meant absence of toxicity or other harmful effects on terrestrial life. Ironically, this meant that there was no place for the CFMs to go but up—up into the stratosphere where ultraviolet photolysis could occur. Chemists then recognized that if this occurred, the resultant chlorine species, Cl and ClO, could enter into their own catalytic cycle, destroying ozone in a manner exactly analogous to the destruction caused by the oxides of nitrogen.

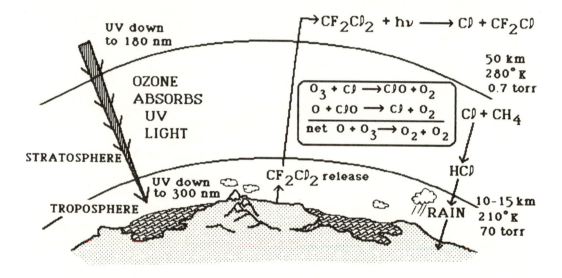

Once this possibility had been recognized, analysis of the whole stratospheric ozone chemistry began in earnest. An international committee of scientific experts assembled by the National Academy of Sciences examined in detail the state of our knowledge of every aspect of the problem. It became clear that the additional chemistry introduced to the stratosphere added not just these 2 catalytic chemical reactions to the roster, but a total of about 40 new reactions involving such species as Cl, ClO, HCl, HOCl, $ClONO_2$, the halocarbons, and several others. Most of these reactions had never before been studied in the laboratory.

Laboratory kineticists and photochemists responded to the challenge by

providing reliable rate constants and absorbances for
the proposed processes using
the growing arsenal of modern experimental methods.
Recent progress in the experimental accomplishments of
this field has been remarkable. It has become possible,
for example, to generate
nearly any desired reactive
molecular species in the laboratory in a variety of ways, to
bring them together with
other reactive species, and to

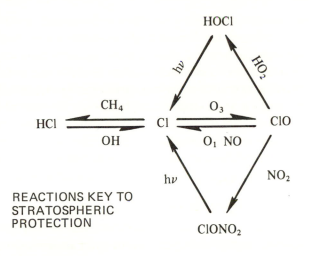

REACTIONS KEY TO
STRATOSPHERIC
PROTECTION

measure their rates of reaction under known, controlled conditions. Such direct
measurements of these extremely rapid reactions were only a distant goal a
decade ago, but they are now a reality.

Finally, field measurements of minor atmospheric species have been revolutionized by some of the recent advances in analytical chemistry. Methods
originally developed for ultra-sensitive detection of extremely reactive species
in laboratory studies have been modified and adapted to measure such constituents as O, OH, Cl, ClO and others at parts-per-trillion concentrations in the
natural stratosphere. This has been accomplished recently in experiments in
which a helium-filled balloon carries an elaborate instrument package to the
top of the stratosphere where the package is dropped while suspended by a
parachute. As the instrument traverses the stratosphere, it measures concentrations of several important trace chemical species and telemeters the information to a ground station. Very recently, the first successful reel-down
experiment was performed in which the instrument package was lowered 10 to
15 km from a stationary balloon platform and reeled back up again like a giant
yo-yo. This method results in a huge increase in the amount of data that can be
obtained in a single balloon flight. It will also allow for the first time a study of
the time evolution and variability of the stratosphere.

Much has been accomplished in the past 10 years. Many of the needed 100 to
150 photochemical and rate processes have been measured in the laboratory,
and many of the trace species measured in the atmosphere. Yet, research
remains to be done. For example, two of the important chemical species
containing chlorine, HOCl and $ClONO_2$, have yet to be measured anywhere in
the stratosphere. Refinements in the reaction rates for many of the important
processes are still required, and exact product distributions for many of the
reactions are still lacking. Nevertheless, the original NAS study, the research

programs it spawned, and the subsequent follow-up studies provided a firm and timely basis for legislative decisions about regulation of CFM use. Industrial chemists produced alternative, more readily degradable substances to replace the CFMs in some applications. Monitoring programs are in place so that trends in the stratospheric composition can be watched. The stratospheric ozone issue provides a showcase example of how science can examine, clarify, and point to solutions for a potential environmental disturbance. Premature initiation of regulation was avoided because the problem was recognized early enough to permit deliberate, objective analysis and focused research to narrow the uncertainty ranges. From first recognition on, chemists played a lead role.

Reducing Acid Rain

Acid rain is one of the more obvious and pressing results of degradation of air quality. Acidic substances and their precursors are formed when fossil fuels are burned to generate power and provide transportation. These substances are principally acids derived from oxides of sulfur and nitrogen. There are some natural sources of these compounds such as lightning, volcanos, burning biomass, and microbial activity, but, except for rare volcanic eruptions, these are relatively small compared with emissions from power plants, smelters, and vehicles in industrial regions.

The effects of acidic rainfall are most evident and highly publicized in Europe and the northeastern United States, but areas at risk include Canada and

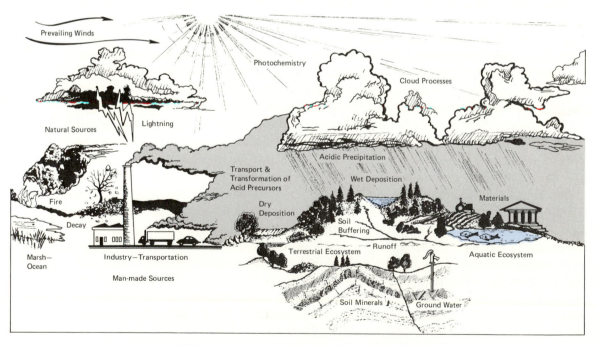

ACID RAIN — SOURCES HERE, IMPACT THERE

perhaps the California Sierras, the Rocky Mountains, and China. In some places precipitation as acidic as vinegar has occasionally been observed. The extent of the effects of acid rain is the subject of continuing controversy. Damage to aquatic life in lakes and streams was the original focus of attention. More recently, damage to buildings, bridges, and equipment has been recognized as another costly consequence of acid rain. The effect of polluted air on human health is the most difficult to quantify.

Greatest damage is done to lakes that are poorly buffered. When naturally alkaline buffers are present, the acidic compounds in acid rain, largely sulfuric acid, nitric acid, and smaller amounts of organic acids, are neutralized, at least until this alkalinity is consumed. However, lakes lying on granitic (acidic) strata are susceptible to immediate damage because acids in precipitation can dissolve metal ions, such as aluminum and manganese, causing reduction in biological productivity and, in some lakes, the decline or elimination of fish populations. Damage to plants from pollution ranges from adverse effects on foliage to destruction of fine root systems.

In a region such as the northeastern United States the principal candidates for pollutant reduction are the power plants burning coal with high sulfur content. Chemical scrubbers that prevent the emission of the pollutants offer one of the possible remedies. Catalysts that reduce oxides of nitrogen emissions from both stationary and mobile sources offer yet another example of the role that chemistry can play in improving air quality.

The various strategies for reducing acid rain involve possible investments of billions of dollars annually. With the stakes so high, it is imperative that the atmospheric processes determining the transport, chemical transformation, and fate of pollutants be well understood.

Acid deposition consists of both "wet" precipitation (as in rain and snow) and dry deposition (in which aerosols or gaseous acidic compounds are deposited on surfaces such as soil particles, plant leaves, etc.). What is finally deposited has usually been injected into the atmosphere in a quite different chemical form. For example, sulfur in coal is oxidized to sulfur dioxide, the gaseous form in which it is emitted from smokestacks. As it moves through the atmo-

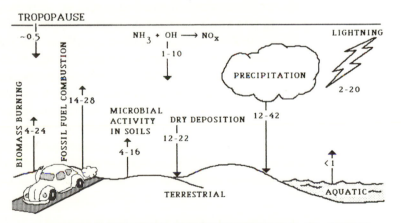

LARGE UNCERTAINTIES REMAIN IN THE GLOBAL NO_x BUDGET

sphere, it is slowly oxidized and reacts with water to form sulfuric acid—the form in which it may be deposited hundreds of miles downwind.

The pathways by which oxides of nitrogen are formed, undergo chemical transformation, and are eventually removed from the atmosphere are also very complex. Nitrogen and oxygen, when heated at high temperatures in power plants, home furnaces, and vehicle engines, form nitric oxide, NO, which reacts with oxidants to form nitrogen dioxide, NO_2, and eventually nitric acid, HNO_3. Quantitative estimates of the global budget for the oxides of nitrogen still contain unacceptably wide uncertainty ranges.

It can readily be seen that without a thorough knowledge of the biogeochemical cycles for the various chemical forms of nitrogen, sulfur, and carbon, and of the global compartments from which these species arise and are partitioned into, it will be difficult to select air pollution control strategies with confidence. Atmospheric and environmental chemistry are central to a clearer and more healthful environment. Development of reliable methods of measurement of trace species in air, kinetics of important atmospheric reactions, and the discovery of new, more effective, chemical processes for reducing pollutant emission are goals that should receive a national commitment for the coming decade.

To minimize acid rain in a cost-effective manner, we must develop a better understanding of the chemistry of the oxides of nitrogen and sulfur as well as hydrogen peroxide, ozone, formaldehyde, and other species in cloud droplets and in the vapor state. The detailed pathways for oxidation of precursors to products are not yet established. Problems are sometimes encountered in extrapolating from laboratory experiments and computer-based models to actual field conditions. Frequently, the rate laws and equilibrium constants established under ideal laboratory conditions become difficult to apply to the more complex mixtures and conditions present in the atmosphere. The role of aqueous phase photochemistry in chemical transformations within clouds is not known. Atmospheric chemistry that occurs in daylight drives reactions to favor products different from those formed at night, so more research is needed at field stations around the clock, as well as in the laboratory.

The roles of reactive species, such as the radicals OH, OOH, and NO_3, in oxidation reactions leading to scavenging of pollutants from the atmosphere need to be better understood in the heterogeneous atmosphere. While systems are easier to study in the gas phase, much important chemistry probably occurs at the liquid droplet-gas phase interfaces, or within the droplets. Most earlier work has focussed on the inorganic constituents of acid precipitation, but certain organic species may potentiate or inhibit reactions. For example, organic compounds in surface organic microlayers covering water droplets may alter mass transport of reactants or act as either catalysts or inhibitors.

Guarding Against Climate Change: The Greenhouse Effect

In the quest for food, goods, heat for homes, and energy for our industrial society, we have increased the concentrations of many trace gases in the atmosphere. Some of them absorb and retain solar energy and may eventually cause inadvertent climate change with catastrophic consequences. If the release of these gases to the atmosphere from man's activities causes significant global warming, results might be flooding due to melting polar ice, loss of productive farmland to desert, and, ultimately, famine. The most publicized of these solar energy traps is carbon dioxide, but the combined effect of increases in nitrous oxide, methane, and other gases could equal that of carbon dioxide.

Approaches used to reduce emission of other pollutants are not appropriate in the case of carbon dioxide, because it is generated in enormous quantities from the burning of fossil fuels and biomass. Here the biogeochemical cycling of carbon assumes great importance. What impact will the "slash and burn" clearing of forests and jungles in the third world countries have? Will increases in biological productivity due to small rises in global temperature result in enhanced photosynthetic removal of carbon dioxide from the atmosphere? What role does methane, which is biogenically produced by termites and other species, play? Are atmospheric particulates coming from human activities likely to block sunlight and offset the effects of increases in carbon dioxide, methane, and nitrous oxide? Large lenses of stratified soot and other aerosols have been observed in Arctic regions. The origin, composition, radiative properties, fates, and effects of these aerosols constituting "Arctic Haze" all need to be clarified.

The behavior of soot in the atmosphere takes on even greater significance in light of the uncertainties about the possible atmospheric effects of nuclear warfare. It was not until 1982 that the hypothesis of global cooling from soot generated by nuclear war was advanced. This concept has since been termed "nuclear winter" because even limited nuclear wars have been predicted to cause the generation and injection into the atmosphere of so much soot that crops would freeze in summertime. Great uncertainties exist concerning the residence time of aerosols in the atmosphere and the effects of soot on radiation balance.

Unlike local pollutants, the global pollutants are vexing because they require action on a global scale, and the citizens of different countries view their priorities differently. What is needed by all is a solid science base, upon which difficult decisions can be based. Whether individual countries have emphasized fossil fuel versus nuclear fuel in the past has been based primarily on economic factors, such as whether that nation had abundant coal reserves. As global threats like carbon dioxide build-up (exacerbated by coal burning) become more clearly defined, we may be forced to re-evaluate the costs and benefits of nuclear power. It takes years to develop sufficient knowledge to allow a wise choice. We must accumulate that knowledge so that we can choose with confidence . . . weighing wisely the real threat posed by carbon dioxide build-up, with possible mitigation strategies, against a clearer picture of the options before us, including the environmental and waste disposal problems of nuclear energy generation.

Cleaner Water and Safe Disposal of Wastes

Our surface and subsurface waters are precious resources. Most of us take it for granted that when we want a drink of water, or to go swimming or fishing, our streams, lakes, and aquifers will be safe to use. Our progress in protecting water bodies from contamination has not generally been as successful as our efforts in cleaning up pollution in the air. Nonetheless, some important progress has been made. Lake Erie, once thought doomed to die biologically from eutrification induced by phosphates and other nutrients, is making a comeback. Improved water treatment, coupled with more rigorous attention to hazardous waste treatment and disposal, holds the key to future advances. To recognize and control the sources of pollution, we must understand the intricacies of pollutant movement and conversion.

Nearly half of the citizens of the United States depend upon wells for their drinking water. A recent NAS assessment of groundwater contamination estimated that about 1 percent of the aquifers in the continental United States may be contaminated to some extent. Evidence of subsurface migration of pollutants makes it increasingly important to protect, with the best science and technology available, the aquifers feeding those wells.

A number of disposal practices and waste repositories involving burial in the ground have been used for many years with only minimal groundwater contamination. Procedures have been predicated on the assumptions that the waste material was unlikely to migrate and that, over time, the compounds would be oxidized, hydrolyzed, or microbially decomposed to harmless products. Now, however, some instances of serious groundwater contamination have appeared. Some compounds have proven to be more stable and mobile than expected, while some of them are bacterially converted into more toxic and mobile forms. In retrospect, it is clear that the scientific knowledge base for the earlier decisions was inadequate.

Proposals currently under consideration for recovering seriously contaminated aquifers are soberingly expensive. For example, estimated costs for "containment" efforts at the Rocky Mountain Arsenal near Denver, Colorado, are about $100M and for "total decontamination" up to $1B. Such enormous prospective clean-up costs require thoughtful weighing of the cost/benefit trade-offs to society in deciding what to do. More relevant here is the inescapable conclusion that it is only prudent to invest the much smaller amounts of public funds into research that will better define clean-up options and lessen the chances of recurrence.

If the subsurface is to be used as a repository for our wastes, we must have much more thorough understandings of the physical/chemical/biological system it presents. We must be able to predict the movement and fate of waste compounds with greater confidence than is now possible. Laboratory and field studies must examine migration of compounds and ions through subsurface strata, and we must develop new analytical techniques for detecting and

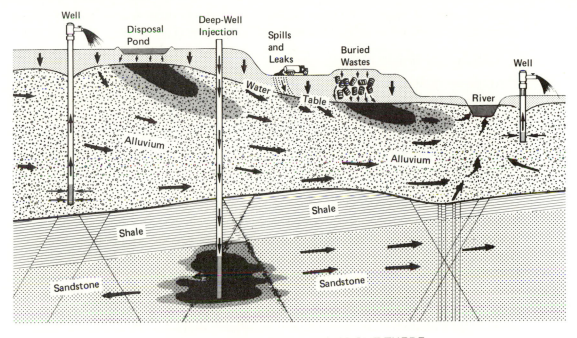

IT GOES IN HERE — BUT IT COMES OUT THERE

following the movement of polluted subsurface plumes (e.g., by measuring subsurface soil gases).

Groundwater quality can also be improved by developing better methods for treating wastewaters, including industrial wastewaters containing especially stable contaminants. Conventional wastewater treatment depends upon combinations of chemical and biological processes. While this is effective for some types of wastes, research is needed on advanced techniques, such as ozonization, "wet air oxidation" (high temperature and pressure aqueous oxidation), plasma and high temperature incineration, and adsorbents and resins for pollutant removal (including hybrid systems involving biological degradation).

Innovative methods for recapture and recycle of valuable substances, such as metals that would otherwise contribute to water pollution, are also needed. Solvent extraction, ion exchange, reverse osmosis, and other chemical separation processes deserve study. Mines pose special problems. Acid mine drainage and mobilization of radioactive mine tailings are subjects of continuing studies that should reduce adverse effects.

Agriculture has depended increasingly on pesticides to control disease and insects and to lower the cost of food production. An undesired result has been inadvertant contamination of water supplies in some areas. Assessment of the fate of pesticides and development of acceptable alternatives are important research objectives.

It seems clear that chemists, geologists, and environmental engineers will need to address many of these problems in water and waste treatment at increasing levels of activity to safeguard our water resources.

Radioactive Waste Management

At present, it is thought that the best place to store radioactive waste is underground. This means that an understanding of the fundamental geochemistry is required. We must be able to make reliable predictions concerning possible radionuclide migration through the media surrounding the repository. However, mathematical modeling of the transport process to calculate the capability of a given site to contain stored radionuclides requires knowledge in several key areas. These begin with the response of the geochemical system (groundwater chemistry and mineralogy, for example) to the repository environment (radiation and temperature effects). Next we must learn about the manner in which radionuclides are transported under repository and natural conditions (e.g., complexation by organic and inorganic ligands, and transport by colloids and particulates). Then, mechanisms for radionuclide retardation must be better understood. Among these are solubility behaviors of both fission products and transuranic elements (the physical chemistry of multivalent elements in near-neutral solution), sorption mechanisms, and the effects of long-term nonequilibrium water-rock interactions. Then, we must face the challenge of validating predictions for 10^5 years or so into the future, perhaps by comparison with observations from the geologic record, including those connected with the Oklo natural reactor sites. Finally, we should be looking into ways to cope with radioactive wastes other than underground storage in perpetuity. Perhaps fully recoverable, monitorable, temporary storage (either surface or underground) would give more well-defined risk control and, at the same time, be more practical. Again, a variety of chemical problems needing research arise here—the optimum chemical form of the stored radioactive elements, cladding, corrosion—but none seems to rule out this option in advance.

V-B.   Continued Economic Competitiveness

Introduction

The chemical industry is difficult to describe briefly. It encompasses inorganic and organic chemicals employed in industry, plastics, drugs and other biomedical products, rubber, fertilizers and pesticides, paints, soaps, cosmetics, adhesives, inks, explosives, and on and on. The value of U.S. chemical sales in recent years has been in the neighborhood of $175-180B annually, with a favorable balance of exports over imports of about $10-12B. Employment in U.S. chemical and allied product industries is more than a million, including more than 150,000 professional scientists and engineers. The numbers are as imprecise as the definitions of fields, but they are large and the effect on the economy is important. However, the narrow context of the foregoing numbers does not adequately indicate the pervasive presence and impact of chemistry in our society. Chemical products are in many cases supplied to other industries to be processed and resold with value added. Beyond this aspect, chemistry extends beyond the range of chemical products and materials. Chemical processes are abundant and growing in modern manufacturing sequences. Mechanical operations, such as cutting, bending, drilling, and riveting, are being replaced by processes such as etching, plating, polymerization, cross-linking, and sintering. For example, electronic microcircuits are produced through a sequence of perhaps a hundred chemical process steps. Finally, chemistry is the science on which our ability to understand and manipulate living systems is based. Heredity is now understood in terms of the chemical structure of genetic material. Disease and treatment are chemical processes. Every medicine that a doctor prescribes is a chemical compound whose effectiveness depends upon the chemical reactions it stimulates or controls.

The business climate of the chemical industry is complex and changing. The U.S. situation is particularly difficult owing to the confluence of many diverse factors that are unique or more advanced than in other countries. Antitrust law and enforcement in the United States strongly discourages cooperative actions on the part of U.S. corporations. This results in competition between individual U.S. companies and consortia of foreign corporations and governments. Governmental policies in regard to industries based on science are frequently more favorable abroad than in the United States. No easy solution is in sight.

International competition in the petrochemical arena is becoming severe as nations controlling cheap and abundant feedstocks establish their own manufacturing complexes to refine crude oil and produce polymers and other products higher on the value scale. It is probably too early to measure the impact of this movement, but large-volume producers in developed nations are wary. It seems probable that the threat will be concentrated in commodities (e.g., ethylene glycol, polyethylene) with the largest established markets. It remains to be seen in which markets producers in less developed countries can effectively compete, lacking, as yet, a strong base in marketing and research.

The chemical industry is also confronted with an active and growing public concern for health and safety as these relate to exposure to chemicals. The movement is most advanced in the United States where diverse responses range from sensible prudence to unreasoning panic. It manifests itself economically in increasing costs for environmental maintenance and worker safety, for proving safety and effectiveness of new products, and for protection against product liability. The soundness of individual concerns aside, it can be seen that the cost to the competitiveness of the U.S. chemical industry has been enormous, the more so in view of the fact that comparable industries abroad have not yet felt the full impact of these pressures of public concern.

Thus it is not surprising that the profitability of chemical companies in the United States has become a cause for national concern. The uniquely advanced standard of living in the United States owes a great deal to innovations and productivity of the nation's chemical businesses. Preservation of this quality of life requires that the United States remain a strong and leading competitor in chemistry and other technologies. A key issue responsible for past success has been the strength of U.S. university research and the effective employment of its productivity. Vigorous support of this academic research community is a critical first requirement for maintaining the competitive position of the U.S. chemical industry.

Past Successes and Recent Trends

The history of chemistry over the last century is filled with examples of research advances that led to new products and concepts. A hundred years ago, dyestuff chemistry was active. The petrochemical industry was small in 1940, but it is immense today, and polymer innovations run in parallel. New pharmaceutical products have grown vigorously on the basis of highly sophisticated synthetic chemistry. Recent studies, however, have led to the conclusion that the pace of innovation in commodity and industrial chemicals is diminishing, and the power of these parts of the industry to sustain their growth is in question. Classification and analysis of innovations indicate that chemical product and process advances have fallen off alarmingly over the past 10 years. The trend permits some observers to portray chemistry as a mature field that has exhausted its opportunities to replace natural materials with superior synthetic materials. These are sobering thoughts both for the industry and, more seriously, for the nation itself.

Another analysis is possible, however. The time scale of the recently perceived decline is short, and projections are risky. The only prediction that is easily made is that changes are inevitable. New products are sure to enter the marketplace. Will a significant fraction of them be ours? New processes are certain to be needed as people worldwide move to new feedstocks and new energy sources. In this country, we are learning to accommodate to pressures for increased attention to health and environmental impacts—pressures that are just beginning to be felt by foreign competitors. This is not a time to assume that we should be resigned to paying royalties abroad and to surrendering our positive balance of trade in chemicals. Innovations take years to develop, and we should be looking to our future in a time when the field of chemistry is changing and international competition is keen. Our future lies in the health of our research effort in chemistry. It must be maintained and strengthened.

Energy and Feedstocks

Energy and chemical feedstocks are intrinsically tied together through their overwhelming dependence on petroleum. Energy uses account for most of the consumption of organic materials. Burning of petroleum goes on at an ever-increasing pace, and the future crisis of supply is directly related to this fact. Throughout much of the world, people have come to take petroleum-derived heat and transportation for granted. Thus the inevitable depletion of the earth's petroleum resources will strongly affect the style and standard of living of people everywhere. The effects of depletion should become evident within two decades and become severe within four decades. Hubbert estimated in 1970 that 80 percent of the world's ultimate

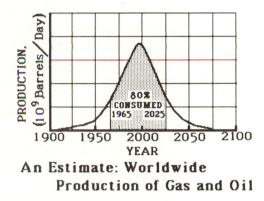

An Estimate: Worldwide Production of Gas and Oil

production of oil and gas will be consumed between 1965 and 2025. The estimate seems to be receiving confirmation in current discovery and consumption rates, but its alarming implications are clearly not grasped by the public.

Petrochemical uses of petroleum account for only a few percent of the total—3 to 5 percent by most estimates. Thus the chemical industry is not the cause of the approaching era of depletion, but the effects will be felt within the industry as feedstocks and processes change. The effects on feedstocks will probably be less dramatic than the reductions in energy uses. Petrochemical uses are characterized by higher value added, and they can withstand the coming price increases brought on by depletion better than uses involving combustion. Further, processes are already known for the conversion of coal to suitable forms for use as feedstocks, and coal deposits are more abundant. Therefore, it is expected that the repercussions of petroleum depletion in chemical feedstocks will be much less important than in energy production.

Renewing Our Industries

International competition is a general problem for U.S. industry and is generally recognized as such. Steel, automobiles, communications, textiles, and machine tools are examples of industries that have had significant problems. It is instructive to consider the response to these pressures in the specific case of automobiles to illustrate the central role of chemistry in maintaining and improving the U.S. position.

The U.S. automobile industry evolved into a gigantic business during the first half of this century. In the 1950s and 1960s American products took on a character that enjoyed excellent success. The vehicles were large, heavy, and powerful. Fuel was abundant and inexpensive, so, with little incentive to conserve, fuel economy was not an important consideration. The cars were built for the American market and few were exported. Similarly, few foreign-built cars made their way to North America. By the mid-1960s, however, Volkswagon had become a significant supplier to the U.S. market with sales of more than half a million small economy cars per year. During the 1970s the market was further invaded by cars of Japanese manufacture. Pursuing an aggressive policy of collecting design, technology, engineering, and assembly information, much of it from the United States, the Japanese developed the most automated and efficient car building facilities in the world. These facilities, and a commitment to quality, produced the world's most fuel-efficient and least expensive cars.

At the same time, legislation was passed in the United States that specified mandatory fuel economy objectives and placed strict limits on air pollution from automobile emissions. The American car was required to change dramatically, and the investment required by the manufacturers was high, approximately $80B. The objectives are being achieved through a variety of developments, every one involving chemistry: new and lighter materials, better combustion control and engine efficiency, catalytic exhaust treatment, reduced corrosion, smaller size, transmission improvements, etc.

Polymers, aluminum, and high-strength alloy steels are employed for weight reduction. New chemicals for oil additives and improved rubber formulations for underhood tube and hose applications are solving problems of engine compartment temperature brought on by aerodynamic designs featuring sloping hoods. The riding comfort of the smaller cars is being improved through the use of vibration damping butyl rubber. Tire tread compounds are being reformulated to reduce rolling resistance. New, high-solid, solvent-based paints are being developed to reduce air pollution. Chemically based rust proofing systems are being introduced to prolong life. Contemporary U.S. cars contain more than 500 pounds of plastics, rubbers, fluids, coatings, sealants, and lubricants, all products of the chemical industry.

Further inroads of plastic materials can be expected as research leads to the process innovations that are needed. Reaction injection molding is a recently introduced process for making large parts like fenders and hoods. High-performance composites, i.e., stiff fibers in a polymer matrix, have already appeared as drive shafts and leaf springs. Some advanced models have frames and bodies made of composites. Long cycle times caused by slow cure of the matrix resins is an economic limitation that is receiving research attention. In this connection, it should be noted that new designs for light aircraft (i.e., general aviation) have airframes that are almost entirely composites. For automobiles, the use of composites may lead to new design-fabrication methods that will greatly reduce the number of parts to be assembled. Chemistry lies at the root of all of these advances.

Clearly the problems faced by the American automobile industry are complex mixtures of historical preferences, social pressure, legislation, and vigorous outside competition. Chemistry is an essential technology in any successful response to these pressures.

New Horizons

The chemical industry is changing, and chemical science is becoming importantly interwined with other areas of science and technology. To an increasing degree chemists must be adept at dealing with subjects and practitioners of allied technologies. Chemistry is critical in providing materials and processes for American industries, meeting their needs across the spectrum from mature industries (new electrode materials for aluminum production, low-cost sweeteners for the food industry, etc.) to rapidly growing, high-technology areas (high-performance composites for aircraft, improved ceramics for electroncs and engines, protein pharmaceuticals, etc.). Each of these areas requires development of chemical products that respond to markets outside of chemistry, as in the representative examples given below.

Biotechnology

Biotechnology is not new. The ancients knew how to bake and brew thousand of years ago. The processes of fermentation, separation, and purification have long been familiar. Until recent years the field might have been labeled applied microbiology. As the molecular structure and basic chemistry of genetic material became known, a new era of biotechnology opened up. It led to gene-splicing procedures that enabled biochemists to cause bacteria to produce complex molecules that exhibit important biological activity. Enzymes have been found that will break chemical bonds in DNA chains at specific points and allow foreign DNA to be inserted with new chemical bonds. The altered DNA then produces proteins according to its revised code. The protein products can be hormones, antibodies, or other complex chemical compounds with specific properties and functions. Interferon, produced by bacteria with a human gene spliced in place, is expected to be valuable in treating a variety of diseases. Human insulin is already being marketed. Activity is intense, and commercial enterprises are emerging rapidly.

The area of biotechnology is an exciting and exuberant realm for scientists, engineers, and investors. Although some of the expectations appear to be extravagant, there can be no doubt that this is an area that will see many important economic developments in the coming decades. The United States is at present the world leader, with basic chemical and molecular biological research feeding an effective commercial community. Europe, with strong, relevant research, and Japan, with a leading position in fermentation processes, can be expected to challenge the U.S. position. The advances that will determine the future of the field will accrue through the practice of pure chemistry at its most sophisticated reach. Increasingly, progress depends upon a deep understanding of biology at the molecular level. Basic research on the molecular structure and chemistry of biological molecules will be a crucial ingredient as we try to maintain our current leadership position in biotechnology.

High-Technology Ceramics

Ceramics are materials with high temperature stability and hardness; they tend to be brittle, and they are difficult to shape. Ceramics are now of major commercial interest for components of electrical devices, engines, tools, and a wide range of other applications in which hardness, stiffness, and stability at high temperatures are essential. Major advances in their use can be anticipated because of new chemical compositions and novel fabrication techniques.

For many, many centuries, ceramic pieces have been made from a slurry or paste of a finely ground natural mineral. The slurry is formed or cast in the desired shape and then "fired," i.e., heated to a temperature high enough to burn away the added slurry components and to melt and join the mineral particles where they touch. The strength of the final object is critically limited by small imperfections.

A number of new chemical techniques are now being developed to synthesize ceramic precursors and to produce final products more free of defects. These techniques depend upon control of reaction kinetics and tailoring of molecular properties. Thus controlled hydrolysis of organometallic compounds is used to generate highly uniform ceramic particles ("sol-gel technology"). Organometallic polymers can be spun into fibers and pyrolyzed to produce important materials like silicon carbide. Reaction of volatile chemical precursors at high temperature in the vapor phase, followed by controlled deposition of the reaction products, can give highly uniform temperature-resistant coatings to preshaped objects. Addition of suitable impurities ("doping agents") can change properties dramatically. For example, alumina ceramics can be significantly toughened by addition of zirconia.

The production of ceramics has a major economic role that will surely grow as new materials are discovered and developed. Chemical advances will be essential to this growth by providing new precursors and more controlled production techniques. The potentialities have been recognized abroad, where major research programs on ceramics have been launched (particularly in Japan). To remain competitive, U.S. research efforts must be strengthened.

Advanced Composites and Engineering Plastics

The discovery of ultrahigh-strength fibers based upon graphite embedded in a matrix of organic polymer has led to development of a new class of materials now referred to as "advanced composites." A fiber, such as a graphitic carbon chain, a mineral fiber, or an extended hydrocarbon polymer, is suspended in a conventional high-polymer matrix, such as epoxy. The resulting composite can exhibit tensile strength comparable to that of structural steel but at a much lower density. Because of this high strength-to-weight ratio, such composites are finding abundant applications in the aerospace industry. Significant weight reductions are achieved in commercial and military aircraft that use airframes and other aircraft components made of composites. Other applications include space hardware, sporting goods, automotive components (e.g., drive shafts and leaf springs), and boat hulls.

There has also been a rapid development in tailoring polymer mixtures to obtain particular properties or behavior. Success with these polymer "alloys" or "blends" has required a high degree of chemical understanding of the molecular interactions at phase boundaries between two polymers that are not mutually soluble. An example is the commercial polymer blend called Zytel Y.T.®, a thermoplastic nylon toughened with a hydrocarbon elastomer. The development of this high-performance plastic was based upon extensive studies of interactions at interfaces between different polymers.

Plastics are also being developed for high temperature applications, such as engine blocks for automobiles. A prototype "plastic engine" based on reinforced polyamide and polyimide resins has been demonstrated in a competitive racing car. An engine-weight reduction of 200 pounds can be achieved, with obvious benefit to fuel economy.

These technologies are moving forward rapidly around the world. Carbon fiber production is currently dominated by Japan, while the United States leads in high-strength polymeric fibers. Research will figure importantly in the evolution of such leaderships. New rapid-curing matrix materials are needed. The nature of the bonding region between the fiber and its composite matrix environment is an important factor in structural performance but poorly understood chemically. These and other fundamental questions remain to be investigated. Other countries have initiated strong programs to address these questions: Japan has identified composite materials as a thrust area; Germany has established a new Max Planck Institute in this field; other countries are actively pursuing the opportunities. While U.S. industrial laboratories have recorded some gratifying commercial successes, our basic research activity must be more strongly encouraged and stimulated to ensure continued U.S. competitiveness on the world scene.

Photoimaging

The purpose of photography is to produce an accurate and lasting record of the image of an object or a scene. With a history of 150 years, the silver halide process has evolved from complex procedures conducted by specialists with a working knowledge of photochemistry into a pastime through which untrained individuals can produce likenesses of outstanding clarity and accuracy. The individual presides over remarkable feats of optics and chemistry to produce these pictures on the spot, usually without having the faintest appreciation of what goes on in the camera or on the film. The result brings pleasure and useful pictorial images to people throughout the world.

The chemistry of the photographic process can be usefully divided into the inorganic photochemistry of the silver halide and the organic chemistry of sensitization, development, and dye formation. When radiation strikes a microcrystal of a silver halide, a latent image is formed that is believed to consist of a few atoms of metallic silver. The metallic silver functions as a catalyst for the reduction of the entire grain under the chemical action of a reducing agent, the developer. The silver halide grains in a photographic film are typically of the order of a micrometer in size, and control of the size and shape of the particles is important. Although silver halides are sensitive only to light at the blue end of the spectrum, the grains can be activated at longer wavelengths with sensitizing dyes absorbed on the crystal surface. These molecules are coated onto the silver halide surface in layers less than one-thousandth-of-a-millimeter thick. Color is achieved when the oxidized form of the developer reacts with a color coupler to give a dye of the required hue. By combining the 3 color primaries, 11 colors can be achieved. Conventional color photography involves several carefully controlled chemical processes, including development, bleaching, fixing, and washing.

In color instant photography these steps must be combined in a single planar unit, which can be processed in the light without temperature control. A typical instant film contains over a dozen separate layers with thicknesses of the order of 1 micrometer each. Physical chemical factors, such as solubility and diffusion, are critical as are the chemical reactions occurring in the various layers during processing. The sophistication of the chemistry of instant color photography is difficult to comprehend and presents a striking contrast with the simplicity of operations required of the user.

In this important area of our economy, new technological achievements continue to appear, ranging from amateur photography to such demanding and esoteric uses as photoresists for semiconductor production (see below) and infrared mapping of the earth's resources from satellites. Competition from abroad is strong, particularly in the mass market area. The United States has been the world leader in photographic technology for many years in an industry where the connection with our traditional research strength in photochemistry is clear. We must keep it so.

Microelectronic Devices

The microelectronics revolution has already had an enormous impact on the industrialized world, and it is clear that there is a great deal more to come. The best known device is the microprocessor, a remarkably intricate and functionally integrated electrical circuit built on a tiny silicon "chip." Some microprocessors and the latest high-capacity computer memory chips contain hundreds of thousands of individual transistors or other solid state components squeezed onto a piece of silicon about one-quarter-of-an-inch square.

These "chips" are currently made from highly purified, elemental silicon containing impurities deliberately implanted in specific locales to form individual devices with desired electronic functions: amplification, rectification, switching, storage of on-off logic information, etc. These minute devices are then interconnected by metal "wires" on a microscopic scale. All this is clearly inorganic chemistry; there is no organic material present finally other than an organic polymer coating for protection against deterioration. However, an important point not generally realized is that the fabrication of these exquisitely complex devices depends critically on thin (less than 1 micron thick) organic films of radiation sensitive polymers whose technology involves organic chemistry, photochemistry, and polymer chemistry.

The purpose of the films is to permit selective doping in the pattern of a desired electrical circuit. Because steps in the process involve high temperature, a thin layer of silicon dioxide is used as the masking layer that determines whether or not the underlying silicon is acceptable for doping. Organic materials called photoresists are used to form the primary pattern that is transferred into the silicon dioxide layer.

In photolithography, chemical changes in the photoresist material are initiated by exposure to light. In these changes, covalent chemical bonds are ruptured (or formed) through light-sensitive functional groups attached to the polymer structure. The chemical bond changes result in a local increase (or decrease) of the photoresist solubility in a suitable solvent. Thus after exposure through a mask, an image of the mask can be developed merely by washing in the solvent. What is not generally appreciated is that this solubility is achieved through carefully designed polymer photochemistry.

Existing organic photore-

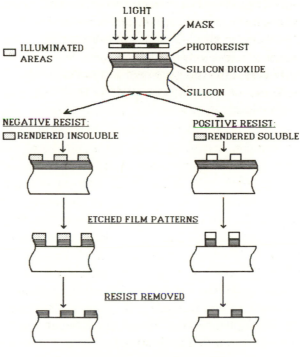

KEY STEPS IN THE FABRICATION OF SILICON INTEGRATED CIRCUITS USING PHOTORESISTS

sists could achieve the spatial resolution that wasconsidered adequate up to the early 1970s when individual integrated circuit feature sizes were in the range of 3 to 10 microns. However, the inexorable desire for continued increase in device density has demanded ever smaller features. A decade ago it became apparent that new photoresists would be needed because existing materials were not capable of defining the feature sizes (1 to 2 microns) soon to be required. The development of these materials has been made possible by research advances in polymer chemistry, photochemistry, and radiation chemistry. Because these feature sizes are close to the wavelength of light used for conventional optical imaging (.4 microns), diffraction effects caused by the features on the mask (a mask is analogous to a photographic negative) become important. These effects can be reduced by using shorter wavelength radiation. There has been extensive development of resist materials that are chemically sensitive to exposure with electron beams, X-rays, and short-wavelength ultraviolet light instead of the near ultraviolet light now used.

Masks are made by chemically etching thin chromium films deposited on glass, using a resist that is patterned by exposure to a computer-controlled electron beam. The development of the organic resist material used for defining the metal pattern rests on relatively recent research in both polymer chemistry and radiation chemistry. Many new types of chemical reactions are involved, and the advances in integrated circuit complexity could not have occurred if these new materials had not been available. Virtually none of them existed in 1970. Examples of new electron-beam resists are the copolymers of various alkenes and sulfur dioxide whose synthesis and radiation sensitivity were discovered in fundamental studies over the last two decades.

Because optical technology is both well established and the simplest type to implement, it is receiving strong support. New high-resolution photosensitive organic materials are under development in the United States, Japan, and Europe. Researchers have taken advantage of such diverse photochemistry as that of ortho-nitrobenzyl and other photochemically removable protective groups that were designed for protein and natural product synthesis. There has also been some success in using theoretical organic chemistry in the design of materials with specific optical absorption band changes.

A current trend in semiconductor fabrication is to use reactive gas plasmas instead of liquid solutions to etch the substrate under the photoresist mask. Most organic materials are not sufficiently resistant to these vigorous conditions, and it has taken much research to provide a few useful materials. It is difficult to design materials having the necessary combination of physical and chemical properties. Their development will draw on continued research advances in polymer chemistry and photochemistry, including laser-induced chemistry. Progress in the relevant areas of chemistry will be one of the important factors if we are to retain competitive advantage in this rapidly moving and economically critical technology.

Analytical Instrumentation

The greatly increased demand for analyses in important applications, such as industrial processes, the environment, and health, has pushed worldwide sales of analytical instruments from $300M to $3B per year in the last decade. U.S. manufacturers have dominated this market, with a currently favorable trade balance of nearly $1B. Instrument obsolesence times are commonly 6 years or fewer, placing great emphasis on innovative research and new applications.

While innovations are coming from physics, electronics, computer sciences, and biology, chemistry remains central to continued leadership in this area. To cite two examples, U.S. chemists have been at the forefront of exciting new developments using lasers and computers. As described elsewhere in this report, laser excitation can provide specific, sensitive data on elements and molecules and their environments, with the variety of new methods increasing on an almost daily basis. Dedicated computers are taking over more and more of the task of operating complex instruments, handling their high data rates, and even producing final reports.

Like the increasing pervasiveness of the computer in modern society, the development of analytical instruments of improved accuracy, speed, and specificity at lower prices will certainly lead to new applications, such as those in automated industries, preventative medicine, and environmental warning systems, as well as greatly improved research efficiency. Retaining and increasing U.S. leadership in analytical instrumentation should thus bring benefits far beyond an attractive balance of trade.

Molecular-Scale Computers

Miniaturization of electrical devices has been one of the most significant factors in the rapid advances that have made modern computers possible. Circuit elements in present silicon chips have dimensions near 1 micrometer, i.e., in the range of 10,000 Å. However, it may be that fabrication of microscopic devices based upon silicon and other semiconductor methods is beginning to push against natural barriers that will limit continued movement toward increasingly compact devices. Thereafter, breakthroughs will be needed. Where will we turn when existing technologies are blocked by intrinsic natural limits? Irresistibly, we must contemplate molecular circuit elements that will permit us to move well inside the 10,000 Å limit. We are led to picture computer devices on the molecular scale.

As is normal, adventurous concepts generate exciting, often emotional controversy. Advocates tend to be glowingly enthusiastic, in both expectations and claims. At the other extreme, there can be outright disdain from those dedicated to currently successful and still advancing technologies that would be made obsolete by the new directions. However, the arguments of even the most sophisticated detractors are disarmed (contradicted?) by the fact that this intelligent opposition is being generated in a working computer using exactly the structure under challenge, the human brain! In an age of machine synthesis of DNA segments and laboratory design of artificial enzymes, it would be excessively timid to say that we can neither learn nor mimic the elegant circuits that each of us depends upon to read and consider these printed words.

In a three-dimensional architecture, use of molecular circuit elements with 100 Å spacing would provide packing a million times more dense than any now achievable. The materials under discussion range from entirely synthetic electrically conducting polymers to natural proteins. Molecular switches, the basic memory elements of the proposed computer, might be based upon double bond movement in polyacetylene, photochromism, or molecular orientation in solids. Ideas about connecting the molecular elements to external devices are still vague.

There are those who dismiss as far-fetched the idea of man-made molecular scale computers. Only a few decades ago, however, these same individuals might have classified as science fiction a proposal that someday there would be a man on the Moon, that fertility could be controlled by taking a pill, or that we could learn the structure of DNA. But since we know that molecular computers are routine accessories in all animals from ants to zebras, it would be prudent to change the question from *whether* there will be man-made counterparts to questions concerning *when* they will come into existence and *who* will be leading in their development. The *when* question will be answered on the basis of fundamental research in chemistry; the *who* question will depend on which countries commit the required resources and creativity to the search. The United States will want to be in the forefront, and we must be sufficiently bold to support the fundamental research programs that will move us toward this goal.

Conclusion

The field of chemistry in the United States has great industrial and economic importance. The consistent and significant positive balance of payments, even in the era of an over-strong dollar, is an indication of intrinsic strength. The continuing flow of innovations that benefit society is encouraging. U.S. universities are the best in the world, and year by year they draw students from throughout the world for graduate study. In each of these aspects, the United States leads the world.

Even so, there are abundant challenges to the chemical strength of the United States from Europe, from Japan, and from some of the less-developed countries. The United States must work hard and creatively to maintain its leadership in view of unfavorable antitrust regulation, environmental restrictions, health and safety requirements, wage rates, and currency leverage, all of which make the competitive position of U.S. chemical products difficult to retain. Answers lie in objective justification of any restraints imposed by legislation, with balanced concern for the important social values represented in current regulations. And we must continue to stimulate the academic and industrial research that maintains the knowledge base from which we derive our competitive edge. To this end, efforts must be made to attract an adequate share of the finest young minds to the field of chemistry. Support for university research in chemistry must be enhanced to produce the best-equipped laboratories in the world and retain the most gifted faculties. Only a sustained and vigorous approach will be effective in maintaining our position in the essential field of chemistry, so necessary to any high-technology society.

V-C.   Increased National Security

The nation's security depends upon its people being well and healthy, having an adequate food supply, and living in a safe environment. It depends upon there being an ample, assured supply of appropriate energy sources for transportation, production, and communication. Still another requirement is an adequate domestic store of critical materials, as well as alternative materials for the most important applications and for those materials whose supply is most vulnerable to interruption or termination. Maintaining national security requires not only that health, food, environment, energy, and materials be adequate today, but also that we can ensure that they will still be adequate for future generations and changed geo-political circumstances. This requires, and indeed is critically dependent upon, basic chemical research. Other sections of this report document the ways in which meeting these basic needs will depend upon advances in chemical research.

The nation's security also depends upon having a strong, healthy economy that leads to full employment, a desirable standard of living, domestic well-being, and productive flexibility. Here also, as illustrated in the preceding section of this report, it is clear that the contribution of chemical research to industrial productivity has a large influence on national employment and upon the nation's position in international trade. A stable, secure economy is one that can compete internationally and whose strength is not critically dependent upon events outside the nation's control.

Finally and ultimately, national security depends upon the ability of the nation to defend itself and to deter and prevent armed conflict. In these areas, chemistry, "the central science," again plays a critical part.

Strategic and Critical Materials

As noted in Section III-C, a "material" is a chemical substance out of which useful things are made—including things like armor plate, jet engine turbine blades, spacecraft heat shields, air frames, submarine hulls, flak-jackets, and infrared detectors. When an application has crucial importance to our national defense, the requisite material is called a *strategic* material. When an application has crucial importance to our industrial strength, the requisite material is called a *critical* material. An important element of our national security is connected with identifying those strategic and critical materials whose availability might be limited or cut off by political developments abroad. Fundamental research areas that lead to new and alternative materials add to our options in the event of such cut-off—they furnish appropriate places for defense investment.

By the same token, the possibilities for new defensive systems and weapons depend to a great extent on the invention and development of new materials with which to make them. Advanced weapons need materials that are lighter, stronger, tougher, and cheaper than presently available. The pursuit of new materials and the study of chemistry are inextricably linked through the need to understand material behavior at the molecular level and the need to synthesize new chemical compounds. Efficient processing of new materials requires development of on-line chemical analytical techniques.

New ways of controlling surface, solid state, and polymer chemistry will play a lead role in developing materials of superior hardness, shatter resistance, weight, flow properties, corrosion protection, and wear resistance, for use in non-nuclear and nuclear defense systems and weapons. These materials may be alloys, polymers, ceramics, or fiber-reinforced composites. Fundamental advances in understanding the structure, bonding, and chemical reactivity at surfaces should also result in the development of improved coatings for antiradar, reduced drag, and resistance to intense laser radiation.

There are four areas of chemistry that will make particularly significant contributions in the development of new materials and of new pathways to existing materials.

Surface Chemistry

Innovative applications of surface chemistry and integration with mutually supportive advances in other aspects of surface science are needed for corrosion protection, coating adhesion, welding and joining, hardness, and wear resistance—all of which contribute to and determine the effectiveness, cost, and useful life of weapons systems. Inhibiting corrosion alone is a major expense of military hardware. Enhanced understanding of interfacial chemistry will also facilitate better coatings, such as antiradar (stealth) coatings for aircraft, missiles, satellites, reentry vehicles, and ships; antisonar coatings for ships and submarines; reduced-drag coatings for attack submarines; enhanced reflectivity coatings for high-power-laser mirrors, and many others. The development of high-performance, fiber-reinforced composites of metals, ceramics, or polymers depends on a better understanding of the surface chemistry at the fiber/matrix interface.

Synthesis and Properties of New Solid State Materials

An important part of future defense strategy is superior electronic warfare, consisting of command, control, communications, intelligence, and electronic countermeasures. Advances in this area depend upon development of new nonlinear optic, electro-optic, and electronic materials. For example, we need ultrafast electronics that are intrinsically resistant to damage by X-rays, gamma rays, neutrons, and particle beams. We also need high-power-laser frequency multipliers, infrared and ultraviolet electro-optic materials, and nonlinear optical absorbers to protect against laser beams. Advances in these areas will come through research into the optical, electronic, and crystal structure of new chemical compounds. Such research permits us to design substances with desired macroscopic properties, and it provides the synthetic techniques needed to make those substances.

Modern weapons and weapon concepts depend increasingly upon the use of polymers and polymer composites as materials to meet stringent physical requirements of weight, density, and strength. Development of these new polymers is the task of the polymer chemist working with other polymer scientists. As described in Section III-C, new polymers have potential for applications ranging from structural materials that compete with steel to novel electronic materials that may be our future semiconductors.

Long-term storage of nuclear weapons adds to the demands for new materials. Crucial to stockpile lifetime and reliability are the questions of how, why, and when materials age and deteriorate, including underexposure to radioactivity. Because composite materials are of increasing importance, this knowledge must include basic understanding of the chemistry at the component interfaces within a composite and how that chemistry is affected by prolonged degradation in hostile environments.

Catalysis

The development of more specific, faster, more uniform catalysts will radically change the cost and availability of advanced chemicals and materials. For example, the study of catalysts has led to new techniques of polymer synthesis that have allowed new polymers to be developed and made advanced polymer alloys available for modern weapons. In addition to offering the possibility of new and better materials, highly specific catalysts can also reduce the cost of militarily important chemicals and thus make them available for practical use (see Sections VII-A, III-B, and V-D).

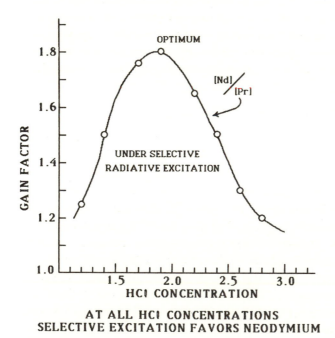

AT ALL HCl CONCENTRATIONS SELECTIVE EXCITATION FAVORS NEODYMIUM

Separations Chemistry

Separations chemistry is the application of chemical principles, properties, and techniques to the separation of specific elements and compounds from extraneous materials (including mineral ores) and from each other. It has applications in such diverse areas as the nuclear fuel cycle, analytical chemistry, and biochemistry. It capitalizes on the differences in such properties as solubility, volatility, adsorbability, extractability, stereochemistry, and ion properties of elements and molecules. As an exam-

TABLE V-1 Essential Defense Uses of Some Materials

System	Material[a]									
	Be	Carbon Fiber	Cr	Co	Ge	Mn	Pt	Quartz	Ta	Ti
Satellites	X	X	X	X		X		X	X	X
Aircraft	X	X	X	X		X				X
Engines			X	X		X			X	X
Helicopters		X	X	X	X	X				X
Missiles	X	X	X	X	X	X		X	X	X
Tanks			X	X	X	X		X	X	X
Artillery			X	X		X				
Ammunition			X			X				X
Ships			X	X		X				
Submarines	X		X	X		X			X	
Mines			X	X		X			X	
Electronics	X		X	X		X	X	X	X	
Support industries			X	X		X	X			X

[a] Be—Beryllium   Mn—Manganese
Cr—Chromium   Pt—Platinum
Co—Cobalt   Ta—Tantalum
Ge—Germanium   Ti—Titanium

ple, the rare earth elements neodymium (Nd) and praeseodymium (Pr), important in laser manufacture, must be separated from the mineral monazite. A difficult part of this extraction is the separation from chemically similar cerium. Photochemical studies show that this separation can be enhanced manyfold by selective excitation that exploits the different chemistries of the elements under excitation with light.

Many vital materials result from application of separations chemistry. They range from biochemicals separated from living organisms to the chromium needed to produce the stainless steels used in defense, medical, and industrial products. They include catalysts, pigments for protective coatings, fertilizers, and materials used to produce energy and to facilitate communication and transportation.

The availability of critical and strategic materials to U.S. industry and the military is dependent in many instances on the development of practical, economical chemical separations methods. Table V-1 illustrates the essential defense uses of some materials, all but two of which are imported. Table V-2 adds quantitative data on U.S. dependence on imports for some critical metals and minerals. Future availability of such elements as chromium, the platinum group elements, and others may depend critically upon developing chemical separations pro-

TABLE V-2 U.S. Import Dependence, Selected Elements (Imports as Percent of Apparent Consumption)

	1950	1980
Manganese	77	97
Aluminum (bauxite)	71	94
Cobalt	92	93
Chromium	100	91
Platinum	91	87
Nickel	99	73
Zinc	37	58
Tungsten	80	54
Iron (ore)	5	22
Copper	35	14
Lead	59	<10

cesses for chemical mining or for their extraction from low-grade but indigenous ores or geothermal brines. In those cases where substitutes based upon more abundant elements can be found for the critical materials, chemical separations processes will be needed for increased economical recovery of many of the substitutes.

Historically, high-technology defense materials that have come from defense research of the types described above have quickly moved into the private sector to yield additional positive economic and social benefits.

Surveillance and Intelligence

Many important applications of chemical procedures relate to the prevention or early warning of armed conflict. Examples include sensor development to identify rocket plumes or high-explosive phenomena; the use of neutron and gamma emission data, instrumentation, and techniques for safeguard surveillance to ensure the nonproliferation and control of nuclear materials; the analysis of radioactive debris from nuclear events; and the development of methods for identification of specific trace chemicals resulting from various potentially military-related chemical processes. These technologies clearly have implications in surveillance and treaty verification, and the resulting analytical and modeling efforts greatly affect our defensive posture in the prevention of armed conflict.

Past efforts in these areas have brought about substantial advances in defense capabilities, as well as an appreciation for the capabilities of other nations. For example, much of what we now know about advanced foreign nuclear weapons technology comes from gas and particle analysis, remote from the scene of use, coupled with appropriate modeling. More detailed knowledge of actinide and fission product behavior than we currently have is required if we are to be ready for probable future developments.

Many of the techniques developed for nuclear surveillence (and for defense against chemical and biological warfare) are also used to detect and counter potential terrorist activities. However, the remote detection of explosives remains a difficult problem and is the subject of current and future research into the development of appropriate noninvasive trace chemical analyses.

Case History: Theoretical Chemistry and Rocket Surveillance

Of concern to all Americans is defense against intercontinental ballistic missile attack. Early warning and activation of a defense system is crucial. Much of the current defense approach is based upon detection of a missile plume's characteristic emission of light, termed its signature. The signature identifies the origin of the rocket and provides a mechanism for an antimissile device to key onto the intruding missile and destroy it.

The radiation from the rocket plume is responsible for the plume signature. This radiation is characteristic of the fuel components used to propel the rocket and is partially caused by collisions among molecules produced in fuel combustion and the components of the upper atmosphere. Such collisions cause plume molecules, such as H_2O and CO_2, to be excited into higher-lying energy states, which subsequently emit radiation.

One must know the details of this radiation to design detection devices, and the details require a knowledge of the probabilities that collisions among plume and atmospheric compounds will cause excitation. In this example, the requisite information was not available from experiment. As an alternative, ab initio quantum chemistry and molecular dynamics methods were used to obtain the required information. Potential energy surfaces that govern the collision of $O(^3P)$ atoms, the principal component of the upper atmosphere, with H_2O and CO_2 molecules were calculated using highly accurate, many-body methods. Employing these surfaces, quasi-classical dynamics methods were used to obtain the excitation probabilities. The results served as an essential input to the detector design.

Similar theoretical approaches have been used to calculate the radiation signature resulting from nuclear explosives.

Nuclear Power and Nuclear Weapons

Since their participation in the discoveries of nuclear fission and of the first transuranium elements, nuclear chemists have played indispensable roles in the nuclear energy program in this country. This has been equally true in both the military and civilian applications of nuclear energy. The technological requirements of these programs are often so closely related to fundamental research that it becomes difficult to separate the two.

A prime example of close relationship between applied and basic research is found in the chemistry of the transuranium elements. The chemical properties of these elements were first established by following their radiations when the elements were available only in unweighably small quantities. A cadre of skilled chemists were able to apply their fundamental knowledge of chemistry to synthesize and separate the new element plutonium. They were also able to extend our knowledge and synthesize a whole new region of the Periodic Table—that of the transuranium nuclides. The methods devised for the original, large-scale processes to separate plutonium from irradiated uranium fuel, based on the knowledge of actinide and fission product chemistry at that time, are still in use. A present concern in the United States should be to maintain and extend our knowledge of fundamental actinide and radiochemistry; many experts are nearing retirement, and replacements are not being generated at the universities because of the interdisciplinary nature of the field, the expense of adequate training, and, in part, public attitudes toward uses of nuclear energy. Yet, a new generation of such experts will surely be needed, no matter what future course is followed regarding manufacture or disposal of nuclear weaponry or use of nuclear power. We must still be able to deal effectively with the radioactive materials and wastes already in existence.

Nuclear Reactors

Nuclear reactors play a part in national defense in the production of electrical power, in the production of plutonium and tritium, and in propulsion, especially of submarines. The design and operation of nuclear reactors are primarily the province of reactor physicists and engineers, but scores of problems encountered in reactor construction and operation call for the skills of the nuclear chemist. Monitoring the purity of materials needed for construction depends upon chemical analytical techniques. Detailed understanding of the neutron economy in a reactor requires nuclear chemists to establish rates of plutonium production and destruction, efficiency of use of the fissionable material, and breeding capabilities. In the design of new types of reactors, extensive studies of the nuclear reaction and disintegration probabilities of individual isotopes of the heavy elements are often crucial. These studies are carried out usually to obtain fundamental data on the stability and reactivity of nuclei.

Tritium Production

Tritium is also required for nuclear weapons, not only for development of new weapons, but for maintenance of existing weapons. Because of its relatively short half-life of only 12 years, it cannot be stockpiled and must be continually produced in fission reactors via the reaction of thermal neutrons with lithium-6. New production, extraction, and purification technologies at existing facilities as well as the design of new reactors that would combine tritium production with power production can be envisioned. Fundamental chemistry to develop new target materials and a study of tritium retention and binding as well as studies of tritium diffusion mechanisms are needed. Improved and more economical methods for separation of tritium from other hydrogen isotopes are possible.

Actinide Chemistry

Development of nuclear reactors, power sources, and weapons requires the production and chemical separation, not only of the fissionable materials, plutonium and uranium, but of a number of other unusual elements as well. A knowledge of their chemistry and their complex metallurgy is essential. The actinide elements (including uranium) constitute a frontier region of the Periodic Table. Their properties can neither be interpolated nor simply extrapolated from those of the lighter elements. It is possible to develop new, more efficient methods for separation of these elements (as well as plutonium) from irradiated fuel. For example, new methods (photochemical, pyrochemical, electrochemical) for adjusting oxidation states that do not require addition of large volumes of solution or additives requiring costly waste disposal would result in large savings and less impact on the environment. More efficient and economical methods of isotope separation are also possible, including methods based upon laser processing or chemical exchange.

Laser Isotope Separation

The application of lasers to isotope separation must be counted an important national security development because of its potential applicability to purification of fissionable isotopes. Multiphoton excitation has been discussed in Section III-D with reference to the possible separation of fissionable isotopes through selective laser excitation. A number of tuned-laser excitation schemes have been tried, and chemists were usually involved. The multiple photon excitation of SF_6 (or its structural analogue, UF_6) with a tuned infrared laser is most clearly a chemical process. First, the excitation ruptures a chemical bond to produce two reactive fragments, SF_5 (or UF_5) and F atom, which must then be chemically trapped to retain the isotopic specificity. Clearly, research on any such scheme that shows promise must be pursued. Any such process, if successful in decreasing costs, would increase access to fissionable materials, both here and abroad, plainly a matter that affects our national security.

Radiochemical Detection

A continuing problem in the development of nuclear weapons is the assessment of the performance of new designs. Nuclear and radiochemistry have provided the basis for sophisticated and detailed analysis of the performance of nuclear devices. Ultrasensitive and selective analyses have been devised, including high-sensitivity mass spectrometry, such as resonance ionization and accelerator-based mass spectrometry, isotope separation, sensitive radiation measurement instrumentation, and radiochemical separations for nearly every element in the Periodic Table. As a particular example, nuclear bomb testing disperses in the atmosphere large amounts of fission products whose presence reveals both the event and the type of nuclear testing. Many of these fission product elements already exist in the environment from natural sources; their presence can interfere with detection of the more telltale elements present only because of a fission event. Lutecium is an example of the latter, but its detection can be obscured by the much larger natural background levels of chemically similar ytterbium. A solution is provided by tuned laser excitation in a mass spectrometer. At the resonant laser frequencies at which lutecium can be photoexcited to ionization, the ytterbium back-

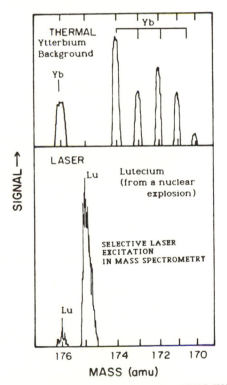

MONITORING NUCLEAR TESTING WITH SELECTIVE MASS SPECTROMETRY

ground can be completely suppressed so that minute levels of lutecium and its isotopic distribution can be measured.

In addition to analyzing for the fissile materials and fission products from a nuclear device, sensitive analyses are performed for the nuclear reaction products of specific elements added as so-called "radiochemical detectors." To interpret the results of these analyses, relevant nuclear data such as neutron cross sections, fission yields, and neutron emission for various fissioning systems must be measured. In this way, thermonuclear as well as fission yields and efficiency can be measured, and neutron fluxes and energies can be determined.

Processing and Reprocessing

The recent emergence of plutonium pyrochemical processes (electrolytic or chemical processes that use oxidation-reduction reactions to effect chemical separations at elevated temperatures) has resulted in a dramatic increase in the ability to produce high-purity plutonium metal from scrap residues. These processes resulted from basic chemical studies during the sixties. Currently, ton amounts of metal are produced by pyrochemical processes each year, but many tons still remain tied up in scrap residues. Advanced pyrochemical methods promise more efficient recovery based on recent research progress in molten salt-molten metal chemistry. For example, present plutonium pyrochemical operations are limited to plutonium-rich metal systems with melting points less than 800°C; processes are needed for uranium-plutonium systems with melting points of about 1000°C. Basic chemical studies are required to identify materials and equipment for high temperature operation and to identify low-melting multicomponent metal systems that could be used as solvents for high-melting scrap. Pyrochemical processes have the advantage of generating few new waste streams. Most of the waste streams that are produced are discarded to retrievable storage. The high cost of disposal and storage, however, suggests that much of this waste should be purified and recycled rather than discarded. For example, waste $CaCl_2$-CaO salts generated during the reduction of PuO_2 to metal could be reused by conversion of CaO to $CaCl_2$.

Currently, the only nuclear reprocessing being done in the United States is related to national defense. Increasing the efficiency of this operation will increase the recovery of materials needed for the nuclear weapons program and also reduce the waste disposal problem. Of course, it remains a national responsibility to provide for the safe storage and isolation of radioactive waste generated by our nuclear weapons program.

High-Speed Chemistry: Explosives and Fuels

The design and production of improved fuels and explosives for propulsion and munitions continues to be of central importance to our national security. This area will be moved ahead rapidly on the basis of the rich opportunities before us in reaction dynamics, molecular dynamics, theoretical chemistry, and solid state chemistry.

Even though the chemistry of explosives has been studied for hundreds of years, the underlying principles that would lead to predictive models for synthesis of better explosives are only now on the threshold of being understood. There are two areas where considerable progress is expected in the coming years.

Detonation Chemistry

Conventional condensed-phase explosives yield detonation waves with velocities in the order of 9 m/μsec, densities greater than 2 g/cm^3, temperatures of several thousand degrees, pressures of the order of 500 Kbar, and a chemical reaction zone where the energy necessary to sustain the detonation is released in less than 10 nsec. The study of chemical reactions under any one of these experimental conditions is difficult, and their combination pushes the limits of chemical science.

Recently, several nonlinear laser diagnostic techniques have been demonstrated that allow spectroscopic examination of shock-compressed materials. For example, using a laser method called "backward stimulated Raman scattering" in shock-compressed benzene, molecular vibrational frequency shifts have been measured as a function of pressure. Such data permit determination of pressure and temperature-induced changes in the intermolecular potentials. Other recently developed laser-based methods, such as "reflected broadband coherent anti-Stokes scattering," have allowed simultaneous spectroscopic monitoring of several constituents in shockcompressed systems. Finally, subpicosecond (i.e., less than one-trillionth of a second) laser diagnostics are being developed to determine the important energy transfer pathways at the molecular level in detonating systems.

Synthesis of New, Tailored Explosives

Recently, there has been considerable advance in our ability to predict the densities of organic compounds. Since density is an important factor in the energy of an explosive, this advance has stimulated and guided synthetic efforts toward new explosive molecules. Extension of these density prediction techniques to the prediction of crystal structures may provide a route toward the estimation of other important physical properties of proposed explosives and aid the search for high-pressure synthetic methods to produce unusually dense structures.

These fundamental studies may also lead to an understanding and mitigation of the events that lead to the accidental initiation of explosions and to techniques for formulating energetic explosives research that have improved both mechanical and safety properties. Other basic questions in explosives research involve understanding and improving the relatively poor efficiency (10

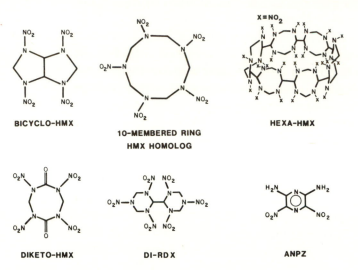

HETEROCYCLIC RING COMPOUNDS : POSSIBLE NEW EXPLOSIVES ?

to 20 percent) with which an explosive material's chemical energy is transformed into explosive (translational) energy.

Somewhat analogous to the studies of detonation and explosion initiation are studies of the basic mechanisms of chemical reaction that occur in the combustion of solid and liquid fuels and propellants. Use of modern spectroscopic diagnostic techniques to unravel rapid, complex chemistry at the molecular level is considerably more advanced and pervasive in the study of propellants than it is in the study of explosives. The underlying theme is that fundamental understanding will lead to improved efficiency—saving weight, energy, and money—and, perhaps, to new "exotic" fuels. Areas of particular current interest are:

Chemical Kinetics of Combustion

The larger fraction of our propulsion and transportation system depends upon combustion processes (vehicles, ships, planes, rockets, etc). As presented in Section III-B and expanded in III-D, this is a time of special opportunity for understanding the basic chemical steps involved in combustion initiation, flame extinction, flammability limits, energy pathways among molecular degrees of freedom, and combustion instabilities. Plainly such understandings will strengthen our weapons and defense systems. They will help us inhibit or prevent unwanted combustion events—fires and accidental explosions—and enable us to increase the rate of heat release and the combustion intensity in practical systems. Even when fuels or combustibles are not gaseous, gaseous reaction rates may control the chemical behavior. Illustrations include the extinction of burning fuel droplets and the production of soot in burning oil sprays. Both national security and nonmilitary applications of combustion processes warrant full exploitation of this active research frontier.

Containment or Treatment of Hot Combustion Products

This field requires knowledge of fluid flows and advanced cooling techniques, catalytic and corrosive reactions on hot surfaces, and participate formation and deposition from hot gases. It also prescribes improved high temperature materials (metals, ceramics, lubricants).

Enhanced Diagnostic Techniques

Combustion systems, with their multiphase nature and rapidly fluctuating variables, have long represented a formidable challenge to experimental diagnosis. Now many advanced laser spectroscopic techniques are yielding valuable chemical information on gaseous constituents and their temporal and energy behavior. As an example, it is now possible to map the temperature within a flame by recording the vibrational excitation of a combustion product across a two-dimensional slice through the flame. Thus, two tuned lasers can simultaneously excite fluorescence of OH molecules, one laser probing the vibrationally "cold" OH molecules (v = 0), the other laser probing the vibrationally "hot" OH molecules (v = 1). The relative populations of the two states furnishes a local thermometer at the site of fluorescence. With linear array detectors, vidicons, digitizers, and computer-controlled representations, an accurate, two-dimensional temperature map within the flame can now be recorded.

As such powerful techniques are extended and become more widely available, the accurate characterization of flame temperature and concentration profiles will permit fundamental refinement of kinetic models. These will help us understand and control flame propagation velocity, ignition delay, ignition energy, quenching distance, flammability limits, and stability limits. Perhaps we will also learn more about detonation velocity and the response of energetic chemicals to combustion suppressants. The latter are of importance with respect to fire hazards.

Modeling of Turbulent Combustion Systems

Mathematical models that appropriately simulate turbulent systems must be developed to aid designers of combustion systems; key experimental parameters have to be identified to test the theories. The flow in nearly all practical combustion devices, especially efficient pulsed combustors, is turbulent. Therefore, it is of key importance to consider the effect of the turbulence on the chemistry of flames, as well as the interaction of these features with the multiphase character of most practical combustors. In many instances, the chemical reaction rates are sufficiently fast relative to the turbulence time frame that reactions are effectively over as soon as the reactants contact each other on a molecular scale. In other instances, chemical reactions may lag significantly behind the turbulent fluid-mixing time scales. In most hot, chemically reacting systems, a mix of rates prevails. The chemical kinetics and turbulent fluid-mixing rates are intertwined in a complex fashion, offering a challenge to both theory and experiment.

Such research has obvious relevance to propulsion systems and hence to defense goals. It is likely, as well, that advances here would have valuable applicability to problems faced by the chemical industries in their attempts to find reliable methods for destruction of hazardous wastes by combustion process.

Chemical and Biological Defense

Chemistry plays a critical role in developing defenses against non-nuclear weapons and in strengthening our non-nuclear deterence. For those who see potential retaliation as an effective deterrent, there is concern that the United States, having unilaterally stopped the research, development, and production of chemical and biological stockpiles from 1969 to 1983, is vulnerable to attack by forces with superior offensive and defensive chemical and biological weapons. Surely we cannot assume that a potential enemy of the United States would also refrain from developing such weapons and categorically refuse to use them. Hence, we must keep aware of the state-of-the-art and be ready with adequate sensing and monitoring methods. We must have in place a sound defensive capability that includes the ability to detect such agents, to sound alarm, and to take protective countermeasures. Acquisition of these abilities and the development of optimum strategies for destroying and counteracting the effects of chemical and biological agents will require the development of novel analytical and spectroscopic methods, a definition of the basis of action at the molecular level, and identification of populations at risk because of the intrinsic and environmentally induced variability of response.

Chemical and Biological Agent Detection

The rapid detection and unequivocal identification of chemical and biological agents is a key ingredient in defending against agent attack. As a consequence there is major emphasis on the development and deployment of ultrasensitive and highly specific (i.e., low false alarm rate) methods for agent detection. While the molecular species of interest differ greatly, the desired end plainly has much in common with environmental monitoring. For example, the techniques under study for remote sensing of atmospheric pollutants are clearly applicable (e.g., long-path in situ Fourier transform infrared methods and laser-based "lidar": see Section V-A). More generally, advances in analytical chemistry and biochemistry will play a pivotal role in meeting this objective, with several notable techniques already demonstrated and currently under further development.

One such example is tandem mass spectrometry (MS/MS), a technique whose unusual specificity, sensitivity, and response speed make it promising as a universal detector for vaporized chemical agents. In operation, the atmospheric sample flows continuously through an electrical discharge, and the ions produced are drawn through a differentially pumped orifice into the first mass spectrometer, where ion masses corresponding to the targeted compounds are selected. Each of the mass species is then fragmented separately to produce a characteristic mass spectrum (usually dozens of peaks) measured in the second mass spectrometer. To produce a false alarm, a stray substance must not only yield the same primary mass, but its secondary products must have the same masses and abundances. Subpicogram sensitivities and subsecond response times have been demonstrated when only a few targeted compounds are sought. For more comprehensive sets of possible agents, the Fourier transform MS/MS is promising in that it simultaneously separates all masses (rather than scanning masses sequentially) and can measure the resulting secondary spectra simultaneously at high resolution. Instrument size and simplicity is a challenging problem. However, the critical analytical information relevant to the absence of life on Mars provided by a double-focusing mass spectrometer weighing only 12 pounds (aboard the 1972 Mars Viking Lander) shows what can be accomplished. Furthermore, laboratory detection limits for continuous monitoring of deliberately added contaminants have been demonstrated in the parts-per-trillion range (bromine, 70 ppt; pyridine, 2 ppt; aflatoxin, 10 ppt; and tetrachlorobenzodioxin, 10^{-12} grams).

A second example is "metastable atom-induced fluorescence," a technique that has significant potential as a detector for chemical agents. In this approach, highly energetic inert gas atoms (e.g., helium, argon) produced by a low-voltage electrical discharge are mixed with a trace impurity. The metastable atoms are sufficiently energetic to cause decomposition of the trace molecules into excited fragments characteristic of the impurity. Each excited fragment emits a unique optical spectrum that makes possible its identification. Thus, the atom-induced spectra of various chemical agents (nerve, mustard, blood) provide much less ambiguous identifications because of the unique groupings of fragments. Furthermore, such spectra are capable of extremely sensitive detection. At this writing, 50 parts per trillion of the mustard simulant 2-chloroethylethylsulfide (2-CEES) in air has been detected.

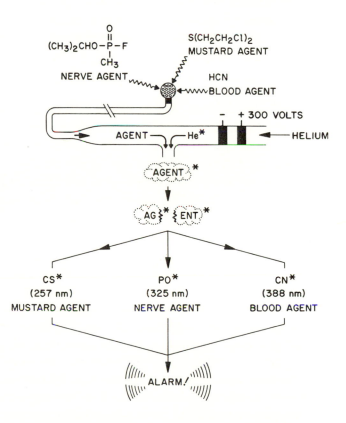

DETECTION of CHEMICAL AGENTS

Circular intensity differential scattering (CIDS) is a potentially powerful

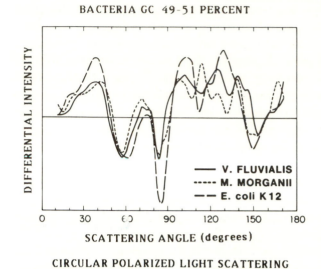

BACTERIA GC 49-51 PERCENT

CIRCULAR POLARIZED LIGHT SCATTERING
DIFFERENTIATES SIMILAR BACTERIAL AGENTS

technique for detecting biological agents. In CIDS the differential scattering of left and right circularly polarized light is observed. It is very sensitive to differences in long-range order among biological macromolecules, such as the DNA or RNA in a virus or bacterium. This probe has been used to distinguish among a wide variety of microorganisms. For example, it is capable of clear discrimination among bacteria having a similar guanine-cytosine nuclei acid base content. Such discrimination is, of course, a necessary first step toward protection and defense.

Currently, an aerosol CIDS flow cytometer for detecting bacterial aerosols as a first line of defense against biological agent attack is being evaluated.

Protection

Novel ways are being developed to promote the induction of protective responses in humans (e.g., through the synthesis of specific immunoglobulins and other proteins) that will greatly reduce the toxicity stemming from exposure to chemical warfare agents. Studies to date have focused on ways of enhancing protective response in cells that reduce cell killing associated with exposure to alkylating agents by factors in excess of 100-fold. Major effort has been directed toward devising means for increasing the magnitude of the protective response to poisons and toward investigating the underlying mechanisms.

Similarly, contamination of equipment as a result of chemical or biological attack could render it harmful to the user. Methods must be developed that allow for safe, nondestructive decontamination. They could take the form of novel protective coating materials or noncorrosive/nontoxic decontaminating fluids. Complementary chemical systems using both of these approaches may be required. Furthermore, periodically, stores of obsolete munitions containing chemical agents must be destroyed. Methods currently available are prohibitively costly and hazardous. The development of efficient, environmentally acceptable processes would be a major contribution to national security and, again, it would probably help us deal with potentially hazardous industrial wastes.

New Frontiers in Defense

New directions in defense include increasing research emphasis on sophisticated detection, reliable defensive weapons that counter other weapons, and high-technology weaponry, including chemical lasers. In these developments, chemistry plays a vital part, as exemplified by spectroscopic-based detection schemes, lightweight polymer-based materials, stealth coatings, and laser-resistant coatings.

The growing emphasis on the importance of space to national strategic defense requires development of new materials that can perform reliably in a vacuum environment. Emphasis on space may also lead to the reality of people living and working away from the planet earth. The first step will be the establishment of space stations in earth orbit. The greatest barrier to the establishment of man's continued presence in space is the cost and difficulty of transporting construction materials from the earth's surface to orbit. In the long term, we must see if these materials could be made from lunar resources. Space or lunar materials processing will require vision and creativity across all scientific and engineering disciplines. Chemists will play a major role as we develop maintainable lunar habitat atmospheres, invent novel processes for producing construction and propellant materials from lunar resources, and develop novel lunar-based electrical power generation processes.

Conclusion

The ingredients that make for a healthy and satisfied populace, in both the nation and the world, are the key factors underlying national security. Chemistry plays a major role here in areas ranging from agriculture, health, and environment to a dynamic, productive economy. In addition, however, the nation needs the ability to defend itself and to prevent and deter armed conflict. In these areas also, chemistry plays a vital role, touching all aspects of defense from propulsion, weapons materials, and classical munitions to the most advanced strategic concepts.

CHEMISTRY is a central science
that responds to societal needs.

It is critical in Man's attempt to...
monitor and protect our environment

Libraries into Space

Unbelievable though it sounds, we may have to place whole libraries in a space-like environment over the next decade! This strange proposal is not made because our orbiting astronauts need more reading material, but because if we don't do that or something similar, most of our books won't be around very long for the rest of us to read. An alarming and little known problem faces mankind today—the vast majority of books, those printed since the 1850s, are relentlessly yellowing and crumbling to dust. The library at the University of California at Berkeley alone stands to lose 60,000 books and periodicals per year to decomposition. This is not because of air pollution; the source of the destruction lies in the very paper on which the books are printed. Now, some clever chemists have discovered that, surprisingly, a trip into an environment similar to space provides at least one solution to this vexing problem.

Papermaking processes used since the 1850s universally employ an alumrosin sizing to keep ink from "feathering" or spreading on the paper. Slowly, this paper-maker's alum—aluminum sulfate—combines with moisture in the pages and in the air to form sulfuric acid. This aggressive substance, in turn, facilitates attack on the cellulose fibers in the paper, breaking them into smaller and smaller fragments and, ultimately, to dust. Between 75 and 95 percent of the deterioration in "modern" paper is caused by such acid attack.

In recent years, chemists have developed a number of acid-neutralizing processes for books. One of these, developed in the Library of Congress research laboratory, suggests that the chemical diethyl zinc may be ideal for the job. Diethyl zinc is a gas, so its molecules can easily permeate even a *closed* book. Once inside, the substance deacidifies each book and then looks ahead to the future by leaving an alkaline residue of zinc oxy-carbonate. This residue, uniformly distributed throughout the paper fibers, protects the book from any future acid attack.

Ironically, this life-saving agent, diethyl zinc, bursts into flame on contact with air and explodes when it touches water. How does a chemist work with a compound that cannot be exposed to air or water? In a deep space environment, of course. A suitable location was found at NASA's Goddard Flight Center, where 5,000 books from the Library of Congress took a simulated flight, not on a rocket into space, but in a laboratory space-simulating vacuum chamber.

First, the books were thoroughly dried by warming under vacuum for about 3 days. Then, with all oxygen removed from the chamber, gaseous diethyl zinc was introduced and allowed to diffuse into the books. As the neutralizing reaction proceeds, harmless ethane gas is produced and pumped away. Then the protective zinc oxy-carbonate is formed. The results have been extremely promising, and, as the technology is perfected, libraries across the nation will be looking to install huge deacidification facilities. These countermeasures, coupled with the new "alkaline reserve" papers now used in modern printing, promise that the precious heritage of the world's libraries, including the enormous Library of Congress, will be preserved for future generations to enjoy, and profit from, just as we do today.

V-D.　Intellectual Frontiers

This chapter has shown how chemistry offers societal benefit connected with better environment, sustained economic competitiveness, and increased national security. These benefits draw upon the entire spectrum of chemistry, and they flow from research discoveries across the whole range. Nevertheless, some intellectual frontiers are specially well placed here. For example, the surface sciences, with their implications for new heterogeneous catalysts furnish a wellspring of critical importance in international competitiveness. Condensed phase chemistry and new separations techniques also can be expected to contribute fruitful new dimensions to our competitiveness in foreign markets. Next, the new frontiers in analytical chemistry support and contribute to advances in all other areas of chemistry. Analytical chemistry is the cornerstone upon which our monitoring and management of the environment is built. Finally, nuclear chemistry was nurtured in the World War II Manhattan Project and its health continues to be of prime importance, since world peace depends upon a balance of nuclear arms.

In each of these subjects, there are opening frontiers and rewarding intellectual opportunities to be pursued.

Chemistry at Solid Surfaces

The surfaces of metals and ionic solids are intrinsically chemically reactive. The reason is clear: the bulk crystal takes a structure that provides for each interior atom optimum chemical bonding to neighboring atoms around it in all three dimensions. At the surface, however, the atoms have unsatisfied bonding capacity because the neighboring atoms are missing in one direction. Hence, this is a region of special chemical behavior, one of unusual interest to chemists. The importance of this special behavior simply cannot be exaggerated. Corrosion occurs, of course, at iron surfaces, with obvious deleterious effect on many structures of great utility, from the lofty Eiffel Tower to the lowly nail. It has been estimated that corrosion costs the U.S. economy billions of dollars annually. At aluminum surfaces, there is rapid reaction on exposure to air that forms a protective and quite inert oxide coating. Hence we can safely have the convenience of aluminum foil in the kitchen, despite the fact that aluminum is flammable. But by far the greatest importance of surface chemistry is that it confers upon some surfaces extremely effective catalytic activity. This capacity of a solid surface to speed up chemical reactions by many orders of magnitude without being consumed is called heterogeneous catalysis. Its significance has been extolled in Sections III-A and III-B as the basis for commercial processes of immense economic value. It is one of the most important and active frontiers of chemistry.

Heterogeneous catalysis is not new. What is new is the array of powerful instruments developed over the last 15 years that provide, at last, experimental access to the chemistry on a surface *while that chemistry is taking place.*

Without such techniques, catalysis has remained over many decades largely an empirical art. Now we have instruments with which to characterize precisely the nature of the catalyst surface and to study molecules while they are reacting there. Now we are accumulating the store of quantitative data needed for catalysis to become a science. Already, catalyst design and fabrication has become a high-technology industry. The intellectual challenge to understand the chemical behavior of surface-adsorbed monolayers has propelled surface science into the mainstream of fundamental research in departments of chemistry and chemical engineering. This research will have impact on many important technologies.

The instrumentation of the surface sciences will be described in Section V-E. Some research highlights and productive frontiers are described below.

The Structure of Solid Surfaces

Metallic crystals can exhibit a variety of surfaces depending upon the angle of the surface relative to the natural crystal axes. The most stable surfaces tend to be flat and close-packed with each surface atom surrounded by a large number of nearest neighbors. Other surfaces may be formed, however, that are stepped, with terraces several atoms wide and separated by steps of monatomic height. Atoms at these ledges are even more exposed, hence more reactive than surface atoms embedded in the smooth terraces. Further, there may be kinks in the steps, or the surface may be "rough" with atomic-size openings between surface atoms with, again, special reactivity. Such chemically important surface irregularities can now be identified by low-energy electron diffraction (LEED).

FLAT (1,0,0)   **FLAT (1,1,1)**

TERRACED (7,7,5)   **KINKED (10,8,7)**

CHEMISTRY ON A PLATINUM SURFACE DEPENDS ON THE SURFACE EXPOSED

How important this can be is illustrated in the catalytic production of ammonia from nitrogen and hydrogen on single crystals of an iron catalyst. The effectiveness of a catalyst depends upon how rapidly each surface site can adsorb reactants, encourage them to rearrange chemically, and then release the products so that the site can begin the process again. The iron crystal face designated (1,1,1) is about 430 times more active than the closest-packed (1,1,0) crystal face and 13 times more active than the simpler (1,0,0) face. It is now believed that the rate-limiting step is the rupture of the strong nitrogen-nitrogen bond of N_2 (225 kcal/mole) and that this occurs with an activation energy near 3 kcal/mole on the (1,0,0) face but with nearly zero activation energy on the specially active (1,1,1) surface.

A second, equally important, example is the use of a platinum catalyst to restructure alkane hydrocarbons to forms with better combustion properties (e.g., octane number, volatility). Now, it is possible to discern which catalyst surfaces optimize the desired products. Thus, *n*-hexane, an extended-chain structure with low-octane number, can be converted to forms with higher-octane numbers, such as benzene and branched or cyclic alkanes, using a platinum catalyst in the presence of hydrogen. We now know that benzene is favored on the flat (1,1,1) surface or on stepped surfaces with terraces of (1,1,1) orientation, like (7,5,5). In contrast, formation of branched or cyclic alkanes is favored on the flat, (1,0,0) surface or stepped sur-

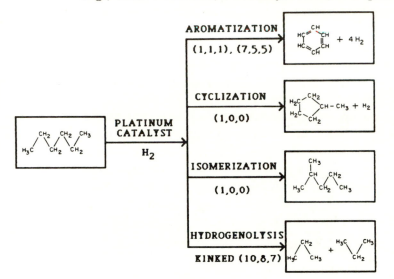

DIFFERENT SURFACES FAVOR DIFFERENT PRODUCTS

faces with (1,0,0) terraces. Kinked surfaces, like (10,8,7), tend to produce less desirable products like propane and ethane. Knowing this, we can seek a reagent that will permanently bind to and block ("poison") these active "kink" sites to eliminate their less desirable products.

Because of their influence on catalytic action, surface structures are attracting much research interest. Small particles tend to display many different surfaces, depending on method of preparation. As the metallic particle grows, it becomes more like the bulk material and tends to disfavor surfaces with terraces and kinks. Atoms in the surface layer may take an equilibrium spacing from the second layer several percent closer than is found for interior layer spacing. Even more drastic, because of the incomplete bonding of surface atoms, they may seek equilibrium positions different from the packing in the bulk material in order to optimize their bonding. Such "surface reconstruction" has been found for platinum, gold, silicon, and germanium.

Another important question that can now be experimentally explored is the surface composition. Even the purest samples will have some impurities, and these may noticeably affect some properties of metals and semiconductors. Relevant to surface chemistry is the question of the extent to which a given impurity preferentially concentrates at the surface. Indeed, this may be the rule rather than the exception. The difference in bonding between host and impurity atoms explains why the bulk material tends to reject the impurity. The same difference may cause the impurity to be a welcome addition to the surface, where host atoms alone cannot satisfy their bonding capability. There are cases in which impurities at the parts-per-million level are so concentrated at the surface that they can cover it completely.

Of course, this issue is always present in binary or multicomponent alloy systems. There is excess silver at the surfaces of silver-gold alloys, copper at copper-nickel alloy surfaces, and gold at gold-tin alloy surfaces. Some metals that are not miscible in bulk are found to be completely miscible (mutually soluble) on a surface. Thermodynamic models are being developed to predict the surface composition to be expected for a given bulk composition. Experimental data and understandings are especially needed at this time when a variety of binary and ternary substances are under study because of their interfacial electrical properties.

In summary, determination of the atomic structure of surfaces and surface composition is basic to understanding the wide variety of surface properties now finding important practical applications. They are the starting point for advancing corrosion science, heterogeneous catalysis, lubrication and adhesion, as well as for producing new surfaces and interfaces with novel electronic properties.

Adsorbed Molecules: Chemical Bonding at the Surface

For many decades, the adherence of a substance to a surface was measured by the ease of its removal on warming. Some substances are easily removed at temperatures near or below room temperature. Such a situation is traditionally categorized as "physisorption": the adsorbed substance retains its molecular integrity and is bound to the surface only by weak forces, such as van der Waals or hydrogen bonding interactions. Other substances are more tightly held by the surface and can be removed only by heating to much higher temperatures—perhaps 200 to 600°C. Here, covalent bonding to the surface is involved, and the molecular structure of the adsorbate can be expected to differ from what it was before adsorption. This situation is called "chemisorption," and it is usually if not always involved at some stage in any heterogeneous catalysis. Hence, understanding of the molecular structure and chemical properties of chemisorbed molecules lies at the heart of heterogeneous catalysis.

Among small molecules, carbon monoxide on metal surfaces has historically been given most attention, in part because of especially favorable spectroscopic properties that facilitated detection of the small number of molecules on the surface. This history turns out to be fortunate, for one of today's pressing problems is the conversion of coal to useful hydrocarbon feedstocks, and many catalytic schemes use carbon monoxide as an intermediate via "syn gas," a mixture of CO and H_2 derived from coal (see Section III-A and Table III-4 in Section III-B).

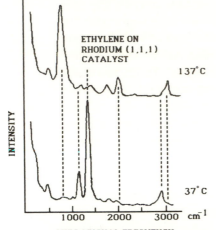

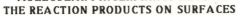

MOLECULAR FINGERPRINTS REVEAL THE REACTION PRODUCTS ON SURFACES

A second key example is that of adsorption of ethylene on catalytic metal surfaces. It has been known, from its thermal behavior, that ethylene chemisorbs on platinum and rhodium catalysts. Now, we can add information about the structures that are formed on the surface through direct observation of the vibrational frequencies of the adsorbed species. While direct observation of these frequencies through infrared absorption spectroscopy is sometimes possible, the advent of electron energy loss spectroscopy (EELS) has greatly accelerated such studies. The characteristic molecular frequencies are imprinted on the energy distribution of electrons bounced off the metal surface, and they provide a fingerprint that is readily interpreted by a chemist experienced in relating infrared spectra to molecular structures.

For ethylene on rhodium, the EELS spectrum plainly shows that, after adsorption, the ethylene molecule has been structurally altered even at room temperature. Then, on warming 50°C or so, the spectrum begins to change still more. By the time the temperature has changed by 100°C, the spectrum shows that reactions have taken place, and the hydrocarbons now present on the surface have new structures. These EELS spectra reveal, then, which of the possible surface structures, C_2H_3, C_2H_2, C_2H, CH_3, CH_2, and CH are present at a given temperature and, hence, the sequence of their formation as the temperature is raised. Such intimate knowledge of the chemical events taking place on the catalyst surface furnishes the basis for a detailed understanding of the catalytic dehydrogenation and hydrogenation of ethylene.

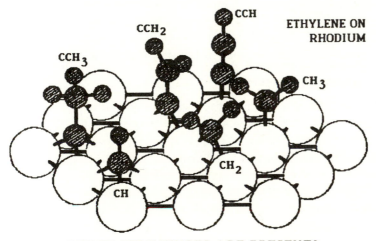

WHICH STRUCTURES ARE PRESENT?

Co-Adsorption on Surfaces

The realm of chemistry on surfaces takes on new dimension when two substances are adsorbed on the same surface. Then attention shifts from the interaction of the adsorbate with the surface to the interaction of two different species when they share the special environment provided by the surface.

The first way in which this interaction can occur is when one adsorbate changes the special environment seen by the second adsorbate. An example has already been mentioned in which one adsorbate attaches so strongly to particular sites that another adsorbate is denied access to them. For example, a clean molybdenum metal surface will decompose the sulfur-containing molecule, thiophene, C_4H_5S. However, if elemental sulfur is co-adsorbed, it chemisorbs quite strongly at the active sites needed for thiophene decomposition. Thus sulfur "poisons" the catalyst for this particular reaction.

As a second example, carbon monoxide is physisorbed on rhodium, as shown both by its ease of removal on warming and its vibrational frequency on the surface, which is close to that of gaseous carbon monoxide. If, however, the rhodium is 50 percent covered by co-adsorbed potassium, CO becomes chemisorbed. The EELS spectrum shows a CO vibrational frequency appropriate to a bridged structure with a double-bond carbon-oxygen frequency. Under these conditions, hydrogenation of CO is facilitated with the desirable outcome that higher molecular weight alkanes and alkenes are obtained. Explanations are based upon the ease of ionization of potassium and the effect of such electron-release in the presence of the metal surface.

Still to be mentioned is the direct reaction between the two adsorbates. In the future, this will be seen as the most prolific source of the new chemistry that can take place in this special reaction domain. An obvious example has been cited— the hydrogenation of ethylene. When hydrogen adsorbs on platinum or rhodium, the H_2 molecule is split and the two atoms are separately bonded to metal atoms. Now, when ethylene is co-adsorbed, it does not encounter H_2 at all. Instead, it finds individual hydrogen atoms attached to the surface. Plainly, if co-adsorbed hydrogen and ethylene react, they will follow a reaction path characteristic of the species on the surface and governed by activation energies unrelated to those associated with a gas phase encounter between H_2 and C_2H_4.

Energy Transfer During Gas-Surface Collisions

Currently the energy transfer between molecules impinging on the surface of a solid is under active investigation. The purpose is to learn how translational and internal energies of incident molecules are exchanged with the characteristic vibrations of the crystalline surface. Such data should be relevant to residence time and energy content of molecules as they adsorb and desorb. Molecular beams are used, and the results to date have contained surprises. Energy transfer to the surface is less facile than expected, and it can be surface structure-sensitive. Rotational and vibrational energy contents are separately influenced by the surface temperature but not in simple ways. More experimental data and theoretical treatments are needed so that we can accurately describe surface dynamic phenomena.

Surface Electrical Properties

A nonconducting material invariably displays an electrical space-charge at an interface with vacuum or other media. These space-charges find important applications in the colloid sciences, semiconductor surface devices, and in modern printing and copying technologies. Surface ionization, field ionization, and photoelectron emission are electrical characteristics of surfaces that are coming under scrutiny and finding a variety of applications.

Novel Spectroscopic Technologies

Many of the most modern techniques of surface science require that the measurement be carried out in ultrahigh vacuum (i.e., below 10^{-9} torr). This is a considerable limitation because every practical application of surface behavior occurs in the presence of gas, liquid, or another solid at the interface (including, of course, all catalysis). Desperately needed are comparably sensitive experimental techniques that permit study of chemical behavior at the interface between a solid surface and a second medium at significant density. Attenuated total reflectance IR and grazing-incidence infrared spectroscopy have been in use for some time, and the new Fourier transform difference techniques are significantly improving our ability to detect the tiny infrared absorbances offered by less than monolayer coverages. Tunable infrared lasers offer further improvement that has not yet been exploited. New discoveries and developments can be anticipated to join the two already mentioned in Section III-A—surface-enhanced Raman and surface-enhanced second harmonic generation. Up to million-fold enhancements of Raman intensities for surface-adsorbed molecules have been demonstrated for particular adsorbants on particular surfaces. It is already clear that surface preparation is an important factor, and there is not yet sufficient clarity in the theoretical explanations under consideration to specify the range of applicability to be expected. Perhaps more general applicability will be provided by second-harmonic generation, using laser sources, since the effect depends upon the intrinsic dielectric asymmetry provided by a phase boundary. In principle, small surface asymmetries can be dealt with by using higher laser power—the nonlinear behavior can be proportional to the cube of the power. Furthermore, pulsed lasers can be used, which suggests the possibility of temporal studies on the nanosecond to picosecond time scale.

We have only begun to explore the range of potentialities that has been opened by the new instrumental techniques for studying chemistry at interfaces. Vapor and plasma depositions are providing opportunities for thin-film depositions that affect a variety of surface behaviors. Epitaxial influences are being exploited. Energetic ion implantation permits controlled injection of desired impurities near or on the surface of a metal or semiconductor. Rapid energy-deposition from lasers permits melting and rapid cooling of surface regions that can freeze into glassy form or with a high temperature composition and structure. Conducting polymer films may alter or reroute electrochemical phenomena that exhibit luminescence or function as molecular switches or molecular logic devices. Many biological processes, too, take place at solid-liquid interfaces; surface science research may provide molecular-level scrutiny of such processes as they may be taking place in vivo, conceivably in the cell, in the brain, in bone, etc.

Applications have already appeared and more can be expected in better control of abrasion, corrosion, and high temperature performance, as well as in design and fabrication of new semiconductors and other electrical devices. Most important, however, will undoubtedly be the full exploitation of surfaces as a new reaction domain, as we develop our fundamental understandings of heterogeneous catalysis.

Condensed Phase Studies

The study of condensed phases illustrates in an especially clear way the central position of chemistry, both as an intellectual discipline and as an applied field. The great challenges facing solid state science, earth science, biochemistry, and biophysics all involve the ability to understand and manipulate the properties of condensed phases. These properties result directly from the interatomic and intermolecular forces between chemical entities present in these phases. In addition, almost all useful materials and the majority of practical processes involve one or more condensed phases.

Optical and Electronic Properties of Solids

Over the past 15 to 20 years, high pressure has proved to be a powerful tool in the study of electronic phenomena in solids. Basically, increased compression increases overlap among adjacent electronic orbitals. Since different types of orbitals have different spatial characteristics, they are perturbed to different degrees. This "pressure tuning" is the element that makes pressure effects a powerful tool for characterizing electronic states and excitations, testing theories, and uncovering electronic transitions to new ground states with different physical and chemical properties.

Conceptual areas to which pressure effects are adding important new insights include ligand field theory, van Vleck's theory of high-spin to low-spin transitions, and Mulliken's theory of electron donor-acceptor complexes. Pressure effects are also extending the Forster-Dexter theory of energy transfer in phosphors and theories of the efficiency of a variety of laser materials, including II-VI and III-V compounds that exhibit the zincblende structure, and rare earth oxides and chelates.

Many instances of electronic transitions that show pronounced and meaningful response to high pressure have been found. For example, the insulator-conductor transitions for 9 elements and 40-50 compounds (the first organic superconductor exhibited superconductivity between 6 and 18 kilobars). Other cases are paramagnetic-diamagnetic transitions in ferrous compounds, a ferromagnetic-diamagnetic transition in iron, photochromic-thermochromic transitions in anils, spiropyrans, and bianthrones, and electron transfer transitions in 20-30 ethylene diamine complexes with resultant chemical reactivity of a new type.

Liquids

Many of the fundamental processes of nature and industry take place in the liquid state. The rate of transport of molecules in solution can limit the speed with which a synthetic chemical reaction can occur, a nerve can fire, a battery can generate current, and chemicals can be purified and isolated by separation. A properly chosen liquid solvent can accelerate a chemical reaction by a million-fold or slow it down by a comparable factor. Molecules in liquids can be highly efficient agents for storing or transferring energy. The structure of liquid water influences the course and nature of biochemical processes essential to life. In recent years there has been significant progress towards a better understanding of the liquid state based both on theoretical and experimental work. These advances have been fueled by developments in three areas: experimental techniques, large-scale computer simulation, and new theoretical tools. The enormous progress in the field of liquids can be traced in no small measure to the constant interplay among these areas.

The structure and dynamics of a wide range of fluids, from liquid hydrogen to molten silicates, can be investigated by a number of spectroscopic techniques, such as X-ray and neutron diffraction, nuclear magnetic resonance, laser Raman, and Rayleigh scattering. In the context of experimental studies, it is important to note that pressure as an experimental variable provides much information about molecular motions and interactions in liquids. However, constant pressure, constant volume, and constant temperature experiments are all needed to test, rigorously, theoretical models of liquids and establish a firm experimental basis for the development of new models. Among the newer experimental approaches, relaxation techniques are particularly powerful. The techniques of nonlinear laser spectroscopy provide new information on the picosecond time scale (10^{-12} sec) about the freedom of movement of a solute molecule in its solvent cage. Now we can watch fundamental chemical events as they take place: how two iodine atoms combine in a liquid to produce an iodine molecule, how a stilbene molecule interconverts between different conformations, how electrons released in liquid water become "trapped," or "solvated," and how energy deposited in a solute molecule like nitrogen or benzene is transferred to its solvent environment. Quite a different opportunity area is connected with liquid-solid phase transitions in small clusters. We have a variety of new experimental methods for producing and studying small clusters as well as the theoretical tools with which to interpret the results. We can look ahead to an understanding of how bulk phase transition properties emerge as cluster size increases.

Another major stimulus to progress in studies of liquids is in computational technology: the impressive calculational power of high-speed computers has been brought to bear on liquid-state structure and dynamics. In the Monte Carlo computer technique, hundreds of thousands of configurations of the molecules are sampled by probability methods. The output is two-fold. First, thermodynamic data is generated for fundamental studies, for comparison with experiments, and for predictions under conditions difficult to obtain experimentally. Second, detailed descriptions of the structure are provided in many cases at a molecular level beyond that experimentally accessible at this time. An example is the simulation of ionic solution structure near an electrified surface, as in an electrochemical cell.

Quite a different computer-based technique has been labeled "molecular dynamics" (MD). The positions and orientations of hundreds of molecules can be simulated and tracked in their time evolution under thermal agitation to provide a detailed picture of both liquid-state structure and dynamics. The MD methodology has now been applied to quite an array of fundamental problems of the liquid state. Favorite and important objectives of such simulations are to model the properties of water and of proteins as they exist in water. Beyond these, even a limited listing of applications conveys the scope of the method: molecular motion and energy transfer, chemical reactions, liquid-solid and liquid-gas interfaces, phase transitions, ionic solutions, molten salts, and glasses.

The remaining source of advance in liquid-state science has been the development of new theoretical approaches and methods. In the area of structural and equilibrium properties, powerful new perturbation theories based on the key features of intermolecular forces have been proposed and focused on liquids of considerable complexity, e.g., a new theory for the hydrophobic effect, which plays an influential role in the stability of biologically important macromolecules in water. Both theory and computer simulation add more depth to our understanding of this crucial factor in the organization and function of biological systems.

In the area of liquid-state dynamics—transport, energy transfer, and reaction—the introduction and development of the time correlation function method has had a profound impact on theory. The theorist has new analytical methods with which to attack the calculation of transport, energy relaxation, and chemical rate properties. For example, coherent, pulsed laser excitation of a solute molecule provides evidence about molecular reorientation times in the liquid state, but time correlation functions are needed to interpret such data.

Until recently, most experimental work has focused on investigation of single-molecule properties, such as reorientation and vibrational dephasing, which reflect only indirectly the influence of the intermolecular interactions. However, by studying spectra induced by such molecular interactions, one can obtain direct information about the interactions. There should be increased emphasis on studies of density effects on collision-induced scattering. Other areas that show special promise for future work are chemical reaction dynamics in liquids, phase transitions involving liquids, solids, and mesophases, such as liquid crystals, and interfacial phenomena involving liquids.

Chemical synthesis in liquids under high pressure deserves special mention. Chemical reaction as it takes place under high pressure (e.g., at thousands of atmospheres pressure) gives unique insight into reaction mechanisms and, as pointed out by example in Section III-D, control over product distribution. High-pressure studies reveal the volume profile of a reaction—including during its passage through the rate-limiting transition state—and in this way a new type of information is gained about reaction pathways. Thus we can learn about the concertedness of a multiple-bond reorganization, solvation reorganization during reaction, and location of the transition state along the reaction coordinate. Additionally, the PV work term becomes comparable to the energy and entropy barriers for reaction. Thus the role of pressures in excess of 10 kilobars is a valuable new dimension of organic synthesis in solutions, a dimension, as yet, little explored.

Critical Phenomena

For any fluid, there is a range of temperature and pressure within which the liquid and gaseous states cannot be differentiated. Fluid behavior under these "critical conditions" can differ markedly from normal behavior and give rise to new phenomena. The past 20 years have seen a revolution in our understanding of such critical phenomena. Undoubtedly the most important single theoretical advance in our understanding in the last 15 years has been the development of the renormalization group approach. The theory is couched in relatively new conceptual terms (nonclassical critical exponents, scaling, and universality classes). It shows computational promise for quantitative expression of the functional form and exponents in our description of fluid properties and their dependence upon the molecular parameters and the experimental variables (the scaling equation of state). The theory has predictive capability that recently received striking verification by experiment.

The discovery of tricritical points, at which three phases become simultaneously identical, and the theoretical and experimental elucidation of the properties at these points has been another significant development of the last decade. Surfaces and interfaces of near-critical fluids and fluid mixtures can themselves exhibit transitions and critical phenomena. The surface tension and interfacial profile between near-critical coexisting phases exhibit unusual (nonclassical) critical behavior that has been treated theoretically and measured experimentally. The discovery that a polymer unit isolated in a good solvent is itself a near-critical object and that statistical models already developed to treat other phenomena (e.g., magnetism) are applicable to dilute polymer solutions has enriched the study of both critical phenomena and polymers. An example is provided by the polymerization transition in pure liquid sulfur at 160°C, which is related to critical phenomena in ferromagnets.

The past 15 years have seen the intoduction of the critical point and critical phenomena into practical and engineering applications. The use of critical point drying is now a standard sample preparation method in electron microscopy. "Super-critical" extraction is now used in research applications in liquid chromatography and commercially in the preparation of a wide variety of products. The latter include extraction of perfume essences and the removal of caffeine from some instant coffees. The dramatic changes in solvent power with very small changes in pressure or temperature near the critical point make it seem likely that increasing use will be made of near-critical fluids for other practical applications.

Chemistry of the Earth and Extraterrestrial Materials

Geochemical phenomena involve complex mixtures, frequently with a number of phases as well as very high pressures and temperatures. Recent advances in high-pressure technology have made possible studies that duplicate conditions well into the Earth's core. In recent years many Earth scientists have studied the "geochemical cycles" of elements—that is, the changing chemical and physical environment of a given element during such Earth processes as crystallization, dissolution, metamorphism, and weathering. These processes may lead to concentration (e.g., ore deposits) or dispersion of an element. The geochemical cycle of carbon has provided a focus for the reawakened field of organic geochemistry. Research on the stability, conformation, and decomposition reactions of fossil organic molecules has led to greater understanding of the genesis and constituents of coal, oil, and other organic deposits. Such knowledge has obvious value that extends from guiding our exploration for new fossil fuel deposits to helping us decide how to use the ones we have.

Radioactive isotope geochemistry first received widespread notice and application as a dating technique. Now there are many new applications, including some that involve stable isotopes in studies of fluid flow and reaction kinetics relevant to geochemical processes. Furthermore, the Earth's unique isotopic signature imposes severe constraints on theories of the origin and chemical evolution of the Earth.

Meteorites are of considerable chemical interest because they include the oldest solar system materials available for research, and they sample a wide range of parent bodies—some primitive, some highly evolved. Meteorites carry decipherable records of certain solar and galactic effects and yield data otherwise unobtainable about the genesis, evolution, and composition of the Earth and other planets, satellites, asteroids, and the Sun. Isotopic anomalies in many metals and gaseous elements and compositional data—particularly trace elements—have shed light on all stages of meterorite parent body (asteroidal) formation, evolution, and destruction. Organic compounds found in some meteorites might provide clues to those compounds that were precursors to life, to interstellar molecules, and to cometary material.

Analytical Chemistry

Characterization and measurement of atomic and molecular species—qualitative and quantitative analytical chemistry—uniquely contribute to and benefit from the current rapid progress in science. Basic discoveries in physics, chemistry, and biology are providing the bases for new analytical methods and computerized instrumentation. In reciprocation, these new capabilities are central to research progress in chemistry, other sciences, and medicine, as well as to applications in environmental monitoring, industrial control, health, geology, agriculture, defense, and law enforcement (for the Hitler diaries, the disagreements of historians and handwriting experts were settled quickly through chemical analysis). Further, the 10-fold growth of the analytical instrumentation industry to $3B sales worldwide has been led by the United States with its nearly $1B positive balance of trade in this area.

A key factor in this growth has been the incorporation of computers into analytical instrumentation. The benefit is well-deserved because the advances in solid state technology critical for modern computers have been dependent on analytical advances, such as new capabilities to analyze trace impurities in silicon. Now microprobe analyzers using computer imaging techniques are answering questions critical to making microcircuitry even smaller, producing computers that are faster, more reliable, and cheaper. Closing such loops challenges the best basic chemistry, and it also generates unusual intellectual opportunities at the frontiers of science. A few examples illustrate the broad range of the challenges.

Analytical Separations

Analysis of many complex mixtures is possible only after fractionation into components. Then, a variety of identification and quantitative measurement schemes become effective that would be ambiguous or impossible if applied to the unseparated mixture. Hence, devising new separations for use in an analytical context is an active field of research.

There is no single technique more effective and generally applicable than the chromatographic method. The basic principle depends upon the fact that each molecular species, whether gaseous or in solution, has its own characteristic strength of attachment to and ease of detachment from any surface it encounters. The differences in these attachment strengths can furnish a basis for separation. The differences can depend upon heat of adsorption, volatability, solvation, molecular shape (including stereogeometry), charge and charge distribution, and even functional chemistry. Great ingenuity has made it possible to use the whole range of molecular properties for analytical separations that can require only tiny amounts of material.

The different instrumental methods of chromatography will be discussed in Section V-E. For our discussion here, a few examples will illustrate the potential. Liquid chromatography, in which a solution of the mixture of interest passes through a column loaded with a suitable particulate material, can separate and reveal the presence of as little as 10^{-12} grams of a substance in a mixture. For gaseous samples, the technique can discriminate literally thousands of components in mixtures such as those from flavors, insect communication chemicals, and petroleum samples. It is even possible to separate compounds that differ only in isotopic composition (e.g., deuterium for hydrogen).

Two-dimensional chromatography can give additional specificity, resolution, and sensitivity when coupled with techniques such as isoelectric focusing. For example, 2-D electrophoresis can resolve 2000 blood proteins by separating a mixture spot linearly under one set of conditions, and then using another set of conditions to separate further the initial line of spots at right angles. Spot locations and amounts can be measured quantitatively with computerized scanning based on NASA programs developed for satellite pictures.

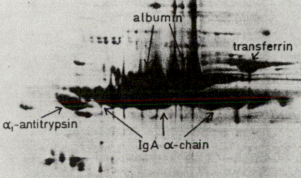

PROTEIN GEL PATTERN
HUMAN MYALOMA SERUM
5 $\mu\ell$

Optical Spectroscopy

The intellectual opportunities in this field, which introduce a host of valuable analytical techniques, can be illustrated by two notable achievements of the last decade: the incorporation of computers as an integral part of most instrumentation and the detection of single atoms and molecules. "Smart" commercial instruments now have microcomputers preprogrammed to carry out a wide variety of experimental procedures and sophisticated data analyses. The more powerful computers of the future will digest the huge volumes of data from spectroscopic methods (especially Fourier transform and two-dimensional methods) much more efficiently. This will further improve resolution, detection limits, interpretation, spectral file searching, and presentation of the results with 3-D color graphics in "real-time" to permit direct human interaction with the experiment.

Intense laser sources of electromagnetic radiation are revolutionizing analytical optical spectroscopy. An obvious benefit is increased sensitivity. In special cases, resonance-enhanced multiphoton ionization has achieved the ultimate sensitivity—detection of a single atom (cesium) or molecule (naphthalene)—and achievements in laser-induced fluorescence are approaching this limit. Laser remote sensing, such as for atmospheric pollutants, is effective at distances of

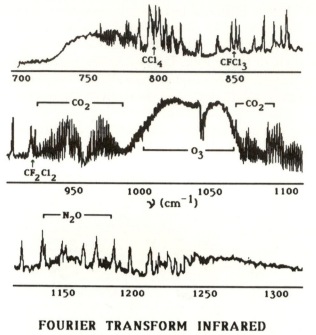

**FOURIER TRANSFORM INFRARED
NIGHT SKY SPECTRUM**

over 1 mile; fluorescence excitation and pulsed laser Raman with time-resolved ranging are particularly promising.

To use the wavelength selectivity of the laser to give specificity for mixture analysis often requires the development of new strategies because many atomic and molecular transitions are much broader than the laser line width. For example, dramatic line narrowing results from cooling through supersonic expansion for gases or with liquid helium for molecules embedded in a cryogenic solid (matrix isolation). These complementary techniques minimize interference by rotational and vibrational transitions and substantially improve detection sensitivity and diagnostic capability.

The spectroscopic potentialities of synchrotron sources have barely been tapped, and free-electron lasers as light sources are on the horizon. Synchrotron light sources designed to bridge the gap between laser ultraviolet sources through the vacuum ultraviolet to the soft X-ray region will undoubtedly open up a variety of unique analytical applications. Free electron lasers, too, show great promise for extremely high brightness at whatever design wavelength is selected, beginning at the microwave range, extending through the far- and mid-infrared, and reaching to the ultraviolet. For example, analytical applications in chemistry would surely result if these design specifications were to be directed toward developing an intense, continuously tunable, short-duration pulse (10 picoseconds) mid-infrared light source.

Mass Spectrometry

Because this method involves separation of gaseous charged species according to their mass, its intellectual frontiers embrace ionic structure, thermochemistry, and gas phase reactivity, and they provide important insights into solution reactions and theoretical chemistry. On the other hand, the methodology offers unusual analytical advantages of sensitivity (detection of single ions), specificity (peaks at 10^2 to 10^6 possible mass values) and speed (10^{-2} sec response) attributes making for a nearly ideal marriage to the dedicated computer. In the celebrated Viking Mars Probe, mass spectrometry was the basis for both the upper atmosphere analysis and the search for organic material in the planetary soil. Such sensitive soil sniffing to detect hydrocarbons might become a fast method for oil exploration. A special tandem-accelerator/ MS can detect three atoms of ^{14}C in 10^{16} atoms of ^{12}C, which corresponds to a radio-carbon age of 70,000 years. The broad applications of mass spectrometry include the analysis of elements, iso-topes, and molecules for the semiconductor, metallurgi-cal, nuclear, chemical, petro-leum, and pharmaceutical in-dustries.

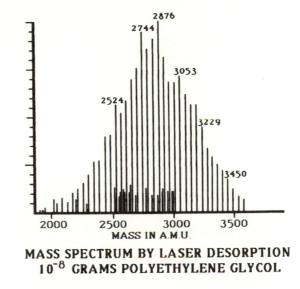

**MASS SPECTRUM BY LASER DESORPTION
10^{-8} GRAMS POLYETHYLENE GLYCOL**

*Large Molecules Vital to
Biomedicine and Industry*

A recently developed series of related techniques uses ion, neutral, and photon bombardment (see Table V-3) to desorb ions from solid samples. These techniques dramatically increase the molecular weight range of mass spectrometry. Plasma desorption with ^{252}Cf has given molecular ions of molecular weight 23,000 from the polypeptide trypsin, while FAB has provided extensive structure information on a glyco-protein of molecular weight above 15,000. Laser and field desorption have produced molecular ion mass spectra displaying the oligomer distribution of

TABLE V-3   Desorption Ionization Techniques for Analysis of High-Molecular-Weight Substances

Field Desorption (FD). Samples placed on a fine, carbon-coated wire are subjected to heat and high electric fields. Commercially available, somewhat erratic, but has been productively employed.

Plasma Desorption (PD). Samples placed on thin foil are bombarded with high energy fission fragments from radioactive californium (^{252}Cf) or ions from an accelerator. Not commercially available.

Secondary Ion Mass Spectrometry (SIMS). Solid samples are bombarded with kilovolt electrons. Low electron fluxes are used for molecular SIMS; high fluxes for inorganic analysis and depth profiling. Commercially available.

Electrohydrodynamic Ionization (EHMS). Samples are dissolved in a glycerol-electrolyte solvent. Desorption from solution occurs under high electric fields and without heating. Almost no molecular fragmentation! Not commercially available.

Laser Desorption (LD). Both reflection and transmission experiments and various sample preparations can be used. Tendency toward thermal degradation. Commercially available with time-of-flight mass analysis.

Thermal Desorption (TD). Sample is placed on probe tip which is heated to desorb ions (no ionization filament is used). Useful for inorganic analysis; recently applied to organic salts.

Fast Atom Bombardment (FAB). Samples in solution (usually glycerol) are bombarded with kilovolt-energy atoms. Fluxes higher than in SIMS. Wide applicability to biological samples, including pharmaceuticals. Commerically available.

polymers. Separation of such complex mixtures is far beyond the capability of other methods.

In "tandem" mass spectrometry, one mass spectrometer (MS-I) feeds ions of a selected mass into a collisional zone that induces fragmentation into a new set of fragment ions for analysis in a second mass spectrometer (MS-II). This technique, abbreviated MS/MS, offers a particularly promising frontier for anaylsis of mixtures of large molecules. "Soft" ionization that avoids extensive fragmentation is used first to produce a mixture of molecular ions. From this mixture, one mass is selected by MS-I, and it is more vigorously fragmented to produce an MS-II spectrum that characterizes the structure of the corresponding component. High speed and molecular specificity are important features of MS/MS. It is a powerful tool for analysis of groups of compounds sharing common structural features. It is particularly effective in removing background signal due to the contaminant species usually present in biological samples. It is now possible to sequence peptides with up to 20 amino acids and, in some instances, with sample sizes as small as a few micrograms.

Instrumentation

Developments in many fields have led to improved MS hardware. The quadrupole mass filter, which is unusually simple and computer-controllable, has revolutionized routine GC/MS analyses and is similarly promising for LC/MS and MS/MS. Inhomogeneous high field magnets developed for high energy accelerators have given a 10-fold increase in mass range for double-focusing instruments to take full advantage of the new methods to ionize high MW compounds. Time-of-flight instruments with their unlimited mass range give accurate molecular weights with ^{252}Cf plasma desorption using subnanosecond timing circuits. The Fourier transform mass spectrometer, based on ion cyclotron resonance and equipped with a superconducting magnet, can give unusual resolution ($>10^6$ at m/z $= 100$), nondestructive and simultaneous measurement of all ions, and the ability to do time-separated mass analyses.

Combined ("Hyphenated") Techniques

There is a growing appreciation for the synergistic benefits of using these computerized instruments in combination, such as the mass spectrometer coupled to a chromatograph (gas or liquid, GC/MS or LC/MS) or to another mass spectrometer (MS/MS), or these coupled with the Fourier transform infrared spectrometer (GC/IR, GC/IR/MS). High-resolution ($1/10^4$) MS gives 1 part-per-trillion ($1/10^{12}$) analyses for the many forms of dioxin (TCDD) to see if they are present in human milk and the adipose tissue of Vietnam war veterans (see Figure, Section V-A). GC/MS is necessary for the specific detection of 2,3,7,8-TCDD, the most toxic dioxin isomer. GC/MS is used routinely for detecting halocarbons in drinking water, polychlorobiphenyls (PCB), vinyl chloride, nitrosamines, and for most of the EPA list of other "priority pollutants." MS/MS with atmospheric pressure ionization can monitor many of these contaminants continuously at the parts-per-billion level, even from a mobile van or helicopter. The high specificity as well as sensitivity of these methods make them especially promising for nerve gases, "yellow rain," and natural toxins in foodstuffs (10^{-11} g vomitoxin in wheat) and plants ("loco weed"). Metabolites found by GC/MS have led to the identification of more than 50 inborn errors of metabolism in newborn infants; early identification is usually critical in preventing severe mental retardation or death. One of the most exciting intellectual frontiers is the possibility that routine profiling of human body fluids may detect incipient disease states; here the molecular complexity will challenge even the combined information provided by chromatographic retention times coupled with infrared and mass spectral data.

Surface Analysis

Most modern techniques for the characterization of surfaces have been developed since 1970. These techniques provide *complementary* information, so that sophisticated research requires multitechnique instrumentation that is, therefore, expensive. Understanding surface chemistry demands unusual information, such as the composition of the first atomic layer of the surface and of the molecular species on the surface. The surface layer can be sampled with secondary ion mass spectrometry (SIMS). Because this method strips away the surface during the measurement, continued bombardment then samples underlying layers for depth profiling. Even horizontal spatial information can be obtained at 400 Å resolution.

Characterizing surface molecular species, which is basic to understanding heterogeneous catalysis, brings additional intellectual challenges. Desorption mass spectrometry can now identify species with molecular weights of several thousand, but the effect of desorption on structure needs further study. Techniques providing detailed information on molecule-surface interactions, such as low-energy electron loss spectroscopy and surface-enhanced Raman, give promise of directly visualizing the dynamics of surface chemistry. Here, special challenges abound: sensitivity requirements are staggering (a 1-mm^2 monolayer of benzene weighs less than 10^{-9} g), and atmospheric pressure reactions require special interfaces to use high-vacuum (10^{-12} atm) surface spectroscopic techniques.

Electroanalytical Chemistry

Electrochemistry is also an interfacial science, and it presents basic challenges to the understanding and control of the properties of surfaces and the processes that occur there. Improved ion selective electrodes demand a deeper understanding of molecular-scale electrochemistry. To obtain picomole sensitivity (10^{-12} moles) and specificity of stripping using pulse voltammetric techniques, we depend heavily on solid state circuitry and microprocessors. Improved sensitivity and miniaturization (electrode area a few square microns) have made possible continuous analysis in living single cells. Other successful applications in difficult environments include flowing rivers, liquid chromatographic detectors, nonaqueous chemical process streams, molten salts, and nuclear reactor core fluids.

Another vital frontier is the direct application of surface science techniques (LEED, Auger, ESCA, and Raman) to the study of electrode surfaces. Fundamental advances in electrochemistry will not only yield important improvements in this nondestructive, inexpensive analytical tool, but also in such commercial devices as batteries and fuel cells.

Computers in Analytical Chemistry

There has been repeated reference to the opportunities for analytical instrumentation opened by the recent growth in both the speed and availability of digital computers. Dedicated microprocessors or minicomputers that increase the cost of an instrument by less than 50 percent can increase its capabilities many fold. Whole body scanners based upon three-dimensional nuclear magnetic resonance techniques would not be practical without fast Fourier transform and data interpretation capabilities. FT/NMR, FT/infrared, and FT/mass spectrometry have led to similar dramatic improvements in the specific detection of complex molecules (NMR, 10^{-8} g; IR, 10^{-10} g; MS, 10^{-13} g). Computer-aided pattern recognition should be applicable when data from several techniques can be obtained. Computer data reduction and interpretation have greatly increased the efficiency of trained scientists. With this revolution has come an increasing awareness of the need for better training to ensure "computer literacy" among scientists, especially analytical chemists. The increasing complexity of science and the explosive growth in the data acquisition rate of instruments will continue to challenge improved computer capabilities for many years.

The current impressive progress in analytical instrumentation and methodology has drawn heavily on fields such as lasers, electronics, computers, chromatography, mass spectrometry, and the surface sciences, in each of which the United States is a world leader. Combining relevant discoveries in these fields with those of chemistry to find better analytical solutions to old and new scientific problems is a current intellectual challenge. The resulting analytical capabilities should be a key element in future progress in these scientific fields and their commercial outlets, as well as in the manufacture of analytical instrumentation.

Separations Sciences

Separations chemistry has already been discussed in Section V-C and again in this section under Analytical Chemistry. Thus, while it is a well-defined body of chemical science, it also cuts across several more or less classical or conventional areas of chemistry. It is well defined in that it is concerned with the application of chemical principles, properties, and techniques to the separation of specific elements and groups of elements from extraneous materials and from each other. It is a cross-cut field in that it has applications in diverse areas as enumerated in Section V-C.

Quite a number of applications of separations chemistry have been mentioned in earlier sections, ranging from biochemicals separated from living organisms to processes that furnish continuous supplies of critical and strategic materials. Research advances in separations will have industrial applications of substantial economic and strategic importance. The example of critical metals mentioned in Section V-C (see Table V-2) provides a case in point. Almost 90 percent of our use of the critical metal platinum, in great demand as a catalyst, is met by imports; mining of the major platinum source in the United States (in Stillwater, Montana) has not yet begun. A second, undoubtedly more important example, concerns our access to uranium. Chemical separations, and their implementation in chemical engineering processes, are vitally important in developing the nuclear fuel cycle. About 13 percent of the nation's electrical energy is derived from nuclear energy. A much larger percentage is provided to the industrialized Northeast. Chemical separations are used at the uranium mill where the very low-grade uranium ores (typically .1 to .3 percent U_3O_8) are treated in highly selective chemical processes to produce a concentrate of greater than 80 percent U_3O_8. Subsequent chemical separations, based on solvent extraction or formation of a volatile fluoride, produce a uranium product pure enough for use in nuclear reactor fuel manufacture. After removal from the reactor, the highly radioactive fuel is subjected to a selective, remotely operable chemical process that separates uranium and plutonium from the fission products to high levels of purity, in a safe reliable manner and on a large scale. Chemical separations processes have also been devised to separate useful fission products from the fission product waste stream.

Research in the separations sciences must have wide scope. It focuses strongly on investigation of the properties of the liquid state at its most fundamental level, including solvent-cage reorientation, solvent-solute interactions, and chemical behaviors of fluids under extreme pressures and temperatures. Separations are typically much less efficient, thermodynamically, than other steps in chemical processing. With new insights, we may learn how to carry out separations more efficiently and how to optimize the rate of the process in view of its intrinsic thermodynamic implications. The chemical engineering community will furnish important contributions; practical applications can be anticipated.

Nuclear Chemistry

Since the days of the Curies, chemists have played a key role in the fundamental exploration of radioactivity and nuclear properties, as well as in nuclear applications to other fields. Most of the advances in our understanding of the atomic nucleus have depended strongly on the complementary skills and approaches of physicists and chemists. Furthermore, the applications of nuclear techniques and nuclear phenomena to such diverse fields as biology, astronomy, geology, archaeology, and medicine as well as various areas of chemistry have often been and continue to be pioneered by people educated as nuclear chemists. Thus the impact of nuclear chemistry is broadly interdisciplinary.

Studies of Nuclei and Their Properties

With over 2600 different nuclear species now known and new ones being discovered every month, there is a vast range of nuclei to explore, and they exhibit a wide spectrum of properties. Some nuclear states are well described in terms of the motion of a few nucleons in an average potential and single-particle or shell-model states, while others involve collective motions such as rotations and vibrations. Nuclear spectroscopy, the systematic study of excited states of nuclei, has greatly advanced since the 1960s and has led to greatly improved models; nuclear chemists have made significant contributions to this field, especially in regions of deformed nuclei, such as the actinides and lanthanides, where rotational, vibrational, and intrinsic single-particle states have been used extensively in testing nuclear models. New phenomena, such as changes of nuclear shape with increasing nuclear spin, have been discovered.

Particularly interesting advances have been made in extending our knowledge of nuclear and chemical species at the upper end of the Periodic Table. In the last 15 years, elements 104 to 109 have been synthesized and positively identified, often by ingenious new techniques necessitated by the fact that the half-lives of these species are very short, down to milliseconds. In addition to these new-element discoveries, many new isotopes of other transuranium elements have been found, and the study of their nuclear properties has played a vital role in advancing our understanding of alpha decay, nuclear fission, and the factors that govern nuclear stability. Fission research in particular has borne rich fruit: totally unexpected changes in fission properties (mass and kinetic-energy distributions of fragments) with changes of only one nucleon in the region of fermium indicate a dominant effect of the doubly closed shell configuration of ^{132}Sn (50 protons, 82 neutrons) among fission fragments. The study of spontaneously fissioning isomers among the heaviest elements has led to the important realization that the potential energy surfaces of nuclei in this region have two minima, and this, in turn, opened the way to a new and powerful approach to calculating such surfaces—the so-called shell correction method.

Along with the advances in understanding nuclear properties goes new insight into the chemistry of the elements at the upper end of the Periodic Table. The prediction that the actinide series ends with lawrencium (element 103) has been confirmed by experiments that have shown element 104 to have the properties expected of a group IVb element. This confirmation has put predictions of the chemical properties of higher-Z elements on a firmer footing.

Further exploration of the limits of nuclear stability is clearly in order, both at the upper end of the table of nuclides and on the neutron-rich and neutron-poor sides of the valley of stability. Newly discovered reaction mechanisms, such as multinucleon transfer reactions at near-Coulomb-barrier energies, promise to give access to more neutron-rich and therefore much longer-lived (minutes to hours) isotopes of elements with $Z > 100$ than have been available. This should open the way to more detailed investigations of the chemistry of these interesting elements at the upper end of the actinide series and beyond, where relativistic effects on the atomic electrons should play an increasingly prominent role. The quest for "superheavy" elements, i.e., nuclear species in or near the predicted "island of stability" around atomic number 114 and neutron number 182, has so far not been successful. However, new attempts in this direction are in preparation because it has recently become clear that the conditions used in past experiments were probably not at all optimal.

Nuclear Reactions

In the realm of nuclear reactions, the last decade has brought to light a new mechanism in heavy-ion induced reactions termed deeply inelastic collisions; this process is characterized by the damping of large amounts of collective nuclear energy through interactions with nucleonic modes of excitation. Studies of such damped collisions give information on the cooperative phenomena and relaxation processes occurring within a small quantal system initially far from equilibrium.

Other major advances that have resulted from nuclear reaction studies have been extensions of the nuclide chart to extremely neutron-rich and neutron-poor nuclides. Spallation reactions with high energy protons, transfer reactions with heavy ions, and multiple neutron capture reactions in high neutron fluxes are among the approaches used in this quest to reach or approach the limits of nuclear stability. Much improved nuclear systematics, new insights into nuclear reaction mechanisms, and even the discovery of new modes of radioactive decay (proton emission and 2-neutron emission) have resulted. The studies are also of relevance to astrophysics, especially for understanding and calculating nucleosynthesis by rapid successive neutron captures, a process believed to be responsible for element building to the highest Z's in stellar environments of extremely high neutron fluxes, such as those that may exist in certain types of supernovae.

Another current challenge in nuclear reaction research is the attempt to produce nuclear matter under extreme conditions of density and temperature that approach those thought to have existed in the earliest stages of the expanding universe. Such conditions can presumably be produced in head-on collisions of heavy ion beams accelerated to relativistic energies, and accelerators capable of producing the requisite beams will soon become available.

Space Exploration

The breadth of applicability of nuclear techniques is demonstrated in the exploration of the Moon and our companion planets during the past two decades.

For example, the unmanned Surveyor missions to the Moon provided the first chemical analyses of the moon, employing a newly developed analytical technique that used the synthetic transuranium isotope ^{242}Cm. The analyses identified and determined the amounts of more than 90 percent of the atoms at three locations on the lunar surface. These analyses, verified later by work on returned samples, provided answers to fundamental questions about the composition and geochemical history of the Moon. Nuclear techniques also played an important role in the chemical analyses performed by Soviet unmanned missions to the Moon and in experiments designed to seek life on the surface of Mars by the U.S. Viking missions. Similarly, activation and isotopic analyses were prominent in the analyses of returned lunar samples of the concurrent intensive studies of meteorites, making possible elucidation of the temporal history of the Moon and meteorites.

Isotopic Anomalies

Ever since the discovery of the isotopic composition of the chemical elements, it has been assumed that this isotopic composition is essentially constant in all samples, an assumption that provides the basis for assigning atomic weights. The only exceptions involved elements with long-lived radioactive isotopes. However, since 1945, human operations have affected the atomic weights of several elements (e.g., Li, B, U) under some circumstances. More fundamentally, it has been discovered that the solar system is not composed of an isotopically homogeneous mixture of chemical elements. Even for an element as abundant as oxygen, variations of the isotopic abundance have been noted for different parts of the solar system. Such isotopic variations have now been established for several chemical elements, and they provide clues to the nucleosynthetic processes that gave rise to the chemical elements, as well as to the conditions that prevailed at the birth of the solar system.

A startlingly large isotopic anomaly was discovered in the uranium of uraninite ore samples from the Oklo mine in Gabon (West Africa) in 1972. Anomalously low isotopic abundances of uranium-235 in these ores led to the astonishing conclusion that, 1.8 billion years before the first manmade nuclear reactor, nature had accidentally assembled a uranium fission reactor in Africa! This reactor was made possible by the higher ^{235}U concentration ($\sim$3 percent instead of the present-day .7 percent) at the time. Massspectrometric analyses of various elements in the Oklo ore not only proved that isotopic compositions labeled them unmistakably as fission products, but also made it possible to deduce such characteristics of the reactor as total neutron fluence (1.5×10^{21} neutrons cm^{-2}), power level ($\sim$20 kW), and duration of the self-sustaining chain reaction ($\sim$10^6 years). An important practical result of the Oklo studies is the fact that most fission products as well as the transuranium elements produced in the reactor did not migrate very far in 1.8 billion years. This has clear implications for the possibility of long-term confinement of radioactive waste products in geologic formations. An interesting scientific fringe benefit of the

Oklo event is that, from detailed analyses of the isotopic composition of the residual fission products, it has been possible to set upper limits, orders of magnitude lower than by any previous method, on the variation with time of some fundamental constants, such as the fine structure constant and the coupling constants for strong and weak interactions. This is significant because such variations are the consequence of certain cosmological theories, and the limits set by the Oklo data help to narrow the choice of acceptable cosmological models.

Solar Neutrino Experiments

For nearly 40 years it has been almost universally accepted that the Sun's energy, on which life on Earth depends, is produced by a series of thermonuclear reactions deep in the solar interior. It is also generally agreed that the only radiations produced in these reactions that can penetrate through the sun and reach us are neutrinos, so that the only experiment to date that can be considered a probe of the postulated reaction sequence is an attempted radiochemical measurement of the neutrino flux from the Sun. Neutrino capture by ^{37}Cl to form radioactive ^{37}Ar has been monitored since 1968 in 650 tons of perchloroethylene in a deep mine in South Dakota. This painstaking experiment—only a few neutrinos are captured per month—indicates a solar neutrino flux about one-fourth of the theoretically predicted value, which casts doubts on the completeness of our understanding of how the sun and other stars generate their energy. This discrepancy between theory and experiment has led to much re-examination of the astrophysical models and of the nuclear data underlying the flux prediction, but no satisfactory resolution has been found. To determine whether the source of the discrepancy is to be sought in the astrophysical models or in fundamental properties of the neutrino, another radiochemical neutrino detection experiment is being prepared. It uses ^{71}Ga as the detector because its response is much less model-dependent than that of ^{37}Cl.

Nuclear Chemistry in Medicine

Nearly 20 million nuclear medicine procedures are performed annually in the United States. Advances in nuclear medicine depend crucially on research in nuclear and radiochemistry. For example, great progress in our knowledge of the chemistry of technetium in the past decade will clearly lead to much more effective applications of ^{99m}Tc, the most widely used radionuclide, because the physical and chemical properties of technetium compounds can be related to their in vivo activity in pathological states.

Another important example is the development of ingenious, rapid online methods for labeling a variety of compounds with cyclotron-produced short-lived positron emitters, such as ^{11}C(20m) and ^{18}F(110m), with very high specific activities. Such compounds, e.g., ^{18}F-2-deoxy-2-fluoro-D-glucose and 1-^{11}C-palmitic acid in conjunction with positron emission tomography (PET), are finding important new research and clinical applications in neurology and cardiology.

Future progress in nuclear medicine will clearly require close collaboration among scientists in various disciplines, including radiochemists and nuclear chemists. One of the challenges is the radionuclide labeling of monoclonal antibodies which, if successful, would open up a whole new area of imaging and therapy.

Stable isotopes, in conjunction with NMR spectroscopy, also have important applications in medicine. With ^{13}C and ^{15}N tracers, NMR spectroscopy of humans will make possible new insights into the molecular nature of diseases, provide a noninvasive method for their early detection and for the clinical management of patients, and make possible in vivo studies of metabolic processes. This has led to one of the most exciting developments of the last few years—large-object imaging. The presence and chemical form of key elements can be mapped in entire human organs in living patients. These powerful, noninvasive techniques were literally undreamt of 15 years ago. They have arisen in response to demands for the ability to study via NMR ever larger biomolecules as well as biological systems in vivo.

V-E.   Instrumentation

As in earlier chapters, sophisticated instrumentation has figured prominently in our discussions of environmental monitoring, international competitiveness, and national security. The techniques of the surface sciences are of dominant importance to the advances being made in catalysis, upon which so many industries depend. Chromatography joins mass spectrometry (Section IV-E) and laser spectroscopy (Section III-E) as a ubiquitous tool in analytical chemistry. Infrared spectroscopy typifies the several optical spectroscopic methods that are finding effective use in environmental monitoring as well as in research applications.

Surface Science Instrumentation

Surface science is one of the most rapidly growing areas of the physical sciences at this time. The development of an array of powerful instruments that can reveal the atomic structure and chemical composition of surfaces has been largely responsible for the rapid rise. The field has been stimulated, as well, by a wide range of important applications. For example, surface and thin film electrical properties, with relevance to miniaturization of semiconductor devices, have attracted the interest of many physicists. Both physicists and chemists are investigating surface etching and epitaxial growth, with the same application in mind. But surely the prospect of understanding catalysis on a fundamental level is one of the most exciting and significant frontiers opened by these new instruments. This is, of course, a realm for chemists. No doubt the historical pattern of NMR will be repeated—physicists have perfected a remarkable set of instruments with which chemists will open the cornucopia of catalysis.

Instruments for the Study of Surfaces

The various techniques of surface science probe the surface with particles or photons. Among the particles that have proven useful are electrons, ions, neutral atoms, neutrons, and electronically excited atoms (metastables). Photon probes extend from the X-ray region to the infrared. When particles are used, either as incident projectiles or as secondary indicators of high energy photon-induced processes (e.g., electron-ejection following X-ray absorption), ultrahigh vacuum environments are essential (10^{-9} to 10^{-10} torr). In contrast, photon probes can be effective when the surface is in contact with a gas at high pressure or a liquid, the conditions under which surface catalysis can occur.

A second aspect of categorization is the type of information provided. A key question about chemistry as it takes place on a surface is the molecular structure of the molecules that have become attached to the surface. Is each molecule essentially intact (physisorbed) with its structure and bonding little changed? If so, the surface may be serving only as a site for reaction, immobilizing the reactant as it awaits its fate. Or does the molecule react with the surface, so that it is attached more strongly (chemisorbed)? If so, it has acquired a new molecular identity, undoubtedly with changed chemical behavior. Second, we would like to know the structure and composition of the surface, for in chemisorption, the surface is itself a reactant. Finally, it is useful to understand the bonding of the solid itself in this zone of discontinuity, where one bulk phase ends and another begins.

Table V-4 lists more than 15 types of the surface science measurements that

TABLE V-4　Surface Science Instrumentation Relevant to Chemistry on Surfaces

Surface Analysis Method	Acronym	Bombard or Irradiate with:	Physical Basis	Information Obtained
Electron energy loss spectroscopy	EELS	Electrons, 1-10 eV	Vibrational excitation of surface molecules by inelastic reflection	Molecular identity, orientation and surface bonding of adsorbed molecules
Infrared spectroscopy	IRS	Infrared light	Vibrational excitation by absorption	(Same as above)
Raman	Raman	Visible light	Raman scattering, resonant, surface-enhanced	Vibrational spectrum adsorbed molecules
Thermal desorption	TDS	Heat	Thermally induced desorption, decomposition of adsorbates	Desorption energetics, surface chemistry of adsorbates
Extended X-ray absorption fine structure	EXAFS	X-rays	Interference effects in photoemitted electron	Atomic structure of surfaces, adsorbates, nearest neighbor distances
Molecular beam scattering	—	Molecules of known energy	Inelastic reflection off surface	Energy transfer to surface
Auger spectroscopy	AES, Auger	Electrons, 2-3 keV X-rays	Electron emission from excited surface atoms	Surface composition
Secondary ion mass spectroscopy	SIMS	Ions, 1-20 keV	Ion beam-induced ejection of surface atoms as ions	Surface composition
Ion sputtering	—	Inert gas ions	Surface atom ejection by ion bombardment	Surface composition, depth profiling
X-ray and UV photoelectron spectroscopy	XPS, UPS, ESCA	X-rays, (synchrotron) UV light (21 eV)	Electron emission from inner shells	Surface composition near surface (100 Å) oxidation states
Ion scattering	ISS	Inert gas ions	Elastic scattering	Atomic structure and composition of surface
Low energy electron diffraction	LEED	Electrons, 10-300 eV	Elastic back scattering, diffraction	Atomic surface structure
Scanning electron microscope	SEM	Electrons	Electron scattering	Surface topology
Laser microprobe mass spectrometry	—	Visible, UV light	Focused light-induced molecular desorption	200-micron surface compositional mapping
Laser-induced second harmonic generation	—	Visible, UV light	High-photon field non-linear effects	Detection of molecules at a solid-solution interface

are now in use. Some of the listings embrace two or more techniques and, even so, the table is not all-inclusive. The first six are the methods most responsive to the first set of questions posed above. The other instruments mainly provide information about the surface itself, its structure, composition, and bonding in the first few layers. Plainly, coupling two or more complementary methods can greatly enhance the significance of any single measurement used alone.

Among the electron probes, low energy electron diffraction (LEED) reveals the atomic structure of clean, ordered surfaces and ordered structures of monolayers of adsorbed atoms and molecules. Its role in determining bond distances and bond angles is the same in surface chemistry as the role played by X-ray diffraction in the structural chemistry of solids. Electron energy loss spectroscopy (EELS) detects the vibrational modes of surface atoms and molecules with an energy resolution of about 40 cm^{-1}. Scanning electron microscopy (SEM) yields surface topology with about a 300 Å spatial resolution. Auger electron spectroscopy determines the surface composition with a sensitivity of about 1 percent of a monolayer for most elements (10^{13} atoms/cm^2). X-ray photoelectron spectroscopy (X-Ray PES) also determines the composition of surfaces and of the near-surface region ($\sim$100 Å), as well as the oxidation states of the surface. Photoelectron diffraction uses the diffraction of photoelectrons for surface structure analysis as they exit from the solid into vacuum. Ultraviolet photoelectron spectroscopy (UVPS) uses He I radiation (21.2 eV) or synchrotron radiation to eject electrons from the valence shell of atoms or molecules or from the valence bands of solids at the surface. In this way, the surface electronic structure is explored.

Ion scattering from surfaces has been used for surface composition analysis with great sensitivity, 10^9 atoms/cm^2. In secondary ion mass spectroscopy (SIMS), neutral and ionized atoms and molecular fragments are ejected by bombardment with high energy (1-20 KeV) inert gas ions. Ion scattering spectroscopy determines the surface composition by the energy change of inert gas ions upon surface scattering. Ion sputtering or ion etching removes atoms from surfaces layer by layer. The combined use of ion sputtering and electron spectroscopy yields a depth profile analysis of the chemical composition in the near-surface region.

Diffraction techniques with helium and other atoms are used to determine surface structure and roughness. Energy transfer during molecular beam-surface scattering yields information about the dynamics of elementary surface reaction steps of adsorption, surface diffusion, surface reactions, and desorption. It also provides information about the nature of the attractive potential between the molecule that approaches the surface and the surface atoms.

Grazing angle X-ray diffraction provides still another method for learning the atomic structure of surfaces and interfaces. Extended X-ray absorption fine structure measurements (EXAFS) can be used to determine nearest neighbor population and interatomic distances for small dispersed particles and surfaces. The availability of high-intensity laser sources is now awakening the development of a new set of surface sensitive techniques. Surface infrared spectroscopy, laser Raman spectroscopy, second harmonic generation surface spectroscopy, and laser ellipsometry all provide information about the surface chemical bonds of adsorbed atoms and molecules. Solid state nuclear magnetic resonance is specially well suited for determination of the structure of high surface area solids like the molecular sieve materials.

Instrument Developments Needed

There are many, well-perfected techniques for the study of surfaces under well-controlled conditions. Developments of the next few years will focus more attention on techniques that clarify the molecular structure and behavior of the adsorbate. EELS is such a technique. While great effort and design skill has been invested in achieving the EELS resolution now available, about 40 cm^{-1}, it is only marginally able to provide the structural information desired. A 10-fold improvement is needed, to a spectral resolution of 5 cm^{-1} or better; such a gain would enormously increase the value of this technique.

Research systems have been built with capacity to move a sample from an ultrahigh vacuum environment into contact with a gas and then to return to the vacuum situation. This is an important capability and should be made available commercially. Surface samples should be readily held at cryogenic temperatures down to 4 K. Laser techniques, too, offer special promise for chemistry-oriented surface studies. Then, to open the door to kinetics of reactions as they take place on surfaces, techniques must be developed for pulsed excitation and subsequent temporal analysis on a short time scale.

Costs

Table V-5 lists some of the most important instruments from Table V-4 and approximate current costs. It is important to realize that rarely can an investigator effectively address a problem of surface chemistry with only one of these techniques. Instead, an effective laboratory will need the synergism and flexibility provided by having access to three or four complementary techniques. For example, the first five entries in Table V-5 are mutually supportive. Thus, the research group of a single investigator will require a capital investment exceeding $500K and, of course, a substantial on-going support to ensure cost-effective maintenance and operation of these systems.

TABLE V-5   Approximate Current (1985) Costs ($) for Surface Science Instruments

Electron energy loss spectrometer	EELS	200-225K
Low energy electron diffraction	LEED	150-175K
Auger electron spectrometer	AES	150-250K
Tunable laser sources and detectors	—	100-150K
Thermal desorption mass spectrometry	TDS	150-200K
X-ray photoelectron spectrometer	XPS	150-200K
Ion-scattering spectrometer	ISS	150-175K
Secondary ion mass spectrometer (static mode)	SIMS	170-200K
Secondary ion mass spectrometer (dynamic mode)	SIMS	650-700K
Rutherford back-scattering system	—	500-600K
Laser microprobe mass spectrometer	—	300-325K
Raman microprobe	—	150-170K
X-ray absorption fine structure attachment to synchrotron	EXAFS	400-500K

The instruments listed in Table V-4 permit us now to inaugurate a new era of investigation of chemistry in the surface domain. Sections III-A, III-B, and V-D show that both the economic and intellectual stakes are high. We must increase chemistry funding levels to place these powerful tools in the hands of those chemists working on catalysis. Only then can we expect to maintain a world-leadership position in this crucial field. The United States cannot afford merely to watch with admiration as the field of catalysis is developed in properly equipped laboratories abroad.

Surface Analysis

As is always the case, sensitive measurement techniques can be regarded as analytical tools. This is the case in the surface sciences. Every one of the capabilities listed in the last column of Table V-1 can be put to analytical use in the pursuit of questions that may be only remotely connected to the surface sciences. As an example, a state-of-the-art laser microprobe device designed to desorb molecules from a solid surface can be used to detect the presence of a pesticide on the leaf of a plant. Such a capability was quite impossible only 10 years ago; today it permits us to contemplate tracking the amount, stability, weathering, and chemistry of a pesticide in field use.

Of course, the analytical technique may, as well, be concerned with monitoring or clarifying chemical changes that take place on a surface or with a surface. Many of these analytical studies relate to catalysis. In Section V-D, examples were given of the use of EELS to determine the molecular structures that exist on a catalyst surface as it functions. Similarly, X-ray photoelectron spectroscopy (ESCA) studies of the cobalt molybdate catalyst show another facet of the chemical role of a catalyst. This catalyst (with 3 percent cobalt) is used commercially to remove sulfur from petroleum (to reduce acid rain).

In actual use, the catalyst surface is first prepared by chemical exposure to hydrogen gas at a high temperature to reduce surface oxides. Then, the catalyst is "activated" by exposing it to a hydrogen sulfide/hydrogen mixture. Understanding how the catalyst has been chemically changed in each of these treatments is a crucial part of understanding how the catalyst works. Present-day ESCA measurements clearly reveal the changes in the cobalt atoms as the oxide coating is removed by hydrogen and then as they are converted to the sulfide.

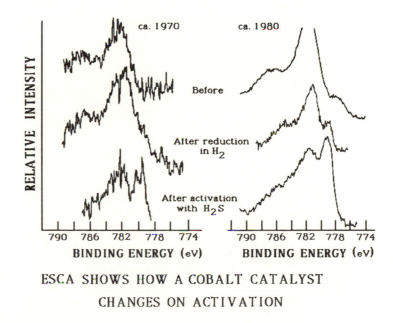

ESCA SHOWS HOW A COBALT CATALYST CHANGES ON ACTIVATION

Fifteen years ago, the best ESCA equipment in existence was unable to distinguish these changes.

The myriad of applications that lie somewhere between the two examples mentioned above has been made possible by the array of surface science instruments shown in Table V-4. These applications have given rise to *surface analysis*, a new subdivision of analytical chemistry.

Applicability

Surface analysis is quite different from bulk analysis; frequently, factors important for surface analysis are not important to bulk analysis. The most common distinguishing feature is the effective sampling depth of the analytical technique used. For each technique, the sampling depth of that technique defines the exact surface sampled. Sampling depth is important because the measuring technique should be appropriate to the phenomenon under study. For example, bonding to the surface, wettability, and catalysis involve only a few atomic layers, whereas passivation and surface hardening treatments involve 10 to 1000 atomic layers. Typical sampling depths for the primary surface analytical techniques are one or two atomic layers for low energy in ion scattering, 5 Å for static SIMS, 20 Å for the ESCA and Auger techniques, and 100 Å for dynamic SIMS. Laser mass spectrometry, the Raman microprobe, and scanning electron microscopy reach into the surface from 1000 to 10,000 Å (i.e., to 1 micron).

Another important matter is the microscopic heterogeneity or microcrystallinity of the sample. The distribution of the species across a surface and its depth distribution inward from the surface can determine the behavior of the surface and must be known. The shallower the sampling depth of the technique, the more finely it is able to define the depth profile of a sample.

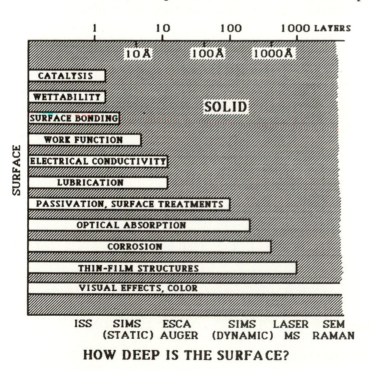

HOW DEEP IS THE SURFACE?

Developments Needed

A major challenge in the development of surface analytical instrumentation is the reinforcement of its quantitative dimension. Most of the examples given have been concerned with *what* is there. We must also be able to determine *how much*. Relative quantitative surface analysis measures a species of interest against a component already present. To quantify surface species without resorting to such internal standards is a difficult problem whose solution will expand surface analysis to many applications, particularly those involving organic species.

Another important problem is the development of microprobes that can provide both chemical and spatial information about surface species. Currently, Auger and ion microprobes are useful in this respect for probing elemental composition, such as the presence and location of the trace contaminants phosphorus and lead in silicon chips. However, they are not able to probe for large organic molecules such as carcinogens or therapeutic drugs. Thus, development of new organic microprobes is an urgent need. Characterization of small particles is another important challenge for surface analysis; this is particularly important in environmental monitoring where the analysis of carcinogenic hydrocarbons on particulates is a current problem. Finally, development of new hardware is important. An example has been mentioned earlier: it is important to interface high-vacuum surface spectroscopic techniques with samples at atmospheric pressure. Development of cells to permit real time examination of surfaces in contact with a reactive gas is a challenging instrumental problem.

Costs

The cost listed in Table V-5 are applicable in analytical uses as well. Just as for research applications, surface analytical problems are seldom solved by a single, stand-alone technique. Instead, the more interesting problems require a combination of instrumental approaches. Therefore, an effective surface analytical laboratory will have to be equipped with several instruments. A considerable capital investment is implied, again approaching or exceeding $500K.

Chromatography

Chromatography separates molecules or ions by partitioning species between a moving and stationary phase. The technique exploits small differences in properties such as solubility, absorbability, volatility, stereochemistry, and ion exchange, so that understanding the fundamental chemistry of these interactions is basic to progress in the field. Liquid chromatography has shown an impressive growth since 1970. The current $400M annual sales are mainly by U.S. manufacturers. The growth has come through innovations, such as high pressure and gradient moving phases to give greater speed and resolution, bonded-molecule stationary phases to give greater selectivity and column life, and electrochemical, fluorometric, and mass spectrometric detectors sensitive to as little as 10^{-12} g. Although gas chromatography is a more mature field by perhaps a decade, important advances continue to appear. High-speed separations can now be accomplished in a few tenths of a second; portable instruments the size of a matchbox are in use. A complex mixture can be separated into literally thousands of components using fused silica capillary columns that are a direct spin-off from optical fiber technology for communications. It is even possible to separate compounds that differ only in isotopic composition.

Despite this well established record of success, chromatography is still expanding its horizons. High-performance liquid chromatography and capillary column chromatography provide convincing examples of new concepts advancing the field.

High-Performance Liquid Chromatography (HPLC)

During the 1970s, theoretical understandings of the complex flow and mass transfer phenomena involved in chromatographic band dispersion helped optimization of column design. During this same period, small diameter (3 to 10 micron) silica particles with controlled porosity were introduced and synthetic advances in silica chemistry led to tailoring of particle diameter, pore diameter, and pore size distribution. Today, 15-cm columns with efficiencies exceeding 10,000 theoretical plates are routine.

The instrumentation ancillary to these high-performance columns required development of specialized pumps to drive liquid flows with high precision and low pulsation through the small particle columns. Detector advances occurred as well. First UV and refractive index, then more selective detectors based on fluorescence and amperometry/coulometry, were developed for HPLC.

Still another major advance of the 1970s was the introduction of chemically bonded phases in which surfaces of porous silica are functionalized with organosilanes. Especially important is the use of hydrocarbonaceous phases (such as *n*-octyl and *n*-octadecyl) in which the mobile liquid phase is typically an organic-aqueous mixture. This is called reversed phase chromatography (RPLC), and it currently provides well over 50 percent of all HPLC separations. It is especially well suited to substances at least partially soluble in water (e.g., drugs, biochemicals, and polynuclear aromatics).

Thus HPLC is a vibrant field with new developments continually affecting many disciplines. New small particle supports based on silica and organic polymeric materials have recently been introduced for the ion exchange and reversed phase HPLC separation of biopolymers. Whereas separations previously required days for completion, today it is becoming possible to accomplish even better resolutions within a few minutes. Column design is improving as well. Instead of the conventional 4- to 5-mm diameters, narrower bore columns from .5-2-mm i.d. are providing routes to sensitive analyses even when the amount of sample is limited. Also, the lower flow rates at the same linear velocity permit coupling of LC to powerful vapor phase detectors, such as mass spectrometry and flame ionization. Open tubular capillary LC columns of 1- to 10-micron inner diameter are being investigated for the potential of generating high resolving power in the separation of extremely complex mixtures (e.g., fossil energy fuels). In all these examples, specially designed instruments are needed to accommodate the small sample sizes.

Finally, the microprocessor/computer is playing an increasing role. "Smart" HPLC instruments are under development that use statistical optimization schemes. Semi-empirical solvent and stationary phase characterization schemes have been developed to enhance the power of these approaches. New detectors of greater sensitivity and selectivity are on the horizon. In particular, laser spectroscopy promises to yield highly sensitive devices for subpicogram detection.

Because of these performance improvements, HPLC is having a major impact on diverse fields of biochemistry, biomedicine, pharmaceutical development, environmental monitoring, and forensic science. Today, peptide analysis and isolation requires HPLC because of its separating power and speed. Analysis of PTH-amino acids in protein/peptide sequencing is conventionally accomplished by RPLC. In clinical analysis, therapeutic drug monitoring can be accomplished by HPLC. The analysis of catecholamines is typically accomplished by RPLC with electrochemical detection. Isoenzyme analysis, important, for example, in assessment of damage after heart attack, can be rapidly accomplished by HPLC. Analysis of parent drugs and their metabolites in a pharmoco-kinetic study is typically accomplished by HPLC. The isolation of synthesized drugs in purified form is typically achieved by HPLC. The analysis of polar and high-molecular-weight organic species in waste streams can be performed by HPLC, while the separation and analysis of phenols by RPLC is recommended. Analysis of narcotics, inks, paints, and blood represent only a few of the samples of forensic relevance.

Capillary Chromatography

This version of chromatography dispenses with the granular materials normally packed into the column. Instead, it uses an open capillary tube with a thin retentive layer on its inner wall. It began with capillary gas chromatography and now is being transferred to use with liquids.

Although many satisfactory GC columns are available today, surface investigations are continuing to improve the general understanding of thin liquid films and related superficial interactions. Glass as an inert material for the preparation of GC capillary columns carried with it a fragility that discouraged many potential users. Now we have flexible, fused-silica capillaries with a polymer overcoat; these columns are a spin-off of fiber-optics technology. The advances in capillary column technology led to intensive commercialization during the 1970s. Today's capillary columns exhibit efficiencies between 10^5 to 10^6 theoretical plates and are capable of separating literally hundreds of components within a narrow boiling-point range. As the corresponding chromatographic peaks are separated by seconds or less, the sample input and output measurements must be comparably rapid. Direct introduction of samples at the nanogram levels has been developed, and much effort has been spent on optimization of gas-phase ionization detectors. Among these detectors are some of the most sensitive measurement devices known. Combined advances in the column and detector areas now make feasible trace analytical determinations below 10^{-12}-gram levels by capillary gas chromatography. The highly sensitive electron capture detector and element-specific detectors, in conjunction with capillary GC, currently find numerous applications in environmental and biomedical research.

Of particular note is the combination of capillary GC with powerful identification methods, such as mass spectrometry and Fourier transform infrared spectroscopy, as mentioned in Section V-D. The combined techniques are now routinely capable of identifying numerous compounds of interest that are present in complex mixtures in only nanogram quantities. They have been used to identify new biologically important molecules, as well as in drug metabolism studies, forensic applications, and identifications of trace environmental pollutants.

During the last decade, microcolumn high-performance liquid chromatography (HPLC) has been under intensive development. Two advantages are the reduced consumption of the expensive and often environmentally undesirable mobile phase and the possibility of exploring new detection methods. Open tubular columns and partially packed columns of "capillary dimensions" have been tried. The open tubular columns for GC typically have 200- to 300-micron inner diameters to obtain optimal solute mass-transfer processes between the two chromatographic phases. Because of radial diffusion rates, liquid chromatography in open tubular columns necessitates considerably smaller column dimensions, as small as 5 to 10 microns, and nanoliter volumes are needed for both sample introduction and detection volumes. Packed capillary columns of dimensions ranging from 40 to 300 microns have now been developed that perform satisfactorily: several hundred thousand theoretical plate performance can now be achieved in several hours' time, and resolution of quite complex mixtures has been demonstrated.

Microcolumn technology has recently found yet another application in capillary high-voltage zone electrophoresis. The small diameters (typically 60 microns) of open tubular columns permit application of voltages in excess of 30,000 volts without overheating. Very efficient separations of certain charged species were already demonstrated, but improvements are still needed.

Capillary supercritical fluid chromatography has recently emerged as a promising approach to the analysis of complex nonvolatile mixtures. As the solute diffusion coefficients and viscosities of supercritical fluids are more favorable than those observed in the normal condensed phase, chromatographic performance is substantially enhanced. Furthermore, the relative optical transparency of supercritical fluids makes them attractive for certain optical detection techniques. Besides its analytical potential, supercritical fluid chromatography appears to be an ideal method for measuring physicochemical parameters in the vicinity of the critical point.

Field-Flow Fractionation (FFF)

Chromatography becomes more difficult to apply as molecular size grows and becomes ineffectual in separating macromolecules and colloidal particles in the size range .01 to 1 micron in diameter. A recent innovation, field flow fractionation, may fill this need.

In FFF, a liquid sample is injected into a thin (.1-.3 mm), ribbon-like flow channel. A thermal, sedimentation, or electric field gradient is applied through the ribbon. Each constituent in the sample distributes itself in a steady-state concentration gradient that is determined by its response to the gradient and its diffusional properties. Since flow through the channel is fastest near the middle of the ribbon, constituents that are pulled close to the wall move more slowly through the ribbon than constituents that reside near the middle of the flow channel. Separations are thus achieved. A useful aspect of this technique is that the strength of the applied field can be varied in a deliberate and programmed way during the course of the separation.

Thermal gradients are effective in separating most synthetic polymers. Sedimentation gradients separate large colloids, and electrical fields are appropriate for charged species. Because of the range of operating parameters, FFT has proven capable of separating both charged and uncharged species in either chain or globular configuration. The method works both in aqueous and nonaqueous media. The mass range of molecules and particles to which FFF has been applied extends from molecular weights of 1000 up to 10^{18}, that is, up to particle sizes of about 100-micron diameters. FFF appears to be applicable to nearly any complex molecular or particulate material within that vast range.

Because the channel geometry and flow are well characterized, the rate of displacement of a given constituent can be related rigorously to such properties as mass, size, diffusivity, density, charge, and thermal diffusion rates. Hence, the above properties can be determined by measuring displacement rates, and FFT becomes an accurate tool for particle characterization.

Applications of FFF have so far included macromolecules and particles of biological and biomedical relevance (proteins, viruses, subcellular particles, liposomes, artificial blood, and whole cells), of industrial importance (both nonpolar and water soluble polymers, lattices, coal liquid residues, emulsions, and colloidal silica), and of environmental significance (waterborne colloids and fly ash).

Costs

Chromatography is an essential tool to every synthetic chemist and to analytical chemists in a variety of fields. An advanced analytical gas chromatograph might cost $20K, an HPLC about the same, and a preparative (large volume) chromatograph somewhat more, perhaps $30K. While each item has only a modest cost, three or four such instruments will be needed as dedicated instruments by each research group. Thus the total may approach $100K, a capital investment that must be available for effective research.

Infrared Spectroscopy

The infrared spectral region reveals molecular vibrational motions. Because these motions are sensitive to bond strengths and molecular architecture, infrared spectroscopy has become one of the routine diagnostic tools of chemistry. A large, research-oriented chemistry department might operate five to ten such instruments with capabilities ranging from rugged, low-resolution instruments for instruction in an advanced first-year chemistry course to high-resolution Fourier transform instruments (FTIR) suited to molecular structure determination and specialized research use.

Computer-Aided Spectrometers

Modern research infrared spectrometers incorporate dedicated computer capability for programmed operation, data collection, and data manipulation. The major impact of computers, however, has been their influence on the accessibility and reliability of Fourier transform interferometers. As mentioned earlier in Section III-E, the perfection of the Fourier transform algorithm plus the reduction in accompanying computer costs brought the interferometer from a trouble-plagued, research-only instrument to a routine, high-performance workhorse. Spectral resolutions of .25 cm^{-1} are readily obtained over a long scan range (e.g., 4000 to 400 cm^{-1}) in 20 or 30 minutes. A notable capability is the ease and accuracy with which difference spectra can be displayed. One important application relates to infrared spectra of biological samples in which evidence of a chemical change associated with a localized biological function can be completely masked by the heavy infrared spectrum of the inactive substrate. The digitized data permit precise spectral subtraction so that the background spectrum can be virtually eliminated to reveal the spectral changes of interest. Another vivid display of the value of the difference capability is provided by photolysis of molecules suspended in a cryogenic solid ("matrix isolation"). If the digitized spectrum before photolysis is subtracted from the spectrum after photolysis, only the features that change are seen. Any molecule that is

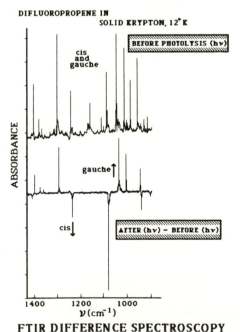

DIFLUOROPROPENE IN SOLID KRYPTON, 12° K

BEFORE PHOTOLYSIS (hν)

cis and gauche

ABSORBANCE

gauche

cis

AFTER (hν) − BEFORE (hν)

1400   1200   1000
ν (cm^{-1})

FTIR DIFFERENCE SPECTROSCOPY SHOWS ROTAMER INTERCONVERSION

being consumed presents its spectral features downward, while the product spectral features extend upwards. This has been used, for example, to distinguish the two rotameric forms (*cis-* and *gauche-*) of 2,3,-difluoropropene in the cluttered spectrum of a complex mixture. Interconversion is caused by laser irradiation of one of the absorptions of one rotamer.

Applications

The coupling of FTIR with gas chromatographic separations in a variety of analytical uses has been discussed in Section V-D. This coupling is facilitated by computerized data collection, and it is made possible by the reduced scan time that accompanies the high-performance characteristics of FTIR instruments. Also as noted in Sections V-A and V-D, infrared spectroscopy is a specially effective method for monitoring and studying atmospheric chemistry. This is because gaseous molecules of low molecular weight are important, including formaldehyde, nitric acid, sulfur dioxide, acetaldehyde, ozone, oxides of chlorine and nitrogen, nitrous oxide, carbon dioxide, and the freons. These substances are influential participants in photochemical smog production, acid rain, stratospheric disturbance of the ozone layer, and the greenhouse effect.

TABLE V-6 Additional Instrumental Techniques in Modern Chemistry

Instrument	Information Obtained	Approximate Cost ($)
Ion cyclotron resonance spectrometer	Reaction rates of gaseous molecular ions	125K
Laser magnetic resonance spectrometer	Precise molecular structures of gaseous free radicals	75K
Laser-Raman spectrometer	Vibrational structure of molecules or of chromophores in complex	60K
Fluorimeter	Energies and lifetimes of electronically excited molecules	40K
Circular dichroism spectrometer	Stereoconformations of complex molecules	50K
Flow cytometer	Laser-activated cell sorter	150K
Protein sequencer	Automated analysis of protein sequence	120K
Oligonucleotide synthesizer	Automated synthesis of design oligonucleotides	40K
Electron diffraction	Molecular structures of gaseous molecules	150K
Scintillation counter	Tracking radio-tracers through chemical reactions	50K

Costs

Fourier transform infrared spectrometers are now sufficiently easy to use—with the high performance described above—that they are becoming ubiquitous. In 1983, perhaps 200 such instruments were sold by U.S. companies, and foreign instruments are appearing (from West Germany and Canada). Costs currently range from \$140K to \$200K, depending upon the resolution and scan range. Accessories permit long-wavelength spectroscopy to 10 cm^{-1} and near-infrared spectroscopy reaching into the visible.

Other Instrumentation

In Sections III-E, IV-E, and V-E, there has been explicit discussion of more than a dozen different classes of instrumentation that are important in defining and advancing the current frontiers of chemistry. By no means, however, is the list all-inclusive. Table V-6 lists additional types of equipment, what kinds of chemical information each one provides, and approximate current costs. Plainly, these, too, contribute to the capital investment needed to sustain frontier research in chemistry.

CHAPTER VI

Manpower and Education

INTRODUCTION

This report focusses on the U.S. research enterprise in the chemical sciences. It shows decisively that the vitality of this enterprise is essential to our economic competitiveness, our national security, our ability to respond to society's needs, and our understanding of the universe and our place in it. The wellspring of this vitality is and always will be the continued entrance of an adequate number of brilliant young scientists to the field. Thus, we are inevitably drawn to consider the health of the educational system that attracts top calibre individuals, that nurtures their creativity, and that effectively prepares them for their professional careers.

There is no room for doubt that the higher levels of professional activity in chemistry depend directly on the educational experiences embodied in the Ph.D. program. The dependence is rooted in the rapid pace of scientific progress over the span of a professional chemists's career. This pace requires ability to cope with and develop new ideas—the heart of Ph.D. thesis work in chemistry. Hence our prime concern will be with the factors that determine the effectiveness of our doctoral educational system.

Of course, the technical manpower issue also raises questions about the requisite predoctoral educational levels. Obviously the individuals who elect to enter a Ph.D. program in chemistry decide to do so on the basis of their baccalaureate and earlier experiences. Thus we must be sure that the baccalaureate educational system is attracting a cadre of excellent candidates to the doctoral programs and preparing them well for it. At the precollege level, we need much more effort to ensure that some of our brightest young people become seriously interested in science with a good fraction looking toward chemistry.

DOCTORAL EDUCATION IN CHEMISTRY

Graduate education in chemistry provides a valuable, career-molding inter-action with a mature scientist who is working productively at an active research frontier. There is a significant one-on-one aspect to the research director-graduate student interaction. In a highly personalized way, the faculty member will encourage individuality and creativity while directing the student toward problems likely to be soluble, interpretable, and significant to the advancement of existing frontiers. As the student matures, he/she assumes more and more responsibility for selecting the next question to be addressed and the experi-mental approach to be followed, for eliminating obstacles as they appear, and for interpreting results as they are obtained.

At the same time, the typical chemistry graduate student will be a member of a group of peers working with the same faculty research director on problems of related character based on similar experimental and theoretical techniques. This group might include several other graduate students and one or two postdoctoral students. The transfer of ideas and techniques within this peer group is another vital and rewarding part of graduate study in chemistry.

Currently, a large proportion of Ph.D. degree recipients continue their educational preparation by conducting 1 or 2 years of postdoctoral study at another institution. This, too, has become an important part of the chemist's career development. It lets the student broaden horizons by venturing into a field different from the thesis work, by interacting with other productive researchers at a different locale, and by assuming more complete responsibility for the course of the research program. The combination of close collegial collaboration with a research-active faculty research director followed by more independent postdoctoral research work identifies chemistry as an excellent prescription for the encouragement and nurturing of individual creativity in talented young scientists.

Thus, graduate education in the sciences can be likened to the time-tested, traditional apprentice-journeyman-master system. In chemistry, *we have an educational process that effectively furnishes the stream of talented and well prepared young scientists essential to the continued vitality of the nation's technology enterprise. Herein lies a substantial basis for the investment of federal resources in the fundamental chemical research conducted in the nation's universities.*

Chemistry Doctorates in U.S.

Table VI-1 shows for the period 1960 to 1981 the number of U.S. degrees awarded in chemistry. It is not to be assumed that most of the Ph.D.s have progressed through the master's degree; quite the opposite, the M.S. is for many the terminal graduate degree, usually received 2 to 3 years after the baccalaure-ate. The larger fraction of the Ph.D. candidates enter graduate school with a

TABLE VI-1 Number of Degrees Awarded in Chemistry, 1960-1981

	Bachelors	Masters	Ph.D.s	$\dfrac{\text{Ph.D. (Year N)}}{\text{Bach. (Year N-4)}} \cdot 100\ (\%)$
1960	7,603	1,228	1,048	17.0
1964	9,724	1,586	1,301	17.1
1968	10,847	2,014	1,757	18.1
1970	11,617	2,146	2,208	22.7
1972	10,721	2,259	1,971	18.2
1974	10,525	2,138	1,828	15.7
1975	10,649	2,006	1,824	16.3
1976	11,107	1,796	1,623	15.2
1977	11,332	1,775	1,571	15.4
1978	11,474	1,892	1,525	14.5
1979	11,643	1,765	1,518	14.0
1980	11,446	1,733	1,551	14.0
1981	11,540	1,667	1,628	14.3

4-year bachelor's degree, and they complete the Ph.D. between 4 and 5 years later.

The last column of Table VI-1 shows that for the 5-year period 1977-1981, about one-seventh of those receiving bachelor's degrees continue on to receive the Ph.D. (as is typical of the physical sciences). For the same period, for chemical engineering it would be one-twelfth, for biological sciences, one-thirteenth, and for mathematics, one-twenty-seventh of the bachelor degree recipients who will ultimately receive the doctorate. The larger fraction for chemistry reflects the direct value of and need for graduate education in the chemistry profession.

The trend in the annual number of Ph.D. degrees awarded has changed dramatically over the last two decades. During the 1960s, the number of Ph.D.s in chemistry doubled, peaking at 2200 Ph.D.s in 1970. Since then there has been a decline that has seemed to level off by the end of the decade at about 1500 Ph.D.s per year. Now, it seems to be rising again. Physics doctorates followed closely the same pattern except, perhaps, in most recent years. These long-range trends are, of course, important from a national manpower point of view even though they are difficult to

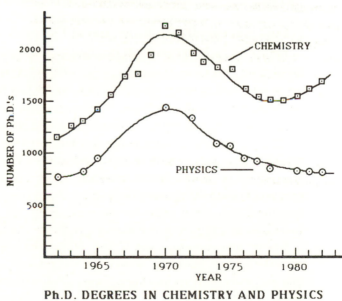

Ph.D. DEGREES IN CHEMISTRY AND PHYSICS

interpret because they span a period of complicated demographic, social, and economic changes. They do, however, suggest that the decline in Ph.D.s during the 1970s has ended, and Ph.D. entry into chemistry is again rising, presumably in response to positive career perceptions.

Career Opportunities for Chemistry Ph.D.s

If that is the perception, it is a reasonable one. Appendix Table A-5 shows that in 1981 business and industry employed more doctoral chemists than the sum of those employed with doctorates in the biological sciences, mathematics, physics, and astronomy combined. Furthermore, Table VI-2 shows that chemistry has a "field mobility" that is quite favorable, one of the higher among doctoral scientists of various disciplines (1977 figures). The "field mobility" expresses the percentage of doctoral recipients employed by business and industry who are actually engaged in professional activities in their own doctoral field. The 1977 data show that 72 percent of the doctorate chemists in industry are finding jobs based in their doctorate field. This can be compared, for example, to 82 percent for engineering and 41 percent for physics.

TABLE VI-2   Field Mobility of Doctoral Scientists and Engineers Employed in Business and Industry, 1977[a]

Field of Doctorate	Percent Employed in Field of Doctorate	Number Employed in All Fields
Computer science	92	600
Engineering	82	20,700
Earth science	82	2,000
Chemistry	72	21,200
Agricultural sciences	69	2,300
Biological sciences	41	5,900
Physics/astronomy	41	6,800
Mathematics	37	1,800

[a] The National Research Council, *Ph.D.'s in Business and Industry.*

Post-Baccalaureate Educational Patterns for Chemists

While considerable variation exists, a typical chemistry Ph.D. graduate experience involves three essential elements: teaching, course work, and thesis research. In many graduate schools, teaching is required for 1 year, sometimes including fellowship holders. The rationale for this element involves several components: teaching is an invaluable educational experience for the graduate, it helps him/her evaluate an academic career as a career goal, it provides stipend support in advance of selection of a research director, and it aids chemistry departments in meeting their large service role in undergraduate education for contiguous disciplines. From the point of view of financial support, teaching can thus provide approximately 20 percent of the stipend support usually received by a chemistry graduate student.

There are several qualifying steps that may be required for successful completion of doctoral study in chemistry: entrance examinations, course grades, cumulative examinations, preliminary examinations, thesis submission, and final defense of thesis. Few schools would use all of these and of those used, there is considerable variation in relative importance. Generally, the most significant screening instruments are cumulative examinations taken during the first 2 years (if used) and the preliminary examination taken during the second or third year. Of course, the ultimate completion of Ph.D. study depends upon submission of an acceptable research-based thesis. However, to a first approximation, the preliminary examination determines who receives the Ph.D., while completion of the thesis determines how long it takes a given student to receive the Ph.D.

In addition to reimbursement for teaching duties (as teaching assistants (TA) paid by the university), chemistry graduate students who do not have fellowship financial aid (NSF, NIH, etc.) can receive research assistantship (RA) stipends. There are a small number of these supported by industrial grants, often to a particular department but sometimes in the name of a particular faculty member, and not uncommonly with some stipulation on the area of chemical research in which the recipient's thesis work must fall. But the majority of RA stipends are drawn from federal grants to an individual faculty member to support the graduate students under his/her direction. Table VI-3 shows for the

TABLE VI-3 Chemistry Graduate and Postdoctoral Students in U.S. Doctoral-Granting Institutions, 1974-1980

Year	Graduate Students			Postdoctoral Students	
	Total Number[a] (% Foreign)[a]	Number w/Research Assistantships[b]	Number R.A. s Federally Supported[b]	Total Number[c] (% Foreign)[d]	Number Federally Supported
1974	11,700 (20)	3111	2388	2379	1789
1975	11,965 (20)	3233	2864	2522	1889
1976	12,360 (20)	3521	2827	2610	2035
1977	12,575 (20)	3597	2883	2658 (47)	2111
1978					
1979	12,790 (21)	4085	3285	2604 (54)	2147
1980		4541	3733	2710	2255

[a] NSF Publication 81-316, Tables B-3 and B-4. Graduate student totals include both Masters and Ph.D. candidates.
[b] "National Patterns of Science and Technology Resources, 1982" NSF 82-319, Tables 62 and 63.
[c] Ref.b, Tables 59 and 60.
[d] Ref.a, Table B-13.

period 1974 to 1980 the number of such RAs and also the number derived from federal grants. Over the 6 years shown, 80 percent of the RAs were federally supported. Taking account of the number of Ph.D. degrees received for each of the years shown in Table VI-3 and the approximate number of years needed to receive the Ph.D., the data indicate that between two-thirds and three-fourths of U.S. doctoral students in chemistry receive either TA or RA stipends. State resources provide almost all of the TA support, and federal resources provide 80 percent of the RA stipends built into individual research grants.

Table VI-3 also shows the number of chemistry postdoctoral students and the number of them who were federally supported. Just as for graduate RAs, about 80 percent of the postdoctoral students are federally supported, and, again, the majority of their stipends are built into individual research grants. Interestingly, for the years 1976 to 1980 the number of postdoctoral stipends each year exceeded the number of Ph.D.s granted that same year by a factor of 1.7 on the average. Since the average postdoctoral tenure is about 2 years, this implies that approximately 70 to 80 percent of the chemistry Ph.D.s are presently entering postdoctoral study. Thus it has become a norm that most Ph.D. chemists engage in a period of postdoctoral training whatever their ultimate employment. The magnitude of a stipend for a postdoctoral student engaged in university research and supported through a federal grant is generally decided by the university or, even more locally, by the department. These stipends vary from university to university but for a new Ph.D., most of them currently fall in the range $16,000 to $21,000. In contrast, 1984 postdoctoral stipends for new chemistry Ph.D.s at National Laboratories averaged around $25K to $27K while at industrial laboratories, it tended to fall in the range $30 to $32K. Thus university stipends for postdoctoral students are only three-fourths as large as those paid by National Laboratories (also from federal funds) and two-thirds as large as those paid by industry.

Remembering that competitive market forces determine industrial stipends and that a postdoctoral student has already invested about 9 years in college and university education, it is reasonable for university postdoctoral stipends to fall in the range defined by those National Laboratories and industries that offer term postdoctoral appointments. *It is recommended that universities raise their postdoctoral salaries for chemists to bring them into the range established by National Laboratory and industrial postdoctoral programs.*

PRECOLLEGE CHEMISTRY EDUCATION

In January 1983, the American Chemical Society assembled a committee of eminent chemists and educators under the chairmanship of Peter E. Yankwich. The charge to the committee was to *"Examine the state of chemistry education in the United States today and make such recommendations as seem appropriate in light of the findings."* The existence of this current and authoritative assessment of chemistry education makes it unnecessary for us to examine in depth the science educational system from which our future chemists will be drawn. Nevertheless, the importance, indeed the urgency, of the recommendations proposed by that committee demands that we summarize here some of its findings. In so doing, we hope to direct wide attention to this important document and to encourage support of its recommendations. Released in June 1984, the Yankwich Report *Tomorrow The Report of the Task Force for the Study of Chemistry Education in the United States* can be obtained from the American Chemical Society, 1155 Sixteenth St., NW, Washington DC 20036.

The ACS initiation of this activity was one of many responses to a mounting public concern that the state of science and mathematics education at the precollege level had declined seriously in quality over the decade of the 1970s. Another important such study was that produced by the National Commission on Excellence in Education led by David P. Gardner. This study, published in 1983, expressed alarm that is epitomized in its title *A Nation at Risk: The Imperative for Educational Reform*. This is one of the more than twenty-five 1982 and 1983 bibliographic entries collected in the Yankwich Report—reports, articles, and commission studies that see problems of crisis proportions in precollege mathematics and science education.

These problems are presented concisely in the Executive Summary of the Yankwich Report. The part referring to precollege education is quoted below:

> "*Executive Summary*. The American Chemical Society Chemistry Education Task Force finds that:
>
> Misunderstanding of science is widespread and the public understanding of chemistry is poor. Too little science is taught in the elementary schools, possibly because too few teachers are well qualified to teach it; neither programs to assist improvement of teacher qualification nor good teaching materials are readily available. Too few teachers of chemistry in high schools are well grounded in the subject; those that are are spread too thin, have too few mechanisms available for maintaining and improving their qualifications, and are too easily wooed away to more satisfying and more remunerative employment. Laboratory exercises are slowly disappearing from general chemistry education in both high schools and colleges. . . ."

We will not address further the critical issues thus placed before us concerning precollege education. However, we emphatically endorse the view that *improvement of science education for all students at the precollege level must be a matter of high national priority*. A substantial improvement there will benefit all citizens because everyone is affected by the rapid techological changes that are inescapably part of our modern society. Hence every individual has both the right and obligation to participate in deciding society's technological course. A generally raised scientific literacy is necessary. It is the basis by which a democratic citizenry can participate wisely in choosing among the technical options that will determine its economic well-being and quality of life.

Baccalaureate Chemistry Education

Because of the basic character of chemistry and its centrality among the sciences, introductory chemistry courses fulfill a crucial service role. A knowledge of the atomic makeup of the world around us is requisite in most of the advanced courses to be taken by the student entering the health and the biological sciences, physics, engineering, geology, oceanography, and even astronomy. Thus, the typical first-year chemistry class is not dominated by majors in chemistry but rather by students entering a variety of fields contiguous to chemistry. This complicates selection of the curricular content of first- and second-year chemistry courses. Surely the instructor cannot focus this content solely on the needs of the smaller number who see themselves moving toward a professional career in chemistry.

The complication is not entirely unfortunate. The reflex response—to segregate introductory courses into several specialty courses aimed at different disciplinary constituencies—may well be the wrong one. It is an extreme version of the long-term trends in higher education toward ever earlier specialization. In our zeal to help our young people toward their announced goals, we may be forcing them to select those goals before they have the breadth of experience and maturity to do so wisely. If so, we should not at the same time add obstacles to change of direction if student experience so dictates. Nor should we configure curricula so that the student gets no exposure to new intellectual horizons out of which such a decision might have evolved.

There is one significant consideration that crosses the disciplinary boundaries, viz., the essential role of laboratory experience in introductory science courses, including chemistry. The importance of this element is persuasively argued in the Yankwich Report and is embodied in their recommendation U5:

> *Whether they are taught to nonscientists, science majors, or chemistry majors, foundational courses in chemistry at the college level must include a substantial component of significant laboratory work.*

The third- and fourth-year courses strive to offer the optimum content for a student aspiring to a career in chemistry. It is not necessary for us to expound on detailed curricular content here. That has been a subject of ongoing healthy debate. Mechanisms for evaluation and accreditation exist, including, most particularly, the Committee on Professional Training of the American Chemical Society. Issues currently under active discussion are enumerated in the Yankwich Report item U9 "The Approved Curriculum in Chemistry."

One of the crucial issues identified in the Yankwich study is the need for a substantial introduction to modern instrumental methods (item U8). Fulfilling this educational goal requires adequate resources. Consistent with a theme repeated over and over in the present report is that meeting this need is not only a matter of capital investment. Even after up-to-date instrumentation is in place, its cost-effective use requires resources for maintenance and repair. This is a pervasive problem in undergraduate education because resources for chemistry education have not been adequate for development of the infrastructure necessary for maintenance. It is important to remember that this is not a problem restricted to graduate research. Even if it is solved at the research-oriented universities with the primary aim of increasing research productivity, the 4-year colleges have similar needs.

In fact, the key role of the 4-year colleges in meeting our national technical manpower needs must be recognized. A significant fraction of the entering graduate students in chemistry, possibly one-third, receive excellent baccalaureate preparation at institutions that do not offer doctoral chemistry programs.

At these institutions, undergraduate research is a specially valuable experience for any student who is considering whether to enter graduate work in chemistry. To have this opportunity available, the 4-year colleges must be able to maintain a sufficient level of research readiness and faculty interest. A variety of support mechanisms can be effective in strengthening this educational dimension.

- *Both research universities and industrial laboratories should welcome summer or sabbatical visiting researchers from nearby college faculties.*
- *Industries should consider passing on serviceable but less than state-of-the art instrumentation to college departments for both educational and research use. Industrial support services (electronics, machining, glassblowing) might be made available for occasional maintenance attention to such equipment.*
- *Federal tax incentives would provide impetus to such industrial equipment gift and maintenance programs.*
- *The federal research-funding agencies, in particular, the National Science Foundation, should play an active role by providing competitive awarded research grants of appropriate size and number of research-active faculty at 4-year colleges.* A model is suggested in Chapter VII (see Tables VII-8 and VII-9).

Resources for Basic Research in the Chemical Sciences

INTRODUCTION

The understandings that follow from basic research in chemistry open new options for addressing societal needs. The benefits may be recognized and realized within only a few years, or they might not come to fruition until decades after the most crucial discoveries. This range of time horizons explains, in part, why research in chemistry is conducted in the United States in various arenas, industrial laboratories, private (not-for-profit) laboratories, national and other federal laboratories, and in our university and college laboratories. Progressively through this sequence, research tends to be increasingly directed toward the fundamental understanding of nature and less practical or goal-oriented. This trend reveals the fact that in the United States, the frontiers of chemistry are primarily explored and expanded in our research universities. This characteristic contrasts with the organization of fundamental research abroad, as witnessed by the considerable dependence upon the Max Planck Institutes in Germany, the CNRS Laboratories in France, and the Academy Institutes in the Soviet Union. The U.S. system has the enormous advantage that it strongly couples the basic research function to the education of the next generation of scientists. Thus it continuously renews our pool of scientific personnel with young scientists whose thesis work has probed the edges of our knowledge.

BASIC CHEMICAL RESEARCH IN INDUSTRY

Because of the clear potentiality for short-term payoff from chemical research, the chemical industry invests heavily in its own in-house research. In 1982, the Chemical and Allied Products industries invested about $4.2B in corporate research and development, of which about $380M might be classified as basic research. These statistics implicitly confirm a major thesis of this report, that research in chemistry pays off in future processes and products used by society. They also show that industrial laboratories furnish an important locus of chemical research. Excellent fundamental research is conducted in this arena but, by and large, attention tends to be focussed on programs that offer prospect for marketable products within a fairly short time, and most of these programs must be proprietary.

Scientists in industrial laboratories depend upon and draw from a reservoir of fundamental knowledge constantly renewed and expanded by university-based research. Industries also rely upon a stream of talented young scientists entering the field and bringing immediate familiarity with the latest discoveries, the recent scientific literature, and the newest instruments and scientific techniques. As tangible evidence of industry's recognition of these dependencies, the chemical industries furnish direct support to university research in amounts estimated to be about $10M to chemistry departments and $10M to departments of chemical engineering in 1983. While this is only a modest fraction of the resources needed to maintain international research leadership for U.S. chemistry, it is an extremely important source of support. Industrial support of university research provides communication and coupling between industrial and academic scientists that facilitate movement of new discoveries into the industrial laboratories where applications can be developed. At the same time it can influence beneficially the graduate educational process, and it gives industry some opportunity to influence the university research agenda. Efforts are being made to strengthen this coupling (e.g., through the Council for Chemical Research) and to increase the amount of this support. A realistic appraisal suggests that industrial support might be as much as double its current amount. Tax incentives to encourage such gains should be explored.

It is recommended that new mechanisms and new incentives be sought for developing stronger links between industrial and academic research and for increasing industrial support for fundamental chemical sciences research conducted in universities.

The most fundamental and adventurous research will remain a modest, though vital, component of industrial research because the likelihood for payoff is too uncertain and the time horizon for application is too remote. Yet, the most fundamental chemical discoveries can offer the most far-reaching benefits to society, most often in directions that could not have been foreseen. This "high-risk," "blue sky" research ultimately furnishes the intellectual basis for our cultural ethos and our technological competitiveness. Hence it is an appropriate place for public investment. It explains and justifies the considerable federal investment in support of scientific research at the national laboratories and at the nation's university laboratories.

Total federal obligations for basic research in chemistry were $349M in fiscal year 1983. When corrected for inflation, this represents a 10.9 percent increase over the federal investment 10 years earlier. During that same period, the sum

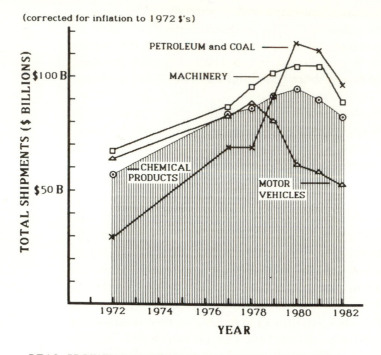

(corrected for inflation to 1972 $'s)

REAL GROWTH FOR CHEMISTRY-BASED INDUSTRIES

of the chemistry-based petroleum, coal, and chemical industries increased in inflation-corrected business volume by more than a factor of two, while machinery deliveries were increasing by only 30 percent and automobile deliveries were 20 percent below 1972 levels. (All figures corrected for inflation.)

Equally important, the international balance of trade for chemical products has steadily remained positive. It has risen from $1.4B in 1965 to about $12B in 1981, second only to machinery. Thus our chemistry-based industries are key to our overall economic well-being, and their future must be assured.

While the FY 1983 federal obligation of $349M for chemistry research may seem a large sum, it is well within bounds defined by federal obligations for other physical sciences that depend upon sophisticated instrumentation (see Table VII-1), which compares federal funding for chemistry, physics, and astronomy over the 10-year period 1973 to 1983.

The parenthetical numbers, corrected with GNP deflators to 1973 dollars, show that while real growth in chemistry funding was 11 percent, physics funding grew 20 percent and astronomy funding 44 percent. At least one criterion by which these figures can be judged is their appropriateness to the need for talented young people in the nation's industries. Thus if one divides the federal obligations (in FY 1983 dollars) by the number of scientists employed in industry, this "normalized" annual investment in chemistry amounts to $4K per year per employed chemist. This is 15-fold less than the comparable investment in physics and astronomy (taken together because there are no separate data on the use of astronomers in industry). A related "normalization" can be based on the number of Ph.D. degrees granted per year. In 1983, about 1700 chemistry Ph.D. degrees were conferred, so the annual investment per Ph.D. joining the work force was $205K. This figure is one-fifth the comparable figure for physics and perhaps one-twentieth that for astronomy. Thus, *the federal investment in chemistry is meagre compared to that received by its companion physical sciences. Clearly, this investment is not commensurate*

TABLE VII-1   Federal Obligations for Basic Research in the Physical Sciences, 1973 and 1983

	Chemistry	Physics	Astronomy
	Current $ (FY 1973 $)[a]	Current $ (FY 1973 $)[a]	Current $ (FY 1973 $)[a]
(1) FY 1973[b]	$146M (146M)	$351M (351M)	$122M (122M)
(2) FY 1983[b]	$349M (162M)	$905M (421M)	$379M (176M)
(3) Scientists[c] employed by industry (1980)	86,600	22,400	
(4) Number Ph.Ds[d] (1983)	1700	830	100
$/Industry scientists (2)/(3)	$4.0K	$57.3K	
$/Ph.D. (2)/(4)	$205K	$1090K	$3800K

[a] Based on GNP deflator, see Science Indicators, 1980.
[b] See Table A-7.
[c] See Table A-4.
[d] See Table VI-1.

with the practical importance of chemistry—both economic and societal—nor with the outstanding intellectual opportunities it now offers.

To frame recommendations directed toward redress of this imbalance, we must examine the budgets of each of the federal agencies that might logically support basic chemical research in the public interest and in the achievement of their respective missions. Table VII-2 shows the distribution of support for chemistry among the five agencies that contribute significantly to fundamental research performed in universities and colleges. These agencies also support research in their own national laboratories, but funding of basic research performed in universities and colleges is a clear-cut and unambiguous indicator of a particular agency's commitment to long-range chemistry research and the renewal of the pool of scientists.

Table VII-2 shows that the largest fraction for the support of chemical research has come from the National Science Foundation over the last decade. This is despite the obvious relevance of chemistry to the congressionally mandated missions of the other agencies listed. The detailed budgets of each of these agencies will be considered in turn. First, however, it is appropriate to consider the "style" of research in chemistry.

CHEMISTRY: AN ACTIVITY OF CREATIVE INDIVIDUALISTS

Today's public image of science is still heavily influenced by the reverberating impact of the World War II Manhattan Project that brought us the atomic bomb and the Apollo Project of the 1960s that let us set foot on the Moon. We are seen to be in an era of Big Science. But embedded in this glamorous, highly organized, and well publicized setting, there are a number of scientific disciplines that have somehow maintained the highly personal characteristics of

TABLE VII-2 Federal Obligations for Basic Research in Chemistry Performed by Universities and Colleges (by Percent of Total)

	NSF	NIH	DOD	DOE	DOA
FY 1974	49.2	24.2	9.2	9.2	3.1
FY 1984	44.7	21.5	16.1	11.0	3.6

classical human creativity: How many writers were needed to create *Hamlet*? How many artists to paint the *Mona Lisa*? How many scientists to propose relativity? Chemistry is one of these disciplines. Somehow it has remained an idiosyncratic and highly competitive activity that depends upon sustained individual initiative and personal creativity. Scientific publications in the field generally involve two or three authors. There are no examples to be found in chemistry to match the multiple authorship—dozens of authors on a single paper—like those announcing the occasional discovery of a new subatomic particle.

Chemistry has remained, worldwide, an innovative "cottage industry" with a *modus operandi* that has been remarkably productive. Tangible evidence of its success is provided by the faster-than-exponential discovery of new compounds (see Chapter I, p. 4). This gratifying record was achieved despite the fact that at any given moment, the molecules easiest to synthesize have already been made; the harder ones remain. Yet discovery is accelerating. The only plausible explanation is that chemistry in the small project mode is an extremely effective enterprise, both here and abroad.

Thus the term "cottage industry" describes a highly individualistic and personally creative activity rather than a consensual one. These characteristics impart a healthy competitiveness and a liberating freedom from bounding paradigms. They make chemistry an ideal field in which to nurture a young scientist's originality and initiative. He or she can be intimately involved and in control of every aspect of an investigation, selecting the question, deciding on the approach, assembling and personally operating the equipment, collecting and analyzing the data, and deciding on the significance of the results. Here is another reason to nourish this central and fundamental science in its present image.

Yet we are in an era in which directors of U.S. federal science-funding agencies will candidly admit that they believe it easier to argue for an enormous increment of funding to sponsor a large machine or a massive project than for a smaller increment to stimulate many smaller projects with comparable or greater expectation for new discoveries and scientific advances that will surely respond to society's needs. Thus the Department of Energy in its 1985 budget devotes 55 percent of its Office of Energy Research budget to two "Big Science" project areas: $548M for high energy physics and $440M for fusion research. Currently under consideration by various agencies are proposals for *incremental* funds to build a hard X-ray synchrotron light source ($160M), a neutron source ($250M), a "next-generation" multimirror telescope ($100M), a set of "supercomputer centers," an array of "engineering centers," and an accelerator with a circumference of 80 miles (~$4B). Each of these new projects will require large, ongoing (and incremental) operating budgets that are irresistibly rooted in huge initial capital investments.

In the presence of such ambitious programs, the incremental resources needed to exploit the rich opportunities before us in chemistry are easily in scale. Because of the societal payoff to be expected from such an incremental investment, it will be readily and persuasively defensible in the individual competitive grant style already known to be effective in chemistry.

PRIORITY AREAS OF CHEMISTRY

The strength of American science has been built on allowing creative, working scientists to decide independently where the best prospects lie for significant new knowledge. Many of the most far-reaching developments, both in concept and application, have come from unexpected directions. Thus, a listing of priority areas may tend to close off or quench some of the most adventurous new directions whose potential is not yet recognized.

Even so, it makes sense to concentrate some resources in specially promising areas. This can be done if we regard our research support as an investment portfolio designed to achieve maximum gain. A significant part of this investment should be directed toward consensually recognized priority areas but with a flexibility that encourages these favored listings to evolve as new frontiers emerge. A second substantial element in this portfolio should be directed toward creative scientists who propose to explore new directions and ideas. Then, a third element must be the essential resources to provide the needed instrumentation and the infrastructure for its cost-effective use in achieving the goals of the entire portfolio.

Where this balance will fall for each of the funding sources will vary, of course. Industrial research will weight rather heavily the currently recognized priority frontiers. At the other extreme, NSF must take as its first responsibility the encouragement of new avenues from which tomorrow's priority lists will be drawn. The other mission agencies should structure their portfolios between.

This report shows decisively that this is a time of special opportunity for intellectual advances in chemistry. Furthermore, the report demonstrates that such advances will not only enrich our cultural heritage, but also will help us respond to human needs and sustain our economic competitiveness. It is in society's interest to exploit these opportunities and to do so with particular attention to those frontiers that deserve high priority because they can be confidently expected to yield high intellectual and social return from the needed additional federal investment. We identify here five areas that meet this criterion.

A. Understanding Chemical Reactivity
B. Chemical Catalysis
C. Chemistry of Life Processes

D. Chemistry Around Us
E. Chemical Behavior Under Extreme Conditions

Understanding Chemical Reactivity

This is surely a time of special opportunity to deepen our fundamental knowledge of why and how chemical changes take place. The advance of the frontiers of reaction dynamics at the molecular level has undergone a revolutionary advance during the last decade. At the same time, synthetic chemists are constantly adding to our arsenal of reaction types and classes of compounds in a way that is eliminating historical distinctions between organic and inorganic chemistry. Much of this remarkable progress is due to the development and application of powerful instrumental and analytical techniques that give us capability to probe far beyond current bounds of knowledge.

In *reaction dynamics*, we can now aspire to elucidate the entire course of chemical reactions, including the unstable structural arrangements intervening between reactants and products. Just as the last three decades saw rich development of our understandings of equilibrium molecular structures and equilibrium chemical thermodynamics, *the next three decades will see elucidation of the temporal aspects of chemical change*. We will be able to ascertain the factors that determine the rates of chemical reactions because of our new abilities to watch the fastest chemical processes in real time, to conduct reliable theoretical calculations of reaction surfaces, to examine chemical changes at the most intimate level ("state-to-state"), to track energy movement within and between molecules, and to exploit hitherto inaccessible nonlinear photon excitation processes ("multi-photon" excitation). These remarkable possibilities are rooted in a powerful array of new instruments, foremost of which are lasers and computers, and including Fourier transform infrared spectrometers, ion cyclotron resonance techniques, molecular beams, and synchrotron radiation sources.

New reaction pathways in synthetic chemistry offer another rapidly advancing frontier. These pathways identify a high leverage opportunity because they *provide the foundation for future development of new products and new processes*. Selectivity, the key challenge in chemical synthesis, is the cornerstone. Control of the different intrinsic reactivity in each bond type (chemoselectivity), the connection of reactant molecules in proper orientation (regioselectivity) and in the desired three-dimensional spatial relations (stereoselectivity) is at last within reach. Our ability to produce a controlled molecular topography has far-reaching implications for catalyst design. The traditional line of demarcation between organic and inorganic chemists has virtually disappeared as the list of fascinating metal-organic compounds continues to grow. We have just begun to elaborate and understand the potentialities of chemical pathways opened using light as a reagent. Finally, chemists are learning how to prepare solids with a wide range of tailored properties that include inorganic solids with contrived cavities as designed catalysts, polymers with structural properties that challenge those of steel, and new families of "electronic chemicals"—inorganic and organic semiconductors, resists, super-lattice materials, optical fibers, nonlinear optical materials—that will accelerate development of microelectronics and information transition.

Again powerful instrumentation plays a central role. Rapid and definitive identification of reaction products, both in composition and structure, account for the speed with which synthetic chemists are able to test and develop adventurous synthetic strategies. Of prime importance are high-resolution Nuclear Magnetic Resonance, computer-controlled X-ray crystallography, and high-resolution mass spectroscopy coupled with the delicate separation capabilities provided by chromatography in its advanced forms.

Chemical Catalysis

A catalyst accelerates a chemical reaction toward equilibrium without being consumed. This acceleration can be as much as 10 orders of magnitude while favoring one particular reaction out of many competing pathways. *There is now in prospect the possibility of obtaining a molecular-level understanding of catalysis to move it from an art to a science.* Rich payoff can be expected because we will be laying the foundation for the development of new technologies. All facets of this critical frontier are opening and synergistically interacting.

Heterogeneous catalysts are solid materials prepared with large surface areas upon which chemical reactions occur at extremely high rate and selectivity. Entirely new kinds of information are now accessible through an arsenal of new detection techniques of such sensitivity that we can hope to watch chemical change take place on a solid surface (low energy electron diffraction, electron energy-loss spectroscopy, Auger spectroscopy, photoelectron spectroscopy, surface-enhanced Raman, etc.). These instruments open the door to understanding and controlling the chemistry in this surface domain.

Homogeneous catalysts are soluble and active in a liquid reaction medium. Often they are complex metal-containing molecules whose structures can be modified to tune reactivity in desired directions to achieve high selectivities. Organometallic chemistry and metal cluster compounds are of particular importance; they reveal homogeneous catalysis as a bridge between heterogeneous catalysis and enzyme catalysis.

Artificial enzyme catalysis is now an exciting frontier because of our instrumental capability to deal with molecular systems of extreme complexity. It permits us to apply the synthetic chemist's ability to produce a molecular topography designed to adsorb selectively a paticular reactant and hold it in a known geometry—the enzyme counterpart to the basic feature of a heterogeneous catalyst. At this structured surface locale, a chemically bound metal atom is placed so that it will impart to the adsorbed guest molecule a desired chemical reactivity—the enzyme counterpart to homogeneous catalysis. Prototype artificial enzymes are in preparation and are on the drawing boards. Revolutionary potentialities for new processes are in prospect.

Electrocatalysis and photocatalysis are adding new dimensions to the field of catalysis. Chemical reactions can now be induced at the interface between a liquid solution and an electrochemical electrode surface, with or without absorption of light by a semiconductor used as an electrode. In either case, our growing knowledge of homogeneous catalysis and of semiconductor behavior is being applied and coupled with the stimulating aspect of the electro- or photochemical energy input. Potential applications range from solar energy storage to photogeneration of liquid fuels, such as methanol from carbon dioxide and water.

Chemistry of Life Processes

In the last decade, chemists have succeeded in recognizing and synthesizing a large number of molecules of exquisite complexity. This capability is most timely because the exciting and largely phenomenological advances of the biosciences now demand explication at the molecular level. Thus, the time is ripe for quite spectacular advances in chemistry at the interface of chemistry and biology. These advances are bound to have applications to human health, animal health, and agriculture. The opportunities are illustrated by three broad types of problems: receptor-substrate interactions, vectorial chemistry at membranes, and genetic engineering.

Receptor-substrate interactions selectively mediate essentially all biological processes. Thus, protein receptors (enzymes, antibody, membrane, or intracellular receptors) interact selectively with one or more substrates (enzyme substrate, antigen, hormone, neurotransmitter, or simple molecule or ion). Chemistry is needed to understand these processes in molecular detail because we must be able to isolate and identify the structures of these substrates, synthesize them in useful quantities, analyze their receptor-interactions in physical-chemical as well as biological terms, and modify their structures to suit desired uses. Medical and biological applications of great value can be foreseen, but the methods of chemistry are needed in order to manipulate these substances.

Vectorial chemistry describes reactions depending upon spatial separation (as by a membrane) of reactants into regions of different concentrations. Because of the importance of such systems in living systems (cells and organelles), we must understand the relations between concentration gradients across membranes and the processes by which chemical bonds are made and broken. Active chemical modelling, at both the synthetic and mechanistic levels, is needed to complement current activity in mechanistic biology. Progress will be directly applicable in pharmacokinetics and drug delivery.

Genetic engineering has become possible as molecular biologists have discovered and exploited the action of certain natural enzymes that affect DNA. Restriction enzymes catalyze the cutting of DNA at special places, and ligation enzymes can join it (or a contrived insert) together again. Through synthesis of DNA and RNA sequences, structural analysis of gene fragments, and development of separations techniques, chemists will play an important and increasing role as we use these capabilities to clarify, on a molecular level, the chemistry of genetics, and as we add to the growing number of applications of genetic engineering.

Chemistry Around Us

The atmosphere, oceans, earth, and biosphere are strongly coupled through the chemical processes that take place in each region. Man's disturbance of this global chemical reactor is no longer negligible. Networks of interlocking chemical cycles involving trace constituents help determine the gr ss structure and behavior of the stratosphere, the troposphere, and, through rain, the soil and lakes that make up our local environment. To protect these local environments, we must understand what chemical substances are present and in what concentrations, as well as what chemical reactions they induce, and at what rates the changes take place. The first two issues involve analytical chemistry, and the second two involve reaction dynamics. Fortunately, both fields are in particularly fruitful states of development.

Analytical chemistry critically determines our ability to advance our understanding of environmental chemistry because much of this chemistry is controlled by reactive molecules present at trace levels—in some cases as low as parts per trillion. Astonishing progress is being made in extending analytical sensitivity limits (How little can we detect?), sharpening analytical specificity (How sure can we be of what we are detecting?), and improving separations (Can we isolate the desired constituent even in miniscule quantities?). Such progress has immediate applicability in the analysis of complex but very dilute mixtures of pollutants, pesticides, and degradation products of both human and natural origin as found in ambient air, toxic wastes, polluted streams and lakes, agricultural soils, and biological samples.

Instrumentation will play a central role in these gains. Analytical chemists are applying our most sophisticated techniques, including tandem mass spectrometry, high-resolution gas chromatography coupled with mass or Fourier Transform infrared spectroscopy, supercritical fluid chromatography, remote detection using laser fluorescence or absorption techniques, ultrasensitive in-cavity and photoacoustic laser methods, chemiluminescence, and computer-aided data collection and manipulation. Increased investment in analytical chemistry will permit us to extend detection well below toxicity bounds so that potential problems can be anticipated and ameliorated long before the hazard level is reached.

Reaction dynamics in environmental chemistry poses some surprisingly difficult problems that define new research fronts. In atmospheric chemistry, complex chains of interlocking reactions can be involved, and reaction rates of highly reactive and elusive molecules can be controlling (e.g., OH, HO_2, NO_3). Because of the reactivity, these rates are difficult to measure, and reliable laboratory methods for measuring the relevant rate constants must be developed. Even the locale of reaction may be in question because of the presence of solid and liquid particulates, including finely divided carbon particles (soot). Reaction rates here may be catalytically enhanced. Nucleation of aqueous clusters induced by such pollutants as sulfur oxides and nitric acid may figure importantly in transport as well as chemistry, so nucleation rates must be known. Hypersaline droplets provide an unfamiliar reaction environment in which aqueous solution chemistry can be strongly perturbed. Photochemistry is a significant factor and adds to the problem because the chemical fate of the photoactive species must be considered in all the potential reaction locales—in the gas phase, adsorbed onto solid particles, or dissolved in droplets (hypersaline or not). For example, little is known about aqueous phase photochemistry in clouds.

Once again, modern laser spectroscopic techniques and computer-aided data collection, usually coupled with traditional kinetic methods, are permitting us to address these challenging questions. We cannot afford to neglect the reaction dynamics aspect of environmental chemistry.

Chemical Behavior Under Extreme Conditions

Most of our knowledge of chemical change has been accumulated within a narrow range of the influential variables, pressure and temperature being the most obvious. Now, as our measurement techniques are becoming more powerful, we can investigate chemical processes as they occur under conditions far removed from those of our normal ambient surroundings. The ability to study chemistry under such extreme conditions expands the number of laboratory variables with which chemical reactivity can be manipulated and controlled. At the same time, these extreme conditions provide critical tests of our basic understanding of chemical processes. With capabilities in hand or close on the horizon, significant progress in new materials, new processes, new devices, and deeper understandings would reward a concentration of effort on the study of chemistry under extreme conditions. The effort should encompass chemistry under exceptionally *high pressure, high temperature, in gaseous discharges* ("plasmas"), and *at temperatures near absolute zero.*

High-pressure chemistry has potentiality on several fronts as it has become possible to examine reactivity at pressures up to and exceeding a million times atmospheric pressure (>1 megabar). High-pressure studies of reactivity reveal the volume profile of reactants so they add an entirely new facet to our description and understanding of the unstable atomic arrangements that intervene between reactants and products. The insights so gained could be one of the important ways that the temporal aspects of reactions (reaction rates) are understood and brought under control. Reaction mechanisms are revealed, and reaction pathways can be manipulated. New processes and chemical products are to be expected.

Next, pressure can have a differential effect on electronically excited states of molecules, thus altering the optical properties of liquids and solids, and it can change the packing of molecules in the solid state to affect electrical properties. The ability to vary the relative energies of electronic states in a continuous manner can provide unique tests of theories of electronic processes, energy transfer processes in phosphors, and behavior of laser materials, such as the II-VI and III-V compounds. It has already been shown to provide control of photochromism, semiconductor-conductor transitions, and superconducting transitions. Further gains in these areas can be expected to result in new devices, such as pressure-tunable display devices, lasers, switches, superconductors, and magnetic devices.

Thirdly, we are seeing a revolution in our understanding of critical phenomena, the behavior of substances at the pressures and temperatures at which the gaseous and liquid states can no longer be distinguished. Powerful new theoretical approaches are responsible, such as the "renormalization group" approach. A further unexpected discovery is that surfaces and interfaces of near-critical fluids can themselves exhibit transistions and critical phenomena. Experimental techniques are keeping pace, as revealed by both prediction and demonstration of "wetting transitions." Applications are in store, such as microemulsions for oil extraction, liquid crystals for display devices, and new polymer transitions.

High temperature chemistry is not new: combustion has been known since prehistoric times. What is new is our ability to sustain temperatures up to 5000 K over large volumes for long times and to produce temperatures very much higher (up to 100,000 K) for shorter times through a variety of pulsed techniques (laser pulses, shock waves, explosions, and electrical discharges). Exploiting these possibilities will result in more efficient use of energy, high temperature materials, high temperature fabrication processes, and new understandings of chemical reactivity, including combustion.

High temperature liquid phases are present in many technological processes (molten metals, silicates, salts, oxides, sulfides, metalloids), but fundamental understandings have lagged those for gases and solids. Unusually strong and sometimes long-range interactions characterize these liquids, and techniques for their study (including pulsed laser, X-ray, neutron diffraction, Raman scattering, NMR and EXAFS) must be adapted to the high temperature regime.

The technological importance of high temperature solids is already obvious and is still increasing. Substitutes made necessary by scarcity (e.g., for chromium alloys) or environmental problems (e.g., for asbestos) and materials that must function at extremely high temperatures (e.g., in gas turbines, nose cones, internal combustion engines) provide examples where substantial gains of practical importance are to be expected.

Finally, the basic foundations for prediction are woefully inadequate at high temperatures where gross excitations of electronic, vibrational, and rotational degrees of freedom make first-order simplifying assumptions (such as separation of these variables) inadequate or inapplicable. Spectroscopic data are needed for high temperature species, both in ground and excited electronic states but with high vibrational and rotational excitation. Bond dissociation energies, heats of formation, ionization energies, and radiation cross sections must be reliably known for the unfamiliar molecular species found in flames and explosions. The applicable thermochemical data base must be filled in and expanded.

Plasmas are produced by an electric discharge through a gas. Extremely high temperatures are characteristic; they can reach a million degrees Kelvin. A nonequilibrium situation can be expected, and the apparent temperature can depend upon the species and the degree of freedom probed. Radiation within and out of the plasma zone can contribute to the behavior. The chemical species present include ions, electrons, and electronically excited and chemically reactive neutrals. These characteristics give plasmas unique and, at this time, poorly known chemistry, so much so that plasmas have been called a new state of matter. Better understanding of plasmas will be of value because of their growing importance in a wide variety of contexts ranging from stellar chemistry to practical applications in semiconductor fabrication (plasma etching) and design of nuclear fusion reactors.

Low temperature chemistry, once thought to be nonexistent, is providing unique information about chemical reactions that take place at temperatures near absolute zero. Such reactions can now be studied both in the gas phase, using supersonic jet cooling, and in solid environments through the matrix isolation method. The supersonic jet cooling technique has helped open the spectroscopic study of weakly bound molecules ("van der Waals molecules"). Coupled with laser-induced fluorescence and molecular beams, it opens new avenues to understanding intramolecular energy transfer and predissociation. Also, the ability to prepare complex molecules in the gas phase but with vibrational and rotational temperatures near absolute zero gives access to spectroscopic detail normally completely obscured. New applications of supersonic jet cooling are still being discovered, and they often provide unique insights.

Suspension of highly reactive molecules in inert gas solids at temperatures near absolute zero (the matrix isolation technique) also yields information difficult to obtain by any other method. The results nicely complement both high temperature studies and supersonic jet cooling because the structures and reactions of the transient molecules that determine the chemistry of flames and explosions can be examined. Recent applications have turned to unusual reactions, such as metal atom insertions into organic molecules and light-induced isomerizations. Laser-selective excitation of cryogenically trapped reactive pairs has provided the first evidence of mode-selectivity in bimolecular reactions, and it has suggested new chemical routes to solar energy storage.

Chemical synthesis at extremely low temperatures has also provided preparative routes to molecular species too reactive to accumulate under normal conditions. A number of cryogenic solvents permit synthesis of complex organic and metal-organic molecules at temperatures reaching down to that of liquid air. Even inert gases can be liquified to use as reaction solvents over a wide range of cryogenic temperatures, using high pressure to broaden the liquid ranges. Finally, evaporation and sputtering of metal atoms into cryogenic organic samples can be used in large-scale preparative processes for unusual metal-organic substances that may have special catalytic activity.

CHEMISTRY AND THE NSF MISSION

The chemistry supported by NSF is judged mainly on its potential for adding to our understanding of nature rather than its presumed relevance to a practical outcome. Because the most far-reaching technological changes tend to stem from unexpected and unpredictable discoveries, the fundamental research supported by NSF is most critical to the long-range technological future of this country.

In NSF, the chemical sciences are supported primarily in three divisions: the Chemistry Division, the Materials Sciences Division, and the Chemical and Process Engineering Division. Chemists also participate to some extent in divisional programs in other NSF directorates: Biochemistry, Atmospheric Chemistry, Geochemistry, and Marine Chemistry. The Materials Sciences Division includes three chemical science-oriented programs: Solid State Chemistry, Polymers, and Metallurgy. Also included are the Materials Research Laboratories (the MRL Program), which block-fund groups of physicists, chemists, and engineers with relatively focussed and applied program goals. Table VII-3 shows the budgets for these programs over the years 1972 to 1984, both in current dollars and corrected with GNP deflators to constant, 1972 dollars.

Table VII-3 shows that over the decade 1972-1983, total NSF funding for the chemical sciences rose in real terms by about 40 percent; but this growth was concentrated in the materials sciences, which grew by 50 percent and in chemical engineering, which grew from a small base by about 90 percent. The Chemistry Division budget grew by 23 percent over the same period, during which costs of scientific instrumentation have increased much faster than inflation, and day-to-day dependence upon such instrumentation has become almost universal across chemistry. Over this same decade, our economy has depended more and more on the health of the chemical industry, as reflected in both the doubling of its contribution to the GNP and the growth of its positive trade balance. These factors, coupled with the exciting opportunities in chemistry, justify considerably larger NSF support.

To assess the extent to which incremental funds are needed, it is necessary to examine in detail the disposition that has been made of the available resources. This can be examined most clearly for the Chemistry Division budget and in terms of three funding dimensions: purchase of large instrumentation for shared use (either on a departmental or regional basis), purchases of expensive instrumentation for dedicated use, and the size of individual research grants. To

TABLE VII-3   NSF Funding of the Chemical Sciences, 1972-1984

Year	Chemistry Division	Materials Science Division[a]	Chemical Engineering	Chemistry Division	Materials Science Division[a]	Chemical Engineering
	(in current-year dollars)			(in constant 1972 dollars)		
1972	24.5M	4.8M		24.5M	4.8M	
1973	25.1	5.0		24.0	4.8	
1974	26.6	5.1		23.7	4.6	
1975	32.7	5.8		26.5	4.7	
1976	34.7	8.2		26.3	6.2	
1977	40.2	9.8		28.6	7.0	
1978	43.1	11.3		28.7	7.5	
1979	45.2	11.5	13.0M	27.6	7.0	8.0M
1980	51.7	14.7	13.9	29.1	8.3	7.8
1981	57.6	14.9	16.7		7.6	8.6
1982	61.4	15.9	20.4	29.4	7.6	9.8
1983	67.6	16.2	22.6	30.8	7.4	10.3
1984 (est.)	80.0	19.5	26.6	33.2	8.1	11.1
1985 (request)	92.1	22.6	32.5	35.6	8.7	12.5
1985 (est.)[b]	87.8	21.5		33.8	8.3	

[a] This is the portion of the MRL budgets received by members of Chemistry and Chemical Engineering Departments, about 20 percent of the total. The remainder is directed to members of Physics and Engineering Departments who receive, respectively, about 45 percent and 35 percent of the total.
[b] After congressional action, as of January 1985.

begin, it is helpful to trace the history of funding by the Chemistry Division for these three elements.

Before 1970, instrumentation accounted for less than 7 percent of the Chemistry Division budget. It was then deliberately raised to about 9 percent for the years 1970 to 1972. Again a deliberate decision in 1973 led to another increase in the percent of the Chemistry Division budget spent for dedicated and shared instrumentation, this time to 17 percent. This percentage slowly rose to 18.6 percent by 1982. Now, in 1984 and 1985 it is about 25 percent.

Through much of this 15-year period, the amount expended for dedicated instrumentation has been essentially constant at about 10.5 percent. The major chang-

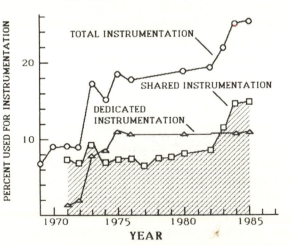

NSF CHEMISTRY DIVISION BUDGET

TOTAL INSTRUMENTATION

SHARED INSTRUMENTATION

DEDICATED INSTRUMENTATION

PERCENT USED FOR INSTRUMENTATION

YEAR

STEADILY RISING INSTRUMENTATION COSTS (IN PERCENT OF CHEMISTRY DIVISION BUDGET)

es have been in response to the pressure for heavier investment in shared instrumentation. Taken together, shared and dedicated instrumentation have eaten away a larger and larger fraction of the Chemistry Division budget with the result that almost no real growth could be directed toward the other costs of performing research. Over the 11-year period 1972 to 1983, the budget less instrumentation rose only 5 percent (corrected for inflation).

The need to divert to instrumentation an increasingly larger fraction of the NSF Chemistry Division budget is but one of the symptoms of resources inadequate to the opportunities we must exploit and develop. To remedy this, we present an analysis of the needed level of resources in each of the major dimensions: shared instrumentation, dedicated instrumentation, and individual grant size. The analysis is based on the following four premises, the first of which is clearly established throughout this report.

—Chemistry is rich with opportunities for intellectual advances, for improvement of the quality of life, and for strengthening our economic competitiveness.

—We wish to assure a U.S. position of international leadership in the exploitation and development of these opportunities.

—We wish to attract to the chemical sciences an appropriate share of most promising young scientists to provide the talented manpower needed in this vital area.

—We wish to be sure that this enterprise engages the full national capability, as is appropriate to the national benefits to be derived.

Shared Instrumentation

The NSF has a proud heritage in its support of departmentally or regionally shared instrumentation. Unfortunately, through the 1970s, the NSF carried most of the load in supplying and maintaining such equipment in chemistry. However, current resources are quite insufficient. Many worthy requests must be declined, up to 50 percent cost-sharing might be required, and no allowance is made for ongoing maintenance. With the above four premises in mind, we offer here a systematic approach to estimating the need.

The NSF shared instrumentation program receives requests for a variety of instruments in the cost range of $200K to $800K. These requests reveal the instrumental techniques needed to conduct frontier research in chemistry. Table VII-4 lists eight examples of costly instrumentation commonly requested. No claim is made that every chemistry department needs every one of these instruments nor even a particular subset of them. We do assert, however, that a research university must maintain state-of-the-art capability for *some* of these instruments to remain front rank. The breadth of the research strength for a particular department will determine how many instruments would be needed to maintain international competitiveness. A large department with full breadth would require six state-of-the-art instruments in its "Departmental Instrument Inventory." With a somewhat narrower range of activity, three

TABLE VII-4   International Competitiveness in Shared Instrumentation

Departmental instrumentation menu	
(1) High-field NMR spectrometer	$750K
(1) Mass spectrometer	500K
(1) X-ray diffractometer	450K
(1) FTIR	200K
(1) Raman	200K
(1) ESR	200K
(1) Departmental computer	300K
(1) Array processor	250K
(8) Instruments	$2850K
Average capital cost per instrument	$355K
Cost share, NSF, 80%	$285K
Maintenance and operation at 20% capital cost/year for 5 years	$355K
Total cost, NSF share per instrument	$640K

instruments might suffice. With a still sharper research focus, two instruments would probably keep a number of research faculty active at their research frontiers. Thus we begin this analysis by considering three "Departmental Instrument Inventory" levels—six, three, or two state-of-the-art instruments from the list in Table VII-4. At each level, the instruments must be replaced often enough to avoid obsolescence.

Experience in industrial research laboratories indicates that replacement time for the modern instrumentation under consideration averages about 6 years, a time determined by technical, not mechanical obsolescence. In other words, well before instrument-maintenance becomes a major problem, new instrument capabilities have become available that redefine the feasible research goals. On the average then, over a 6-year period, a department must have a reasonable chance to compete for continued access to the largest state-of-the-art capability for its Departmental Inventory.

The financing of such a program includes three elements: initial capital investment, cost-sharing policy, and ongoing costs of maintenance and operation. It is time to carry over from physics and astronomy the well-recognized principle that cost-effective use of sophisticated instrumentation requires ongoing support for maintenance and operation. Without this infrastructure support, such instrumentation is used neither at full efficiency nor full effectiveness. On the basis of studies on this issue, about 20 percent of the original capital investment for a 5-year period is needed. *NSF should build into its shared instrumentation program annual operating and maintenance support (20 percent of capital investment) for a period of 5 years after purchase.*

Again we learn from physics and astronomy that cost-sharing by the institution becomes less and less viable as instrument costs continue to rise. Given the current financial stress in universities, we urge that *the federal share of instrumentation capital investment should average at 80 percent.*

With these guiding recommendations on cost-sharing and infrastructure support, Table VII-4 shows that an average cost per shared instrument would require an NSF commitment of $640K.

Finally, we propose a deliberate approach to the question of how many U.S.

research universities can and ought to be in mind as NSF sponsors academic research in chemistry. There are 198 U.S. institutions that grant the Ph.D. degree in chemistry. The corresponding graduate faculty exceeds 4000, the number of postdoctorals is about 2800, and the number of full-time graduate (M.S. and Ph.D.) students exceeds 13,000. Of the 198 degree-granting institutions, we propose that at least 20 of them should be able to compete successfully for a Departmental Instrumentation Inventory of six major instruments. Such an institution could consider replacement of each of these instruments every 6 years, to average one per year. For a larger number of institutions—we propose 40—that competition might be successful every other year. For these, the Departmental Inventory could include three state-of-the-art instruments. For a next tier of 60 institutions, success would average 3 years, to maintain two modern instruments. These estimates—20 first-tier, 40 second-tier, and 60 third-tier institutions—can be seen to be modest in scale by comparing to the number of Max Planck Institutes in Germany. There are a dozen Max Planck Institutes in which chemistry is a central component. These Institutes might be considered analogous to our 20 first-tier research universities because they tend to be more richly endowed with instrumentation than the larger number of German universities also engaged in chemistry research. Scaling on the basis of total population, a dozen Institutes in Germany would correspond to about 40 compettitive institutions in the United States (3.4 times higher). This shows that the level we propose is reasonable and needed if we wish to maintain international competitiveness. The cost of such a shared instrumentation program is shown in Table VII-5 and compared with the projected NSF Departmental Instrumentation budget for FY 1985. The NSF shared instrumentation budget falls far short of the need. ***The NSF Departmental Instrumentation budget for FY 1986 should be augmented by $25M.***

Dedicated Instrumentation

Much fundamental research today depends upon the sophisticated instrumentation just discussed but with such specialized application that shared use is quite impractical. However, the philosophy used above, based upon the same four premises, again furnishes an estimate of the resources needed to maintain U.S. leadership in a number of crucial specialty areas. This time an average cost per instrument is based upon a 15-instrument menu that weights some instruments more than others. Furthermore, it is assumed that no cost-sharing is required (as is

TABLE VII-5 Recommended NSF Program for Shared Instrumentation (Average Cost per Institution, $640K)

Number of Universities	Number of Instruments per Year	Cost per Year ($)
20 (on average)	1	12.8M
40 (on average)	1/2	12.8M
60 (on average)	1/3	12.8M
		38.4M
NSF FY 1985 departmental instrumental budget		13.5M
Needed increment		24.9M

currently customary for dedicated instruments) and that support for maintenance and operation (infrastructure support) is assumed for a 3-year period. The outcome is an average NSF investment of $350K per instrument (see Table VII-6).

The number of such instruments needed is reflected in the number of NSF grants made per year in those programs most dependent upon dedicated instruments. There is no point in making grants without providing the researcher his "tools of the trade." Four such programs are listed in Table VII-7 together with the planned FY 1985 budgetary allocation. To determine the instrumentation needs for international competitiveness, we assume that a reasonable fraction of the grants will be able to compete for one or two of these instruments every 6 years. We suggest that within a 6-year period, the top 10 percent of the grants might win two (different) instruments and that the next 20 percent would compete favorably for one instrument. As Table VII-7 shows, this implies that over a 6-year period, 268 instruments would be purchased, a rate of 45 instruments per year. This annual cost, $15.75M, exceeds by more than a factor of two the amount recently planned. *The planned FY 1985 NSF support of dedicated instrumentation should be augmented by $9.6M.*

TABLE VII-6 International Competitiveness in Dedicated Instrumentation

A dedicated instrumentation menu	
(1) Picosecond spectrometer	$360K
(1) Molecular beam	250K
(2) FTIR	400K
(6) Lasers (Yag Doubled, Raman shifted)	540K
(1) High-resolution mass spectrometer	400K
(1) X-ray diffractometer	500K
(2) Dedicated computer	600K
(1) Array processor	250K
(15) Instruments	$3300K
Average capital cost per instrument	$220K
Cost share, NSF, 100%	$220K
Maintenance and operation at 20% capital cost/year for 3 years	$130K
Total cost, NSF share, per instrument	$350K

Grant Size

As indicated earlier, instrumentation has absorbed almost all the growth in the Chemistry Division budget for the last 15 years. Though the instrumentation needs are by no means met, the impact on grant size has become increasingly acute. The adverse effect of this sustained level funding (corrected for inflation) is revealed by the level of effort supportable by the amount of an average grant. For example, if we begin with the proposed FY 1985 Chemistry Division budget, $92.1M, and subtract the amount planned for Departmental Instrumentation ($13.5M) and the probable amount for dedicated instrumentation (estimated at 10.5 percent, $9.7M), the remainder, $68.7M, is available for individual grants. The planned number of grants, 918, implies an average grant size of $74.8K. Perhaps $30K will be extracted for institutional overhead and fringe benefits, which leaves only $45K for research personnel salary costs and research expenses. This amount will barely support one postdoctoral, one-and-one-half graduate students, and 1 or 2 months' summer salary for the principal investigator.

Table VII-8 presents a range of possible grant sizes based upon various levels of effort and a set of reasonable assumptions about stipends, allotments for services, and supplies and small equipment needs. Overhead and fringe benefit costs are computed at an average value, 67 percent.

The levels of effort A, B, and C proposed in Table VII-8 range from one postdoctoral student and six graduate students (level A) to one postdoctoral and two graduate students (level C). While a single grant at level A would not suffice for quite a number of our highly productive research groups, it defines a substantial research program. Level C, although a much smaller program, is still one with the vitality and continuity needed for effective fundamental research. Table VII-8 adds levels D and E in recognition that research is also actively pursued and should be encouraged at undergraduate institutions and the smaller graduate institutions as an important element of undergraduate education and an effective means of invigorating faculty.

TABLE VII-7 Recommended NSF Program for Dedicated Instrumentation (Average Cost per Instrument, $350K)

NSF Program	Planned No. Grants FY 1985	Proposed FY 1985 Budget ($)
Chemical physics	180	14.8M
Chemical dynamics	180	17.0
Structural and thermochemistry	180	15.5
Analytical	130	11.0
TOTAL	670	58.3M

For international competitiveness

Top 10%, 2 instruments/six years $67.2 = 134$ instruments
Next 20%, 1 instrument/six years $134.1 = \underline{134}$ instruments
                                                           268 instruments

$$\frac{268 \text{ Instruments}}{6 \text{ years}} = 45 \frac{\text{Instruments}}{\text{Year}} \quad 45 \; \$350\text{K} \quad = \quad \$15.75\text{M}$$

Present NSF budget = (0.105) ($58.3M) $\underline{6.12\text{M}}$
(if held at 10.5% of program funds)

Needed increment $9.6 M

TABLE VII-8 Proposed NSF Chemistry Grant Sizes

	Level of effort									
	A		B		C		D		E	
Postdoc, 20K	1	20.0	1	20.0	1	20.0	1/2	10.0	—	—
Grad's, 9K	6	54.0	4	36.0	2	18.0	1/2	4.5	—	—
Faculty summer, 4K/mo	2 mo	8.0	2 mo	8.0	2 mo	8.0	2 mo	8.0	2 mo	8.0
Services, 3.5K	(7)	24.5	(5)	17.5	(4)	14.0	(2)	7.0	(1)	3.5
Supplies, 4.5K	(7)	31.5	(5)	22.5	(4)	18.0	(2)	9.0	(1)	4.5
Subtotal		138.0		104.0		78.0		38.5		16.0
Overhead fringe, 67%		92.5		69.7		52.3		25.8		10.7
Small instruments		8.0		6.0		4.0		2.0		2.0
Total		239K		180K		134K		66K		29K

With these levels in mind, we can now estimate the number of grants at each level needed to implement research programs that would maintain this country's international competitiveness, supply the talented scientific manpower sought by our industrial and government laboratories, and contribute our share to the increase of human knowledge. Table VII-9 shows a model with

TABLE VII-9   NSF Grant Needs for International Competitiveness

Number of Universities	A	B	C	D	E	Total
20	160	100	40	—	—	300
40	60	120	160	—	—	340
60	10	20	30	60	—	120
Colleges	—	—	—	—	80	80
	230	240	230	60	80	840
Cost	$55.0M	$43.2M	$30.8M	$4.0M	$2.3M	$135.3M

For international competitiveness 840 grants		$135.3M
Present NSF Chemistry Division budget	$92.1M	
Less departmenal instrumentation	13.5	
Less dedicated instrumentation	6.1	
Present NSF chemistry division budget Less instrumentation		72.5M
Needed increment		$62.8M

which to judge the present NSF grant program in the Chemistry Division. The model is consistent with and supported by the arguments that accompany Table VII-5.

This model would provide NSF support for 2830 graduate students, about 35 percent of those currently engaged in Ph.D. study, and 730 postdoctoral students, 26 percent of the number currently at this educational level. These percentages are reasonable when compared to the data of Table VII-2 showing that NSF provides 45 percent of the federal support for chemistry research performed in our universities and colleges. Of course, chemistry is supported elsewhere in NSF, which accounts for the remaining contribution NSF makes to the support of this essential science.

Thus the proposed model points to a need for much larger funding in support of individual grants, even if the number of grants is not increased. That outcome does not imply or advocate focussing resources at a small number of established research centers at the expense of others. It does imply and advocate open competition for individual grants within the peer review system, and it assumes that an award, once made, will be adequate to complete the proposed research. It implies less proposal writing, less need for multiple grants to sustain a viable program, and provision for supporting infrastructure at all grant sizes. The discussion uses a tiered model merely to indicate the scope of the national research effort that could and should be aggressively pursuing the opportunities presented in this report. It is not intended that NSF seek to establish such a tiered structure. Nevertheless, the tiered model dramatizes the fact that even with much larger funding for chemistry, the number of institutions that would be fully competitive on the international scene would be well within the aspirations and needs of this nation of 50 proud states.

The startling revelation of Table VII-9 is how far the proposed FY 1985 Chemistry Division budget falls short of these aspirations and needs. Table VII-10 combines this with the analyses of Tables VII-5 on shared instrumentation and Table VII-7 on dedicated instrumentation. The cumulative increment shows the magnitude of the discrepancy between needs for international competitiveness and present support levels. Such inadequate support translates directly into lost opportunities and, in the long run, into lost leadership in science and industry. The nation cannot afford these losses.

TABLE VII-10 NSF Chemistry Division Budget Incremental Needs for International Competitiveness in Today's Frontiers of Chemistry

	FY 1985 Request	Increment Needed	Total Need (in FY 1985 dollars)
Departmental instrumentation	$13.5M	$24.9M	$38.4M
Dedicated instrumentation	6.1	9.6	15.7
Grants	72.5	62.8	135.3
Total	$92.1M	$97.3	$189.4M

Table VII-10 shows that *the NSF Chemistry Division budget should be doubled,* after correction for inflation. For cost-effectiveness, *it is recommended that the NSF begin a 3-year initiative to raise the NSF support for chemistry by 25 percent per year for FY 1987, FY 1988, and FY 1989. The added increment should be used for increasing grant size, ensuring encouragement of young investigators, enhancing the departmental and regional instrumentation program, and increasing the amount for dedicated instrumentation.*

Creativity Within NSF

The Chemistry Division in NSF has a laudable record of innovativeness and flexibility in its funding patterns. Its Young Investigator and Shared Instrumentation programs were responsive to encouragement by the 1965 predecessor to this report. More recently, it has experimented with new contractural mechanisms that cluster grants from a given institution, peer review based on "recent track record," one-time extensions based on creativity, and Regional Instrumentation Facilities. *The Chemistry Division is encouraged to continue seeking new mechanisms of funding that help NSF fulfill its unique role of stimulating adventurous and innovative research with as little constraint on that research as possible.*

In the simplest analysis, NSF should try to support creative people in a fashion that permits them to be creative. This can be done within the peer review system by eliciting judgments from reviewers based as much on their evaluations of the investigator's research promise as on his or her research promises, as stated in the proposal. For established investigators, considerable weight should be placed on originality evident in recent accomplishments. On this basis, perhaps 10 percent of the existing grants might be extended a few years without a new proposal (at the program officer's discretion). (This is now being done in NIH with the so-called "Javitz grants" within the Institute for the Neurosciences). Alternatively, especially creative programs ready for renewal might be supported for longer durations, such as 5 to 7 years.

The NSF should maintain its attention to the special needs of the new investigators whose continued entry into chemistry is essential to its long-range vitality. A current difficulty is the large "start-up" costs associated with initiation of research in almost any area of chemistry. A second problem is the time required for build-up of research productivity. Both require risk-taking that must be open to NSF program officers. Grant duration must be sufficient to avoid forcing young scientists into pedestrian research programs sure to lead to quick publications; 4- and 5-year grants should not be considered excessive. Multiyear grants should accommodate especially large, first-year "start-up" costs.

Finally, within bounds set by reasonable accountability, NSF should strive to minimize the number and length of proposals required for an active and productive investigator to obtain adequate support. The increase in grant size advocated here would immediately reduce both the number of proposals per investigator and the diversion of the research community in the operation of the peer review system. Increased grant duration would have the same salutory effects. Grants of less than 3-year's duration should be avoided, and 5-year grants should not be uncommon. Finally, the current NSF limit on proposal length—about 15 single-spaced pages for the proposal itself—should be enforced. Both program officers and reviewers should be encouraged to return single-investigator proposals that are excessive in length.

CHEMISTRY AND THE DEPARTMENT OF ENERGY MISSION

DOE support of the chemical sciences is embedded in a total R&D FY 1985 budget amounting to $5778M, which rose by 4.1 percent from the FY 1984 level. However, 44 percent of this is directed toward Defense R&D, which rose by 10.3 percent. When these R&D activities are subtracted, the non-Defense R&D total, $3245.9M, is found to fall slightly relative to FY 1984 (by .2 percent).

In another profile of the FY 1985 DOE R&D budget, two-thirds will be expended in the DOE National Laboratories, which, all together, saw their proposed collective budgets rise by 8.5 percent from 1984. By difference, the one-third expended outside the National Laboratories ($1889.8M) fell by 3.8 percent. A component of the difference is attributable to the concentration of the overall budget increase in Defense-related R&D, most of which is conducted in 4 or 5 of the 12 National Laboratories.

Need for a DOE Initiative in Chemistry

With these 1984-1985 changes in mind, it is appropriate to assess the relative emphasis placed on fundamental research in chemistry by DOE in pursuit of its mission. To do so, we have listed in Table VII-11 the FY 1985 budgets of the most fundamental research programs conducted under the DOE headings "Energy Supply" and "General Science and Research." The individual programs are listed in order of size, and the last column shows the percentage of the total for those programs. The table shows that of the programs listed, the Materials Sciences represent 10.9 percent, the Chemical Sciences 5.3 percent, and the Nuclear Sciences (where Nuclear Chemistry is found) 2.5 percent.

The Materials Sciences Program devotes a modest percentage of its budget to chem-

TABLE VII-11 Magnitude of Selected DOE Fundamental Research Programs, FY 1985[a]

High energy physics[b]	$547.8M	30.7%
Magnetic fusion energy	440.1	24.7
Materials sciences[c]	193.6	10.9
Environmental sciences	191.1	10.7
Nuclear physics[b]	180.6	10.1
Chemical sciences[c]	95.1	5.3
Nuclear sciences[c]	44.0	2.5
Applied mathematical sciences[c]	36.8	2.1
Engineering and geosciences[c]	28.3	1.6
Biological energy research[c]	13.1	0.7
Advanced energy projects[c]	11.1	0.6
Total	$1781.6M	

[a] AAAS Report IX: *Research and Development, FY 1985* (following congressional action, as compiled by AAAS in Nov. 1984).
[b] Programs conducted under "General Science and Research."
[c] Programs conducted under "Basic Energy Science" within "Energy Supply."

istry-oriented programs (about 7 percent) including programs on Polymers (1.3 percent), Catalysis (1.9 percent), Corrosion (3.0 percent), and Combustion (.4 percent). About 9.4 percent of the Nuclear Science budget goes to support heavy-element chemistry.

One can explain the sense of urgency implicit in the very large annual investment being made in the development of nuclear fusion, an investment that has been sustained now for almost two decades. It is quite impossible, however, to rationalize the extremely modest emphasis placed on chemistry, as embodied in the 5.3 percent figure. Chemistry and Chemical Engineering will be the dominant sciences in the energy technologies that must be developed and that we will depend upon for the rest of this century. In 1983, 92 percent of the U.S. energy consumption was based upon chemical fuels. The small remainder, 8 percent of our use, was mostly provided by about equal contributions from nuclear and hydroelectric energy.

As the DOE contemplates its mission, *to assure future access to abundant and clean sources of energy*, it must reckon with these challenging expectations for the next three decades:

—by the year 2000 the U.S. annual energy consumption will probably exceed today's use by 20 to 50 percent;

—during the next three decades, growth in the use of nuclear power will be severely constrained by social concerns already in evidence;

—further increase in hydroelectric power has natural limits and is in conflict with widespread desire to minimize environmental encroachment;

—even the most optimistic proponents of nuclear fusion do not see it providing a large fraction of our energy use before well into the 21st century;

—dependence upon high-grade petroleum crudes and high-grade coal deposits must decline as worldwide reserves are depleted and as access to foreign crude oil is capriciously restricted by political developments beyond our control.

These boundary conditions surely point to the need for expanding the knowledge base upon which new energy technologies can be built. Chemical and electrochemical systems provide some of the most compact and efficient means of energy storage. And we can predict with confidence that foremost among the new energy sources will be low-grade chemical fuels, such as high-sulfur-content coal, shale oil, tar sands, peat, lignite, and biomass. For not one of these alternatives does appropriate technology exist today that can economically meet the stringent demand that environmental pollution be avoided despite the higher impurity content of these new feedstocks. Enormous chemical challenges must be met—for new catalysts, new processes, new fuels, new extraction techniques, more efficient combustion conditions, better emission controls, more sensitive environmental monitoring, and many others. Biomass must be brought to practicality to reduce the amount of fossil fuel burned and thus to help check the rate of increase in atmospheric carbon dioxide. (Combustion of biomass grown for fuel cannot return more CO_2 to the atmosphere than was consumed in the photosynthetic processes by which the biomass was produced). Solar energy must be fully exploited including through development of artificial photosynthetic and electrocatalytic techniques that avoid combustion by converting the photon energy directly to electrical or chemical energy. To accelerate our movement toward meeting these critical needs *the Department of Energy should mount a major initiative in those areas of chemistry relevant to the energy technologies of the future.* The same urgency that justifies our powerful program in nuclear fusion dictates a program of comparable magnitude in chemistry. The scope of the initiative should be broad, encompassing all forms of catalysis (homogeneous, heterogeneous, electro-, photo-, and enzymatic-catalysis), exploiting the new potentialities for understanding combustion, developing the plant sciences that will facilitate our use of natural photosynthesis, and adventuring boldly into frontiers that may open new energy avenues (genetic engineering of photosynthetic organisms, development of polymeric photovoltaic devices, etc.). The program should take full advantage of the multidisciplinary capabilities of our National Laboratories. Although its funding is set at a modest level, the Combustion Research Facility at Sandia

Livermore provides a laudable example. *In an appropriate number of our National Laboratories, the defined mission should be reshaped to include a major focus on one or more of the areas of chemistry crucial to energy technologies.* And, most important, the DOE research support to universities must be increased to engage the larger chemistry community in the accomplishment of the Department's mission. While the chemistry activity at the National Laboratories is being increased, *university research programs in energy-relevant areas of chemistry should be raised to be commensurate with those in the National Laboratories. In addition, the interaction between DOE laboratories and universities should be strengthened through visiting faculty researcher programs and long-term collaborative projects.*

A Proposed 5-Year Initiative

A program to approach these goals in a cost-effective way is presented in Table VII-12. It proposes to build toward a level of commitment about half as big

TABLE VII-12   A Proposed 5-Year DOE Initiative in Chemistry (All in FY 1985 Dollars)

	Biological Energy + Chemical Sciences + Catalysis + Combustion	Incremental Growth	National Labs	Universities
FY 1985	$120M	$—	$ 94M	$ 26M
1986	142M	+22M	101M	41M
1987	169M	+27M	110M	59M
1988	201M	+32M	121M	80M
1989	239M	+38M	134M	105M
1990	285M	+46M	149M	136M
Total growth over 5 years		$165M		

as that for magnetic fusion, appropriate to the reality that 90 percent of our energy must come from chemical energy sources for the next quarter-century. *Incremental growth by a factor of about 2.5 is needed in chemistry research programs relevant to the DOE mission.* This level of effort should be roughly equally divided between the National Laboratories and university laboratories. The substantial growth implied is approached over a 5-year period at a real growth rate of 20 percent per year for 5 years to ensure cost-effective distribution of the incremental resources and to provide orderly growth of the DOE program management expertise that will be needed. Each yearly increment in this 5-year program would be divided in a growth pattern that will, first, stimulate the efforts of those National Laboratories that choose to refocus their defined mission toward chemistry-based energy technologies and, second, build the engagement of the academic research community in the areas that undergird these technologies. The FY 1985 baseline is taken to be $120M, based upon the approximate present sum of the Chemical Sciences, the Biological

Energy Research, and the Catalysis, Corrosion, and Combustion programs.

This initiative is intended to be broad in scope to encompass the range of chemistry frontiers at which advances can be expected and which are obviously of relevance to the development of new energy technologies. A desirable distribution of the incremental resources is given in Table VII-13.

TABLE VII-13   A Desirable Deployment of Incremental Resources (All in FY 1985 Dollars)

	1986	1987	1988	1989	1990	5-Year Program Growth
Catalysis						
Heterogeneous	$ 6M	$+6M	$+7M	$+8M	$+10M	$+37M
Homogeneous	+2M	+3M	+4M	+5M	+6M	+20M
Enzymes and artificial enzymes	+2M	+3M	+4M	+5M	+6M	+20M
Electrocatalysis	+3M	+4M	+4M	+5M	+6M	+22M
Reaction dynamics	+3M	+4M	+5M	+6M	+7M	+25M
Photosynthesis and photochemistry	+3M	+4M	+4M	+5M	+6M	+22M
Plant sciences	+3M	+3M	+4M	+4M	+5M	+19M
Increment	$22M	$27M	$32M	$38M	$46M	$165M

Technical Qualifications at the DOE National Laboratories

In light of our recommendation that the DOE mount an initiative in support of chemistry-based energy technologies, it is useful to ask about the distribution of technical qualifications of the scientific staffs at the existing National Laboratories. Furthermore, changes over the last decade in professional qualifications at each of the National Laboratories may indicate changing trends in the way each Laboratory sees its mission evolving. Table VII-14 shows for four National Laboratories the number of physicists and of chemists in 1970, 1980, and 1984. In assessing these figures, it is perhaps relevant to remember that U.S. business employs approximately 2.5 times more Ph.D. chemists than Ph.D. physicists.

The ratios shown in the last column of Table VII-14 are revealing. The only trend discernible is at Oak Ridge where the hiring pattern must reflect a deliberate movement away from chemistry-based technologies. At Argonne and Brookhaven, the hiring pattern seems to signal a general laboratory expansion over the 1970s followed by a retreat or slowdown in growth. However, in neither laboratory is there evidence of significant change toward chemistry-based mission goals. For Los Alamos only current data were available, and they display heavy emphasis on physics-oriented goals. These compositions imply leanings away from chemistry-based technologies, an outcome more or less dictated by and appropriate to the distribution of DOE research resources presented in Table VII-11. The program advocated in Table VII-12 projects an

TABLE VII-14 Distribution of Chemists and Physicists at the DOE National Laboratories

National Laboratory	Year	Number of Ph.D. Physicists		Professionals Chemists		Number of Physicists / Number of Chemists
Argonne	1971	168		128		1.31
	1980	191	+23	159	+31	1.20
	1984	169	−22	132	−27	1.28
Oak Ridge	1970	178		180		.99
	1980	250	+72	176	−4	1.42
	1983	269	+19	166	−10	1.62
Brookhaven	1970	200		82		2.50
	1980	260	+60	133	+51	1.95
	1984	276	+16	134	+1	2.06
Los Alamos	1984	679		242		2.81

overall growth by about 65 percent of the chemistry-oriented research activity at the National Laboratories. It is recommended that *growth in chemistry-oriented research should be concentrated at those National Laboratories that choose to refocus their defined mission toward chemistry-based energy technologies. This growth should add substantially to the cadre of Ph.D. staff with credentials in areas of chemistry appropriate to the new mission.*

CHEMISTRY AND THE NIH MISSION

According to AAAS Report IX: *Research and Development, FY 1985* (see Table II-15, p. 132), the NIH budget in FY 1984 was $4477M, more than 3.5 times the NSF budget for the same year. Of this, $537M was directed to NIH intramural research and $2387M to extramural research projects. Thus, these two elements together account for, respectively, 12.0 and 53.3 percent of the total budget.

In contrast to other federal agencies that support chemical research (NSF, DOE, and DOD), not one of the National Institutes of Health has a program expressly titled "Chemistry." Neither are there any program descriptions that identify as a primary program goal the advance of particular subbranches of chemistry that could be seen to be particularly relevant to the Institute mission. Nevertheless, NIH furnishes a substantial fraction of the U.S. federal support for university research in chemistry, surely in excess of 25 percent. Thus, NIH plays a crucial role in support of basic chemical research in this country.

The fact that chemistry is not overtly supported makes it difficult to track the magnitude and distribution of the substantial NIH funding of research conducted by chemists. This is evident in the 1983 NSF study of federal research support to chemistry, agency by agency (see Appendix Table A-7). The table displays FY 1982 amounts directed toward basic research in chemistry conducted at the nation's universities: by NSF, $76.4M, and by NIH, $38.3M. The

NSF figure can be derived as a fraction of the announced budgets for its divisions; the sum of the NSF Chemistry Division budget and the chemistry part of the Materials Science Division budget is $77.3M (see Table VII-3), and smaller amounts are derived from the Divisions of Biochemistry, Atmospheric Chemistry, Geochemistry, and Marine Chemistry.

Contrast this agreement with the outcome of a more detailed NIH budget analysis sponsored by the Board on Chemical Sciences and Technology of the National Research Council for FY 1982. This analysis was not based on the stated aim of the research (which, perforce, must always be justified in terms of human health) but rather on the total funding of individual investigators whose institutional connection is a chemistry department at a Ph.D.-granting university. The total so obtained was $76M, just double that recorded in Appendix Table A-7. The discrepancy undoubtedly reflects the substantial cross-disciplinary character of chemistry research as conducted in our university chemistry departments and implicitly justifies the substantial support chemistry receives from NIH.

Average Grant Size

Table VII-15 shows some detail on the FY 1982 distribution among the institutes of the funding received by chemists. About 90 percent of the grants are supported by 5 of the 11 Institutes and 54 percent by the Institute for General Medical Sciences. Over all the institutes, the average grant size is $83.2K. This is only slightly larger than the NSF average, $74.8K, and it again will support less than an average level of effort C in Table VII-8 (one postdoctoral and two graduate students). By the same argument made earlier concerning NSF grant sizes, *it is recommended that a fraction of any additional NIH funds into chemistry be used to increase average grant size.* A 30 percent increase in average grant size to level of effort B (Table VII-8) is a reasonable target. Furthermore, somewhat *larger grant size should be considered appropriate for cross-disciplinary collaborative programs that, through joint PI structure, link expertise in chemistry with that in other disciplines* (biology, molecular biology, etc.).

Grant Success Ratio

Through all of its institutes in FY 1982, NIH supported 14,826 individual investigator grants with a total cost of $1.45B. Thus chemistry receives about 6 percent of the research monies distributed by NIH through individual grants and about 3.7 percent of the total resources NIH directs to the conduct of R&D at universities and colleges (in FY 1982, $2.07B). When the data base is expanded to include, as well, departments of biochemistry, pharmacology, and medicinal chemistry, total NIH support in the form of grants to individual investigators rises to some $204M in FY 1982 with 2,256 individual grants. To these four departments, the Institute for General Medical Sciences devotes nearly 40 percent of its budget, over $94M, to grant support. Support from the

National Cancer Institute rises for these four departments to $28M, somewhat less than 10 percent of the total NCI research budget.

The last column of Table VII-15 shows that about 6 percent of all NIH individual investigator grants are made to investigators in university chemistry departments but that the percentage is considerably higher in the Institute for General Medical Sciences, 19.3 percent. For this particular Institute, detailed study of awards made relative to the number of applications received over the period 1974-1982 shows that the percentage of applications awarded has consistently remained a few percentage points *above* the rate to nonchemistry scientists over this period. Thus scientists in chemistry departments are apparently being equitably treated as measured by the success of their applications.

On the other hand, the average success rate for competing research projects has declined from about 60 percent in 1974 to about 40 percent in 1982. Equally damaging is the fact that success rates fluctuate widely from year to year, moving from about 60 percent in 1975 to 40 percent in 1977, back up to 55 percent in 1979, and then down to 37.5 percent in 1982. Such large and apparently capricious variations do not afford the continuity essential for first-class fundamental research. Needless to say, the overall NIH budget did

TABLE VII-15   National Institutes of Health Research Projects to Chemistry Department-Based Principal Investigators, FY 1982[a]

Institute	Dollars[b]	Approximate Number, Research Grants	Percent of Total Number, Res. Grants
General Medical Sciences	42.9M	499	19.3
National Cancer Institute	11.7M	152	5.6
Allergy and Infectious Diseases	4.5M	55	3.8
Heart, Lung, and Blood	6.2M	67	2.9
Arthritis, Diabetes, Digestive, and Kidney Diseases	5.3M	64	2.7
Neurological and Communicative Disorders and Stroke	1.8M	25	1.7
Environmental Health Sciences	1.2M	18	5.5
Aging	.4M	5	1.2
Dental Research	.4M	5	1.4
Eye Institute	1.7M	23	2.3
Child Health and Human Development	.7M	10	0.8
Total all institutes	76.8M	923	5.6

[a] Robert M. Simon, National Research Council, private communication.
[b] These dollar amounts do include institutional overhead.

not display swings of these magnitudes, so other factors are at work in producing these large amplitude fluctuations. Whatever the causes, these rapid

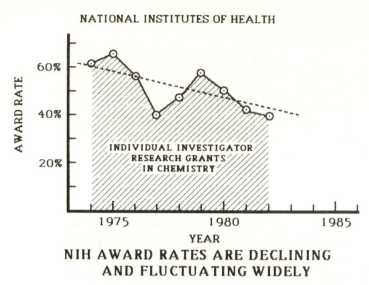

NATIONAL INSTITUTES OF HEALTH

NIH AWARD RATES ARE DECLINING AND FLUCTUATING WIDELY

changes disrupt and damage high-quality research programs, and they are to be avoided. Hence *we applaud and vigorously support the efforts of the National Institutes of Health to build into its yearly budget an extramural grant stabilization program*.

Shared Instrumentation

In the 1960s, NIH began a program of support for the purchase of large instrumentation—mainly NMR and Mass Spectrometers—for shared use at universities. The program stabilized in the support of existing centers without new starts in the early 1970s and gradually was phased out. Nevertheless, NIH had furnished an admirable prototype model for the NSF Departmental Instrumentation program which, from a much smaller funding base, attempted by itself to meet chemistry departmental needs through the 1970s.

Now NIH has reawakened its shared instrumentation program, a timely addition to the existing oversolicited counterpart programs in NSF and DOD. In view of the growing dependence upon sophisticated instrumentation in the health-related sciences, *we recommend that NIH maintain its extramural shared instrumentation program at a level approximately equal to that proposed here for NSF. Further, we urge that initial cost-sharing and support of ongoing maintenance and operations follow the same guidelines proposed earlier for NSF, i.e., 80 percent cost sharing and 5-year maintenance at 20 percent of the initial cost*.

CHEMISTRY AND THE DEPARTMENT OF DEFENSE MISSION

The many ways in which our national security depends upon a vigorous scientific enterprise are enumerated in the introduction in Section V-C. The body of this report presents compelling evidence for the role that basic and applied chemical research has played in this enterprise, with direct impact on the technologies upon which the nation's security is based. Most obvious examples of interest to DOD include fuels and propellants, new polymers for protective garments, structural elements, and nose cones, alloys for jet engine parts, electronic materials, upper atmospheric chemistry, medicines, chemical lasers, and a host of others. Plainly, it is appropriate for the Department of

Defense to devote a deliberate fraction of its resources and attention to the maintenance of the research activity that leads to such advances.

Applied and Basic Research

For near-term exploitation of scientific advances, DOD should invest heavily in applied research, which is designated by categories 6.2, 6.3, and 6.4. At the same time, long-range security interests dictate that DOD should also support fundamental research in those areas that can be seen to underlie technologies of particular relevance to the defense mission. The more fundamental research is designated category 6.1. Over the last two decades, there have been profound changes in the pattern of DOD research activity. When corrected for inflation, the level of support for all R&D declined steadily from 1970 to 1975, remained constant until 1980, and then was raised steeply during the last 5 years. In 1984 the level of activity in applied research exceeded the 1965 level and in the proposed 1985 budget, it is 22 percent higher. When attention is focussed on basic research (6.1), the picture is remarkably different. Viewed as a percentage of the total R&D, in 1965, 5.1 percent of the R&D was directed to fundamental research. In 1980, this figure had dropped to 3.9 percent. In 1984, the 6.1 category accounted for only 3.0 percent of the total R&D, and in the proposed 1985 budget, it drops still further, to 2.7 percent. Expressed in level of effort in inflation-corrected dollars, the proposed 1985 investment in basic research is only two-thirds the 1965 value. ***It is recommended that over the next 5 years, the percentage of the DOD R&D budget directed to basic (6.1) research be increased to restore the 1965 value of 5.0 percent by the year 1990.***

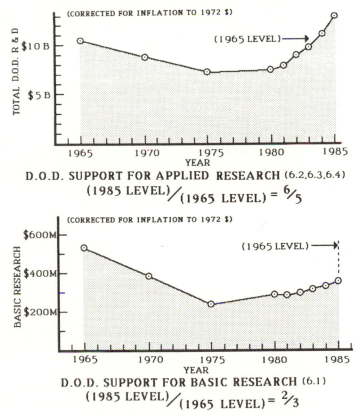

D.O.D. SUPPORT FOR APPLIED RESEARCH (6.2,6.3,6.4)
$$\text{(1985 LEVEL)} \Big/ \text{(1965 LEVEL)} = {}^6\!/_5$$

D.O.D. SUPPORT FOR BASIC RESEARCH (6.1)
$$\text{(1985 LEVEL)} \Big/ \text{(1965 LEVEL)} = {}^2\!/_3$$

Research Areas

A number of broad research areas in chemistry deserve DOD attention because they are likely to provide significant advances relevant to defense technologies.

—Strategic and Critical Materials

—Fuels, Propellants, and Explosives

—Atmospheric Phenomena
—Chemical and Biological Defense
—Nuclear Power and Nuclear Weapons Effects

For each of these broad areas, Table VII-16 lists fundamental studies that will

TABLE VII-16   Defense Needs and Special Opportunities

	Army	Navy	Air Force	DARPA
Strategic and critical materials	✔✔✔	✔✔	✔✔	✔✔✔
Polymers as structural materials	✔	✔	✔	✔
Solid state chemistry	✔	✔	✔	✔
Chemical synthesis	✔	✔	✔	✔
Fuels, propellants, and explosives	✔✔	✔✔	✔✔✔	
Molecular spectroscopy & kinetics	✔	✔	✔	
Chemical synthesis			✔	
Catalysis, surface sciences	✔	✔		
Combustion	✔	✔	✔	
Corrosion	✔	✔		
Chemical lasers			✔	
Fluid transport		✔	✔	
Condensed phases		✔		
Theoretical chemistry		✔	✔	
Atmospheric phenomena	✔✔	✔✔	✔✔✔	
Chemical kinetics	✔	✔	✔	
Atomic & molecular spectroscopy	✔	✔	✔	
Analytical chemistry	✔	✔	✔	
Theoretical chemistry	✔	✔	✔	
Chemical and biological defense	✔✔✔	✔✔		
Biotechnology	✔			
Analytical chemistry	✔	✔		
Marine chemistry		✔		
Organic synthesis	✔			
Nuclear power and nuclear weapons effects	✔✔	✔✔✔	✔✔	
Nuclear chemistry and nuclear processing	✔	✔		
Nuclear stability	✔	✔		

NOTE: ✔ = applicable   ✔✔ = important   ✔✔✔ = critically important

provide the advances that will lead, in the long run, to advanced defense concepts and applications. The table also indicates specific applicabilities to the specialized interests of the various defense arms.

Chemistry Research in Universities

With so many areas of opportunity of special relevance to the DOD mission, there is ample reason for DOD to guarantee the vitality of U.S. research activity in chemistry. Furthermore, there are clear benefits to DOD if these opportunities are pursued, in part, in our university research laboratories. First, university participation builds the technical manpower pool needed to deploy and maintain our increasingly sophisticated defense technologies. Second, it gives DOD significant influence on the university research agenda in directing attention toward advancing our knowledge in those areas of chemistry key to our defense posture.

Plainly, the extent of DOD influence on university research agendas is related to the fraction of the university support coming from DOD sources. This fraction remained close to 10 percent through the decade of the 1970s, a level much too low to secure the desired end. In order for DOD to have a significant impact on building our technical manpower pool while increasing the growth of critical scientific knowledge, its support of chemistry must be comparable to that of other federal agencies. Since four agencies furnish most of the basic research support for the chemical sciences, a reasonable level for DOD support is near 25 percent of the total.

In fact, beginning in 1981, the percent of DOD support has been growing. From 1980 to 1983, DOD funds for university research in chemistry rose from $15.0M to $29.5M, sufficient to bring this percent to 16 percent. This rise paral-

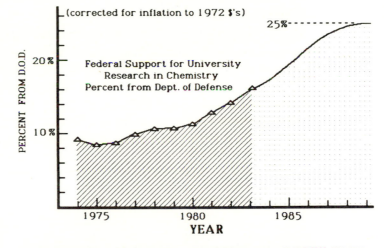

TECHNICAL MANPOWER AND CRITICAL KNOWLEDGE REQUIRE A LARGER D.O.D. INVESTMENT

lelled a corresponding much-needed rise in in-house research investment from $20.7M to $30.4M, which, after inflation, represents a real growth of 4 percent per year. Then, in the years 1984 and 1985, planned support for chemistry research leveled off, just matching inflation at 6.1 percent per year.

It is recommended that *DOD support for university research in the chemical sciences should be raised to about 25 percent of the total federal support. Real growth of 10 percent per year should be sustained until that goal is reached. Because of the central importance of chemistry to our national security, the same proposed growth should be provided to DOD in-house research programs of the 6.1 category.*

6.1 Research in the Various Defense Arms

Table VII-17 shows for the years 1982 to 1985 the total DOD investment in fundamental research, the percentage of these amounts devoted to chemistry and materials programs, and how these amounts were divided among the various arms. The Army, Navy, and Air Force direct approximately equal amounts to the support of chemistry, which is appropriate in view of the opportunities chemistry affords (see Table VII-16).

In the preceding discussion, it was recommended that the benefits to DOD warrant an increase in its current level of support for chemistry of 10 percent real growth per year for 5 years. For each of the three defense arms, *this growth should be focused into the high pay-off research areas identified in Table VII-16. Comparable growth in the Chemistry and the Materials Science programs should exploit the opportunities chemistry offers to provide new strategic materials, fuels, propellants, and explosives, as well as deeper understandings of chemistry relevant to atmospheric phenomena, biological defense, and nuclear power and weapons effects.*

Collaborative Relationships

Since it is to the benefit of both the inhouse DOD laboratories and the broader chemical research community (including both industry and universities), *it is recommended that means be sought to increase the interaction between DOD laboratories and universities.* There are several mechanisms that should be pursued to improve these interactions; they include (a) postdoctoral and visiting faculty programs, (b) long-term collaborative projects, and (c) innovative graduate student support programs. Such interactions are entirely consistent with recommendations of both the Grace Commission and the Packard Committee bearing on the strengthening of federal laboratory, university, and industry interactions.

TABLE VII-17 Department of Defense Research Support for Chemistry and Materials Science, 1982-1985 (6.1, Basic Research)[a]

		1982	1983	1984	1985 (Request)
DOD	Total	$694.1M	$780.0M	$837.9M	$897.9M
	Chemistry	53.1 (7.7%)	58.9 (7.6%)	62.0 (7.4%)	66.3 (7.4%)
	Materials	71.5 (10.3%)	81.0 (10.4%)	82.8 (9.9%)	87.5 (9.7%)
ARMY	Total	$178.1M	$202.4M	$217.5M	$238.8M
	Chemistry	22.2 (12.5%)	23.8 (11.6%)	23.5 (10.8%)	25.4 (10.6%)
	Materials	14.8 (8.3%)	17.1 (8.4%)	17.1 (7.9%)	18.1 (7.6%)
NAVY	Total	$276.0M	$309.3M	$319.3M	$349.7M
	Chemistry	17.1 (6.2%)	18.2 (5.9%)	19.0 (6.0%)	20.9 (6.0%)
	Materials	24.2 (8.8%)	24.0 (7.8%)	25.0 (7.8%)	27.5 (7.9%)
AF	Total	$147.5M	$167.3M	$192.5M	$206.9M
	Chemistry	13.8 (9.4%)	16.9 (10.1%)	19.5 (10.1%)	20.0 (9.7%)
	Materials	18.1 (12.3%)	17.7 (10.6%)	21.9 (11.4%)	22.7 (11.0%)
DARPA	Total	$ 92.5M	$101.0M	$108.6M	$102.5M
	Materials	14.4 (15.6%)	22.3 (22.1%)	18.8 (17.3%)	19.2 (18.7%)

[a] AAAS Report IX: *Research and Development, FY 1985.*

Equipment and Facilities Support

It is now widely recognized—as documented at length in this report—that federal programs supporting science and engineering activities have not adequately recognized the sophistication and cost of the equipment required for modern science. In many cases the equipment found in U.S. laboratories supported by DOD 6.1 and 6.2 programs is greatly outdated compared to the equipment found in laboratories undertaking similar work in U.S. industry or in foreign countries. In 1983 DOD recognized these equipment needs by establishing a special "set aside" program for instrumentation, $30M per year divided equally among its three arms. This heavily oversolicited program has proven to be quite successful, except that maintenance and technician support have not been included as an integral part of the equipment award. Since recipient research groups and their institutions do not have adequate resources to devote to these important purposes, there is a risk that the much needed new instrumentation will be less efficiently employed or will become obsolete more rapidly than would be the case if provision were made to include appropriate levels of maintenance and technician support. *It is recommended that DOD continue its instrumentation program but with the addition of support for maintenance and operation* to ensure cost-effective use of the equipment. *This instrumentation program should not grow at the expense of the direct contract support for research activities.* Evidently the appropriate balance between research support and equipment support is a matter requiring on-going judgment, and continuing attention must be given by DOD to maintaining this balance.

With regard to research facilities at universities and colleges, it is regrettable that the lapse in federal programs has meant that new research laboratories are not being built and that old laboratories and buildings are deteriorating progressively. While the general state of research buildings and laboratories on U.S. campuses is clearly not a principal responsibility of DOD, the Department does have an interest in assuring that campus research facilities are adequate to carry out the research missions and associated technical manpower training for long-run national defense. Accordingly, *DOD should explore mechanisms to support new construction and renovation of university research facilities in particularly critical areas of chemical science.* If attention to such space needs is not forthcoming, it cannot be expected that an adequate research base for DOD needs will be available. In addition, DOD should support OSTP efforts to establish new programs for research facilities generally at the nation's colleges and universities.

CHEMISTRY AND THE DEPARTMENT OF AGRICULTURE MISSION

It is widely recognized abroad that a major strength of the U.S. fundamental research enterprise is the plurality of federal agencies sponsoring it. Each agency exerts its due influence on the research community's agenda by encouraging research at the most fundamental level in areas that underlie and advance that agency's mission. Consequently, it is an unfortunate anomaly and a loss to the nation that the Department of Agriculture has had difficulty mounting a significant competitive grants program to engage the university research community more fully in its mission goals.

The FY 1984 R&D budget for the USDA was $869M, 1.9 percent above the FY 1983 figure. Of this, only 4.5 percent is directed toward research in chemistry ($38.7M in FY 1983). The bulk of this research is performed in-house in seven major research centers under the Agricultural Research Service. In fact, as shown in Table A-7, less than one-fifth of USDA chemistry research is supported through competitive grants at universities and colleges ($6.6M in FY 1983). The result is that USDA provides only about 3.6 percent of the federal support for chemistry performed in the nation's university research laboratories. This is incongruous in the light of chemistry's significant accomplishments relevant to increase in the world's food supply (e.g., in fertilizers, growth hormones, pesticides, herbicides, pheremones, and genetic engineering of plants) and the expanding possibilities for further advances as described in Sections IV-A and IV-D.

Over the last several years, conscientious and laudable attempts have been made by USDA to add to its budget a more substantial competitive grants program that does not detract from the existing activities of the Agricultural Research Service. These attempts have not yet been implemented by Congress. In the public interest, *it is recommended that the Department of Agriculture initiate a substantial competitive grants program in chemistry research. The aim of the program should be to increase over the next 5 years the Department's extramural support of fundamental research in chemistry to an approximate par with its intramural research program.*

CHEMISTRY AND THE NATIONAL AERONAUTICS AND SPACE ADMINISTRATION MISSION

This report identifies several rapidly moving fronts of chemistry in scientific areas where NASA has active interests. Obvious examples are high energy propellants (Initiative A), high temperature materials (Initiative E), chemistry in plasmas (Initiative E), and chemistry in the stratosphere (Initiatives A and D). The current NASA interest in the establishment of a permanent human presence in space offers fascinating challenges in chemistry related to life-sustenance within the closed system of a space station (Initiative C). *It is recommended that NASA direct increased attention toward special opportunities in chemistry relevant to operations in space:*

—high-energy propellants
—chemical behavior under extreme conditions

—reaction kinetics and photochemistry under collision-free conditions
—chemical aspects of life-sustenance in a closed system
—analytical methods for compositional monitoring in both the troposphere and the stratospere

Especially vital is NASA's concern with the chemical composition of the atmosphere, particularly in reference to changes that may be occurring. The importance of a deep understanding of the complex chemical processes operative in the stratosphere has already been well documented in recent concerns about the ozone layer. Now attention is focussing on the atmospheric carbon dioxide concentration, which has clearly increased over the last three decades. Similar changes are being noted in methane and nitrous oxide concentrations, each of which is intimately involved with the earth's biological activity. Understanding of the biogeochemical cycles that move carbon, nitrogen, sulfur, and other elements into and out of the atmosphere is fundamental to the maintenance of favorable conditions for all forms of life. Because of NASA's unique capabilities, it can play a significant role as we seek this understanding.

NASA has been actively engaged in such studies, through downward-looking sensors in satellites, through programs of active measurement in the atmosphere, and through laboratory-backup programs in chemical kinetics. These programs address such crucial problems as the role of trace gases in the atmospheric trapping of infrared radiation (the greenhouse effect), the deposition and chemical fate of acid compounds and their precursors, the chemical interactions that affect stratospheric ozone, and the environmental implications of the changing desert cover in the tropics. Clearly, *NASA should maintain a substantial and continuing commitment to the study of atmospheric chemistry.*

NASA conducts a large and productive research program through its own NASA laboratories, and it depends significantly upon private research contractors. It engages less fully the academic research community in chemistry. In light of the potential contributions of chemistry to the safety, range, and effectiveness of future space operations, *NASA should more actively encourage academic chemists to address problems relevant to the NASA mission through competitive grants for fundamental research.*

CHEMISTRY IN THE ENVIRONMENTAL PROTECTION AGENCY

For FY 1985, EPA proposed to direct 6.5 percent of its $4.25 billion budget request toward R&D. Approximately half of this $278M R&D support would go to programs in which chemistry plays a role: Environmental Engineering and Technology, $50M; Acid Rain, $34M; Monitoring Systems and Quality, $31M; Exploratory Research, $16M; and Environmental Processes and Effects, $1.9M. While the Exploratory Research program is only 5.6 percent of the total EPA R&D program, over 95 percent is currently directed toward extramural activity. This research is largely conducted at eight university-based centers, but it also includes some competitive research grants. Significantly, this small program was incrementally increased by a factor of 2.5 in FY 1984 over the FY 1983 level, and all the growth was placed in the extramural program. Presuming that this Exploratory Research program is intended to nurture long-range research relevant to its mission, *EPA should increase the percentage of its R&D funds placed in its Exploratory Research program and its commitment to extramural fundamental research relevant to environmental problems of the future. Most of this growth should be awarded through competitive grants.*

Initiatives A and D both present opportunities that are applicable to EPA mission goals. When a potential pollutant enters the environment, it will almost always become involved in chemical transformations that influence its movement through and its impact on the environment. Photochemical and biological factors may be active. *The EPA should encourage systematic and fundamental research directed toward clarification of reaction pathways open to molecules, atoms, and ions of environmental interest, both in the gas phase and in aqueous solutions.*

More important, however, *EPA should have as a conscious and publicized goal the detection of potentially undesirable environmental constituents at concentration levels far below known or expected toxicity limits.* To reach this goal, EPA should stimulate the development of new analytical techniques of all kinds. Its program must, of course, include analytical detection of specific substances already known to present environmental issues. In addition, *EPA should take a prominent role in the support of long-range research in analytical chemistry. Program emphases should include extension of sensitivity limits, increase in detection selectivity, and exploration of new concepts.*

APPENDIX A

Chemistry in Industry: Tables

The Chemicals and Allied Products industry is made up of firms primarily manufacturing any of the classes of products listed in Table A-1. The percentages shown there indicate the share of the industry's shipments in 1982. Chemical and Allied Products is a major industry: shipments in 1982, valued at $169B, accounted for 9.0 percent of all U.S. manufacturing industry (see Table A-2). This percentage has steadily risen over the last decade; chemical shipments were only 7.5 percent of the total in 1972.

The Chemicals and Allied Products industry employs 5 percent of the total U.S. work force engaged in manufacture, and 11 percent of all industrial R&D scientists and engineers. Total employment in the industry in 1982 of 1,074,000 included 597,000 production workers (*C&EN*, June 13, 1983, p. 52). The full-time equivalent number of R&D scientists and engineers (Ph.D. level) employed by the industry in 1982 was 60,000 (for 1970-1981, see "National Patterns of Science and Technology Resources, 1982," NSF 82-319, Table 49).

Three major markets affect substantially the sales level of chemicals: transportation equipment, construction, and agriculture. However, chemistry pervades many other industries (see Table A-4). Among the top 100 companies in the United States in terms of chemical sales (*C&EN*, June 13, 1983, pp. 36-37), with cumulative chemical sales value of $118B in 1982, 24 classified in the petroleum or the natural gas industries account for $34B. Another 22, with chemical sales totalling $15B, are primarily in a wide variety of other manufacturing industries, including photographic equipment and supplies, steel, dairy products, machinery, rubber products, glass, alcoholic beverages, agricultural supplies, lumber and wood products, motor vehicle parts, processed foods, nonferrous base metals, specialty metals, aerospace, and nonmetallic minerals products. Each of these 22 companies classified outside the Chemicals and Allied Products industry had chemical sales exceeding $200M in 1982, and 5 had chemical sales exceeding $1B.

While major chemical research is carried on by some companies classified outside the Chemicals and Allied Products industry, companies within that industry have maintained a characteristically large commitment to basic research compared with other industries. Funds for their performance of basic research amounted to $366M in 1979, nearly a third of the $1,155M total for basic research by all U.S. industry (NSF 82-319, Table 43). Funds for basic research in chemistry by all U.S. industry totalled $382M, compared with

$144M in physics/astronomy, $292M in all engineering, $176M in life sciences, $20M in mathematics, $13M in environmental sciences (geology, oceanography, atmospheric sciences), and $128M in other sciences (NSF 82-319, Table 44).

TABLE A-1 The Chemicals and Allied Products Industry

Drugs and related biomedical products	20%
Soap, other detergents, and cosmetics	18%
Industrial organic chemicals	17%
Plastics materials and resins	17%
Industrial inorganic chemicals	9%
Agricultural chemicals (e.g., fertilizers, pesticides)	7%
Paint and allied products	5%
Other chemical products (e.g., adhesives, sealants, explosives, printing ink, carbon black)	7%

Funds for overall R&D by the Chemicals and Allied Products industry—$4,608M in 1980—contain a typically large component from the companies' own resources—$4,201M—the balance of less than 9 percent of the total being derived from the federal government. In contrast, the amount expended on R&D by all manufacturing industry—$42,312M in 1980—includes $13,165M, or more than 30 percent, from federal agencies (NSF 82-319, Tables 38, 39, and 40). The distribution of this R&D expenditure, according to company size, is shown in Table A-6 for the year 1981.

The importance of Chemicals and Allied Products to the net international balance of trade has steadily increased over the last 15 years, a period over which its trade balance rose from +$1.6B to +$12B. The significance to our international trade situation can hardly be overemphasized because, over this same time period, the total for all merchandise was changing from +$5.8B to a negative balance of −$32.3B (see Table A-3).

TABLE A-2 Manufacturers' Shipments in Selected U.S. Industries, 1972-1982 (Billions of Dollars)

	1972	1977	1978	1979	1980	1981	1982
Petroleum and coal products	29	97	104	148	199	220	202
Machinery (nonelectrical)	66	122	143	167	181	204	184
Chemicals and allied products	57	118	130	148	162	175	169
Electrical machinery	53	88	101	116	129	138	138
Motor vehicles	64	118	132	131	105	115	110
Paper and allied products	28	52	57	65	73	80	78
Blast furnace, steel products	34	51	59	67	62	69	47
Nonferrous base metals	24	42	46	56	60	55	46
Rubber and plastic products	21	40	43	47	47	47	43
All manufacturing	756	1358	1523	1727	1851	1995	1885

TABLE A-3 U.S. Net International Trade Balance: Selected Commodity Groups, 1965-1981 (Billions of Dollars)

	1965	1970	1974	1976	1978	1980	1981
Machinery	+5.1	+6.3	+12.5	+16.7	+13.3	+25.0	+25.9
Chemicals	+1.6	+2.3	+ 4.8	+ 5.2	+ 6.2	+12.1	+11.8
Nonferrous base metals	−0.7	−0.6	− 1.7	− 1.8	− 3.4	− 2.2	− 3.3
Iron and steelmill products	−0.5	−0.8	− 2.3	− 2.0	− 5.1	− 3.7	− 7.5
Automobiles (nonmilitary)	−0.3	−2.9	− 5.0	− 5.7	−10.0	−12.9	−13.6
Mineral fuels and related materials	−1.3	−1.5	−22.1	−29.8	−38.2	−74.9	−71.1
All merchandise	+5.8	+2.6	− 3.3	− 7.3	−30.9	−28.2	−32.2

TABLE A-4 Employed Scientists and Engineers in Selected Fields: Distribution by Type of Employer, 1980[a,b]

	Chemistry	Chemical Engineers	Mathematicians	Biological Scientists	Physicists and Astronomers
Business/industry	86,640	63,710	42,190	39,350	22,400
Academic (Ph.D.-granting)	26,940	3,980	52,230	95,240	24,110
	(7,800)	(1,665)	(9,140)	(28,135)	(7,995)
Federal government	9,075	2,025	12,580	16,160	6,585
State and local government	7,940	1,015	4,985	13,685	1,175
Other nonprofit organizations	7,660	580	4,510	22,620	3,115
Military	1,560	510	1,190	1,520	590
Other	1,985	580	1,185	1,525	835
Total	141,800	72,400	118,870	190,100	58,810

[a] "Manufacturers' Shipments, Inventories, and Orders," 1977-81, M3-1.11, and December 1982, M3-1(82)-12, Bureau of the Census, U.S. Department of Commerce.
[b] "Statistical Abstract of the United States: 1982-83," U.S. Bureau of the Census.

TABLE A-5 Employed Doctorate Recipients (Excluding Postdoctoral Students) in Selected Fields: Distribution by Type of Employer, 1981[a,b]

	Chemistry	Engineering	Mathematicians	Biological Scientists	Physicists and Astronomers
Business/industry	24,320	27,600	3,190	8,480	9,220
Academic	14,775	17,425	13,190	35,260	13,355
Federal government	2,420	3,805	1,040	5,185	2,990
State and local government	300	50	35	1,780	80
Other nonprofit organizations	995	1,955	320	1,510	1,250
Hospital/clinic	345	50	35	1,780	300
Other	45	205	90	810	—
Total	43,200	51,400	17,900	54,000	27,200

[a] "U.S. Scientists and Engineers 1980," NSF 82-314, Table B-12; "Academic Science: Scientists and Engineers, January 1981. Detailed Statistical Tables," NSF 82-305, Table B-5.
[b] "Science, Engineering, and Humanities Doctorates in the United States: 1981 Profile," National Academy of Sciences, 1982, Table 1.5A.

TABLE A-6 Number of Companies in the Chemicals and Allied Products Industry Performing R&D and Funds for R&D, 1981[a]

Number of Employees	Number of Companies	Number with Federal Funds for R&D	Company Funds for R&D	Federal Funds for R&D
Less than 1000	187	5	$ 199	$ 11M
1,000-4,999	62	2	519	1
5,000-9,999	15	3	517	1
10,000-24,999	24	7	1,861	16
25,000 or more	11	8	1,846	355
Totals	299	25	4,942	384

[a] M. Pollak, NSF from "Research and Development in Industry, 1981. Funds, 1981; Scientists and Engineers, January, 1982."

TABLE A-7 Federal Obligations for Basic Research in Chemistry: Total Funding[a] (Parenthetical: Amounts to Universities and Colleges)[b] 1967-1983

Fiscal Year	Total (All Federal Agencies)	Major Supporting Agencies				
		NSF	DOE	NIH	DOD	DOA
1967	$117.5M	$23.3M	$37.6M	$10.7M	$14.0M	$13.6M
1970	126.8	21.7	39.0	11.2	15.8	15.3
1973	146.4	30.0	38.9	14.9	15.2	17.2
1974	149.3 (60.8)	33.4 (29.9)	47.8 (5.6)	19.5 (14.7)	12.6 (5.6)	17.5 (1.9)
1975	158.6 (73.5)	43.4 (38.8)	49.2 (7.6)	20.8 (15.6)	13.1 (6.2)	17.2 (1.9)
1976	168.3 (78.6)	40.6 (26.1)	53.8 (12.6)	23.1 (17.2)	19.1 (6.8)	18.5 (2.3)

[a] NSF, "Federal Funds for Research and Development. Federal Obligations for Research and Development by Agency and by Detailed Field of Science; Fiscal Years 1967-1983."
[b] ibid, "Federal Obligations for Research to Universities and Colleges by Agency and by Detailed Field of Science: Fiscal Years 1974-1983."

TABLE A-8 Industrial Support for Research in University Chemistry and Chemical Engineering Departments, 1980[a]

Type of Support	Chemistry Departments	Chemical Engineering Departments
Uncommitted gifts or grants to departments	$1.91M	$3.14M
Committed gifts or grants to specified faculty or research areas	2.47	1.85
Grants or contracts in response to explicit proposals for specific research	5.52	4.48
Other	0.06	0.16
Total industrial support	10.2	10.2
Total extramural support	145.7	44.3

[a] C. Judson King presentation to the Council for Chemical Research, Nov. 3, 1981, as reported in "University-Industry Research Relationships: Myths, Realities, and Potentials," Fourteenth Annual Report of the National Science Board, January 1983.

TABLE A-9 Chemical Fields of American Chemical Society Members (1984)

Organic Chemistry	20,175	Marketing and Economics	658
Analytical Chemistry	16,114	Fuel Chemistry	652
Biochemistry	9284	Chemical Information	640
Physical Chemistry	8563	Pesticide Chemistry	634
Inorganic Chemistry	6717	Rubber Chemistry	622
Industrial and Engineering	6000	Microbial Chemistry	412
Polymer Chemistry	5018	Geochemistry	376
Medicinal Chemistry	4064	Forensic Chemistry	314
Environmental Chemistry	3912	Carbohydrate Chemistry	273
Agriculture and Food Chemistry	2973	Fertilizer and Soil Chemistry	228
Organic Coatings and Plastics	2482	Fluorine Chemistry	119
Chemical Education	1496	Other	2327
Petroleum Chemistry	1464	Total	99,879
Computers in Chemistry	1054		
Colloid and Surface Chemistry	994	Total Membership, ACS	134,019
Nuclear Chemistry	784		
Chemical Health and Safety	773		
Cellulose, Paper and Textile Chemistry	757		

APPENDIX B

Contributors

The Committee to Survey Opportunities in the Chemical Sciences gratefully acknowledges the contributions of the almost 400 colleagues listed below who made thoughtful suggestions, prepared commissioned papers on cutting-edge research, and critiqued drafts. But, of course, the committee is responsible for this report and its recommendations.

ALDER, B.J., Lawrence Livermore National Laboratory
ANDERSON, J., Harvard University
ANDERSON, P.S., Merck Sharp and Dohme Research Laboratories
ANDREWS, D., Hoffmann-LaRoche, Incorporated
ANSON, F., California Institute of Technology
ARNETT, E.M., Duke University
ASHWELL, G., National Institutes of Health
BAER, E., Case Western Reserve University
BAIR, R.A., Argonne National Laboratory
BAIZER, M.M., Monsanto Company
BALDESCHWIELER, J.D., California Institute of Technology
BALDWIN, J.J., Merck Sharp and Dohme Research Laboratories
BARR, D.W., Los Alamos National Laboratory
BARTELL, L.S., University of Michigan
BARTLETT, R.J., Air Force Rocket Propulsion Laboratory
BASEMAN, R.J., University of California, Berkeley
BAUGHCUM, S.L., Los Alamos National Laboratory
BEAUCHAMP, J.L., California Institute of Technology
BECKER, E.D., National Institutes of Health
BELL, A.T., University of California, Berkeley
BENKOVIC, S., Pennsylvania State University
BENNER, S., Harvard University
BENSON, S., University of Southern California
BENTE, P., Hewlett-Packard Company
BERCAW, J., California Institute of Technology
BERGMAN, R., University of California, Berkeley
BERRY, M., Rice University

BERSON, J., Yale University
BIENENSTOCK, A., Stanford University
BIGELEISEN, J., State University of New York, Stony Brook
BLOUT, E.R., Harvard University
BOUDART, M., Stanford University
BRESLOW, R., Columbia University
BREWER, L., University of California, Berkeley
BROWN, M.S., University of Texas, Austin
BUCHI, G., Massachusetts Institute of Technology
BURRIS, R.H., University of Wisconsin, Madison
BURWELL, R., Northwestern University
BUSCH, K.L., Purdue University
BUSS, R.J., University of California, Berkeley
BYER, R.L., Stanford University
CAIRNS, E., Lawrence Berkeley Laboratory
CALVERT, J., National Center for Atmospheric Research
CANE, D.E., Brown University
CAPORALE, L.H., Merck Sharp and Dohme Research Laboratories
CARDILLO, M.J., AT&T Bell Laboratories
CARGILL, G.S., IBM Corporation
CASEY, C.P., University of Wisconsin
CASIDA, J.E., University of California, Berkeley
CECH, T.R., University of Colorado
CHAN, A., Monsanto Company
CHAN, S., California Institute of Technology
CHAN, W.Y., University of Arizona
CHANDLER, D.E., University of Pennsylvania
CHANDROSS, E.A., AT&T Bell Laboratories
CHANG, J., Lawrence Livermore National Laboratory
CHIANELLI, R.R., Exxon Corporation

CHISHOLM, M., University of Indiana
CHOWDHRY, U., E.I. du pont de Nemours and Company, Inc.
CHRISTENSEN, B., Merck Sharp and Dohme Research Laboratories
CLARDY, J., Cornell University
CLARK, J., University of Pennsylvania
CLEMENTI, E., IBM Corporation
CODY, R.B., Jr., Nicolet Analytical Instruments
COLEMAN, J.T., University of Illinois
COLLINS, T.J., California Institute of Technology
COLLMAN, J., Stanford University
COOKS, R.G., Purdue University
COOPER, G., Harvard University
CORDES, E.H., Merck Sharp and Dohme Research Laboratories
COREY, E.J., Harvard University
COTTON, F.A., Texas A&M University
COWAN, D., The Johns Hopkins University
COWLEY, A.H., The University of Texas at Austin
CRAM, D., University of California, Los Angeles
CREMERS, D.A., Los Alamos National Laboratory
DAHL, L.F., University of Wisconsin
DANISHEFSKY, S.J., Yale University
DARMEN, P., University of Arizona
DAUBEN, W., University of California, Berkeley
DAVIDSON, E.R., Indiana University
DELUCA, H.F., University of Wisconsin
DLOTT, D.D., University of Illinois, Urbana
DOLL, J., Los Alamos National Laboratory
DOLPHIN, D., University of British Columbia, Canada
DOMBEK, B.D., Union Carbide Corporation
DONARUMA, L., Polytechnic Institute of New York
DONNELL, E.P., Chemical Abstracts Service
DOYLE, M.P., Trinity University
DUNNING, T., Argonne National Laboratory
DUPUY, C., University of Colorado
EDELSON, E., New York Daily News
ELLIOT, J., BioInformation Associates
ELLIS, P.D., University of South Carolina
ERDAL, B.R., Los Alamos National Laboratory
ESSIGMANN, J., Massachusetts Institute of Technology
EVANS, D., University of Wisconsin
EYRING, L., Arizona State University
FARRAR, T.C., University of Wisconsin, Madison
FAULKNER, L., University of Illinois, Urbana
FELLER, R.L., Carnegie-Mellon Institute of Research
FENSELAU, C., The Johns Hopkins University
FERGUSON, E.E., National Oceanic and Atmospheric Administration
FIELD, R., Massachusetts Institute of Technology
FILNER, P., Plant Cell Research Institute, ARCO
FLYNN, G.W., Columbia University
FORNSHELL, R.L., Exxon Corporation
FORSTER, D., Monsanto Company
FOWLER, J., Brookhaven National Laboratory
FREI, H., University of California, Berkeley
FRIEND, C., Harvard University
GARDNER, J., Hoffmann-LaRoche, Incorporated
GASSMAN, P.G., University of Minnesota
GIDDINGS, J.C., University of Utah
GILBERT, W., Biogen
GLASS, A.M., AT&T Bell Laboratories
GODDARD, W.A., III, California Institute of Technology
GOODBY, J.W., AT&T Bell Laboratories
GRIFFITHS, P.R., University of California, Riverside
GROSS, M.L., University of Nebraska, Lincoln
GROVES, J., University of Michigan
GRUBBS, R., California Institute of Technology
GUTOWSKY, H.S., University of Illinois, Urbana
HADLY, M.E., University of Arizona
HAHN, R.L., Oak Ridge National Laboratory
HALL, K., University of Wisconsin
HAMMES, G.G., Cornell University
HAMMOND, G., Allied Corporation
HARDING, L.B., Argonne National Laboratory
HARMONY, M., University of Kansas
HARTFORD, A., Jr., Los Alamos National Laboratory
HAY, P.J., Los Alamos National Laboratory
HAZEN, R.M., Carnegie Institution, Washington, D.C.
HEATHCOCK, C.J., University of California, Berkeley
HEINEMAN, W.R., University of Cincinnati
HERCULES, D.M., University of Pittsburgh
HEXTER, R.M., University of Minnesota
HIRSCHFELD, T., Lawrence Livermore National Laboratory
HOCHSTRASSER, R., University of Pennsylvania
HOFFMAN, D., University of California, Berkeley
HOFFMAN, M., Kansas State University
HOLM, R., Harvard University
HOLTOM, G., University of Pennsylvania
HOPFIELD, J.J., California Institue of

Technology
HOUSE, G.L., Eastman Kodak Company
HRUBY, V.J., University of Arizona
HUIZENGA, J., University of Rochester
HYNES, J.T., University of Colorado
INCHALIK, E.J., Exxon Research and
Engineering Company
INCHAUK, R., Exxon Corporation
ISENHOUR, T.L., Utah State University
JAKOBSEN, R., Battelle Corporation
JELLUM, E., University of Oslo, Norway
JENCKS, W.P., Brandeis University
JESSON, P., E.I. du Pont de Nemours and
Company, Inc.
JETT, J.H., Los Alamos National Laboratory
JOHNSON, D.R., National Bureau of
Standards
JOHNSON, P.M., State University of New
York, Stony Brook
JONAS, J., University of Illinois
JOYCE, R.M., Hockessin, DE (retired from du
Pont)
JURS, P., Pennsylvania State University
KAISER, E.T., Rockefeller University
KALDOR, A., Exxon Corporation
KAMEN, M., University of California, San
Diego
KARGER, B.L., Northeastern University
KATZ, J.J., Argonne National Laboratory
KATZER, J.R., Cornell University
KAUFMAN, F., University of Pittsburgh
(deceased)
KELLER, R., Los Alamos National Laboratory
(deceased)
KELLER, R.A., State University of New York,
Fredonia
KELLEY, F.N., University of Akron
KING, C.J., University of California, Berkeley
KINSEY, J.L., Massachusetts Institute of
Technology
KIRSHENBAUM, I., Exxon Corporation
KISHI, Y., Harvard University
KISSINGER, P.T., Purdue University
KLEMPERER, W., Harvard University
KNITTEL, J.J., Rutgers University
KOCHI, J., University of Houston
KOENIG, K.E., Monsanto Company
KOHN, G.K., Zoecon Corporation
KONECKY, M.S., Exxon Research and
Engineering Company
KOSHLAND, D., University of California,
Berkeley
KRAUSS, M.A., National Bureau of Standards
KRAUT, J., University of California, San Diego
KRUGER, J., National Bureau of Standards
KUBO, I., University of California, Berkeley
KWIRAM, A., University of Washington

LABANA, S.S., Ford Motor Company
LAMBRECHT, R., Brookhaven National
Laboratory
LANGER, R., Massachusetts Institute of
Technology
LAUDISE, R.A., AT&T Bell Laboratories
LEE, Y.T., University of California, Berkeley
LEFKOWITZ, R.J., Duke University
LEONE, S.R., University of Colorado
LEVY, G.C., Syracuse University
LINEBERGER, W.C., University of Colorado
LIPPARD, S.J., Massachusetts Institute of
Technology
LIPSCHUTZ, M.E., Purdue University
LIU, B., IBM Corporation
LYKOS, P., Illinois Institute of Technology
LYTLE, F.W., Boeing Corporation
LYNN, D., University of Chicago
LYTLE, F.E., Purdue University
MACDIARMID, A., University of Pennsylvania
MACIAS, E.S., Washington University, St.
Louis
MACIEL, G.E., Colorado State University
MADIX, R.J., Stanford University
MANDAVA, B., U.S. Environmental Protection
Agency
MARGRAVE, J., Rice University
MARKS, T.J., Northwestern University
MARTIN, J.C., Los Alamos National
Laboratory
MATWIYOFF, N.A., University of New Mexico
MAXWELL, B., Princeton University
McBRIDE, J.M., Yale University
MCCALL, D.W., AT&T Bell Laboratories
MCCAMMON, J.A., University of Houston
MCDOWELL, R.S., Los Alamos National
Laboratory
MCGARRY, F., Massachusetts Institute of
Technology
MCLEAN, A.D., IBM Corporation
MEINWALD, J., Cornell University
MICHL, J., University of Utah
MILLER, C.M., Los Alamos National
Laboratory
MILLER, E., University of Wisconsin, Madison
MILLER, J., University of Wisconsin, Madison
MILLER, L., University of Minnesota
MILLER. W.H., University of California,
Berkeley
MILNER, P.C., AT&T Bell Laboratories
MITCHELL, J.W., AT&T Bell Laboratories
MOORE, D.S., Los Alamos National Laboratory
MORGAN, J., California Institute of
Technology
MORRIS, D., Monsanto Company
MORRISON, G.H., Cornell University
MOSBERG, H.I., University of Michigan

MUETTERTIES, E., University of California, Berkeley (deceased)

MULLINS, L.J., Los Alamos National Laboratory

MURPHY, D.W., AT&T Bell Laboratories

MURRAY, R., University of North Carolina

NEMETHY, G., Cornell University

NEWNAM, B.E., Los Alamos National Laboratory

NICHOLSON, R.S., National Science Foundation

NOGAR, N.S., Los Alamos National Laboratory

NORRIS, J.R., Argonne National Laboratory

NOVOTNY, M.V., University of Indiana

OHRN, N.Y., University of Florida, Gainesville

OLAH, G.A., University of Southern California

OLDFIELD, E., University of Illinois, Urbana

ORMBERG, J., University of Arizona

ORME-JOHNSON, W., Massachusetts Institute of Technology

OSGOOD, R.M., Columbia University

OSTERYOUNG, J.G., State University of New York, Buffalo

OSTERYOUNG, R.A., State University of New York, Buffalo

OVERBERGER, C., University of Michigan

OVERBURY, S.H., Oak Ridge National Laboratory

OXTOBY, D.W., University of Chicago

PACANSKY, T.J., IBM Corporation

PAQUETTE, L., Ohio State University

PARISER, R., E.I. du Pont de Nemours and Company, Inc.

PARMENTER, C.S., University of Indiana

PARSHALL, G., E.I. du Pont de Nemours and Company, Inc.

PASTAN, I., National Institutes of Health

PATCHETT, A., Merck Sharp and Dohme Research Laboratories

PAUL, M.A., Merrick, NY (retired)

PERLMAN, M., Sloan-Kettering Cancer Institute

PINES, A., University of California, Berkeley

PITTS, J.N., University of California, Riverside

PITZER, K.S., University of California, Berkeley

PLATTNER, R.D., U.S. Department of Agriculture

PORTER, N., Duke University

PORTER, R.S., University of Massachusetts, Amherst

POSKANZER, A.M., Lawrence Berkeley Laboratory

POWERS, D.A., Sandia National Laboratory

PRESTEGAARD, J.H., Yale University

QUIGLEY, G.P., Los Alamos National Laboratory

RABALAIS, J.W., University of Houston

RABINOVITCH, B.S., University of Washington, Seattle

RABINOW, J., National Bureau of Standards

RATSETTER, W.H., Genentech, Incorporated

RAYMOND, K., University of California, Berkeley

RENTZEPIS, P.M., AT&T Bell Laboratories

RICH, A., Massachusetts Institute of Technology

RICHARDS, J.H., California Institute of Technology

RINEHART, K.L., University of Illinois, Urbana

RIVIER, J., The Salk Institute

ROBERTS, D., Rutgers University

ROBINSON, F.M., Merck Sharp and Dohme Research Laboratories

ROCKAWAY, T.W., Bioresearch, Inc.

ROELOFS, W.L., Cornell University

ROGERS, L.B., University of Georgia

ROKACH, J., Merck Sharp and Dohme Research laboratories

ROSENBLATT, G.M., Lawrence Berkeley Laboratory

ROSENBLATT, M., Merck Sharp and Dohme Research Laboratories

ROSS, P., Lawrence Berkeley Laboratory

RYAN, J.W., Dow Corning Corporation

SALZMAN, G.C., Los Alamos National Laboratory

SAMARA, G.A., Sandia National Laboratory

SANDER, R.K., Los Alamos National Laboratory

SAUER, K.H., University of California, Berkeley

SAWYER, T.K., Upjohn Company

SAYKALLY, R.J., University of California, Berkeley

SCHAEFER, H.F., III, University of California, Berkeley

SCHAEFER, W.P., California Institute of Technology

SCHERAGA, H.A., Cornell University

SCHMIDT, L.D., University of Minnesota

SCHWARTZ, J., Princeton University

SCOLNICK, E.M., University of Illinois, Urbana

SETSER, D.W., Kansas State University

SHAIR, F.H., California Institute of Technology

SHANER, J.W., Los Alamos National Laboratory

SHANK, C.V., AT&T Bell Laboratories

SHAPIRO, J., University of Illinois, Urbana

SHARP, P.A., Massachusetts Institute of Technology

SHARPLESS, B., Massachusetts Institute of

Technology
SHECHTER, A., National Institutes of Health
SHEN, T.Y., University of Illinois, Urbana
SHEPARD, R.L., Argonne National Laboratory
SHEPPARD, R.C., MRC Laboratory
SHIELD, L.S., University of Illinois, Urbana
SHIRLEY, D.A., University of California, Berkeley
SHRIVER, D.F., Northwestern University
SIEVERS, R.E., University of Colorado
SILBERKLANG, M., Merck Sharp and Dohme Research Laboratories
SINFELT, J.H., Exxon Corporation
SINSKEY, A.J., Massachusetts Institute of Technology
SMALLEY, R.E., Rice University
SNYDER, J.J., Los Alamos National Laboratory
SRINIVASAN, R., IBM Corporation
STEIN, D.R., The Gmelin Institute, West Germany
STEINFELD, J.I., Massachusetts Institute of Technology
STADTMAN, T.C., National Institutes of Health
STILL, W.C., Columbia University
STRYER, L., Stanford University
SUTIN, N., Brookhaven National Laboratory
TALBERT, W.L., Los Alamos National Laboratory
TAYLOR, D.J., Los Alamos National Laboratory
THOMAS, L.J., Eastman Kodak Company
TIEE, J.J., Los Alamos National Laboratory
TOBIAS, C., University of California, Berkeley
TOLLES, W., U.S. Naval Research Laboratory
TOLMAN, C.A., E.I. du Pont de Nemours and Company, Inc.
TROST, B.M., University of Wisconsin, Madison
TRUHLAR, D.G., University of Minnesota
TULLY, J.C., AT&T Bell Laboratories
TURKEVICH, A., University of Chicago
TURRO, N.J., Columbia University
VALE, W.W., The Salk Institute
VALENTINE, J., University of California, Los Angeles
VAN DUYNE, R.P., Northwestern University
VAN HOVE, M.A., University of California, Berkeley
VENKATARAGHARAN, R., Lederle Laboratory
WADT, W.R., Los Alamos National Laboratory

WAGNER, A.F., Argonne National Laboratory
WALLACE, T.C., Los Alamos National Laboratory
WANG, D.I.C., Massachusetts Institute of Technology
WASSERMAN, E., E.I. du Pont de Nemours and Company, Inc.
WATANABE, K.A., Sloan-Kettering Cancer Institute
WAUGH, J.S., Massachusetts Institute of Technology
WEEKS, J.D., AT&T Bell Laboratories
WEI, J.R., Massachusetts Institute of Technology
WEISZ, P.B., Mobil Research and Development Corporation
WENDER, P., Stanford University
WERNICK, J.H., Bell Communications Research
WESSEL, J., Aerospace Corporation
WESTHEIMER, F.H., Harvard University
WETZEL, R., Genentech, Incorporated
WHEELER, J.C., University of California, San Diego
WHITE, J.M., The University of Texas at Austin
WHITESIDES, T.H., Eastman Kodak Corporation
WIBERG, K.B., Yale University
WIGHTMAN, M., University of Indiana
WILKINS, C.L., Northeastern University
WILSON, T.P., Union Carbide Corporation
WINOGRAD, N., Pennsylvania State University
WIPKE, W.T., University of California, Santa Cruz
WITTIG, C., University of Southern California
WOLF, A.P., Brookhaven National Laboratory
WOOD, J.M., University of Minnesota
WRIGHTON, M., Massachusetts Institute of Technology
WYATT, R.E., The University of Texas at Austin
WYMER, R.G., Oak Ridge National Laboratory
YATES, J., University of Pittsburgh
YEAGER, E., Case Western Reserve University
ZARE, R.N., Stanford University
ZENER, N., Case Western Reserve University
ZEWAIL, A.H., California Institute of Technology
ZIMMERMAN, H.E., University of Wisconsin, Madison
ZURER, P.S., Chemical and Engineering News

Index